Transit Systems Theory

Transit Systems Theory

J. Edward Anderson
University of Minnesota

Lexington Books
D.C. Heath and Company
Lexington, Massachusetts
Toronto

Library of Congress Cataloging in Publication Data

Anderson, John Edward.
    Transit systems theory.

    Includes bibliographical references and index.
    1. Urban transportation.   2.   Local transit.
I.   Title.
TA1205.A5   388.4   77-011856
ISBN 0-669-01902-X

Published simultaneously in Canada

Printed in the United States of America

International Standard Book Number: 0-669-01902-x

Library of Congress Catalog Card Number: 77-011856

**To my wife
Cynthia Louise Anderson**

Contents

List of Figures

List of Tables

Foreword

Urban transportation, as Professor Anderson cites it in his introduction, "refers to the totality of movement within an urban area by public and private means." Thus, urban transportation consists of transit, which refers to the process of transferring goods and people in urban areas by public conveyances; and private conveyances, which almost always move on publicly financed roads. This book addresses itself to transit systems theory and in so doing, fills a void which has existed for decades and provides a means for the organized presentation of principles for study and seeking of solutions.

It is safe to state that there has been more written and said about urban transportation and transit systems, particularly, since the advent of participation by the Urban Mass Transportation Administration in urban transportation matters than ever before. There is a good reason for this. Historically, urban transit systems, particularly in the United States, were a private business and a very highly successful business until the overwhelming success of the private automobile caused the changes in the style of living of urban America which in turn resulted in the collapse of urban transit as a viable and profitable business enterprise. Urban transit even under private ownership has always performed a public service. As the privately owned transit systems were increasingly taken over by public bodies, however, the fundamental nature of transit has changed. Thus, today it is looked upon as a vital public service whose level of service is determined by societal needs within limits of societal means. It is this public service nature of urban transit, which puts it in competition for local resources with health, education and welfare and other societal services, that causes much of the difficult controversy surrounding transit. It is partly because of this competition for public funds that frequently it is observed that transit is not a problem amenable to technological solutions, but rather a matter for institutional and financial solutions. Nevertheless, there are many of us who cannot accept the proposition that, in the last quarter of the twentieth century, technology is incapable of providing some solutions, if not all the answers, to frequently debated urban transportation problems. The fundamental modes of conventional transit have been around for a half to three quarters of a century and some of them even longer. It is only since the 1950's, and predominantly since the 1960's, that modern technology and those pursuing modern technology are increasingly focusing and seeking technological solutions to transit problems.

While this book addresses many forms of urban transit, it by design emphasizes the network characteristics of transit and focuses heavily on automated transit systems. Technology can undoubtedly contribute to each and every mode of transportation, including urban transit, by improving componentry, reducing cost of operations, and improving performance. Yet, automation is probably the only new technology which can potentially contribute to revolutionary improvements in transit performance.

Automation through the evolution of electronics, digital computers, systems analysis and systems technology is indeed the product of the mid-twentieth century. While it has penetrated life all around us, it has made relatively few inroads into the operations of urban transit systems. There is good reason for this. Automation achieved its most spectacular initial successes with the military and in aerospace. In all those applications, the perceived benefits over the cost of automation are usually extremely high and therefore automation was readily accepted. Because of very high perceived benefit-cost ratios, even the initial difficulties in achieving high reliability through automation were accepted, or better, circumvented by the generous application of redundancies to assure any required mission success criteria. Automation, however, also succeeded in commercial, civilian business. It surrounds us in the form of airlines reservation systems, automated communications in our telephone networks, business data processing, check clearances, bank and insurance applications as well as manufacturing process control. These are all areas in which automation has produced such a significant quantum jump in producitivity that the occasional failure of automation was readily tolerated because the time lost due to repairing the failed componentry was quickly made up by the high productivity of the automated process.

Transit may be unique in this respect. It is unlike the military or aerospace class of activities, where one can afford sufficient redundancies to achieve a high probability of success and where, in the interest of national security, or national prestige, economic considerations are not as critical as in other areas. On the other hand, transit cannot be compared with the manufacturing process control or reservations or banking systems of civilian undertakings because in transit, the temporary loss of service, if it occurs frequently, cannot be tolerate by the citizens. The most important performance characteristic of transit is probably its dependability to carry people reliably to their destination. Thus, transit may be the highest challenge to the introduction of automation because, on one hand, one cannot afford the redundancies customary in military and aerospace application while, on the other hand, one cannot afford the occasional downtimes associated with the off-line functions that automation usually performs in business. To meet automated operations dependably and at affordable costs is then the challenge to automated transit in urban applications.

Professor J. Edward Anderson understands this challenge and it is not by accident that he devotes such significant segments of this book to life cycle cost, theory of reliability allocation, redundancy, and failure mode and effect analysis. The reader might have different ideas and conclusions about the relative merits of a variety of approaches to automated transit systems, but nobody can quarrel with the need for the concept expressed in the title of Chapter 11, "Design for Maximum Cost Effectiveness."

It is because of this deep understanding of the environment in which automated transit needs to be deployed and can provide its contribution that Professor Anderson's book is highly recommended not only for students of modern technology but also for all of us who are interested in improving urban transportation.

G.J. Pastor
Associate Administrator for Technology
Development and Deployment
Urban Mass Transportation Administration

Preface

The past decade has witnessed a revival of interest in alternative means for movement of people in cities. Hundreds of schemes have been proposed, dozens of which have reached the test-track stage, and a few of which are in operation. Debate over alternative concepts has been intense and heated, indicating the strength of feeling many people have about the subject. All too often, based on inadequate analysis, a great deal of money has been spent on concepts which are later found to be of limited utility. There has been a need to develop a theoretical foundation for the analysis and synthesis of transit systems in a form that can be taught in schools and assimilated by practicing engineers, many of whom enter the transit field with no formal training in the subject. This book is offered as a step in the fulfillment of such a need. It is written as an engineering textbook with sufficient material for a one-year course, and should be understandable to persons with the background in mathematics and the physical sciences usually attained by students in the senior and first-year graduate levels of engineering. While the emphasis is on the technical aspects of transit, it is important to keep in mind that transit is an interdisciplinary subject and that a rounded transit engineer needs to understand many subjects beyond the scope of this book.

For reasons stated in the introduction to chapter 11, most but not all of this book pertains to the theory of automated guideway transit. There has been some discussion of standardization of these systems, but before systems can be standardized they must be classified and the relative merits of each system must be understood. But even then each of the classified systems can be cost effective to a greater or lesser degree depending on how its variable properties are chosen. Before standardization makes sense, the optimum parameters must be known, that is, those parameters that result in maximum cost effectiveness, usually measured by the cost per trip or per kilometer-trip. In a recent study of automated guideway transit systems by the Office of Technology Assessment, it was proposed that AGT systems be classified as either shuttle-loop, group rapid transit, or personal rapid transit. Unfortunately, the first of these refers to the geometry of the lines and the second and third to the service characteristics. Classification into just three types may have apparent advantages for policy makers, but it is much too simplistic for detailed understanding of AGT systems. As a start the classification matrix presented in the summary of chapter 4, which results in identification of twenty-five types of systems, is suggested. Because of my association with the International Conferences on Personal Rapid Transit, I am usually identified with that concept. Nonetheless, in this book the term personal rapid transit is used only in references. The reason is that the term has been used to identify too wide a range of systems, many of which are very cost ineffective. As a result, the term has in my opinion become worse than useless in that its utterance usually generates more heat than light.

My purpose is and has been to search by rational analysis supported by a factual basis for characteristics of and parameter choices within transit systems that will make it possible to build these systems in such a way that the public can be given the greatest service for the least money consistent with environmental requirements. The best way I know to measure "the greatest service for the least money" is by the total cost per trip, and I don't believe the full potential of transit can be realized until systems that minimize the cost per trip become available. It is not surprising that such a quest, joined by many people all over the world, has resulted in systems radically different from those in operation; nor, because of the fundamental importance of transit and the many specialties within it, is it surprising that new types of systems are resisted. Progress can be made only as the fundamentals of the subject become more widely understood.

Hundreds of people have contributed directly and indirectly to this book through their papers and reports, and through conversations I have been privileged to have with them. Mainly as a result of the aforementioned conferences, I have been able to see and read about the contributions of people to the subject all over the globe. The development of much of the material began at the University of Minnesota under the sponsorship of a grant from the Minnesota State Legislature, without which little could have been done. Grants from the Urban Mass Transportation Administration also contributed needed support. The bulk of the work was completed while the author was on leave first with the Colorado Regional Transportation District, and then with the Raytheon Company in Bedford, Massachusetts. Upon returning to the University of Minnesota, the author used much of the material in a two-quarter course, where it was improved by student comments. The moral support and encouragement of many laypersons, whose stake in improving transit can come only with improved transit service, has been essential, and much helpful advice and encouragement has come from many of the members of the Advanced Transit Association. Finally, without the patience and understanding of my wife, Cindy, this book could not have been written.

Transit Systems Theory

1

Introduction

Transit is a word of many meanings. As used in this book, it refers to the process of transporting people and goods within urban areas by public conveyances. The term "urban transportation" is used in contemporary literature to refer to the totality of movement within an urban area by public and private means, even though the private conveyances must almost always move on publicly financed roadways. The term "transit system" refers in this book to all of the hardware needed to provide the function of transit. The hardware may include vehicles, roadways or guideways, stations, and central facilities for operation and maintenance. Transit systems theory is the underlying system of general principles of design, operation, and performance that provide a reasoned basis for selection of specific characteristics and parameters of transit systems. No author can claim to set in print all of transit systems theory but one can hope to pick up where others have left off and present such a body of knowledge in a more general and consistent form. Transit systems theory cannot be developed in a vacuum, but only after the development, operation, and public evaluation of many types of transit systems over a period of many years. As a parallel, the technology of heat engines developed on an ad hoc basis for many decades before the science of thermodynamics led to a fundamental understanding of the thermal processes within the engine and from that to a marked improvement in the performance and efficiency of heat engines.

The beginnings of transit occurred in the early part of the nineteenth century with horse-drawn streetcars[1], a forerunner of which was the stagecoach, which was limited in weight and size because of the condition of the roadways. By operating on a guideway of steel rails instead of mud roads, a team of horses could pull a load many times as great at higher speeds. Because it permitted the cost of the horse and driver to be amortized over many more patrons, and it decreased the trip time, the horse-drawn streetcar became very popular. With the advent of the electric motor and the central-station dynamo later in the nineteenth century, it was natural to electrify the streetcar; however, the history of this development shows many failures before the electric streetcar of the twentieth century emerged. A problem with the streetcar, which became more and more severe in dense cities, was its interference with other traffic, which resulted in slow operating speeds and many accidents. This problem could be solved with then-existing technology by building exclusive rights-of-way for the tracks usually either overhead or in tunnels. The concept of rapid rail

1

transit was born and in many large cities became the backbone of the transit system.

Early in the twentieth century, the technology of the heat engine had developed sufficiently to be used to propel carriages, and these were refined and manufactured in ever increasing numbers. With sufficient numbers of the evolving automobile in use, public support increased for better roads. Once the roads and vehicles had improved sufficiently, the original reason for track-bound street cars faded and the transit bus took over its function in more and more cities, until in the mid 1950s the streetcar had all but disappeared. Earlier, in the first two decades of the twentieth century, the need for a more flexible form of transit than the streetcar or rapid rail was met by advancing automotive technology with the jitney, a semi-demand-activated large automobile or bus that picked up and dropped off people along an approximate route. The jitney competed so successfully with the streetcar that the owners of the large and politically powerful streetcar companies succeeded in persuading legislators to pass laws banning it. Operating small vehicles in a demand mode was considered unfair competition for the less flexible trackbound vehicles, and they were permitted to remain only in the form of the taxi, which is too expensive for most people to use for daily travel. The free market system was not permitted to function to allow the most competitive form of transit to evolve.

In the 1930s and 1940s, many people dreamed of owning automobiles because of the complete flexibility of movement, comfort and privacy they provided but could not afford them. During the 1950s, however, increasing affluence and low cost housing loans led to the complete dominance of the automobile as the mode of urban transportation in most cities in North America and to the spread city of today. Public transit could no longer compete and one after another transit companies went bankrupt. By the early 1960s the increased numbers of automobiles and the still present need for transit regardless of cost combined to initiate the revival of transit by Congressional action, which established the Urban Mass Transportation Administration. While a paragraph was included in the law directing UMTA to investigate the promise of totally new types of transit systems, the main driving force behind its creation was evidently the view that revival of the fixed guideway systems of old with modern engineering refinements would solve the problems brought on by dominance of the automobile. In spite of UMTA funded work which showed that a gradual reintroduction of systems of the past would not prevent continued worsening of congestion, the vast bulk of federal funds were invested in conventional systems. A decade and a half later, these conclusions, summarized by Hamilton and Nance[2], seem generally correct. New ideas are still needed. Perhaps the frustration of rising deficits and disappointing performance will increase interest in innovation, notwithstanding early experiences.

In developing theory of transit systems, this book builds on a great deal of activity in development of new transit systems made possible by a wide variety of technological advances since World War II[3]. Theory is developed, not only of existing systems, but of new systems by considering the "transit system" as a field of initially undetermined characteristics and parameters subject to a field of requirements coming from analyses of the needs of the public. On examination of the results of dozens of transit system development programs, it is clear that most have failed or will fail because characteristics or parameter choices were made on the basis of unsubstantiated but plausible assumptions. People have dreamed for perhaps as long as they have populated the earth of better means of getting to where they want to go. In recent times people have dreamed of and have invested money in many transport ideas, all but a few of which have proved or will prove to be impractical because of the high cost per ride, or because of another fault, which if corrected leads to high cost per ride. Unsupported intuition has provided much misguidance in developing new transit systems which will at a sufficiently low cost meet needs and expectations of the public. Transit systems theory is needed to find optimized solutions based on serving the public as well as possible for the least money subject to environmental and performance constraints.

This book presents basic areas of transit systems theory applicable to a wide variety of types of transit systems. In the final chapter, the previously developed theory is synthesized into characteristics of transit systems optimized to the extent permitted by the knowledge obtained. In chapter 2, basic performance relationships used over and over again in transit systems analysis are developed. These refer to the longitudinal motion of vehicles, and involve limits on acceleration and rate of change of acceleration (jerk) permissible based on the criterion of human comfort in normal and emergency circumstances. The limits used are in the range generally accepted; however, insufficient testing has been done to establish these firmly for all classes of riders. Therefore, the reader should keep in mind the basic algebraic relations in making computations for specific systems. Chapter 3 deals with similar requirements for lateral motion but here these requirements lead to the specification of curvature limits for guideways in various practical situations. Chapter 4 then builds on previous work in development of geometric and performance relationships for various types of transit systems classified as indicated in its summary. In chapter 5, general cost equations are developed for all types of transit, cost effectiveness relationships are developed and discussed, and the general formulas are applied to a field of specific types of systems. In chapter 5, patronage is a parameter. It is important to use patronage this way in initial calculations to give the analyst and policy maker a good representation of the variation of the cost effectiveness parameters with patronage. Then in chapter 6 the subject of patronage analysis is introduced in enough detail to give the systems engineer a good feeling for the subject, but not in the exhaustive detail needed for specific recommendations. Patronage analysis is the heart of the whole transit problem for it deals directly with factors that measure the attractiveness of specific transit features to the potential transit-riding public. It is behavioral, however, and beyond the professional competence of most engineers. Consequent superficial treatment of the subject is the probable cause of failure of many transit concepts.

The three remaining subjects in chapters 7, 8 and 9, and 10, can be studied in any order. Chapter 7 develops the theory of safe operation and leads to specific performance limitations and recommended vehicle features. Chapters 8 and 9 develop a new theory of reliability requirements and reliability allocation based on minimization of life cycle cost subject to the constraint of a given level of service availability. It results in specific recommendations for equipment needed to insure adequate service availability in the systems discussed and quantifies the changes in system reliability associated with changing equipment and equipment parameters. Chapter 10 considers the problem of optimization of the characteristics of elevated transit guideways in such a way that cost per unit length is minimized. Finally, as mentioned above, in chapter 11 the previous theory is used to synthesize the transit systems characteristics that minimize the cost per trip.

The title of this book is *Transit Systems Theory*, not *The Theory of Transit Systems*, because it is not all inclusive. Other topics such as detailed patronage analysis techniques, the theory of control, operational analysis of station and interchange flows, and the theory of large-scale network simulations could and perhaps should be included in such a work. The author believes, however, that the topics included form a fundamental background useful to all transit systems engineers, and that, for the most part, beyond these the topics become specialized and can be pursued in the periodical literature. The book provides the basis for determining what should be controlled, but it leaves to others the detailed implementation of control.

Notes

1. A more detailed and illustrated history of transit development is given in the *Lea Transit Compendium,* Vol. 2, No. 1, 1975, published by the N.D. Lea Transportation Research Corporation, 123 Green Street, Huntsville, Alabama 35801.

2. William F. Hamilton and Dana K. Nance, "Systems Analysis of Urban Transportation," *Scientific American,* Vol. 221, No. 1, July 1969.

3. Much of this work can be found summarized in three volumes of papers: *Personal Rapid Transit, Personal Rapid Transit II,* and *Personal Rapid Transit III,* distributed by the Audio Visual Library Services, University of Minnesota, 3300 University Avenue S. E., Minneapolis, Minnesota 55414. The most comprehensive earlier work on the theory of transit system known to the author appeared in a series of reports published between 1969 and 1972 on the Cabtrack System by the Royal Aircraft Establishment, Ministry of Defence, Farnborough, Hants, England. Unfortunately, these reports have never been released for general circulation. The first post World War II book that gives a systematic presentation of transit concepts and leads to conclusions in general agreement with those of this book is *Individualized Automatic Transit and the City* by Donn Fichter, 1430 East 60th Place, Chicago, Illinois 60637.

2

Basic Performance Relationships

In transit systems analysis the need continually arises to relate kinematic characteristics such as trip time, time to stop, trip length, and stopping distance to line speed, maximum acceleration, and maximum jerk. These relationships are derived and presented in this chapter for future reference.

In deriving the kinematical relationships, it is necessary to make use of the experimental fact that, for comfort of the riders, the ratio of jerk to acceleration should not exceed unity in units of seconds. Stated in another way, the acceleration should not build up to its maximum value or decrease from its maximum value to zero in less than one second. Occasional use is also made of the generally accepted value of maximum service acceleration of about one eighth times gravity for standing-passenger vehicles, and one quarter times gravity for vehicles in which all passengers are seated.

Because they follow directly from the kinematical relationships, relationships for acceleration power and average energy per trip are derived and presented in this chapter.

2.1 The Acceleration Profile

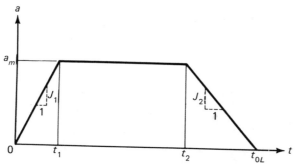

Figure 2-1. The Acceleration Profile

Consider the acceleration of a vehicle from rest to line speed V_L. The maximum acceleration during the maneuver is a a_m. Consideration of human comfort requires that a_m be obtained in a finite time and at a maximum rate J_1, called the jerk. As the vehicle approaches line speed, the acceleration a_m is caused to diminish to zero at a finite rate J_2, which may, for reasons discussed in Section 2.3, not equal J_1.

For mathematical convenience, the acceleration profile just described is assumed to be composed of a series of straight lines as shown in figure 2-1. This is an idealization of an actual acceleration profile, which is continuous in its derivatives, because forces, and even rates of change of forces, cannot be applied in zero time.

The area under the acceleration-time curve from $t = 0$ to t is the velocity at time t. Thus the velocity at time t_1 is

$$V_1 \equiv V(t_1) = \tfrac{1}{2}a_m t_1 \tag{2.1.1}$$

But

$$t_1 = \frac{a_m}{J_1} \tag{2.1.2}$$

Therefore

$$V_1 = \frac{a_m^2}{2J_1} \tag{2.1.3}$$

Similarly, the velocity at time t_2 is

$$V_2 = V_1 + a_m(t_2 - t_1) \tag{2.1.4}$$

and, by analogy with equation (2.1.3),

$$V_L - V_2 = \frac{a_m^2}{2J_2} \tag{2.1.5}$$

In analogy with equation (2.1.2)

$$t_{0L} - t_2 = \frac{a_m}{J_2} \tag{2.1.6}$$

Combining equations (2.1.2) through (2.1.6), we have

$$t_{0L} = \frac{V_L}{a_m} + \frac{a_m}{2J_1} + \frac{a_m}{2J_2} \tag{2.1.7}$$

If $J_1 = J_2 = J$, equation (2.1.7) takes the easily remembered form

$$t_{0L} = \frac{V_L}{a_m} + \frac{a_m}{J} \tag{2.1.8}$$

The time t_{0L} can be interpreted as either the time required to reach speed V_L from rest, or by symmetry the time required to stop from speed V_L.

The jerk J should be high as possible to minimize t_{0L}, but comfort considerations dictate that J be less than or equal to a_m in seconds units. Thus, the contribution of a_m/J to t_{0L} is usually about one second, usually small compared to V_L/a_m.

2.2 The Velocity Profile and Stopping Distance

The curve of figure 2-2 is the integral of the curve of figure 2-1. The area under it is the distance travelled. In the region from $t = 0$ to $t = t_1$, the acceleration is

$$a = J_1 t$$

the velocity is

$$V = \frac{1}{2} J_1 t^2$$

and the distance travelled is

$$D = \frac{J_1 t^3}{6}$$

Substituting equation (2.1.2)

$$D(t_1) \equiv D_1 = \frac{a_m^3}{6 J_1^2} \qquad (2.2.1)$$

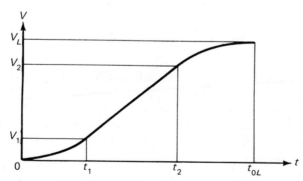

Figure 2-2. The Velocity Profile

By analogy, and using equation (2.1.6),

$$D_{0L} - D_2 = V_L(t_{0L} - t_2) - \frac{a_m^3}{6J_2^2}$$

$$= \frac{a_m}{J_2}\left(V_L - \frac{a_m^2}{6J_2}\right) \tag{2.2.2}$$

From figure 2-2, the area of the trapezoid between t_1 and t_2 is

$$D_2 - D_1 = \frac{(V_1 + V_2)}{2}(t_2 - t_1)$$

Substitute for $t_2 - t_1$ from equation (2.1.4) and multiply the expression out. Then substitute for V_2 from equation (2.1.5) and for V_1 from equation (2.1.3). The result is

$$D_2 - D_1 = \frac{1}{2a_m}\left[\left(V_L - \frac{a_m^2}{2J_2}\right)^2 - \left(\frac{a_m^2}{2J_1}\right)^2\right] \tag{2.2.3}$$

Adding equations (2.2.1), (2.2.2), and (2.2.3), we have

$$D_{0L} = \frac{V_L}{2}\left(\frac{V_L}{a_m} + \frac{a_m}{J_2}\right)$$

$$- \frac{a_m^3}{24}\left(\frac{1}{J_2^2} - \frac{1}{J_1^2}\right) \tag{2.2.4}$$

in which equation (2.1.6) has been substituted.

Following equation (2.1.8) it was indicated that under usual circumstances J is approximately equal to a_m. The maximum value of a_m considered acceptable from the standpoint of comfort is about 2.5m/s^2 or 0.25 gee. Therefore a_m^3/J^2 is approximately 2.5, and the term in equation (2.2.4) proportional to a_m^3 contributes no more than 10 cm to D_{0L}. Therefore, to a good approximation,

$$D_{0L} = \frac{V_L^2}{2a_m} + \frac{V_L a_m}{2J_2} \tag{2.2.5}$$

The value D_{0L} given by equation (2.2.5) is the distance the vehicle travels while its velocity changes by V_L with the indicated values of acceleration and jerk. The word "changes" is used to emphasize that the result is the same if the transition is from rest to line speed or from line speed to rest, if the change in velocity is V_L. Thus equation (2.2.5) can be referred to as the stopping distance. In the case of deceleration, however, the problem of power limitation, discussed in section 2.3, does not exist and we can set $J_1 = J_2 = J$. Then

$$\text{Stopping Distance} = \frac{V_L^2}{2a_m} + \frac{V_L a_m}{2J} \qquad (2.2.6)$$

2.3 Acceleration Power

Power is force times velocity. The acceleration force $F = ma$, where m is the mass of the vehicle and a is the acceleration. Thus

$$\text{Acceleration Power} = P_a = maV \qquad (2.3.1)$$

The energy required to accelerate an object from rest to velocity V is

$$\text{Energy} = \int_0^t P_a\, dt = m \int_0^t aV\, dt$$

But $a = dV/dt$. Therefore

$$\text{Energy} = m \int_0^V V\, dV = \frac{mV^2}{2} \qquad (2.3.2.)$$

the well-known formula for kinetic energy.

In accelerating a transit vehicle, we are interested in the maximum power required to overcome inertia, air drag, and road resistance. This will be dealt with in more detail in section 2.6, but here we concentrate on acceleration power given by equation (2.3.1) to determine how power limitations effect D_{0L} and t_{0L}. The product aV increases linearly from t_1 to t_2 in figure 2-1 and then must fall off to zero at t_{0L} where $a = 0$ after possibly exceeding the value at t_2. It can be shown, however, that unless V_L is less than $1.5\ a_m^2/J_2$, aV reaches its maximum value at t_2. This is assumed in the following paragraph.

The reason for possibly making J_2 less than J_1 is to limit the power required and hence the size of the motors. In this circumstance, we can assume that a_m remains constant until the power reaches P_{max}, following which the acceleration is reduced to zero at rate J_2. In this case, using equation (2.2.5),

$$P_{max} = ma_m V(t_2) = m \left(a_m V_L - \frac{a_m^3}{2J_2} \right) \qquad (2.3.3)$$

in which equation (2.1.5) has been used. If the maximum available power for acceleration is known, equation (2.3.3) can be used directly to compute the maximum permissible value of J_2.

To determine the effect of power limitations on D_{0L} and t_{0L}, consider the following changes due to reduction in J_2:

From equation (2.3.3)

$$\Delta P_{max} = - \frac{ma_m^3}{2} \Delta \left(\frac{1}{J_2} \right) \qquad (2.3.4)$$

From equation (2.2.4)

$$\Delta D_{0L} = \frac{V_L a_m}{2} \Delta \left(\frac{1}{J_2} \right) - \frac{a_m^3}{24} \Delta \left(\frac{1}{J_2^2} \right)$$

$$\qquad (2.3.5)$$

$$= \frac{a_m}{2} \left[V_L - \frac{a_m^2}{12} \left(\frac{1}{J_1'} + \frac{1}{J_2} \right) \right] \Delta \left(\frac{1}{J_2} \right)$$

From equation (2.1.7)

$$\Delta t_{0L} = \frac{a_m}{2} \Delta \left(\frac{1}{J_2} \right) \qquad (2.3.6)$$

For purposes of rough estimates, let

$$P_{\max} \approx m a_m V_L \qquad D_{0L} \approx \frac{V_L^2}{2 a_m} \qquad t_{0L} \approx \frac{V_L}{a_m}$$

Then, if we divide equation (2.3.5) by equation (2.3.4), the result can be written in the form

$$\frac{\Delta D_{0L}}{D_{0L}} = -2 \frac{\Delta P_{\max}}{P_{\max}} \left[1 - \frac{a_m^2}{12 V_L} \left(\frac{1}{J_1} + \frac{1}{J_2} \right) \right] \qquad (2.3.7)$$

and, if we divide equation (2.3.6) by equation (2.3.4), the result can be written in the form

$$\frac{\Delta t_{0L}}{t_{0L}} = - \frac{\Delta P_{\max}}{P_{\max}} \qquad (2.3.8)$$

We see that a given percentage reduction in the maximum power increases D_{0L} by somewhat less than twice that percentage, and t_{0L} by the same percentage. This magnitude of change in t_{0L} is usually insignificant because t_{0L} is a small fraction of the total trip time. If the stations are on the main line, the indicated change in D_{0L} is not significant unless the stations are so close together that V_L can no longer be reached. Thus, with on-line stations, reduction in J_2 below J_1 is usually advantageous. If the stations are off line, however, increasing D_{0L} directly increases the length of the acceleration ramps, thus adding directly to the cost of the system. Since reserve power is needed to operate on grades and in high winds, it is doubtful that a given percentage reduction in $P_{\max}$ will reduce overall cost enough to offset twice that percentage increase in off-line ramp cost and visual impact. Thus, in dealing with off-line station systems we will always assume $J_2 = J_1$.

2.4 Trip Time and Average Velocity

Each trip is composed of one or more maneuvers of the type depicted in figure 2-3. The vehicle begins to move at $t = 0$, reaches maximum velocity at $t = t_a$, cruises to $t = t_b$, decelerates and reaches zero velocity at t_c, waits at a station for a time t_D (called the station dwell time), and repeats its cycle. Let the station-to-station time be denoted by t_s. Then, from Figure 2-3,

$$t_s = t_D + t_a + (t_c - t_b) + (t_b - t_a)$$

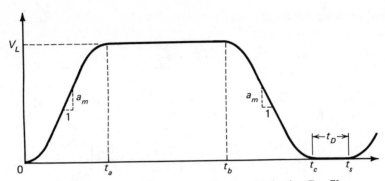

Figure 2-3. The Station-to-Station Velocity Profile

We assume that t_a is given by equation (2.1.7) with $J_1 \neq J_2$, and $t_c - t_b$ with $J_1 = J_2$. Then

$$t_s = t_D + \frac{2V_L}{a_m} + \frac{3a_m}{2J_1} + \frac{a_m}{2J_2} + (t_b - t_a) \qquad (2.4.1)$$

Let D_s be the distance between stations, that is, the area under the velocity profile of figure 2-3. The distance travelled from $t = 0$ to $t = t_a$ is given by equation (2.2.4) with $J_1 \neq J_2$, and from $t = t_b$ to $t = t_c$ by the same equation with $J_1 = J_2$. The distance from $t = t_a$ to $t = t_b$ is $V_L(t_b - t_a)$ in which $(t_b - t_a)$ is given by equation (2.4.1). Thus, D_s can be written in the form

$$\frac{D_s}{V_L} = \frac{V_L}{a_m} + \frac{a_m}{2}\left(\frac{1}{J_2} + \frac{1}{J_1}\right)$$

$$-\frac{a_m^3}{24V_L}\left(\frac{1}{J_2^2} - \frac{1}{J_1^2}\right) + (t_b - t_a) \qquad (2.4.2)$$

Subtracting equation (2.4.2) from equation (2.4.1) eliminates $(t_b - t_a)$ and we have

$$t_s = t_D + \frac{D_s}{V_L} + \frac{V_L}{a_m}$$

$$+ \frac{a_m}{J_1} + \frac{a_m^3}{24V_L}\left(\frac{1}{J_2^2} - \frac{1}{J_1^2}\right)$$

Suppose $J_2 = 0.5J_1$, $J_1 = a_m$, $a_m = 2.5$ m/s², and $V_L = 10$ m/s. In this case the rightmost term is only 0.03 s. Thus in practical cases we can neglect the rightmost term and obtain

$$t_s = t_D + \frac{D_s}{V_L} + \frac{V_L}{a_m} + \frac{a_m}{J_1} \qquad (2.4.3)$$

It will be noticed that the form of this equation makes it very easy to remember. The trip time is simply the sum of terms like equation (2.4.3), one corresponding to each stop. If the vehicle must slow down somewhere enroute, a formula for the additional delay is given by equation (2.5.3).

The average velocity V_{av} is simply D_s/t_s. Using equation (2.4.3),

$$V_{av} = \frac{D_s}{t_D + \dfrac{D_s}{V_L} + \dfrac{V_L}{a_m} + \dfrac{a_m}{J_1}}$$

or

$$\frac{V_{av}}{V_L} = \frac{D_s}{D_s + \tilde{D}} \qquad (2.4.4)$$

in which

$$\tilde{D} = V_L \tilde{t}_D + \frac{V_L^2}{a_m} \qquad (2.4.5)$$

and

$$\tilde{t}_D = t_D + \frac{a_m}{J_1} \qquad (2.4.6)$$

By comparing equation (2.4.5) with equation (2.2.6), we note that when $t_D = 0$, $\tilde{D}$ is the minimum D_s which will permit speed V_L to be reached. Equations (2.4.4) and (2.4.5) are plotted in figure 2-4 in such a way that V_{av}/V_L can be read directly as a function of four variables: D_s, V_L, a_m, and t_D. If the figure is rotated 90 degrees counterclockwise, the right-hand graph is a plot of equation (2.4.5) for five values of t_D, two values of a_m, and for $a_m = J_1$. The lower value of a_m is generally accepted as the appropriate normal acceleration and deceleration for vehicles in which standees are permitted, and the higher value of a_m is the corresponding value if all passengers are seated. The five values of t_D to cover the range used in practice. Note that the five dashed curves are shifted upward from the corresponding set of solid curves.

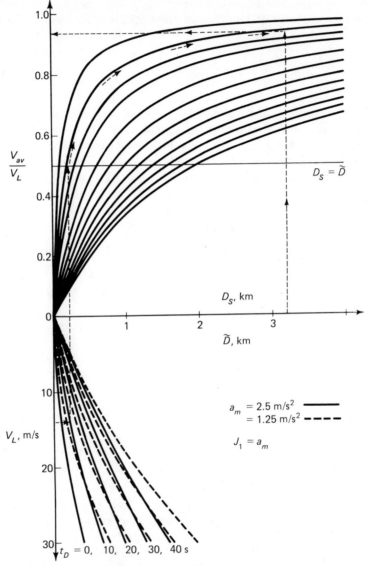

Figure 2-4. The Average Velocity

If we rotate the figure back to its original position, the upper set of curves is a plot of V_{av}/V_L on the ordinate and D_s on the abscissa, with the abscissa taken common to the ordinate of the lower curve. From equation (2.4.4) we see that $D_s = \tilde{D}$ when $V_{av}/V_L = 0.5$. Therefore connection between the lower and upper sets of curves can be made along the line $V_{av}/V_L = 0.5$. Arrows on the curves illustrate their use in an example in which the input variables in the lower set of curves are $t_D = 10$ s, $a_m = 2.5$ m/s², and $V_L = 14$ m/s. These values give $\tilde{D} = 0.22$ km. Follow the dotted line through $\tilde{D} = 0.22$ km up to $V_{av}/V_L = 0.5$. Here $\tilde{D} = D_s$, therefore the solution for V_{av}/V_L lies on the curve which passes through the point $V_{av}/V_L = 0.5$, $D_s = 0.22$ km. The family of values of V_{av}/V_L for various D_s fall along this curve, outlined by arrows. For the specific value $D_s = 3.2$ km, we find that $V_{av}/V_L = 0.936$. Often V_{av} will be specified from patronage considerations. Then a family of solutions can be found by picking values of V_L and finding D_s from the graph in a similar fashion.

2.5 Time and Distance Loss due to Speed Reduction

Often it is necessary to compute the time lost in slowing from line speed V_L to a reduced speed V^*, in which the reduced speed is maintained for a distance D^* and a time interval D^*/V^*. An example is going around a curve. The situation is shown in figure 2-5, in which we assume the transition occurs with the acceleration profile shown in figure 2-1, with $J_2 = J_1$ on deceleration and J_1 greater than or equal to J_2 on acceleration. The values D_{a_1} and D_{a_2} in figure 2-5 are taken from equation (2.2.4), with the term proportional to a_m^3 neglected, by substituting $V_L - V^*$ for V_L. Thus

$$D_{a_{1,2}} = \frac{(V_L - V^*)}{2}\left(\frac{V_L - V^*}{a_m} + \frac{a_m}{J_{1,2}}\right) \tag{2.5.1}$$

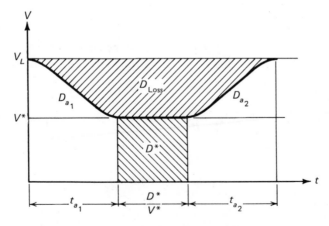

Figure 2-5. Velocity Profile in Speed Reduction

The time intervals t_{a_1} and t_{a_2} are given by equation (2.1.7) with V_L replaced by $V_L - V^*$, and with $J_2 = J_1$ and $J_2 \leqslant J_1$, respectively. Then from figure 2-5,

$$D_{\text{LOSS}} = (V_L - V^*) \left(t_{a_1} + \frac{D^*}{V^*} + t_{a_2} \right) - D_{a_1} - D_{a_2}$$

$$= (V_L - V^*) \left(\frac{V_L - V^*}{a_m} + \frac{a_m}{J_1} + \frac{D^*}{V^*} \right) \qquad (2.5.2)$$

Finally, the time loss is simply the time required to make up the distance D_{LOSS} at speed V_L. Thus

$$t_{\text{LOSS}} = \frac{D_{\text{LOSS}}}{V_L} \qquad (2.5.3)$$

2.6 Average Power Consumption

Consider a train of n_T vehicles, each of mass M_v and frontal area A_v, following the velocity profile of figure 2-3. The total energy input to the vehicle from $t = 0$ to t_s divided by t_s is the average power consumption. The energy input is given by

$$E(t_s) = \int_0^{t_s} \frac{FV}{\eta(V)} \, dt + n_T P_{\text{aux}} t_s \qquad (2.6.1)$$

in which P_{aux} is the auxiliary power consumed per vehicle, $\eta(V)$ is the efficiency of the motors, and F is the retarding force. The force is given by

$$= (1 - \mathcal{R}) n_T M_v \frac{dV}{dt} + \tfrac{1}{2}\rho \, [V^2 + <V_w^2>] \, C_D A_v$$

$$+ n_T M_v \left[F_r(V) + g \, \frac{dz}{dx} \right] \qquad (2.6.2)$$

in which $\mathcal{R}$ is the energy recovery factor as a result of regenerative braking,

ρ is the air density, C_D is the coefficient of air drag, $<V_w^2>$ is the mean square wind velocity, $F_r(V)$ is the road resistance per unit mass, and dz/dx is the slope of the path. The wind velocity appears as indicated because the mean of the local wind velocity squared is

$$<(V + V_w)^2> = <V^2 + 2VV_w + V_w^2>$$

$$= V^2 + 2V<V_w> + <V_w^2>$$

in which the mean wind speed relative to vehicles travelling in all directions, $<V_w>$, is zero. The road resistance term can usually be expressed adequately[1] in the form

$$F_r(V) = C_1 + C_2 V \tag{2.6.3}$$

If the motor efficiency is a strong function of velocity, the integral in equation (2.6.1) cannot be performed in general. However, we can always define an average efficiency $\bar{\eta}$ by the equation

$$\frac{1}{\bar{\eta}} \int_0^{t_s} FV \, dt = \int_0^{t_s} \frac{FV}{\eta(V)} \, dt \tag{2.6.4}$$

Substitute equation (2.6.3) into equation (2.6.2). Then

$$\int_0^{t_s} FV \, dt = (1 - \mathscr{R})n_T \frac{M_v V_L^2}{2} + \tfrac{1}{2}\rho C_D A_V \left[\int_0^{t_s} V^3 dt + <V_w^2> \int_0^{t_s} V \, dt \right]$$

$$+ n_T M_V \left[C_1 \int_0^{t_s} V \, dt + C_2 \int_0^{t_s} V^2 \, dt + g \int_0^{t_s} \frac{dz}{dx} \frac{dx}{dt} \, dt \right] \tag{2.6.5}$$

in which

$$\int_0^{t_s} V \, dt = D_s$$

and $dx/dt = V$.

Sufficient accuracy in the remaining two integrals can be obtained by assuming in the velocity profile of figure 2-3 that $J = \infty$. Then

$$\int_0^{t_s} V^2 dt = V_L D_s - \frac{V_L^3}{3a_m}$$

and

$$\int_0^{t_s} V^3 dt = V_L^2 D_s - \frac{V_L^4}{2a_m}$$

Substituting the three integrals into equation (2.6.5) and using equation (2.6.4), equation (2.6.1) becomes

$$E(t_s) = \frac{1}{\eta} \left\{ (1 - \mathcal{R}) n_T \frac{M_V V_L^2}{2} + \frac{1}{2} \rho C_D A_V \left[(V_L^2 + <V_w^2>) D_s - \frac{V_L^4}{2a_m} \right] \right.$$

$$\left. + n_T M_V \left[C_1 D_s + C_2 V_L \left(D_s - \frac{V_L^2}{3a_m} \right) + g\,z \right] \right\} + n_T P_{\text{aux}} t_s \qquad (2.6.6)$$

in which z is the change in elevation from the beginning to the end of the trip. From equation (2.4.3), t_s can be approximated by the equation

$$t_s = t_D + \frac{D_s}{V_L} + \frac{V_L}{a_m} \qquad (2.6.7)$$

Then the average power consumption is

$$P_{av} = \frac{E(t_s)}{t_s} \qquad (2.6.8)$$

in which, in the term $E(t_s)$, D_s is the average distance between stops.

2.7 Summary

Chapter 2 derives and collects basic performance equations which are used over and over again in the analysis of transit systems. These formulas are not exact because the time-position curves of vehicle motion cannot be defined precisely; however, they are developed based on idealized velocity-time curves sufficiently accurate for the purposes for which they are used. Approximations are based on generally accepted values of maximum service acceleration and jerk, and, by inference, higher order derivatives of acceleration need not be considered. The formulas derived include the time required to travel from rest to a given line speed, the stopping distance from a given line speed, the maximum power output required during acceleration, the time of a nonstop trip at a given line (or cruise) speed, the average velocity counting stops and dwells, and the time and distance lost due to a speed reduction. Since the relationship between line speed and average speed as it depends on station spacing is particularly important, it is plotted in figure 2-4. Finally, a general formula (2.6.6) for the energy per trip is developed.

Problems

1. Show that the acceleration power of an accelerating vehicle reaches its maximum at the point of transition from constant acceleration to constant jerk, if $V_L > 3a_m^2/2J_2$.
2. Consider a 10,000-kg standing-passenger vehicle moving between stops at a line speed of 30 m/s and conforming to standard comfort criteria. Compute the maximum acceleration power in kilowatts if the maximum comfort value of jerk is applied in all cases. If the power available for acceleration is reduced by 30 percent from the computed value,
   (1) by what factor must jerk be reduced as line speed is approached?
   (2) what is the penalty in increasing distance to reach maximum speed?
   (3) what is the penalty in increased time between stops?
3. It is desired to achieve an average speed of 50 km/hr in a transit system with on-line stations and standing-passenger vehicles. If the average station delay is 20 seconds, plot a curve of station spacing versus line speed. What is the minimum station spacing and at what line speed does it occur? What is the physical significance of the minimum point? If the maximum obtainable line speed is 75 km/hr, what is the minimum permissible station spacing.
4. It is desired to achieve an average speed of 50 km/hr in a transit system with off-line stations and seated-passenger vehicles. If the average trip length is 6 km and the trips are nonstop, what is the required line speed if the station delay is 20 seconds, 10 seconds?

5. In going around a right-angle curve, a seated-passenger transit vehicle is restricted to a lateral acceleration of 0.25 g. If the normal line speed is 15 m/s and the curve radius is 35 m, the vehicle must slow down in going around the curve. What is the time loss in negotiating the curve?

6. The ACME Transit Company's standing-passenger transit vehicle is to be considered in an application in which the station spacing is two km and the line speed is 80 km/hr. If the rms wind speed is 16 km/hr, the auxiliary power is 2 kw per vehicle, the propulsion efficiency is 35 percent, and the station delay is 15 seconds, what percent of the energy is saved if the cars operate in two-car trains rather than as single vehicles if regenerative braking is 50 percent effective? By what factor does energy use increase if there is no regenerative braking?

Reference

1. Thomas McGean, *Urban Transportation Technology*, Lexington Books, D.C. Heath and Company, Lexington, Mass., 1976.

3

Transitions from Straight to Curved Guideways

Chapter 2 deals with longitudinal performance relationships which can be applied on both straight and curved sections of guideway. To understand the layout of the specific network configurations discussed in chapter 4, we also need to consider what may be called "lateral performance relationships." These deal with limitations on lateral curvature and rate of change of curvature of guideways due to comfort limitations on lateral acceleration and jerk.

If the stiffness of lateral support between the vehicle and guideway is high, the lateral jerk limitation results in a requirement for spiral transition sections from straight to curved sections of guideway. Spiral transitions will be treated first. Among these there are two types of practical importance: one in which the velocity of the vehicle is constant, and the other in which the vehicle is subject to constant deceleration or acceleration.

If it is practical to reduce the stiffness of the lateral vehicle support device, abrupt changes in guideway curvature can be tolerated under certain conditions. Since allowing these abrupt changes may reduce the cost of manufacture of the guideway, the conditions under which they can be tolerated are derived.

Finally, the minimum radius of curvature of a guideway can be reduced if the curve is superelevated. Reducing the minimum radius of curvature permits greater freedom of design of networks in street systems, reduces the possibility that buildings will have to be removed at curves, and reduces the length and hence, the cost of curves. For these reasons, formulas for design of superelevated curves are derived.

3.1 The Differential Equation for the Transition Curve

Consider the curve shown in figure 3-1, which passes through the origin of the $x - y$ coordinates with zero slope and zero curvature. The arc length from the origin to an arbitrary point P is s, the angle between the velocity vector $\mathbf{V}$ and the x-axis at P is θ, the tangential unit vector in the direction of $\mathbf{V}$ is $\hat{t}$, and the normal unit vector is $\hat{n}$. As point P moves to the right at velocity $\mathbf{V}$, the unit vectors rotate according to the relationships

$$d\hat{t} = \hat{n}d\theta$$

$$d\hat{n} = -\hat{t}d\theta$$

(3.1.1)

23

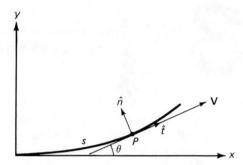

Figure 3-1. Notation in a Transition Curve

Let V be the magnitude of $\mathbf{V}$, $\mathbf{a}$ be the acceleration of point P, and $\mathbf{J}$ be its jerk. Then

$$\mathbf{V} = V\hat{t} \qquad (3.1.2)$$

$$\mathbf{a} = \frac{d\mathbf{V}}{dt} = \frac{dV}{dt}\,\hat{t} + V\,\frac{d\theta}{dt}\,\hat{n} \qquad (3.1.3)$$

$$\mathbf{J} = \frac{d\mathbf{a}}{dt} = \frac{d^2V}{dt^2}\,\hat{t} + 2\,\frac{dV}{dt}\,\frac{d\theta}{dt}\,\hat{n}$$

$$+ V\frac{d^2\theta}{dt^2}\hat{n} - V\left(\frac{d\theta}{dt}\right)^2\hat{t} \qquad (3.1.4)$$

From equation (3.1.4), the tangential jerk is

$$J_t = \frac{d^2V}{dt^2} - V\left(\frac{d\theta}{dt}\right)^2 \qquad (3.1.5)$$

and the normal jerk is

$$J_n = V\,\frac{d^2\theta}{dt^2} + 2\,\frac{dV}{dt}\,\frac{d\theta}{dt} \qquad (3.1.6)$$

We wish to determine the shape of the guideway (the curve of figure 3-1), therefore, we make the transformation

$$\frac{d}{dt} = \frac{ds}{dt}\frac{d}{ds} = V\frac{d}{ds} \tag{3.1.7}$$

hence

$$\frac{d\theta}{dt} = V\frac{d\theta}{ds} \tag{3.1.8}$$

and

$$\frac{d^2\theta}{dt^2} = V^2\frac{d^2\theta}{ds^2} + \frac{dV}{dt}\frac{d\theta}{ds} \tag{3.1.9}$$

and equations (3.1.5) and (3.1.6) can be written

$$J_t = \frac{d^2V}{dt^2} - V^3\left(\frac{d\theta}{ds}\right)^2 \tag{3.1.10}$$

$$J_n = V^3\frac{d^2\theta}{ds^2} + 3V\frac{dV}{dt}\frac{d\theta}{ds} \tag{3.1.11}$$

Equation (3.1.11) with J_n constant defines the transition curve. Once it is found, J_t can be found from equation (3.1.10) to determine if it exceeds the comfort criterion.

In practical cases we will consider $d^2V/dt^2 = 0$; therefore, equation (3.1.10) becomes

$$J_t = -\frac{1}{V}\left(V^2\frac{d\theta}{ds}\right)^2 \tag{3.1.12}$$

But from equation (3.1.3) and (3.1.8), the normal acceleration is

$$a_n = V^2\frac{d\theta}{ds} = \frac{V^2}{R} \tag{3.1.13}$$

in which $d\theta/ds$ is the curvature and R is the radius of curvature. Thus, equation (3.1.12) becomes

$$J_t = -\frac{a_n^2}{V} \qquad (3.1.14)$$

If the limit value of a_n and the minimum value of V are substituted into equation (3.1.14), and the result is below the jerk limit, the acceleration limit determines the length of the spiral transition; otherwise, the limit is determined by jerk. Since the acceleration and jerk limits are approximately equal in units of seconds, the acceleration limit governs if a_n is less than V_{min}, a condition which is usually satisfied.

3.2 The Constant Speed Spiral

If V is constant, equation (3.1.11) can be written

$$\frac{d^2\theta}{ds^2} = \frac{J_n}{V^3} \qquad (3.2.1)$$

At $s = 0$, $\theta = d\theta/ds = 0$; therefore, the curvature is

$$\frac{d\theta}{ds} = \frac{J_n s}{V^3} \qquad (3.2.2)$$

and, from equation (3.1.13), the normal acceleration is

$$a_n = \frac{J_n s}{V} \qquad (3.2.3)$$

Integrating equation (3.2.2), we have

$$\theta = \frac{J_n s^2}{2V^3} \qquad (3.2.4)$$

If equation (3.2.3) is solved for s and substituted into equation (3.2.4),

$$\theta = \frac{a_n^2}{2J_n V} \qquad (3.2.5)$$

With the limit values of a_n and J_n substituted into equations (3.2.5) and

(3.2.3), we obtain the maximum values of θ and s, respectively, along the constant velocity spiral. With $a_n = J_n$ in units of seconds,

$$\theta_{max} = \frac{a_n}{2V} \tag{3.2.6}$$

and

$$s_{max} = V \tag{3.2.7}$$

The equation of the constant velocity spiral in rectangular coordinates (x, y) is found from the differential relationships

$$\left.\begin{aligned} dx &= ds \cos \theta \\ dy &= ds \sin \theta \end{aligned}\right\} \tag{3.2.8}$$

in which all terms are defined in figure 3-1.

The equation of the spiral transition section is therefore given parametrically by the equations

$$\left.\begin{aligned} x &= \int_0^s \cos \theta(s) \, ds \\ y &= \int_0^s \sin \theta(s) \, ds \end{aligned}\right\} \tag{3.2.9}$$

in which $\theta(s)$ is given by equation (3.2.4).

The angle $\theta(s)$ is limited to the value given by equation (3.2.6). In an extreme case, we can assume $a_n = 2.5 \text{ m/s}^2$ and $V = 5 \text{ m/s}^2$. In this case, $\theta_{max} = 0.25$ radian. In most cases, θ_{max} is much smaller; therefore, use of only the first term in the Taylor series expansions of the sine and cosine is sufficient. At θ_{max}, the second terms in the Taylor series expansions

$$\cos \theta = 1 - \frac{\theta^2}{2} + \ldots$$

$$\sin \theta = \theta - \frac{\theta^3}{3!} + \ldots$$

produce an error less than $\theta_{max}^2/2 = 1/32$ compared to unity. Therefore, substituting $\cos \theta = 1$ and $\sin \theta = \theta$ into equations (3.2.9), and then equation (3.2.4), we have

$$\left.\begin{aligned} x &= s \\ y &= \frac{J_n s^3}{6V^3} \end{aligned}\right\} \tag{3.2.10}$$

The equation of the spiral is, therefore

$$y = \frac{J_n x^3}{6V^3} \qquad (3.2.11)$$

If we define the dimensionless variables

$$\bar{s} = \frac{s}{\sqrt{2V^3/J_n}}$$

$$\bar{x} = \frac{x}{\sqrt{2V^3/J_n}} \qquad (3.2.12)$$

$$\bar{y} = \frac{y}{\sqrt{2V^3/J_n}}$$

equation (3.2.4) becomes

$$\theta = \bar{s}^2 \qquad (3.2.13)$$

and equation (3.2.11) becomes

$$\bar{y} = \frac{\bar{x}^3}{3} \qquad (3.2.14)$$

Since these equations contain no parameter, we see that the family of constant velocity spirals scale in proportion to the parameters $\sqrt{2V^3/J_n}$, that is, in proportion to $V^{3/2}$. From equation (3.2.7) we note, however, that the maximum length of the constant speed spiral is proportional to V.

3.3 A Right-Angle Curve at Constant Speed

In this section, the theory of section 3.2 is applied to the specification of a right-angle curve in which the vehicles are to maintain constant line speed V. A constant speed spiral forms the transition from a straight guideway to a guideway of constant radius of curvature R, which, from equation (3.1.13), is

$$R = \frac{V^2}{a_n} \qquad (3.3.1)$$

in which, a_n is specified from comfort conditions. A second spiral, which is the mirror image of the first rotated 90 degrees counterclockwise forms the transition from the constant curvature section back to a straight section. The problem of this section is to determine the coordinates required to lay out the entire curve, and the length of the curved sections.

Let the origin of the $(x - y)$ coordinates be at the point of transition from the straight section to the spiral transition section, with the velocity vector at the origin pointed in the $+ x$ direction. Then the equation of the first transition spiral is, without transformation, equation (3.2.11). Call the end point of this transition section (x_1, y_1). Then the coordinates x_1 and y_1 are found by substituting s_{max} from the equation (3.2.7) into equation (3.2.10).

Thus

$$\left. \begin{array}{l} x_1 = V \\[2em] y_1 = \dfrac{J_n}{6} \end{array} \right\} \tag{3.3.2}$$

The length of the first transition section is V in units of seconds, and the guideway at (x_1, y_1) makes an angle θ, with the x-axis, where from equation (3.2.6)

$$\theta_1 = \frac{a_n}{2V} \tag{3.3.3}$$

Let (x_2, y_2) be the coordinates of the center of curvature of the section of constant curvature. Then, from a simple geometric construction,

$$x_2 = x_1 - R \sin \theta_1$$

$$y_2 = y_1 + R \cos \theta_1$$

Since θ_1 is a small angle, let $\sin \theta_1 = \theta_1$ and, $\cos \theta_1 = 1$. Then substitute from equations (3.3.1), (3.3.2) and (3.3.3) to obtain

$$\left. \begin{array}{l} x_2 = \dfrac{V}{2} \\[2em] y_2 = \dfrac{J_n}{6} + \dfrac{V^2}{a_n} \end{array} \right\} \tag{3.3.4}$$

Let (x_3, y_3) be the coordinates of the center point of the section of constant curvature. This point is important because it determines the clearance required for the curve. From a geometric construction,

$$x_3 = x_2 + R/\sqrt{2}$$

$$y_3 = y_2 - R/\sqrt{2}$$

Substituting equations (3.3.1) and (3.3.4),

$$\left. \begin{array}{l} x_3 = \dfrac{V}{2} + 0.707 \ \dfrac{V^2}{a_n} \\[3mm] y_3 = \dfrac{J_n}{6} + 0.293 \ \dfrac{V^2}{a_n} \end{array} \right\} \qquad (3.3.5)$$

Let (x_4, y_4) be the coordinates of the end point of the section of constant curvature. Then

$$x_4 = x_2 + R \cos \theta_1$$

$$y_4 = y_2 - R \sin \theta_1$$

Making the small angle assumption and substituting from equations (3.3.1), (3.3.3), and (3.3.4),

$$\left. \begin{array}{l} x_4 = \dfrac{V}{2} + \dfrac{V^2}{a_n} \\[3mm] y_4 = \dfrac{J_n}{6} + \dfrac{V^2}{a_n} - \dfrac{V}{2} \end{array} \right\} \qquad (3.3.6)$$

Finally, let (x_5, y_5) be the end point of the spiral transition from curved back to straight guideway. Then,

$$x_5 = x_4 + y_1$$

$$y_5 = y_4 + x_1$$

Substituting from equations (3.3.2) and (3.3.6),

$$x_5 = y_5 = \frac{J_n}{6} + \frac{V}{2} + \frac{V^2}{a_n} \qquad (3.3.7)$$

The length of the section of constant curvature is $R(\pi/2 - 2\theta_1)$, therefore, using equations (3.3.1), (3.3.3), and (3.2.7), the total length of curved guideway is

$$\text{Curved Guideway Length} = R \left(\pi/2 - 2\theta_1 \right) + 2V$$

$$= \frac{\pi}{2} \frac{V^2}{a_n} + V \qquad (3.3.8)$$

Thus, the addition of a spiral transition adds a length V (in units of seconds) to the total length of curved guideway.

3.4 Transition to an Off-Line Station at Constant Speed

In this section, the theory of section 3.2 is applied to the design of a constant speed transition from a mainline guideway onto a parallel guideway separated by a distance H from the mainline. The transition, shown in figure 3-2, is made up of four constant speed spirals of the type given by equation (3.2.11), connected so that the slope and curvature are everywhere continuous. We let the total length of the transition section in the direction of flow be denoted by L.

The section of the transition shown in figure 3-2, between $x = 0$, and $x = L/4$, is computed from equation (3.2.11) without transformation. The curvature is a maximum at point $x = L/4$ and vanishes at points $x = 0$, $L/2$. Therefore, the transition section from $x = L/4$ to $x = L/2$ is a mirror image of the first section about the perpendicular bisector of the line connecting the origin with the point $x = L/2$, $y = H/2$. The section from $x = L/2$ to $x = L$ is obtained by rotating the first half of the transition 180 degrees in the plane of the paper about the midpoint.

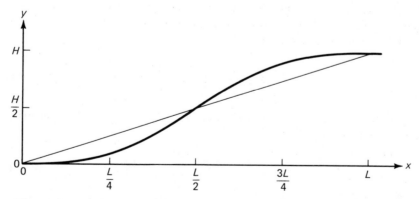

Figure 3-2. A Spiral Transition to a Parallel Line at Constant Speed

In the derivation of the relationship between L and H, it is convenient to use the dimensionless notation defined by equations (3.2.12). Thus, let

$$\bar{H} = \frac{H}{\sqrt{2V^3/J_n}}$$

and

$$\left. \begin{array}{c} \\ \\ \end{array} \right\} \qquad (3.4.1)$$

$$\bar{L} = \frac{L}{\sqrt{2V^3/J_n}}$$

and consider the dimensionless form of the equation for the spiral, equation (3.2.14). From figure 3-2, and equation (3.2.14), we see that at $\bar{x} = \bar{L}/4$

$$\frac{d\bar{y}}{d\bar{x}} = \bar{x}^2 = \frac{\bar{H}}{\bar{L}}$$

Substituting $\bar{x} = \bar{L}/4$, we have

$$\bar{H} = \frac{\bar{L}^3}{16} \qquad (3.4.2)$$

Since equation (3.4.2) and equation (3.2.14) contain only the dimensionless values and no parameters, the transition spiral scales in proportion to the parameter $\sqrt{2V^3/J_n}$, that is, in proportion to $V^{3/2}$. Substituting equations (3.4.1) into equation (3.4.2), we find that

$$L = V\left(\frac{32H}{J_n} \right)^{1/3} \qquad (3.4.3)$$

Thus, for a given value of H, L increases in proportion to V.

The maximum magnitude of the normal acceleration a_n occurs at $x = L/4$ and at $x = 3L/4$. Therefore, in equation (3.2.3), substitute $s = x = L/4$, and then equation (3.4.3). We obtain

$$a_n = \frac{J_n L}{4V} = \left(\frac{J_n^2 H}{2} \right)^{1/3} \qquad (3.4.4)$$

Hence, for given maximum values of J_n and a_n, the maximum permissible value of H is

$$H_{max} = \frac{2a_n^3}{J_n^2} = 2a_n \qquad (3.4.5)$$

in seconds units if $(a_n)_{max} = J_n$. If a lateral displacement larger than H_{max} is required, a straight section must be inserted at $x = L/2$ in figure 3-2. From symmetry, the slope of the straight section is $2H/L$. If H_{max} is substituted into equation (3.4.3) and $a_n = J_n$,

$$L_{max} = 4V \tag{3.4.6}$$

The minimum radius of curvature is found by substituting equation (3.4.4) into equation (3.1.13). Thus

$$R_{min} = V^2 \left(\frac{2}{J_n^2 H} \right)^{1/3} \tag{3.4.7}$$

3.5 The Constant Deceleration Spiral

This case is defined by the equation

$$\frac{dV}{dt} = -a \tag{3.5.1}$$

Substituting equation (3.5.1) into equation (3.1.11) gives, J_n constant, the equation of the constant deceleration spiral. This equation can be integrated if we note that, by substituting equation (3.1.7) into equation (3.5.1),

$$ds = \frac{-V \, dV}{a} \tag{3.5.2}$$

from which

$$\frac{d\theta}{ds} = - \frac{a}{V} \frac{d\theta}{dV} \tag{3.5.3}$$

and

$$\frac{d^2\theta}{ds^2} = \frac{a^2}{V} \frac{d}{dV} \left(\frac{d\theta}{V \, dV} \right) \tag{3.5.4}$$

Thus, with V as the independent variable, equation (3.1.11) becomes

$$a^2 V^2 \frac{d}{dV} \left(\frac{d\theta}{V \, dV} \right) + 3a^2 \frac{d\theta}{dV} = J_n$$

If we multiply both sides of this equation by V, the left side becomes a perfect differential:

$$\frac{d}{dV}\left(V^2\,\frac{d\theta}{dV}\right) = \frac{J_n V}{a^2} \tag{3.5.5}$$

The initial conditions at $s = 0$ are $V = V_0$ and $\theta = d\theta/ds = 0$; thus, from equation (3.5.3), $d\theta/dV = 0$. Therefore, the integral of equation (3.5.5) can be written

$$\frac{d\theta}{dV} = -\frac{J_n}{2a^2}\left(\frac{V_0^2}{V^2} - 1\right) \tag{3.5.6}$$

Integrating again, θ can be written in the form

$$\theta = \frac{J_n V_0}{a^2}\,\frac{(1 - V/V_0)^2}{2V/V_0} \tag{3.5.7}$$

By substituting equation (3.5.6) into equation (3.5.3), we obtain the curvature of the decelerating spiral.

$$\frac{1}{R} = \frac{d\theta}{ds} = \frac{J_n}{2aV_0}\,\frac{V_0}{V}\left(\frac{V_0^2}{V^2} - 1\right) \tag{3.5.8}$$

in which R is the radius of curvature. Using equation (3.1.13), the normal acceleration is

$$a_n = \frac{V^2}{R} = \frac{J_n}{2a}\,V\left(\frac{V_0^2}{V^2} - 1\right) \tag{3.5.9}$$

With the limit value of a_n substituted, the minimum value of V is the positive root of equation (3.5.9) solved for V:

$$V_{\min} = \frac{a a_n}{J_n}\left[\sqrt{1 + \left(\frac{V_0 J_n}{a a_n}\right)^2} - 1\right] \tag{3.5.10}$$

Substitution of equation (3.5.10) into equations (3.5.7) and (3.5.8) gives the maximum value of θ and the minimum value of R, respectively.

As an example, let $J_n = a_n = a = 2.5$ m/s², and $V_0 = 10$ m/s. Then, from equation (3.5.10), $V_{min} = 7.81$ m/s. Substituting V_{min} into equations (3.5.7) and (3.5.8),

$$\theta_{max} = 7.05° \text{ and } R_{min} = 24.4 \text{ m}$$

In practical cases, speed is decreased to obtain the minimum radius of curvature, and hence the smallest requirement for clearance. In this case, both a_n and R_{min} are specified, and V_m is found from the equation

$$V_{min} = \sqrt{a_n R_{min}} \tag{3.5.11}$$

Then, from equation (3.5.9), the velocity at the beginning of the spiral transition should be

$$V_0 = V_{min} \left(1 + \frac{2aa_n}{J_n V_{min}} \right)^{1/2} \tag{3.5.12}$$

that is, the line speed should be slowed to V_0 before entering the spiral.

The length of the decelerating spiral is found by integrating equation (3.5.2) with the initial condition $s = 0$ when $V = V_0$. The result may be written

$$s = \frac{V_0^2}{2a} \left(1 - \frac{V^2}{V_0^2} \right) \tag{3.5.13}$$

Then, in the above example, the maximum length of the spiral is obtained by substituting into equation (3.5.13) the values $V_0 = 10$ m/s, $V = 7.81$ m/s, and $a = 2.5$ m/s². Then $s_{max} = 7.8$ m.

The equation of the spiral is found by substituting equation (3.5.7) into equation (3.2.8) in which we substitute equation (3.5.2). The resulting equation can be integrated in dimensionless form if we define the following dimensionless variables:

$$\beta = \frac{J_n V_0}{2a^2} \tag{3.5.14}$$

$$\xi = \frac{V}{V_0} \tag{3.5.15}$$

$$X = ax/V_0^2$$
$$Y = ay/V_0^2$$

(3.5.16)

Thus,

$$X = \int_{V/V_0}^{1} \cos\left[\frac{\beta(1-\xi)^2}{\xi}\right]\xi\,d\xi$$

$$Y = \int_{V/V_0}^{1} \sin\left[\frac{\beta(1-\xi)^2}{\xi}\right]\xi\,d\xi$$

(3.5.17)

If it can be assumed that $\theta^2/2$ is much less than 1, these equations become:

$$X = \int_{V/V_0}^{1}\xi\,d\xi = \tfrac{1}{2}\left(1 - \frac{V^2}{V_0^2}\right)$$

$$Y = \beta\int_{V/V_0}^{1}(1-\xi)^2 d\xi = \frac{\beta}{3}\left(1 - \frac{V}{V_0}\right)^3$$

(3.5.18)

Solving the first of these equations for V/V_0 and substituting into the second, we have the equation of the decelerating spiral for small angles:

$$Y = \frac{\beta}{3}\left[1 - (1 - 2X)^{1/2}\right]^3$$

(3.5.19)

The specification of a right angle curve with deceleration is found by following the procedure of section 3.3, in which the coordinates of the endpoint of the spiral are found from equations (3.5.18) and the endpoint angle from equation (3.5.7), both for the appropriate value of V_{min}/V_0.

3.6 The Lateral Response of a Vehicle due to a Sudden Change in the Curvature of the Path

In some cases, spiral guideways have been found to be more expensive to manufacture than guideways of constant curvature. Therefore, it is useful

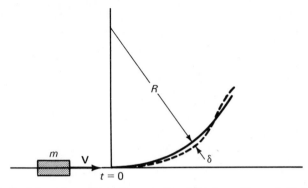

Figure 3-3. A Sudden Transition from a Straight to a Curved Guideway

to know the conditions under which spiral sections can be approximated by sections of constant curvature. The problem reduces to the determination of the lateral response of a vehicle due to a sudden change in the curvature of the path.

Consider a vehicle of mass m moving to the right in figure 3-3 with speed V. The vehicle has a lateral suspension system with spring constant k, damping coefficient ζ, and maximum permissible lateral deflection δ_m. At the point $t = 0$, the guideway curvature suddenly changes from zero to $1/R$. For t greater than 0, the acceleration of the vehicle (and passengers) in the direction normal to the curved path is $\ddot{\delta} - V^2/R$ in which δ is the deflection of the lateral suspension system, positive if away from the center of curvature as indicated in figure 3-3. The lateral equation of motion can be written in the form

$$\ddot{\delta} + 2\zeta\omega\dot{\delta} + \omega^2\delta = a_c \qquad (3.6.1)$$

in which

$$\omega = \sqrt{\frac{k}{m}} \qquad (3.6.2)$$

and

$$a_c = \frac{V^2}{R} \qquad (3.6.3)$$

Also, let

$$\omega' = \omega\sqrt{1 - \zeta^2} \qquad (3.6.4)$$

Then, subject to the initial conditions $\delta(0) = \dot{\delta}(0) = 0$, the solution to equation (3.6.1) is

$$\delta = \frac{a_c}{\omega^2}\left[1 - e^{-\omega\zeta t}\left(\frac{\zeta}{\sqrt{1 - \zeta^2}}\sin \omega't + \cos \omega't\right)\right] \tag{3.6.5}$$

Differentiating,

$$\dot{\delta} = \frac{a_c}{\omega\sqrt{1 - \zeta^2}} e^{-\omega\zeta t}\sin \omega't \tag{3.6.6}$$

$$\ddot{\delta} = a_c e^{-\omega\zeta t}\left(\cos \omega't - \frac{\zeta}{\sqrt{1 - \zeta^2}}\sin \omega't\right) \tag{3.6.7}$$

$$\dddot{\delta} = -a_c\omega e^{-\omega\zeta t}\left[\frac{(1 - 2\zeta^2)}{\sqrt{1 - \zeta^2}}\sin \omega't + 2\zeta \cos \omega't\right] \tag{3.6.8}$$

$$\ddddot{\delta} = -a_c\omega^2 e^{-\omega\zeta t}\left[(1 - 4\zeta^2) \cos \omega't - \frac{\zeta(3 - 4\zeta^2)}{\sqrt{1 - \zeta^2}}\sin \omega't\right] \tag{3.6.9}$$

Note that the lateral acceleration of the vehicle is $\ddot{\delta} - a_c$, which is zero at $t = 0$.

The maximum value of δ occurs at the first zero of $\dot{\delta}$ for t greater than 0, which, from equation (3.6.6), occurs at $\omega't = \pi$. Substituting this value in equation (3.6.5),

$$\delta_m = a_c/\omega^2 \, (1 + e^{-\pi\zeta/\sqrt{1-\zeta^2}}) \tag{3.6.10}$$

With δ_m given by design, k should be chosen for a given m (see equation (3.6.2)) so that

$$\omega^2 = \frac{a_c}{\delta_m}\left(1 + e^{-\pi\zeta/\sqrt{1 - \zeta^2}}\right) \tag{3.6.11}$$

in which ζ is yet to be determined. By setting $\dddot{\delta} = 0$, solving for $\omega't$, and substitution into equation (3.6.7), it can be shown that the maximum lateral acceleration of the passengers, $|\ddot{\delta} - a_c|$, occurs at $t = \infty$. Thus, to satisfy the comfort criterion, we need to compute the maximum value of jerk, $\dddot{\delta}$. The maximum value of the function $\dddot{\delta}(\omega't)$ corresponds to the first zero of $\ddddot{\delta}$.

From equations (3.6.8) and (3.6.9), we see that if $\zeta = 0$, $\ddot{\delta}(0) = 0$ and the first maximum in $\ddot{\delta}$ occurs at $\omega't = \pi/2$. As the damping ratio increases, the first zero of $\dddot{\delta}(\omega't)$ moves to earlier values of $\omega't$ until at $\zeta = 0.5$ the first zero of $\dddot{\delta}(\omega't)$ occurs at $\omega't = 0$. For ζ slightly larger than 0.5, both terms in equations (3.6.9) are negative from $\omega't = 0$ to a value slightly less than $\omega't = \pi$. But, because of the exponential decay term, the value $\ddot{\delta}(0)$ is greater than at the first zero of $\ddot{\delta}$ for $\omega't$ greater than 0. At $\zeta = \sqrt{3/4}$, the first zero of $\ddot{\delta}$ has moved back to $\omega't = \pi/2$, but again $\ddot{\delta}(0)$ greater than $\ddot{\delta}(\pi/2)$. Thus, for $0 < \zeta < \frac{1}{2}$, the maximum value of $\ddot{\delta}(\omega't)$ is found by setting $\dddot{\delta}(\omega't) = 0$. From equation (3.6.9), we then find

$$\tan \omega't = \frac{\sqrt{1 - \zeta^2}}{\zeta}\left(\frac{1 - 4\zeta^2}{3 - 4\zeta^2}\right) \tag{3.6.12}$$

If we use the trigonometric identity $\cos \theta = (1 + \tan^2\theta)^{-1/2}$ and substitute equation (3.6.12) into equation (3.6.8), the bracketed term reduces to unity, and the maximum jerk becomes

$$J_m = a_c\omega \exp\left\{\frac{-\zeta}{\sqrt{1 - \zeta^2}}\tan^{-1}\left[\frac{\sqrt{1 - \zeta^2}}{\zeta}\left(\frac{1 - 4\zeta^2}{3 - 4\zeta^2}\right)\right]\right\} \tag{3.6.13}$$

If $\zeta > \frac{1}{2}$, the maximum jerk is

$$\ddot{\delta}(0) = J_m = 2a_c\omega\zeta \tag{3.6.14}$$

In general, let

$$J_m = a_c\omega\, F(\zeta) \tag{3.6.15}$$

in which the meaning of $F(\delta)$ is found from equation (3.6.13) or (3.6.14). Then square equation (3.6.15) and substitute for ω^2 from equation (3.6.11). The results may be written

$$J_m^2 = \frac{a_c^3}{\delta_m}\left(1 + e^{-\pi\zeta/\sqrt{1-\zeta^2}}\right) F^2(\zeta) \tag{3.6.16}$$

We wish to know how small the radius of curvature, R, can be before J_m

reaches the comfort limit. Therefore, solve equations (3.6.3) for R and substitute for a_c from equation (3.6.16). The result may be written

$$R = \frac{V^2}{J_m^{2/3}\delta_m^{1/3}}\; G(\zeta) \qquad (3.6.17)$$

in which

$$G(\zeta) = \left[1 + \exp\left(\frac{-\pi\zeta}{\sqrt{1-\zeta^2}}\right)\right]^{1/3} \times$$

$$\exp\left\{\frac{-2\zeta}{3\sqrt{1-\zeta^2}}\tan^{-1}\left[\frac{\sqrt{1-\zeta^2}}{\zeta}\left(\frac{1-4\zeta^2}{3-4\zeta^2}\right)\right]\right\} \qquad (0 \le \zeta \le \tfrac{1}{2})$$

$$= \left[1 + \exp\left(\frac{-\pi\zeta}{\sqrt{1-\zeta^2}}\right)\right]^{1/3}(2\zeta)^{2/3} \qquad (\tfrac{1}{2} \le \zeta \le 1) \qquad (3.6.18)$$

The choice of ζ depends on the degree of damping desired, which can be measured by the ratio of the second extremum in the function $|\delta(\omega' t) - \delta(\infty)|$ to the first. Thus,

$$\frac{\delta_{m_2}}{\delta_{m_1}} = \left|\frac{\delta(2\pi) - \delta(\infty)}{\delta(\pi) - \delta(\infty)}\right| = \exp\left(\frac{-\pi\zeta}{\sqrt{1-\zeta^2}}\right) \qquad (3.6.19)$$

The function $\delta_{m_2}/\delta_{m_1}$ and $G(\zeta)$ are plotted in figure 3-4.

Figure 3-4 together with equation (3.6.17) show that the radius of curvature that can be negotiated for a given comfort criterion, given by J_m, is minimized if $\zeta = 1/3$. At this value, the ratio $\delta_{m_2}/\delta_{m_1} = 0.329$, which would appear to be a satisfactory degree of damping. The minimum value of $G(\zeta)$ is $G(1/3) = 0.966$. Therefore, from equation (3.6.17),

$$R_{\min} = 0.966 \frac{V^2}{J_m^{2/3}\delta_m^{1/3}} \qquad (3.6.20)$$

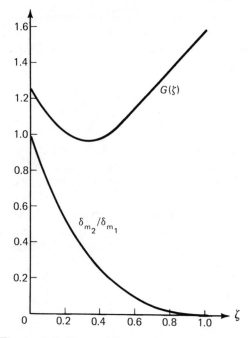

Figure 3-4. Lateral Damping Functions

As an example, let $V = 10$ m/s, $J_m = 2.5$ m/s³, and $\delta_m = 0.05$ m. Then $R_{\min} = 142$ m. Substituting into equation (3.6.3), $a_c = 0.70$ m/s² which is less than the acceleration limit $(a_m)_{\max} = J_m$. Therefore, the curve is determined by the jerk limit and R is given by equation (3.6.20). In general, R is determined by the jerk limit, not the acceleration limit if

$$\frac{J_m^{2/3}\delta_m^{1/3}}{0.966} < (a_c)_{\lim}$$

But $J_m = (a_c)_{\lim}$ in units of seconds. Therefore

$$\delta_m^{1/3} < 0.966\, J_m^{1/3}$$

or

$$\delta_m < 0.901\, J_m$$

if the limit is determined by jerk. Thus, if δ_m is less than approximately one meter, certainly always true, the radius of curvature is limited by equation (3.6.20).

An additional interpretation of equation (3.6.20) is found by solving it for J_m:

$$J_m = 0.949 \quad \frac{V^3}{R^{3/2}\delta_m^{1/2}} \qquad (3.6.21)$$

For a given lateral suspension system defined by δ_m and ζ, and given abrupt changes in curvature characterized by R, equation (3.6.21) shows that the uncomfortableness of the ride, characterized by J_m, worsens as the cube of the velocity.

Suppose a vehicle is on a path of curvature $1/R_1$, and suddenly enters a path of curvature $1/R_2$, in which $R_2 < R_1$. Then, if R is given by equation (3.6.20), the minimum value of R_2 that will meet the comfort criterion is found from the equation

$$\frac{1}{R_2} - \frac{1}{R_1} = \frac{1}{R}$$

from which

$$R_2 = \frac{R_1 R}{R_1 + R} \qquad (3.6.22)$$

If R_2 is substituted into equation (3.6.3) and the computed value of a_c is less than the limit value, equation (3.6.22) determines the curve. Suppose we wish to design a right-angle turn in the guideway in circular arc segments so that the criterion on maximum lateral jerk is always satisfied. Then, from equation (3.6.22), the radius of curvature of successive segments are $R_2 = R$, $R/2$, $R/3$, $R/4$, and so on. In practice, however, it is unlikely that more than two different curvatures will be used.

3.7 Superelevation

The minimum radius in a turn at a given speed can be reduced by means of superelevation. Consider a superelevated, curved guideway, a cross section of which is shown in figure 3-5 at a point at which the speed is V and the superelevation angle is e. The resultant of the vectors representing the centrifugal force $\mathbf{a}_n$, and the gravity force $\mathbf{g}$, makes an angle φ with the normal to the floor of the vehicle. It is the angle φ that is specified to meet comfort criteria. From figure 3-5 we have

$$a_n = g \tan (\varphi + e) \approx g(\varphi + e) \qquad (3.7.1)$$

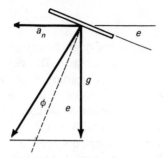

Figure 3-5. A Superelevated Guideway

in which the small angle approximation is sufficiently accurate.

From equation (3.1.13), the minimum radius of curvature is given by

$$R = \frac{V^2}{a_n}$$

if a_n is the largest permissible value of this quantity. Substituting from equation (3.7.1),

$$R_{min} = \frac{V^2}{g(\varphi + e)} \tag{3.7.2}$$

in which φ is the maximum permissible lateral acceleration in a curve divided by g.

The permissible angle e is limited by the possibility that the vehicle might have to stop on curves to a value of about 12 degrees or 0.2 radian. With standing passengers, φ is limited to about 1/8 radian, and if all passengers are seated to about 1/4 radian. Thus, with superelevation the minimum radius of curvature can be reduced by the ratio

$$\frac{R_{e=0}}{R_{e\neq0}} = 1 + \frac{e}{\varphi} \tag{3.7.3}$$

For standing passengers and $e = 0.2$ radian, $e/\varphi = 1.6$, and for seated passengers, $e/\varphi = 0.8$. Thus, the reduction in R_{min} is very significant and worth pursuing. In designing a superelevated curve, the spiral (or varying curvature) transition section must be twisted as well as curved in the horizontal plane. The angle of twist is zero at the zero-curvature end of the spiral and increases uniformly to a value of e of about 12 degrees at the end of maximum curvature.

3.8 Summary

In the layout design of almost every guideway transit system, some sections of curved guideway are necessary. The design of specific systems must therefore be delayed until the student has an appreciation of the design of transitions from straight to curved guideway. These transitions must be designed so that the magnitude of lateral motions are acceptable from the standpoint of comfort. Comfort depends on keeping the maximum lateral acceleration and rate of change of acceleration (jerk) below specified values. This results in the requirement that transitions from straight guideways to guideways of constant curvature must be separated by sections of constantly increasing curvature or spirals. If the speed is constant throughout the transition, the spiral section can generally be approximated by a simple cubic given by equation (3.2.11). Two important applications of the cubic transition are derived: (1) the right-angle curve, and (2) the transition to a parallel guideway, such as used in entry into an off-line station. In both cases enough information is given so that each of these types of curves can be specified. From the equations derived, it is straightforward to derive the transition between two straight lines of arbitrary angle.

Curved guideway costs more than straight guideway, therefore it is desirable to reduce the length of curved guideway wherever possible. In the transition to an off-line station, this is possible if the vehicle starts to decelerate before entering the transition, because sharper curves can be negotiated at the same level of comfort at lower speeds. Thus, if the transition curve is designed to take advantage of the lower speed, it will be shorter. The solution to this problem is lengthy, but it is included because of its importance in reducing guideway cost in certain applications. Instead of a simple cubic, the transition curve is given by the more complex expression, equation (3.5.19).

Spiral guideway can be more expensive to manufacture than guideway of constant curvature, therefore it is useful to know under what circumstances it is possible to approximate a spiral section by one or more sections of constant curvature. Such a transition may be possible within the jerk-comfort limit if the lateral suspension system of the vehicles can compensate for the lack of a spiral transition. Thus the problem is solved by considering a vehicle with given lateral suspension dynamics negotiating an abrupt change in curvature in the guideway. For the case of a linear spring-dashpot suspension system, the solution is worked out in detail. Equation (3.6.17) and figure 3-4 show that the greatest change in curvature can be permitted if the damping ratio if the lateral suspension system is one third. With this damping ratio, the minimum tolerable radius of curvature is given as a function of line speed, maximum tolerable jerk, and maximum suspension system deflection by equation (3.6.20). This equation possesses an interpretation of more general interest: It shows that, with a given change in curvature and a given suspension system, the maximum jerk experienced by the passengers is proportional to the cube of the speed. If a change in curvature is considered as a typical imperfection in the straightness of the guideway due to manufacturing tolerances, erection tolerances, or ground shifts, then in general the discomfort of the ride in terms of jerk worsens in proportion to the cube of the speed, and indicates why it is so much more important to keep the track straight at high speeds. The required tolerances are relaxed if the lateral deflection capability of the lateral suspension system is as large as possible, and if the damping ratio is properly chosen. More analysis is needed to determine if the optimum value of one third computed for the case considered would be different with different kinds of imperfections.

Finally, superelevation as a method of reducing the length and radius of curves is considered in enough detail to provide necessary design information. It is shown that the reduction in the radius of curvature practically possible is a factor of about 1.8 for seated passengers, and 2.6 for standing passengers. Thus, superelevation is well worth considering.

Problems

1. A seated-passenger guideway vehicle system is to be designed to permit right-angle turns at constant speed on city streets for which clearance available for the guideways is 40 m to the centerline of the guideways, that is, if two sets of parallel lines 40 m apart are drawn perpendicular to each other, the centerline of the guideway in making a right-angle turn must lie inside the boundaries of these lines.

   a. Sketch the curve and label all parts.
   b. With no superelevation, what is the maximum velocity for which the curve can be designed.
   c. Assuming the maximum velocity, compute the coordinates of the endpoints of the transition segments with respect to the street corner intersected 45° through the curve, and plot the curve.
   d. If the normal line speed is 20 m/s, what is the deceleration length that must be allowed for before the curve is negotiated.
   e. What is the length of each spiral section, and what is the length of the section of constant curvature? (Make all length computations to the nearest cm.)

2. For a seated-passenger vehicle system in which the line speed is 20 m/s, design a constant velocity transition to a parallel guideway ten meters away.

a. Make a careful sketch of the transition and label all parts. (Note comment following equation (3.4.5).)

b. Compute the coordinates and slopes of all points between transition sections and lay out the transition curve on graph paper making use of symmetry properties where possible.

c. Write an equation for the total length of the transition in terms of V, H, and a_n, and compute the length. By what percentage is the length greater than the maximum length of an all-spiral transition at the same velocity?

d. What is the percent error in length of the transition as computed by equation (3.2.10) instead of by the exact formula (3.2.9). (Hint: integrate the second term in the expansion of $\cos \theta$.)

3. With standing-passenger vehicles, a constant deceleration spiral is designed to turn the guideway through the maximum possible angle with $V_0 = 10$ m/s.

a. Compute V_{min}.

b. Compute θ_{max}.

c. Compute the length of the spiral section.

d. Compute the $x - y$ coordinates of the end point.

e. What is the length of a constant velocity spiral with $V = V_0$ and the same θ_{max}?

4. For standing-passenger vehicles with lateral suspension systems having a maximum permissible deflection of 10 cm and an optimum damping ratio, the line speed is 15 m/s. It is desired to build a right-angle turn using a minimum length of curved guideway, using segments of two different constant curvatures, and maintaining constant line speed.

a. Sketch the curve and label all parts.

b. If two cycles of oscillation of the lateral suspension system must be completed before entering the second segment, what is the length of each segment.

c. What is the total length of the minimum length right-angle curve?

d. What are the coordinates of the endpoint of the total right-angle transition with respect to the initial point? (Hint: Follow the derivations of equations (3.3.2) to (3.3.7.)

5. Assume the constant curvature section of the transition curve of Problem 1 is superelevated a maximum permissible amount. With the same velocity as computed in Problem 1, how much narrower could the width of the streets have been as a percentage of the given width? How much higher could the velocity have been with the same width of streets as a percentage of the velocity with no superelevation?

4

Performance Relationships for Specific Systems

In this chapter, automated transit systems are classified and studied according to the geometry of the lines. There are four classifications: shuttle, loop, line haul, and network. All transit systems are composed of one or more of these types. Hence, the performance of any transit system may be studied using the relationships developed.

4.1 Shuttle Systems

Simple Shuttle

A simple shuttle is diagrammed in figure 4-1. Only one vehicle can be used, and it follows the velocity profile of figure 2-3 in moving from one station to the other. The distance D_s between stations is measured to the center of the stopped vehicle. For a given V_L, the minimum possible value of D_s is the value of $\bar{D}$ in figure 2-4 for the case $t_D = 0$, or twice the stopping distance given by equation (2.2.6).

The travel time from one station to the other counting the dwell time t_D at either station is derived in section 2.4 and is given as t_s by equation (2.4.3). Because V_L appears in the denominator in the second term and in the numerator in the third, a value of V_L exists that minimizes t_s. By differentiation, it is seen that t_s is minimum if $V_L^2 = D_s a_m$. But, discounting jerk, $D_s = V_L^2/a_m$ is twice the stopping distance. Thus, t_s is minimized if the vehicle accelerates to the midpoint between stations, then decelerates to a stop. As D_s increases, the corresponding value of V_L to minimize t_s quickly becomes to large to be practical, and minimum t_s cannot be attained.

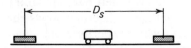

Figure 4-1. A Simple Shuttle

Three useful characteristic times for shuttles can be derived from t_s:

T_1: The time to wait for a vehicle called from the other station

T_2: The average wait time if the vehicle continuously shuttles back and forth and waits t_D seconds at each end

T_3: The effective time headway

These quantities are given by the following equations:

$$T_1 = t_s - t_D = \frac{D_s}{V_L} + \frac{V_L}{a_m} + 1 \text{ second} \tag{4.1.1}$$

$$T_2 = T_1 + t_D = t_s \tag{4.1.2}$$

$$T_3 = 2T_2 \tag{4.1.3}$$

in which we have assumed $a_m/J_1 = 1$ second because this value gives the maximum value of J_1 permissible from the standpoint of comfort.

The capacity of a shuttle in terms of the effective number of vehicles per hour passing a fixed point in one direction is

$$\text{Capacity} = \frac{3600}{T_3} = \frac{1800V_L}{D_s + V_L(t_D + \frac{V_L}{a_m} + 1)} \tag{4.1.4}$$

Equations (4.1.1) through (4.1.4) are plotted in figure 4-2. The upper right-hand quadrant is a plot of equation (4.1.1) for $a_m = 1.25$ m/s². This value is appropriate for standing-passenger vehicles. It is used for shuttles because the round-trip time for a shuttle is long enough so that it is necessary to accommodate all the people who wish service on a particular trip, but short enough that provision for seating is unnecessary. Also, with no seats the vehicle can be used for transporting beds, food carts, and other objects as well as people. The lines of T_1 versus D_s terminate on the left end at the minimum value of D_s possible for the given value of V_L. The envelope of the end points of these lines is a parabola.

The upper left-hand quadrant is a plot of equation (4.1.2) for several practical values of t_D. The lower left-hand quadrant is a plot of equation (4.1.3), and the lower right-hand quadrant shows equation (4.1.4). Plotted in this manner, all of the necessary performance characteristics of a shuttle can be understood from a single chart. The dashed lines in figure 4-2 provide an example for the case $D_s = 600$ m, $V_L = 10$ m/s, and $t_D = 20$ s. Enter the chart at $D_s = 0.6$ km and move up to the curve corresponding to $V_L = 10$

49

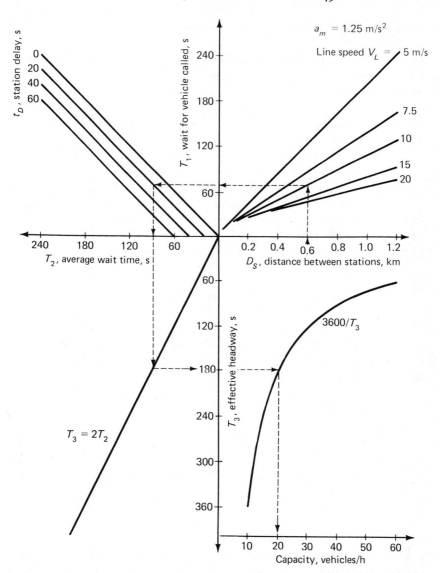

Figure 4-2. Characteristic Times for and Capacity of Simple Shuttles

m/s. Move left to the T_1 ordinate and read $T_1 = 69$ s. Continue left to the diagonal line corresponding to $t_D = 20$ s and turn 90 degrees down to the T_2 axis and read $T_2 = 89$ s. Continue down to the diagonal line labeled $T_3 = 2T_2$ and turn right to the T_3 ordinate. Read $T_3 = 178$ s and continue right to the hyperbola labeled $3600/T_3$. Turn down to the capacity abscissa and read 20.2 vehicles per hour.

Simple Shuttle With Intermediate Stations

Consider the configuration shown in figure 4-3. In the time and capacity relationships derived, we will assume there are n stations separated by arbitrary distances D_{s_i}, each greater than the minimum possible value shown in figure 4-2. Such a configuration is exactly analogous to an elevator and can be referred to as a "horizontal elevator." It would operate in an on-demand mode exactly as an elevator.

The time characteristics can be found from equations (4.1.1 through 4.1.3) and figure 4-2. The time to wait for the vehicle called from any other station nonstop is the value of T_1 in figure 4-2 corresponding to the distance D_s from which the vehicle is called. If, however, the vehicle makes m intermediate stops each with station delay t_D, the wait time is the sum of the values of T_1 corresponding to the $m + 1$ station spacings between m intermediate stops plus mt_D. If the D_{s_i} are all the same, the wait time is

$$T_{1m} = mt_D + (m + 1)\left(\frac{D_s}{V_L} + \frac{V_L}{a_m} + 1 \right) \qquad (4.1.5)$$

The characteristic times T_2 and T_3 have meaning only if the vehicle continues to shuttle back and forth with an average station delay t_D. Then, for an n-station system

$$T_{2_n} = \sum_{i=1}^{n-1}\left(t_D + \frac{D_{s_i}}{V_L} + \frac{V_L}{a_m} + 1 \right)$$

$$= (n - 1)\left(t_D + \frac{D_{s_{av}}}{V_L} + \frac{V_L}{a_m} + 1 \right) \qquad (4.1.6)$$

$$= (n - 1)T_2$$

in which $D_{s_{av}}$ is the average station spacing, and T_2 is found from figure 4-2 corresponding to $D_{s_{av}}$. The effective time headway $T_3 = 2T_{2_n}$ as in equation (4.1.3). The effective capacity is the value given in figure 4-2 corresponding to $D_{s_{av}}$ divided by $n - 1$.

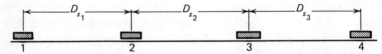

Figure 4-3. Simple Shuttle with Intermediate Stations

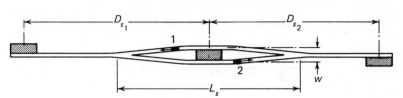

Figure 4-4. A Two-Vehicle Shuttle

Two-Vehicle Shuttle

The major advantage of a simple shuttle is that only one guideway is required. Its major disadvantage is that with only one guideway, only one vehicle can be used, thus limiting capacity. Greater capacity without the expense of a double guideway the entire length can be obtained by using a double guideway around one or more intermediate stations. The Ford Motor Company has used such a configuration in their installation at Bradley Field, Hartford, Connecticut and at the Fairlane Shopping Center in Dearborn, Michigan.

The configuration is in general as shown in figure 4-4, in which it is assumed that D_{s_1} and D_{s_2} may differ, and the middle station uses a central platform. The length of curved guideway is minimized if it is designed according to the theory of section 3.5.

The characteristic times for a two-vehicle shuttle are each one-half the values for a three-station simple shuttle, given by equations (4.1.5) and (4.1.6). The capacity is double that of the three-station shuttle.

Four-Vehicle Shuttle

Consider the concept of figure 4-4 with two intermediate stations, diagrammed in figure 4-5. At time zero the four vehicles are at the two central stations, with vehicles 1 and 3 headed left, and vehicles 2 and 4 headed right. The vehicles advance to new positions in the time interval t_s, where t_s is given by equation (4.1.2) with D_s equal to the largest of the three station spacings shown in figure 4-5. In the first time interval ($t = 0$ to $t = t_s$), vehicle 1 can move to the left end station, and vehicle 4 to the right end station. Only one of vehicles 2 and 3 can move. In the table, the convention is adopted that the vehicle with the lowest number takes priority. Thus, in the first move vehicle 3 waits while vehicle 2 passes the middle segment. In each time step, the vehicle which must wait is encircled. We see that eight time steps are needed to bring the vehicles back to their original positions, and that each of the four vehicles waits out one time step twice.

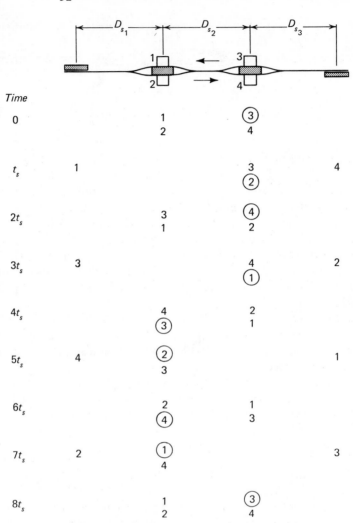

Figure 4-5. Motions of a Four-Vehicle Shuttle

We see that the period of motion is $8t_s$ and that four vehicles pass a given station in a given direction in $8t_s$ seconds. Therefore, the effective time headway between vehicles is $T_3 = 2t_s$, exactly the same as for the simple shuttle (see equation (4.1.3)). Consequently, the capacity is also the same, and is given by figure 4-2.

A similar analysis assuming more than two intermediate stations shows that the capacity remains the same as for a simple shuttle. Only with the configuration of figure 4-4 is the capacity increased over that of a simple shuttle, and in that case by a factor of two. The advantage of shuttle configurations with more than one intermediate station is not to increase capacity, but to keep the capacity constant while increasing the length of the line. Without the intermediate stations, figure 4-2 or equation (4.1.4) shows that the capacity drops rapidly with D_s. As an example, consider a simple shuttle in which $V_L = 10$ m/s, $a_m = 1.25$ m/s^2, and $t_D = 10$ s. Then if D_s is doubled from 300 m to 600 m, the capacity drops from 36.7 vehicles per hour to 22.8 vehicles per hour, or by a factor of 1.6.

4.2 Station Throughput

The capacity of each of the systems discussed in the remainder of this chapter is limited by the number of vehicles or trains per hour that can move through a station, that is, the station throughput. In this section the term vehicle in general refers to either a vehicle or a train. For the purpose of this section, stations can be divided into two types: (1) The common type in which the vehicle flow through the station is unidirectional; and (2) the end-of-the-line station in which the vehicles leave by backing up and then switching to a second line.

Unidirectional Flow Station

Analysis of station throughput is aided by consideration of the distance-time diagrams of two successive vehicles as they pass through a station. Figure 4-6 shows such a diagram for a unidirectional station. The two velocity profiles are assumed to be identical in shape and are as defined in chapter 2. The line velocity, V_L, is the slope of the distance-time line before deceleration begins. The length of each vehicle or train is L, the station delay of vehicle 1 is t_D, and the two vehicles are assumed to be separated in time by an interval T. The problem is to determine how the minimum permissible time headway is related to other essential parameters.

Attention is focused on the trailing time line of vehicle 1 in figure 4-6, and on the leading time line of vehicle 2. Consider the trailing time line of vehicle 1 in a reference frame (x, t) with the origin in time at the moment vehicle 1 begins to leave the station. Then, in a reference frame (x', t') in which time and position move backwards and in which the origin in time is at the moment vehicle 2 stops in the station, the position-time diagram of vehicle 2 is identical to that of vehicle 1. To find it in reference frame x, t, we need only find the position-time diagram of vehicle 1 in $x - t$ coordinates and transform it by means of the equations

$$\left. \begin{array}{l} x' = L - x \\[2mm] t' = T - t_D - t \end{array} \right\} \qquad (4.2.1)$$

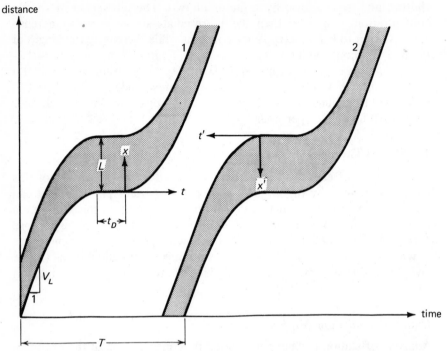

Figure 4-6. The Distance-Time Diagrams of Two Successive Vehicles Entering and Leaving a Station

Generally T will be an order of magnitude or more longer than terms in the position-time equations dependent on jerk. Therefore, in this analysis, jerk will be neglected. Then, if a is the acceleration, the position-time line of vehicle 1 is

$$x_1 = \frac{at^2}{2} \tag{4.2.2}$$

and

$$\dot{x}_1 = at \tag{4.2.3}$$

for $\upsilon \le t \le V_L/a$. For $t > V_L/a$

$$x_1 = V_L t - \frac{V_L^2}{2a} \tag{4.2.4}$$

Therefore, the position-time line of vehicle 2 is

$$x_2' = \frac{at'^2}{2} \qquad\qquad 0 \le t' \le V_L/a$$

$$= V_L t' - \frac{V_L^2}{2a} \qquad\qquad t' > V_L/a$$

Substituting these equations into equations (4.2.1),

$$x_2 = L - a/2(T - t_D - t)^2 \qquad 0 \leqslant t' \leqslant V_L/a$$

$$= L - V_L(T - t_D - t) + V_L^2/2a \qquad t' > V_L/a$$

(4.2.5)

If $T - t_D$ is greater than or equal to $2V_L/a$, the closest separation between x_1 and x_2 at a given t occurs when the velocities of both vehicles are V_L. Thus, $x_1 - x_2$ is found by subtracting the second of equations (4.2.5) from equation (4.2.4) to give

$$\Delta x_{min} = V_L(T - t_D) - V_L^2/a - L \qquad T - t_D \geqslant 2V_L/a \quad (4.2.6)$$

The velocities of both vehicles are equal to V_L when $x_1 - x_2 = \Delta x_{min}$.

If $T - t_D$ is less than $2V_L/a$, the closest separation occurs at velocities less than V_L. Thus, Δx_{min} is found by subtracting the first of equations (4.2.5) from equation (4.2.2), and

$$\Delta x_{min} = at^2/2 - L + a/2(T - t_D - t)^2$$

In equation (4.2.6), t does not appear; however, in the present case Δx_{min} is a function of time. The minimum value occurs when

$$\frac{d\Delta x}{dt} = 0 = at - a(T - t_D - t)$$

that is, when

$$t = \frac{T - t_D}{2}$$

Thus

$$\Delta x_{min} = \frac{a(T - t_D)^2}{4} - L \quad T - t_D < 2V_L/a \qquad (4.2.7)$$

The minimum permissible separation between two transit vehicles is dealt with in detail in chapter 7; however, for analysis of station flows it is adequate to let

$$\Delta x_{min} = \frac{kV_{min}^2}{2a_e} \qquad (4.2.8)$$

in which V_{min} is the velocity of the trailing vehicle at minimum separation, and a_e is the emergency deceleration rate. Thus, from equations (2.2.6), $V^2_{min}/2a_e$ is the stopping distance of the trailing vehicle at minimum spacing if jerk and control time delay are neglected. The constant k, called the safety factor, is the ratio of minimum separation to stopping distance. The available stopping distance is less than $V^2_{min}/2a_e$ because jerk and control delay have been neglected, but more because the lead vehicle cannot stop instantly.

If equation (4.2.8) is substituted into equation (4.2.7), in which at Δx_{min}

$$V_{min} = \frac{a(T - t_D)}{2}$$

and the result is solved for $T - t_D$, we have

$$T - t_D = 2\sqrt{\frac{L}{a(1 - ka/2a_e)}} \qquad (4.2.9)$$

if $T - t_D \leq 2V_L/a$. If $T - t_D \geq 2V_L/a$, $V_{min} = V_L$. Then substitute equation (4.2.8) into equation (4.2.6) to give

$$T - t_D = \frac{L}{V_L} + \frac{V_L}{a}\left(1 + \frac{ka}{2a_e}\right) \qquad (4.2.10)$$

When $T - t_D = 2V_L/a$, equations (4.2.9) and (4.2.10) give the same result:

$$L = \frac{V^2_L}{a}\left(1 - \frac{ka}{2a_e}\right) \qquad (4.2.11)$$

If L *is greater than the value given by equation (4.2.11), equation (4.2.10) holds; and if less, equation (4.2.9) holds.*

For train systems, k is generally taken equal to at least two, and a_e is chosen only slightly greater than a. Therefore the dimensionless parameter $ka/2a_e$ is approximately equal to 1 and equation (4.2.10) holds for trains of all lengths. If equation (4.2.10) is differentiated with respect to V_L and the result is set equal to zero, it is seen that T reaches a minimum value when

$$V_L = \left(\frac{aL}{1 + \alpha}\right)^{1/2} \qquad (4.2.12)$$

in which

$$\alpha = \frac{ka}{2a_e} \qquad (4.2.13)$$

Substituting equation (4.2.12) into equation (4.2.10),

$$T_{\min} = t_D + 2\left[\frac{(1 + \alpha)L}{a}\right]^{1/2} \qquad (4.2.14)$$

For a ten-car train of 20-m cars, $L = 200$ m, and with $a = 1.25$ m/s^2, $t_D = 15$ s, $\alpha = 1$, $T_{\min} = 50.8$ s, and the corresponding value of V_L is 11.2 m/s. This is generally felt to be too low a line speed to give an adequate average speed. If $V_L = 25$ m/s with the same values of the other parameters the headway increases, from equation (4.2.10), to 63 s.

In order to present the results graphically, introduce, in addition to equation (4.2.13), the dimensionless parameters

$$\tilde{T} = (T - t_D)\frac{a}{V_L} \qquad (4.2.15)$$

$$\tilde{L} = \frac{La}{V_L^2} \qquad (4.2.16)$$

Then, equations (4.2.9) and (4.2.10) become

$$\left.\begin{array}{ll} \tilde{T} = 2\sqrt{\dfrac{\tilde{L}}{1 - \alpha}} & \tilde{T} \leq 2 \\[2ex] \quad = \tilde{L} + 1 + \alpha & \tilde{T} \geq 2 \end{array}\right\} \qquad (4.2.17)$$

Note from equation (4.2.9) that at shorter headways, the headway into a station is independent of line speed. Equations (4.2.17) are plotted as the solid lines in figure 4-7 for a family of values of α. Typically a_e lies in the range from a to $2a$ and k ranges from one to two. Therefore, the curves corresponding to $\alpha = \frac{1}{4}$ to 1 are in the practical range. If α is greater than 1, the second of equations (4.2.17) holds for the whole range of positive values of L. Using equations (4.2.12) and (4.2.16), one can see that as a function of V_L, the second of equations (4.2.17) reaches a minimum when $\tilde{L} = 1 + \alpha$. The dashed line in figure 4-7 connects these minimum points.

End-of-the-Line Station

Consider a station at the end of a transit line, which to save space and conserve on track length is arranged so that a vehicle or train entering it must back up onto a parallel line to continue in the opposite direction. A diagram of the station and the corresponding position-time diagrams are shown in figure 4-8. As before, L is the length of the train, t_D is the station dwell time, V_L is the line speed, and a is the deceleration rate. In the present case, the position-time line turns downward in the reverse direction as the train backs up onto a parallel track. Let L_{swx} be the extra distance the train must move backward, in addition to the train length L, before it is out of the

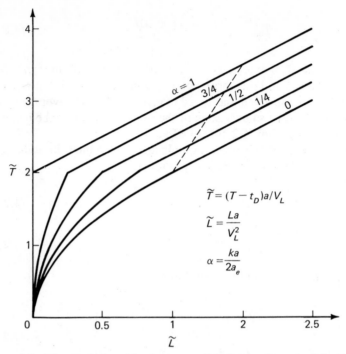

Figure 4-7. The Relationship between Minimum Permissible Headway through Stations and Vehicle Length

way of the next train attempting to enter the station, as shown in figure 4-8.

The minimum L_{swx} can be found from the theory of section 3.4. For a train, the displacement between parallel tracks, H, is generally greater than the value $2a_n$ given by equation (3.4.5). Therefore, as indicated below this equation, a straight section must be inserted between spiral segments. Its length, using equation (3.4.6), is $(H - 2a_n) (4V/2H)$. Therefore the total transition length is $L_{swx} = 4V(1.5 - a_n/H)$. For $a_n = 1.25$ m/s² and, say, V =20m/s and $H = 4$m; $L_{swx} = 95$m.

Consider figure 4-8. Back-up stations are generally considered with train systems in which there are up to ten cars per train. Thus, if each car is say 20 m long, L is on the order of 200 m. The speed V_L corresponding to a stopping distance of $L + L_{swx} = 295$ m is

$$\sqrt{2a(L + L_{swx})} = 27 \text{ m/s} = 61 \text{ mi/h}$$

Thus if V_L is less than this value, which will usually be the case, the train begins to stop inside the distance $L + L_{swx}$. Therefore, the time required to

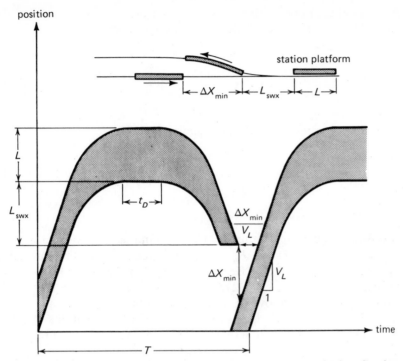

Figure 4-8. The Position-Time Diagram for an End-of-Line Station

stop from a distance $L + L_{swx}$ can be found from equation (4.2.4) by substituting $x_1 = L + L_{swx}$. Then from figure 4-8,

$$T = t_D + 2 \left(\frac{L + L_{swx}}{V_L} + \frac{V_L}{2a} \right) + \frac{\Delta x_{min}}{V_L}$$

The velocity of the train approaching the station is still V_L when its front is L_{swx} from the station platform. Therefore substitute Δx_{min} in the above equation from equation (4.2.8) with $V_{min} = V_L$. Then

$$T = t_D + \frac{V_L}{a} (1 + \alpha) + \frac{2}{V_L} (L + L_{swx}) \qquad (4.2.18)$$

in which α is given by equation (4.2.13). Equation (4.2.18) gives the time headway between trains if the trains are travelling at a constant speed V_L when the front passes the point a distance L_{swx} in front of the platform. After this point, the train begins slowing down.

Since V_L is in the numerator of the second term in equation (4.2.18) and in the denominator of the third term, $T(V_L)$ possesses a minimum point. By setting $\partial T/\partial V_L = 0$, the minimum point is seen to correspond to

$$V_L = \sqrt{\frac{2a(L + L_{swx})}{1 + \alpha}} \tag{4.2.19}$$

Substituting equation (4.2.19) into equation (4.2.18),

$$T_{min} = t_D + 2\sqrt{\frac{2(1 + \alpha)}{a} \; (L + L_{swx})} \tag{4.2.20}$$

Consider a numerical example. If $k = 2$ and $a_e = a$ (typical of train systems), $t_D = 15$ s, and $L + L_{swx} = 230$ m, T reaches the minimum value $T_{min} = 69.3$ s if $V_L = 17.0$ m/s. By comparison, from equation (4.2.18), if $V_L = 22$ m/s, $T = 71.1$ s, or if $V_L = 12$ m/s, $T = 72.5$ s. Thus a minimum headway of say 75 s is applicable over a wide range of speeds.

In terms of the dimensionless variables given by equations (4.2.13), (4.2.15) and (4.2.16), equation (4.2.18) becomes

$$\tilde{T} = 1 + \alpha + 2(\tilde{L} + \tilde{L}_{swx}) \tag{4.2.21}$$

Comparing with equation (4.2.17), one can see that with back-up stations, the headway increases twice as rapidly with train length at a given speed than with flow-through stations. If V_L is well above the minimum value given by equation (4.2.19), a penalty in capacity for back-up stations can be avoided by reducing V_L as the end station is approached. Thus, in equation (4.2.18), reduce V_L enough so that T computed from this equation equals the value computed from equation (4.2.10) with the normal V_L. This procedure will add to the round-trip time of the vehicles but will maintain capacity, if necessary. In determining the loop or line-haul system minimum headway, if different values of T are found due to different conditions at different stations, clearly the largest headway determines the system capacity. Note that nominal headway is constant around the loop.

4.3 Loop Systems

Consider a loop transit system of arbitrary shape as shown in figure 4-9. Let there be n stations numbered in the direction of flow, and let the distance between the ith and $(i + 1)$th stations be $\ell_{i,i+1}$. The stations may be either on line or off line, and the vehicles may run singly or in trains.

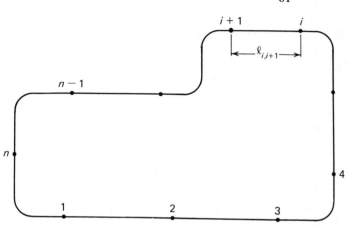

Figure 4-9. Schematic Diagram of a One-Way Transit System

The Maximum Number of Vehicles or Trains

If the stations are on line, the average velocity of a vehicle or train, V_{av}, is given by figure 2-4 as a function of station spacing, station dwell time, line speed, and acceleration level; and the trip time between stations is given by equation (2.4.3). Therefore, the time required to travel completely around the loop is

$$T_Q = nT_{ex} + \frac{\ell_Q}{V_L} \qquad (4.3.1)$$

in which T_{ex} is the excess time given by

$$T_{ex} = t_D + \frac{V_L}{a_m} + \frac{a_m}{J_1} \qquad (4.3.2)$$

and

$$\ell_Q = \sum_{i=1}^{n} \ell_{i,i+1} \qquad (4.3.3)$$

is the distance around the loop. Hence, the average velocity around the loop is

$$V_{av_Q} = \ell_Q/T_Q \qquad (4.3.4)$$

With on-line stations, figure 4-6 gives the minimum permissible time headway T_{min} between vehicles or trains. Therefore the maximum number of vehicles or trains that can be accommodated is

$$N_{max} = \frac{\ell_Q}{V_{av_Q}T_{min}} = \frac{T_Q}{T_{min}} \qquad (4.3.5)$$

In practical daily operation it is doubtful if the actual number of units will be more than half N_{max}.

If the stations are off line, the average velocity can be found from figure 2-4 if D_s is interpreted as the average trip length. However, the maximum number of vehicles that can be accommodated on line is now based on the on-line speed V_L. The theory of minimum headway is developed in detail in chapter 7, but for most purposes it can be expressed adequately by the equation

$$T_{min} = \frac{L + H}{V_L} \tag{4.3.6}$$

in which L is the vehicle length and H is the minimum rear-to-front spacing between vehicles, given by

$$H = V_L t_c + \frac{V_L^2}{2}\left(\frac{1}{a_e} - \frac{1}{a_f}\right) \tag{4.3.7}$$

in which t_c is the time constant for application of the braking force that produces the emergency deceleration a_e, and a_f is the failure deceleration rate. Using equation (4.3.6) and V_L for V_{avg} in equation (4.3.5), the maximum permissible number of vehicles is found for loop systems with off-line stations. Again, the practical maximum number of vehicles may be less by a factor of two. With off-line stations, the maximum achievable throughput of the stations is given by figure 4-6. If the vehicles operate in platoons, L is the platoon length. Station throughput with off-line stations has been treated by computer simulation by several investigators, the work of which is reported in the book *Personal Rapid Transit II* (see note 3 in chapter 1 of this book).

The Trip-Time and Demand Matrices

For each origin station i in figure 4-9, there are $n - 1$ possible destinations. Therefore it is useful in the following analysis to represent all of the trip times in the form of a matrix.

$$T_{ij} = \begin{pmatrix} T_{11} & T_{12} & T_{13} & \cdots & T_{1n} \\ T_{21} & T_{22} & T_{23} & \cdots & T_{2n} \\ T_{31} & T_{32} & T_{33} & \cdots & T_{3n} \\ \cdot & \cdot & \cdot & & \cdot \\ \cdot & \cdot & \cdot & & \cdot \\ \cdot & \cdot & \cdot & & \cdot \\ T_{n1} & T_{n2} & T_{n3} & \cdots & T_{nn} \end{pmatrix} \tag{4.3.8}$$

The first index represents an origin station, and the second a destination. Thus, for example, T_{25} is the time required to travel from station 2 to station 5 counting station dwell time of the vehicles but not the time the patron must wait for a vehicle. It would be trivial to let the major diagonal terms represent the non-trip, therefore let $T_{kk} = T_Q$ for $k = 1,\ldots, n$, where T_Q is the time for a complete circuit given by equation (4.3.1). Note that the diagonal terms of the form $T_{i,i+1}$ and T_{n1} represent the set of n trip times from one station to the next.

The trip time, not counting the time the patron must wait for a vehicle, is given by equation (2.4.3), where D_s is the distance between stops. In on-line station systems

$$T_{ij} = T_{i,i+1} + T_{i+1,i+2} + \ldots + T_{j-1,j}$$

If we let the excess time in equation (2.4.3) due to station dwell and acceleration be as given by equation (4.3.2), then

$$T_{ij} = (j - i)T_{ex} + \frac{\ell_{ij}}{V_L} \qquad \text{(on-line)} \qquad (4.3.9)$$

In systems with off-line stations and nonstop travel from origin to destination

$$T_{ij} = T_{ex} + \frac{\ell_{ij}}{V_L} \qquad \text{(off-line)} \qquad (4.3.10)$$

Some systems have off-line stations but an elevator-type service in which the vehicle can be called into a station on demand and the ride shared. In these systems, T_{ij} is not unique and each case must be treated individually.

Travel demand in person-trips per hour can also be represented by a matrix

$$[D_{ij}]$$

in which the index i represents the trip origin and j the destination. The major diagonal D_{kk} represents the round trip and is zero unless recreational trips are included. There are no simple general relationships among the D_{ij}; however, special cases such as uniform demand in which all the D_{ij} are the same will be treated to gain some insight. Let

$$D_{i\sigma} = \sum_{j=i+1}^{n-1+i} D_{ij} \qquad (4.3.11)$$

and

$$D_{\sigma j} = \sum_{i=j+1}^{n-1+j} D_{ij} \tag{4.3.12}$$

By understanding the meaning of D_{ij}, one can see that $D_{i\sigma}$ is the total flow in people per hour into station i and requesting service on the system. $D_{\sigma j}$ is the total number of people per hour terminating their trips at station j. In general the matrix D_{ij} is a function of time; however, to determine the number of vehicles required it can be assumed independent of time with the terms representing the traffic in the busiest period.

In terms of D_{ij}, the total flow in link i, $i + 1$ in people per hour can be expressed in the form

$$F_{i,i+1} = \sum_{j=i+1}^{n+i-1} D_{ij} + \sum_{j=i+1}^{n+i-2} D_{i-1,j} + \dots + D_{i+2,i+1}$$

$$= \sum_{k=0}^{n-2} \sum_{j=i+1}^{n+i-k-1} D_{i-k,j} \tag{4.3.13}$$

The average line flow is

$$F_{av} = \frac{1}{n} \sum_{i=1}^{n} F_{i,i+1} \text{ people per hour} \tag{4.3.14}$$

If, in an on-line station system, the headway T is known, the average number of people per vehicle (or per train if vehicles are coupled) is simply

$$p_v = F_{av} T \tag{4.3.15}$$

In an on-line station system, the maximum number of people per vehicle is the maximum $F_{i,i+1}$ multiplied by T.

The Average Trip Length in One-Way Loops

This is a useful concept if it is interpreted as the average weighted in accordance with the amount of travel, that is, let

Average trip length = $<L_t>$ = passenger-miles per passenger

Thus

$$<L_t> = \frac{\sum\limits_{i=1}^{n} \sum\limits_{j=i+1}^{n-1+i} D_{ij}\ell_{ij}}{\sum\limits_{i=1}^{n} \sum\limits_{j=i+1}^{n-1+i} D_{ij}} \qquad (4.3.16)$$

in which n is subtracted from any index $n - 1 + i$ greater than n, and

$$\ell_{ij} = \sum_{k=i}^{j-1} \ell_{k,k+1} \qquad (4.3.17)$$

Consider the case of uniform flow, in which all of the D_{ij} are the same. They can then be factored out of the numerator and denominator of equation (4.3.16). Then if equation (4.3.17) is substituted into equation (4.3.16),

$$<L_t>_{uf} = \frac{1}{n(n-1)} \sum_{i=1}^{n} \sum_{j=i+1}^{n-1+i} \sum_{k=i}^{j-1} \ell_{k,k+1} \qquad (4.3.18)$$

By writing out the terms one can see that

$$\sum_{j=i+1}^{n-1+i} \sum_{k=i}^{j-1} \ell_{k,k+1} = \sum_{k=0}^{n-2} \sum_{j=0}^{k} \ell_{i+j,i+j+1}$$

in which the dummy indices have different meanings on the two sides. The advantage of the new form is that the index i no longer appears in the summation limits. Thus, because of the commutative property of ordinary addition, the outer summation in equation (4.3.18) can be brought inside so that

$$<L_t>_{uf} = \frac{1}{n(n-1)} \sum_{k=0}^{n-2} \sum_{j=0}^{k} \sum_{i=1}^{n} \ell_{i+j,i+j+1}$$

But

$$\frac{1}{n} \sum_{i=1}^{n} \ell_{i+j,i+j+1} = \ell_s \qquad (4.3.19)$$

where ℓ_s is the average distance between stations and it is recognized that the result is independent of the index j. Thus

$$<L_t>_{uf} = \frac{\ell_s}{n-1} \sum_{k=0}^{n-2} \sum_{j=0}^{k} 1 = \frac{\ell_s}{n-1} (1 + 2 + 3 + \ldots + n - 1)$$

But, by adding the arithmetic series to itself written backwards, the well known result

$$\begin{array}{cccccc}
1 & + & 2 & + 3 & + \ldots + & (n-1) \\
+ (n-1) & + & (n-2) & + . & \ldots + & 1 \\
\hline
n & + & n & + n & + \ldots + & n
\end{array} = (n-1)n$$

is obtained. Thus

$$<L_t>_{uf} = \frac{\ell_s n}{2} \qquad (4.3.20)$$

The Average Trip Length in Two-Way Loops

If the loop system of figure 4-9 provides for flows of vehicles in both directions, it can be assumed that each patron will opt to travel the shortest route to his destination. If attention is focused on one of these directions, say the counterclockwise direction shown in figure 4-9, the demand is zero for trips more than half way around the loop. Thus, instead of equation (4.3.16), the average trip length is

$$<L_t> = \frac{\displaystyle\sum_{i=1}^{n} \sum_{j=i+1}^{m+i} D_{ij}\ell_{ij}}{\displaystyle\sum_{i=1}^{n} \sum_{j=i+1}^{m+i} D_{ij}} \qquad (4.3.21)$$

in which the limit index m replaces $n - 1$. If the stations are approximately equally placed and n is odd, $m = (n - 1)/2$. If n is even, the most remote station is just as far away in either direction. Therefore split the demand to it in half. Thus

$$<L_t> = \frac{\displaystyle\sum_{i=1}^{n} \left(\sum_{j=i+1}^{i+n/2-1} D_{ij}\ell_{ij} + \tfrac{1}{2}D_{i,i+n/2}\ell_{i,i+n/2} \right)}{\displaystyle\sum_{i=1}^{n} \left(\sum_{j=i+1}^{i+n/2-1} D_{ij} + \tfrac{1}{2}D_{i,i+n/2} \right)} \qquad (4.3.22)$$

With uniform flow and an odd number of stations, by following the process which led to equation (4.3.20) it can be verified that

$$<L_t>_{uf} = \frac{\ell_s(n + 1)}{4} \qquad (n \text{ odd}) \qquad (4.3.23)$$

Similarly, equation (4.3.22) becomes

$$<L_t>_{uf} = \frac{\ell_s}{4} \frac{n^2}{(n - 1)} \qquad (n \text{ even}) \qquad (4.3.24)$$

The average trip lengths for one-way and two-way systems with uniform flow are summarized in table 4-1.

Table 4-1 Average Trip Lengths

Number of Stations :	2	3	4	5	6	7	8	9	10	11	12
$\dfrac{<L_t>}{l_s}$ } One-way :	1	1.5	2	2.5	3	3.5	4	4.5	5	5.5	6
Two-way :	1	1	1.38	1.5	1.8	2	2.29	2.5	2.78	3	3.27
One-way/two-way :	1	1.5	1.5	1.67	1.67	1.75	1.75	1.8	1.8	1.83	1.83

The Station Delay Time, t_D

Station delay time is a very important parameter in determining the performance of automated transit systems. It is clearly dependent upon vehicle configuration and flow. If the vehicle has only three seats abreast, simple timing of the exit and entry maneuver shows that five or six seconds may be adequate for t_D. With six seats, three forward and three backward and one door, it may take roughly twice as long to vacate and reload a vehicle. In larger vehicles somewhat less time per person per door is required, and the result depends on the width of the doorway.

The average walk speed is about two miles per hour or three feet per second, therefore the maximum rate of discharge of passengers per door is roughly one per second, one abreast, or two per second, two abreast. These kinds of considerations tempered with simple experiments and observations at transit stations can determine the mean time required for egress and ingress for a given vehicle configuration. Unfortunately, at the time of writing the author cannot point to any literature that presents data on passenger flow in and out of vehicles. Accepted standard values of station dwell are needed for the purpose of predicting the performance of various types of transit systems.

The Required Vehicle Fleet Size

The required size of the vehicle fleet is given by

$$N = N_o + N_e + N_m \qquad (4.3.25)$$

in which

N_o is the required number of occupied vehicles needed to meet the peak demand if there are p_v people per vehicle;

N_e is the number of empty vehicles in circulation during the peak demand period as a result of nonuniform demand; and

N_m is the size of the maintenance float, that is, the number of extra vehicles required to account for the possibility of rush period breakdowns.

The number of occupied vehicles, N_o, is simply the number of people riding at any one time during the peak period, divided by the average number of people per vehicle, p_v. The number of people riding at any one time is the peak period flow in people per unit time multiplied by the average trip time. The peak period flow used to determine N_o must be averaged over an accepted period such as fifteen minutes or one hour. If a shorter period is used for averaging, a larger fleet will result, but the average wait time for service in the peak period will be reduced.

It is a policy decision to balance the desire for minimum wait with the added cost in vehicles needed to provide it. For the sake of economy, a certain measure of staggering of demand is needed. Any transit system can be swamped at some time by too great a demand, and the author's experience is that the public understands this and will either accept the need to wait longer in unusually busy periods or individually adjust their schedules to avoid the busiest periods. With these thoughts in mind, the author recommends that in public transit applications, the peak flow for computation of N_o be obtained as the average flow over the busiest hour. On the other hand, if the application is to carry students between classes in which the break period is say 15 minutes, then the peak flow used to compute N_o must be the flow averaged over the time period between the earliest and latest arrivals at the stations that permit the students to arrive at the next class on time. This is an interval of approximately seven minutes if the break period is fifteen minutes. If the starting times between classes are say thirty minutes apart, obtained by staggering class schedules on different campuses, then the average can be taken over a period of $30 - 8 = 22$ minutes, instead of $15 - 8 = 7$ minutes. Thus, by such a change in class scheduling, the peak flow is reduced to 32 percent of its former value.

Using the notation of the demand and trip-time matrices,

$$N_o = \frac{1}{p_v} \sum_{i=1}^{n} \sum_{j=i+1}^{i+n-1} D_{ij} T_{ij} \quad \text{(one-way)} \quad (4.3.26)$$

in which the terms of the demand matrix are averaged over an appropriate peak period as discussed above, and one-way flow is assumed. Let

$$\bar{D}_{\text{peak}} = \sum_{i=1}^{n} \sum_{j=i+1}^{i+n-1} D_{ij} \quad (4.3.27)$$

be the average peak flow on the whole loop system, regardless of flow direction. Then, using equations (4.3.9), (4.3.10), and (4.3.16), equation (4.3.26) can be written

$$N_o = \frac{1}{p_v} \left[\gamma T_{\text{ex}} + \frac{<L_t>}{V_L} \right] \bar{D}_{\text{peak}} \quad \text{(one-way)} \quad (4.3.28)$$

in which $<L_t>$ is given in general by equation (4.3.16), and for the case of uniform flow by equation (4.3.20). In on-line station systems,

$$\gamma = \frac{1}{\bar{D}_{\text{peak}}} \sum_{i=1}^{n} \sum_{j=i+1}^{i+n-1} (j - i) D_{ij} \quad (4.3.29a)$$

and, in off-line station, nonstop systems,

$$\gamma = 1 \quad (4.3.29b)$$

In the case of uniform flow, D_{ij} is the same for all i and j. Then equation (4.3.27) becomes

$$\bar{D}_{\text{peak}} = n(n - 1)D_{ij} \quad (4.3.30)$$

and

$$\gamma_{\text{on-line}} = \frac{1}{n(n-1)} \sum_{i=1}^{n} \sum_{j=i+1}^{i+n-1} (j-i)$$

$$= \frac{1}{n(n-1)} \left[\sum_{i=1}^{n} \sum_{j=i+1}^{i+n-1} j - \sum_{i=1}^{n} i \sum_{j=i+1}^{i+n-1} 1 \right]$$

$$= \frac{1}{n(n-1)} \left\{ \sum_{i=1}^{n} \left[i(n-1) + \sum_{j=1}^{n-1} j \right] - (n-1) \sum_{i=1}^{n} i \right\}$$

$$= \frac{1}{n(n-1)} \left(\sum_{i=1}^{n} 1 \right) \left(\sum_{j=1}^{n-1} j \right) = \frac{n}{2} \tag{4.3.31}$$

The ratio of the number of vehicles required in an on-line station system to the number required in an off-line station system is of interest. In the case of uniform flow and one-way loop traffic, this ratio is found from equations (4.3.28), (4.3.29b), and (4.3.31). Thus

$$\frac{N_o(\text{on-line})}{N_o(\text{off-line})} = \frac{\dfrac{n}{2} + \dfrac{<L_t>/V_L}{T_{\text{ex}}}}{1 + \dfrac{<L_t>/V_L}{T_{\text{ex}}}} \tag{4.3.32}$$

Consider a typical example in which $V_L = 15$ m/s, $a_m = J_1 = 2.5$ m/s, and $t_D = 15$ s. Then, from equation (4.3.2), $T_{\text{ex}} = 22$ s. Let $n = 7$ stations and $<L_t> = 1.5$ mi $= 2400$ m. Then $<L_t>/V_L T_{\text{ex}} = 7.27$, and the ratio of equation (4.3.32) is 1.30. Thus, in this case, if all parameters are equal, an on-line station system requires 30 percent more occupied vehicles to serve a given demand than an off-line station system.

In two-way systems, the number of vehicles on each track is obtained from an equation analogous to equation (4.3.26) if the upper limit on the inner sum is changed as in equations (4.3.21) and (4.3.22). If the demand is roughly equal in the two directions, and n is odd, the total number of occupied vehicles required in both directions is

$$N_o = \frac{2}{p_v} \left[\gamma T_{\text{ex}} + \frac{<L_t>}{V_L} \right] \sum_{i=1}^{n} \sum_{j=i+1}^{i+(n-1)/2} D_{ij}$$

$$= \frac{1}{p_v} \left[\gamma T_{\text{ex}} + \frac{<L_t>}{V_L} \right] \bar{D}_{\text{peak}} \quad \text{(two-way)} \tag{4.3.33}$$

in which $<L_t>$ is given by equation (4.3.21) in general, or by equation (4.3.23) in the case of uniform flow. With off-line stations, $\gamma = 1$ as before, and with on-line stations and n odd,

$$\gamma = \frac{\sum\limits_{i=1}^{n} \sum\limits_{j=i+1}^{i+(n-1)/2} (j - i) D_{ij}}{\sum\limits_{i=1}^{n} \sum\limits_{j=i+1}^{i+(n-1)/2} D_{ij}} \qquad \begin{array}{l} (n \text{ odd}) \\ \text{two-way} \end{array} \qquad (4.3.34)$$

In the uniform flow case, by following the derivation of equation (4.3.31), it can be verified that, if n is odd,

$$\gamma = \frac{n + 1}{4} \qquad (n \text{ odd}) \qquad (4.3.35)$$

The computation of N_0 is summarized in table 4-2 (T_{ex} is always found from equation (4.3.2)), and is based on the form of equation (4.3.28).

Returning to equation (4.3.25), consider the computation of N_e. In on-line station systems, service is scheduled and the concept of dispatching

Table 4-2 Computation of the Required Number of Occupied Vehicles

Case	Flow Directions	Stations		γ	$<L_t>$	$\bar{D}_{peak}$
General	One-way	On-Line		(26a)	(4.3.16)[a]	(4.3.27)
		Off-Line		1	(4.3.16)	(4.3.27)
	Two-Way	On-Line	odd no.	(31)	(4.3.21)	(4.3.27)
			even no.	(19)[b]	(4.3.22)	(4.3.27)
		Off-Line	odd no.	1	(4.3.21)	(4.3.27)
			even no.	1	(4.3.22)	(4.3.27)
Uniform Flow	One-Way	On-Line		$n/2$	(4.3.20)	(4.3.30)
		Off-Line		1	(4.3.20)	(4.3.30)
	Two-Way	On-Line	odd no.	$(n + 1)/4$	(4.3.23)	(4.3.30)
			even no.	$\dfrac{n^2}{4(n - 1)}$	(4.3.24)	(4.3.30)
		Off-Line	odd no.	1	(4.3.23)	(4.3.30)
			even no.	1	(4.3.24)	(4.3.30)

[a]Numbers in parentheses are equation numbers.
[b]Obtained from equation 4.3.22 by the substitutions l_{ij} becomes $j - i$; $l_{1,1 + n/2}$ becomes $n_l/2$.

empty vehicles to meet demands is not applicable, therefore all vehicles are considered occupied, and $N_e = 0$. The number of empty vehicles required in off-line station systems is zero if the demand is completely uniform, and depends on the nonuniformity in demand. Let EX_{vj} be the excess flow of vehicles into station j, that is, the number of vehicles in excess of those needed to meet the demand for service at station j. Then, in one-way systems,

$$EX_{vj} = \frac{1}{p_v} \sum_{i=j+1}^{n+j-1} (D_{ij} - D_{ji}) \qquad (4.3.36)$$

If $EX_{vj} > 0$, there is an excess of vehicles at station j; and if $EX_{vj} < 0$ there is a shortage. If the quantities EX_{vj} are known for all j, they can then be used to compute a schedule of empty vehicle dispatching commands to provide vehicles where needed. The total excess of vehicles is

$$\sum_{j=1}^{n} EX_{vj} = 0 \qquad (4.3.37)$$

as may be seen by noting from equation (4.3.27) that $\bar{D}_{\text{peak}}$ can be found by first summing over all destinations from a given origin, or first over all origins to a given destination. Therefore, the problem is one of optimal redistribution of empties.

The number of empty vehicles required is determined by summing the products

$$EX_{vj}T_{ji}$$

in which j corresponds to the stations for which $EX_{vj} > 0$, and T_{ji} is the time required for these vehicles to reach their destination stations. This is a logic operation and can be written in general in the form of a computer program but not neatly in an equation. It is more transparent, however, to consider each case directly once the EX_{vj} have been computed from the demand matrix. Consider the counterclockwise loop system illustrated in figure 4-10.

The small integers are the station numbers and the bold number next to station i is EX_{v_i} in vehicles per minute. In a loop system with off-line stations, under the restriction that no empty vehicle travels the full circuit,

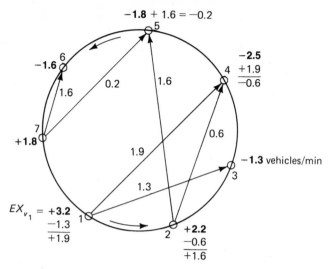

Figure 4-10. Example Computation of the Empty-Vehicle Fleet

it makes no difference in the total number of empty vehicle miles travelled to which stations the excess vehicles are dispatched. Then, consider the dispatching schedule. Arbitrarily start with station 1. If $EX_{v_1} > 0$, as is true in the example of figure 4-9, mentally start 3.2 vehicles per minute (one vehicle every 18.7 seconds) moving around the loop looking for vehicle shortages. The first "sink" ($EX_{v_i} < 0$) is station 3 which demands 1.3 vehicles per minute. Since $EX_{v_1} > |EX_{v_3}|$, station 1 can supply all vehicles needed at station 3. At station 1, subtract 1.3 v/min from the total excess to get 1.9 v/min remaining. Station 4 can use more than this number, therefore dispatch 1.9 v/min from station 1 to station 4. Deducting this number from $EX_{v_4} = -2.5$ leaves -0.6 v./min. All vehicles from station 1 have found destinations. Therefore move to station 2 and repeat the process. Then move to station 3 and note that its requirement is satisfied. Similarly, the need for vehicles at station 4 is satisfied. The remaining shortages at station 5 and 6 are then made up by circulation of vehicles from station 7. By drawing flow lines from "sources" to "sinks" and labelling them with the vehicle flows, an equation for N_e can be written directly from the diagram. Thus

$$N_e = 1.3T_{13} + 1.9T_{14} + 0.6T_{24} + 1.6T_2 + 0.2T_{75} + 1.6T_{76}$$

Using equation (4.3.10), $T_{ij} = T_{ex} + \ell_{ij}/V_L$,

$$N_e = T_{ex}\sum_{+}EX_{vj} + 1/V_L \sum \text{FLOW}_{ij}\ell_{ij}$$

$$(4.3.38)$$

in which $+EX_{vj}$ is the sum of all positive EX_{vj}, and in the example is 7.2 v/m. The second sum, in the example, is

$$\sum FLOW_{ij}\ell_{ij} = \quad 1.3(\ell_{12} + \ell_{23})$$

$$+1.9(\ell_{12} + \ell_{23} + \ell_{34})$$

$$+0.6(\qquad \ell_{23} + \ell_{34})$$

$$+1.6(\qquad \ell_{23} + \ell_{34} + \ell_{45})$$

$$+0.2(\ell_{12} + \ell_{23} + \ell_{34} + \ell_{45} + \qquad \ell_{71})$$

$$+1.6(\ell_{12} + \ell_{23} + \ell_{34} + \ell_{45} + \ell_{56} + \ell_{71})$$

$$= 5.0\ell_{12} + 7.2\ell_{23} + 5.9\ell_{34} + 3.4\ell_{45} + 1.6\ell_{56} + 1.8\ell_{71}$$

If the flow is two-way, equation (4.3.36) is replaced by a pair of equations, one for counterclockwise flow in the directions of the indices shown in figure 4-9, and the other for clockwise flow. Thus,

$$EX_{vj} = \frac{1}{p_\iota}\left(\sum_{i=j-m}^{j-1} D_{ij} + \tfrac{1}{2}D_{j-n/2,j} - \sum_{i=j+1}^{j+m} D_{ji} - \tfrac{1}{2}D_{j,j-n/2} \right)$$

$$EX_{vj} = \frac{1}{P_v}\left(\sum_{i=j+1}^{j+m} D_{ij} + \tfrac{1}{2}D_{j-n/2,j} - \sum_{i=j-m}^{j-1} D_{ji} - \tfrac{1}{2}D_{j,j-n/2} \right)$$

$$(4.3.39)$$

in which

$$m = \frac{n-1}{2} \qquad \text{for } n \text{ odd}$$

$$= \frac{n}{2} - 1 \qquad \text{for } n \text{ even}$$

and the terms not under a summation sign are dropped if n is odd. If an index is greater than n, n is subtracted from it; and if an index is less than 1, n is added to it. Based upon equations (4.3.39), the procedure for determining the size of the empty fleet is the same as in the case of one-way loops.

Returning again to equation (4.3.25), consider the computation of N_m. Scheduled maintenance should be done in the off-peak hours, and then does not enter into N_m. The fleet N_m is needed rather to maintain $N_o + N_e$ vehicles in operation during the peak period even though some vehicles may fail and require unscheduled maintenance. Assume that if a vehicle fails during a rush period, it can be returned to service in a time $MTTR$, that is, the mean time to repair. $MTTR$ is made up of the following components:

$MTTR$ = (mean time to dispatch vehicle to maintenance)
+ (mean time to ready vehicle for repair
   including time to obtain needed parts)
+ (mean time to replace faulty part or subsystem)
+ (mean time to dispatch vehicle back in service)

Let the mean time between vehicle failures be $MTBF$, and let T_{rush} be the length of the rush period. Then the number of vehicles that fail during the rush period is

$$(N_o + N_e)\,(T_{\text{rush}}/MTBF)$$

If $MTTR$ is of the order of T_{rush} but not so long that the vehicle cannot be restored to service by the next rush period,

$$N_m = (N_o + N_e)\,(T_{\text{rush}}/MTBF) \qquad (4.3.40a)$$

But, if $MTTR$ is much less than T_{rush},

$$N_m = (N_o + N_e)\,(MTTR/MTBF) \qquad (4.3.40b)$$

Thus, the importance of easy-maintenance design so that subsystems can be quickly replaced is apparent. Life cycle cost is minimized if an expensive vehicle is returned to service as rapidly as possible. In a well-designed system, N_m should be no more than about one percent of $N_o + N_e$.

The Average Number of People per Vehicle and Time Headway

If p_v is given, $N_o + N_e$ can be determined from the theory of the previous section. Then the average time headway between vehicles, T, is found from equation (4.3.5). Thus

$$T = \frac{\ell_Q}{V_{avQ}(N_o + N_e)} = \frac{T_Q}{N_o + N_e} \qquad (4.3.41)$$

In small-vehicle automated systems in which private party service is offered, p_v is the size of the average group traveling together, and is usually assumed to be about 1.5. In larger vehicle systems, however, the service must be scheduled to a given value of T. Then equation (4.3.41) is used to compute $N_o + N_e$, and equation (4.3.15) is used to compute p_v.

Capacity

The capacity of a loop system is the total number of people per hour the system can handle. The achievable capacity depends on the distribution of demand as characterized by the demand matrix. In on-line station systems, it is limited by the achievable station throughput, derived in section 4.2. In off-line station systems, capacity may be limited by either station throughput or line throughput. If there is only a small number of stations, station throughput, determined by the theory of section 4.2, is the limiting factor. But with a small number of stations, off-line stations often cannot be justified. With a large number of off-line stations, the line capacity, determined by equations (4.3.6) and (4.3.7), limits the system capacity. The line flow in each link can readily be determined from the demand matrix D_{ij}.

4.4 Line-Haul Systems

A line-haul system is a collapsed one-way loop which may have either continuous flow or reverse flow at the end stations. As indicated in section 4.2, loop end stations cut the achievable headway at a given line speed almost in half and hence without a speed change almost double the capacity. But they take more space and are more expensive than back-up end stations. Therefore, the back-up end station is often used. Headway with these can be maintained if the trains are caused to slow down well in advance of the end stations. The intermediate stations may use either side platforms or central platforms, the latter of which are more economical of space. As indicated in figure 4-11, the stations of line-haul systems are usually on line. Also, to obtain adequate capacity, the vehicles are usually trained.

The maximum number of trains is given by equation (4.3.5), in which the minimum headway is found from section 4.2. As with on-line station loop systems, the actual number of trains required is found from equation (4.3.5) with the desired scheduled headway T_h substituted for T_{min}. In on-line station systems, there is no deliberate circulation of empty vehicles; therefore, $N_e = 0$ and N_o is the result found by using equation (4.3.5). Equation (4.3.15) is used to find p_v, the average rush period number of

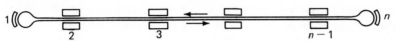

Side-platform stations, end loops

Central-platform stations, back-up ends

Figure 4-11. Line-Haul Configurations

people per train. In line-haul systems, however, the summation limits are different. Using the station designations of figure 4-11 for flow to the right,

$$p_v = \frac{1}{N_o} \sum_{i=1}^{n-1} \sum_{j=i+1}^{n} D_{ij} T_{ij}$$

Substituting equation (4.3.9),

$$p_v = \frac{1}{N_0} \left(\gamma T_{\text{ex}} + \frac{<L_t>}{V_L} \right) \tilde{D}_{\text{peak}} \qquad (4.4.1)$$

in which

$$\tilde{D}_{\text{peak}} = \sum_{i=1}^{n-1} \sum_{j=i+1}^{n} D_{ij} \qquad (4.4.2)$$

$$\gamma = \frac{1}{\tilde{D}_{\text{peak}}} \sum_{i=1}^{n-1} \sum_{j=i+1}^{n} D_{ij}(j - i) \qquad (4.4.3)$$

and

$$<L_t> = \frac{1}{\tilde{D}_{\text{peak}}} \sum_{i=1}^{n-1} \sum_{j=i+1}^{n} D_{ij} \ell_{ij} \qquad (4.4.4)$$

In a given peak period, the terms of the demand matrix D_{ij} corresponding to flow to the right in figure 4-11 are usually quite different from those corresponding to flow to the left. Thus p_v will be different in the two cases, and for the purpose of computing the number of cars per train p_v must of course be taken as the larger of the two values. If the car capacity is given, the number of cars per train is

$$\text{No. cars per train} = \frac{p_v}{(\text{car capacity})(\text{load factor})} \qquad (4.4.5)$$

in which "load factor" is the desired fraction of car capacity used during the rush period averaged over all cars in the system headed in the direction of maximum flow.

4.5 Network Systems

A network transit system is one in which there is more than one path between some of the stations. Fixed route, fixed schedule bus systems are usually network systems; the New York subway system is a network system. If network systems involve transfers from one branch to the other, however, they can be considered as being composed of a series of loops or line-haul branches. In these cases, the theory of sections 4.3 and 4.4 can be applied directly, and further elaboration is unnecessary. Thus, the present analysis is restricted to networks in which the vehicles may transfer from one loop or branch to another. Except in very small networks, the economics favor the use of off-line stations because: (1) they allow use of smaller vehicles and lower maximum line speeds, and hence guideways of lower weight per unit length; (2) they permit lower average trip time and hence reduce both the number of vehicles of a given size required and the total vehicle fleet cost; and (3) they increase patronage because of the reduced trip time. Therefore, the network analysis of this section assumes off-line stations.

Networks may use multilevel interchanges to accomplish vehicle transfer or they may use Y-interchanges. Use of Y-interchanges has the advantage that the guideways can all be at one level and the visual presence at any one location is minimized, but the disadvantage that, at interchanges, vehicles must merge before they diverge thus reducing the capacity. With multilevel interchanges, the vehicle streams diverge before they merge, thus preventing bottlenecks. The disadvantage of the Y-interchange can be reduced by designing the system so that vehicles run both above and below the guideway, thus providing two-way traffic. (A side-by-side two-way system is not practical in network configurations because of the size and complexity of the interchanges.) A two-way, over/under system more than doubles capacity with a given set of line and station locations because, as shown in Table 4-1, the average trip length reduces. With reduced trip length, trip time reduces and with it the number of vehicles. Hence the minimum spacing between vehicles increases. The analysis will, however, treat both multilevel and Y-interchanges; and both one-way and two-way networks.

If a specific network is under consideration; that is, a network with specific line and station locations, and the analyst has the data needed to make a detailed performance, cost, and patronage analysis, then the analysis of performance characteristics should proceed by extending the theory of section 4.3 for loop systems. The same basic framework of analysis is still applicable, but the analyst must take into account that the travel time matrix T_{ij} is not unique, but depends upon the choice of route. The network should be designed, however, so that the nominal path minimizes T_{ij}. Nonminimum paths would be used only in abnormal circumstances such as unusually heavy demand on certain routes, or in the case of breakdowns. Equation (4.3.10) is still valid, therefore the minimum T_{ij} are found by first finding the minimum ℓ_{ij}.

The formula for average trip length is analogous to equation (4.3.16) with the summations extending over all stations; and the theory of the required fleet size follows directly. Equation (4.3.26), with the summations again extended over all stations, shows that the minimum T_{ij} produce the minimum fleet size. The computation of the required empty vehicle fleet size proceeds by first computing the EX_{vj} from equation (4.3.36) with new summation limits. Having the EX_{vj}, the choice of destinations to which the vehicles are routed is more complex than in the case of loops. This problem has been treated by Thangavelu[2], by Irving[3], and by others. A trial selection of the empty vehicle destinations can be made on the basis of minimizing the total empty vehicle travel time. Then the total flow on each link must be computed, and the empty vehicle destinations and routes adjusted until a given link capacity constraint is satisfied.

Rough computations of vehicle fleet size can be made on the following basis: If the flow is completely uniform, $D_{ij} = D_{ji}$, and no empty vehicles are required. On the other hand, if the demand is unidirectional in the sense that if $D_{ij} \neq 0$, $D_{ji} = 0$, the occupied vehicles going from i to j must circulate empty from j to i. In this case half of the vehicles are empty. Therefore, the assumption that one-third of the vehicles circulate empty is a good compromise between these extremes. A number of computer simulations have produced the result of approximately one-third empty vehicles.

In initial analysis of network systems, before specific line and station locations are chosen, it is necessary to be able to estimate the performance and economics in specific situations. Also, a theory of performance and economics of networks at this level is algebraically simple, and it is easy to determine the influence of parameters such as line and station spacing. The theory is developed in two parts: geometric parameters, and performance parameters.

Geometric Parameters

The parameters derived are line density (length of guideways per unit area), station density, intersection point density, and average trip length. Consider the idealized network of figure 4-12. Let the network be square with line spacing L and $n + 1$ lines in each direction. Then the total length of lines is

$$\mathcal{L} = 2nL(n + 1)$$

$$= \frac{2}{L} (nL)^2 \left(1 + \frac{1}{n}\right)$$

But $(nL)^2 = A =$ the area of the network. Therefore,

$$\mathcal{L} = \frac{2}{L} \beta A \tag{4.5.1}$$

where

$$\beta = 1 + L/A^{1/2} \tag{4.5.2}$$

The line density is therefore

$$\rho_\ell = \frac{\mathcal{L}}{A} = \frac{2}{L} \beta \tag{4.5.3}$$

Let the stations be placed at the midpoints as indicated by the dots in figure 4-12. There are three reasons for this: (1) it is awkward to incorporate stations in the intersections and such a procedure increases visual impact at the intersections; (2) for a given L the maximum rectangular walk distance is $L/2$ if the stations are at the midpoints but twice as great if the stations are at the intersections (Even if the street pattern is not a rectangular grid, the rectangular walk distance is more realistic than the shortest distance "as the crow flies."); and (3) for a given line density, the station density is maximized if the stations are at the midpoints. The third reason will be clear from the following analysis.

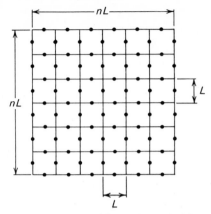

Figure 4-12. An Idealized Transit Network

The number of stations in the network of figure 4-12 is

$$n_s = 2n(n + 1) = \frac{2}{L^2} \beta A \qquad (4.5.4)$$

The station density is therefore

$$\rho_s = \frac{2}{L^2} \beta \qquad (4.5.5)$$

The number of intersections in the network of figure 4-12 is

$$n_I = (n + 1)^2 = \frac{1}{L^2} \beta^2 A \qquad (4.5.6)$$

Hence the intersection density is

$$\rho_I = \frac{\beta^2}{L^2} \qquad (4.5.7)$$

Thus the ratio of station density to intersection density is

$$\rho_s/\rho_I = \frac{2}{\beta} \qquad (4.5.8)$$

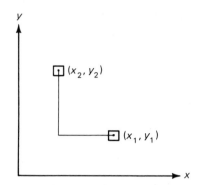

Figure 4-13. Idealization of the Average Trip Length

Thus, for a given line density, the station density is almost twice as great if the stations are at the midpoints rather than at the intersections. On the other hand, for a given station density (the parameter that determines the patronage), the line density is greater by $2/\beta$ if the stations are at the intersections rather than at the midpoints.

Consider the average trip length $<L_t>$ on the network of figure 4-12. If n is large, $<L_t>$ can be approximated by integrating the rectangular trip length over the network area, as shown in Figure 4-13, and by assuming every station is both an equally likely origin for travel and an equally likely destination. This is the assumption of uniform travel as introduced in section 4.3. If n is large, reference to figure 4-13 gives

$$<L_t> = \frac{1}{(nL)^4} \int_0^{nL} \int_0^{nL} \int_0^{nL} \int_0^{nL} (|x_1 - x_2| + |y_1 - y_2|) dx_1 \, dy_1 \, dx_2 \, dy_2$$

$$= \frac{2}{(nL)^2} \int_0^{nL} dx_2 \left[\int_0^{x_2} (x_2 - x_1) dx_1 + \int_{x_2}^{nL} (x_1 - x_2) dx_1 \right]$$

$$= \frac{2}{(nL)^2} \int_0^{nL} \left[\frac{(nL)^2}{2} - nLx_2 + x_2^2 \right] dx_2$$

$$= \frac{2}{3} (nL) = \frac{2}{3} A^{1/2} \tag{4.5.9}$$

Thus, in the limit as n approaches infinity, the average trip length with

Figure 4-14. Four-Station Square Loop

uniform demand is two-thirds the square root of the network area. In finite networks, $<L_t>$ is larger than this limit value because of indirect routing. Consider the series of cases illustrated by figures 4-14 through 4-17 with uniform demand.

Figure 4-14 shows the simplest case, consisting of the basic four-station square loop. Let the distance between stations be L. Then for one-way travel,

$$<L_t> = \frac{(1 + 2 + 3)}{3} \ L = 2L = 2A^{1/2} \qquad (4.5.10)$$

and for two-way travel

$$<L_t> = \frac{(1 + 2 + 1)}{3} \ L = 4/3 \ L = 1.33A^{1/2} \qquad (4.5.11)$$

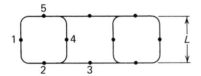

Figure 4-15. A Two-Loop Network

Figure 4-15 shows the next level of complexity. If the flow is *one way,* say counterclockwise, the average trip lengths from each of the five numbered stations are different and are as follows:

Origin Station	$<L_t>_i/L$
1	32/9
2	26/9
3	40/9
4	44/9
5	38/9

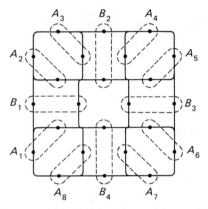

Figure 4-16. A Five-Loop Network

By symmetry, the average trip length from the other five stations are the same. Therefore, the average trip length for the two-loop network with one-way flow and uniform demand is

$$<L_t> = \frac{180}{5(9)} L = 4L = 2.31A^{1/2} \qquad \text{(one-way flow)} \qquad (4.5.12)$$

Similarly

$$<L_t> = \frac{256}{90} L = 2.88L = 1.66A^{1/2} \qquad \text{(two-way flow)} \qquad (4.5.13)$$

The next level of complexity is illustrated in figure 4-16. In this case the process of calculating the trip lengths is complex enough that a systematic procedure is desirable. Let the stations be divided into two types of groups of two stations each: A groups and B groups as shown in figure 4-16. Let $A_i \rightarrow A_j$ represents the trips from each of the stations in group A_i to each of the stations in group A_j, and note that there are four such trips. Then

$$A \rightarrow A = \sum_i \sum_j A_i \rightarrow A_j \\ i \neq j$$

represents all of the trips between A groups except for the trips internal to each A group. These are denoted by

$$A_I = \sum_i A_i \rightarrow A_i$$

The totality of trips in the network of figure 4-16 can be represented by the expression

$$A_I + (A \to A) + (A \to B) + B_I + (B \to A) + (B \to B)$$
$$16 + \quad 8(28) + \quad 8(16) + 8 \ + \quad 4(32) + \quad 4(12) = 552 \text{ trips}$$

The numbers under the group symbols are the numbers of trips generated in each type of group combination. Since the total number of stations is 24, the total number of trips is $24(23) = 552$. The total length of trips in each of the six groups is given in table 4-3 for one-way and two-way flow,

Table 4-3 Computation of Average Trip Length in Five-Loop Network

Group	Number of Trips	Total Length of Trips/L One-Way Flow	Two-Way Flow
A_I	16	8(4)	8(2)
$A \to A$	224	8(120)	8(108)
$A \to B$	128	8(64)	8(54)
B_I	8	4(8)	4(8)
$B \to A$	128	4(152)	4(112)
$B \to B$	48	4(60)	4(52)
	552	2384	2000
$<L_t>$		$1.44A^{1/2}$	$1.21A^{1/2}$

in which $A^{1/2} = 3L$.

The network of figure 4-17 has 60 stations and $60(59) = 3540$ trips. Using the same types of groupings as in figure 4-16, the average trip lengths are determined in a similar manner and are as given in table 4-4. Recognition of symmetries greatly simplifies the process of counting the trip lengths.

In Figure 4-18, the average trip lengths corresponding to the square networks of figures 4-14, 4-16 and 4-17 are plotted. Also, the limit given by equation (4.5.9) is shown as a dashed line. This information is as much as is useful to obtain for the case of uniform flow.

Performance Parameters

The parameters derived are fleet size, average headway, line flow, station flow, and nonstop wait time. The fleet size is given by equation (4.3.25) and

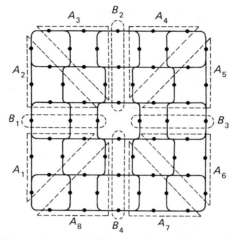

Figure 4-17. A Thirteen-Loop Network

the derivation of each term in that equation proceeds in the same manner as for loops. With networks, however, it is useful to define the parameters

$$\sigma = \frac{N}{N_o + N_e} \tag{4.5.14}$$

$$f_p = \frac{N_o}{N_o + N_e} \tag{4.5.15}$$

Then

$$N = \frac{\sigma N_o}{f_p} \tag{a}$$

Table 4-4 Computation of Average Trip Length in Thirteen-Loop Network

Group	Number of Trips	Total Length of Trips One-Way Flow	Two-Way Flow
A_I	8(30)	8(132)	8(98)
$A \rightarrow A$	8(252)	8(3262)	8(1370)
$A \rightarrow B$	8(72)	8(840)	8(326)
B_I	4(6)	4(24)	4(24)
$B \rightarrow A$	4(144)	4(804)	4(648)
$B \rightarrow B$	4(27)	4(142)	4(124)
	3540	21,344	17,536
$<L_t>$		$1.21A^{1/2}$	$0.99A^{1/2}$

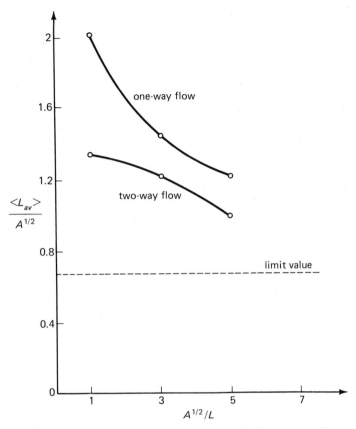

Figure 4-18. The Average Trip Length in Finite Networks with Uniform Demand

In analogy with equation (4.3.26)

$$N_o = (\tilde{t}_h A) T_{\text{trip}} / p_v \tag{b}$$

in which $\tilde{t}_h$ is the trip density, that is, the number of trips carried on the network system per hour per unit area, A is the network area, and p_v is the average number of people per occupied vehicle. In analogy with equation (4.3.10), the average trip time is

$$T_{\text{trip}} = T_{\text{ex}} + \frac{<L_t>}{V_L} \tag{4.5.16}$$

Combining equations (a), (b), and (4.5.16), the fleet size is

$$N = \frac{\sigma \tilde{t}_h}{p_v f_p}\left(T_{\text{ex}} + \frac{<L_t>}{V_L}\right)A \qquad (4.5.17)$$

If the vehicle makes intermediate stops, T_{ex} must be multiplied by the average number of intermediate stops, as indicated by equation (4.3.9).

The average time headway, T_{av}, is found from an equation analogous to equation (4.3.5), that is, by observing that the number of vehicles on line, N/σ, is equal to the total line length $\mathscr{L}$ (equation 4.5.1)) divided by the average nose-to-nose spacing between vehicles. The latter quantity is $T_{av}V_{av}$, where V_{av} is the average velocity. Thus, using equations (4.5.1), (4.5.17) and (4.5.16),

$$T_{av} = \frac{\mathscr{L}}{(N/\sigma)V_{av}} = \frac{2\beta p_v f_p}{\tilde{t}_h L T_{\text{trip}} V_{av}}$$

But $T_{\text{trip}}V_{av} = <L_t>$. (Note by combining equations (2.4.5) and (4.3.2) we see that $V_L T_L T_{\text{ex}} = \tilde{D}$.) Thus

$$T_{av} = \frac{2\beta p_v f_p}{\tilde{t}_h L <L_t>} \qquad (4.5.18)$$

and, as can be expected, for a given trip density, T_{av} is independent of A.

The average line flow in people per unit time, f_{av}, is the line flow in vehicles per unit time, $1/T_{av}$, multiplied by the number of people per vehicle, $p_v f_p$. Thus, using equation (4.5.18),

$$f_{av} = \frac{p_v f_p}{T_{av}} = \frac{\tilde{t}_h L <L_t>}{2\beta} \qquad (4.5.19)$$

The average station flow in people per unit time, fs_{av}, is the total demand per unit time, $\tilde{t}_h A$, divided by the number of stations. Using equation (4.5.4),

$$fs_{av} = \frac{\tilde{t}_h A}{n_s} = \frac{\tilde{t}_h L^2}{2\beta} \qquad (4.5.20)$$

and it is interesting to observe that

$$f_{av} = fs_{av} \ (<L_t>/L) \tag{4.5.21}$$

Finally, the nonstop wait time T_{nswt} is the average time a vehicle must wait at a station after one party has boarded for a second party headed for the same destination to arrive and board. This quantity is the average time headway between arrivals of parties at a station, p_v/fs_{av}, multiplied by the number of possible destinations $(n_s - 1)$. Thus

$$T_{nswt} = \frac{p_v(n_s - 1)}{fs_{av}} = \frac{p_v(n_s - 1)n_s}{\bar{\imath}_h A}$$

For $n_s \gg 1$, and using equation (4.5.4),

$$T_{nswt} = \frac{4p_v\beta^2}{\bar{\imath}_h L^4} A = \frac{4p_v}{\bar{\imath}_h L^2} \left(\frac{A^{1/2}}{L} + 1 \right)^2 \tag{4.5.22}$$

This equation is meaningful if the demand is relatively uniform, but T_{nswt} will in general differ a great deal between station pairs. Note that, for a given trip density, the nonstop wait time increases with the area of the network. Thus, for a given trip density, the type of service that requires a party to wait in a vehicle until a second party boards becomes increasingly unattractive as the network grows. Also, such a service concept increases the total trip time and hence the vehicle fleet size. Other service concepts can be considered. For example, if intermediate stops are permitted and the average number of stops counting the trip end stop is s, the average time to wait at a station for a second party going to one of these s stops is T_{nswt}/s. In another case, if it is desired to increase the vehicle load factor further by waiting for n_p extra parties going to any one of s stops, the wait time of the vehicle and the first party is $n_p T_{nswt}/s$. Thus knowledge of T_{nswt} determines the vehicle wait time for a range of service concepts.

4.6 Summary

The purpose of this chapter has been to develop the theory of performance of various types of transit systems. By "performance" we mean quantities such as characteristic times, trip lengths, average speeds, line flows, station flows, required numbers of vehicles, and average vehicle occupancy. Table 4-5 gives a classification of types of transit systems. Four basic types, classified according to the geometry of the lines—shuttle, loop, line-haul, and network—form the headings of the major sections of the chapter. Each of the four basic types may be further classified according to the geometry of the lines and stations, as indicated in table 4-5, and according to the type of service provided. Dropping the nonapplicable classifications, twenty-five different possibilities remain. In exploring the basic types of systems more deeply, we find that further subclassifications are practical, and discuss these in individual sections.

In section 4.1, shuttle systems are considered. First the simple shuttle is analyzed and it is found that all of its characteristic times can be described in one chart—figure 4-2. Here, based on the distance between the two stations and the line speed, the wait time to call a vehicle from the other end is found. Then, given the average station delay or dwell time, the average wait time, effective headway, and capacity in vehicles per hour are found. Next, the shuttle with intermediate stations is considered. This case is exactly the same as that of an elevator with stops at intermediate floors. It is shown how to find the characteristic times from figure 4-2 and that the capacity in vehicles per hour is found by dividing the value given in figure 4-2 corresponding to the distance between stops by $n - 1$, where n is the number of stations. If a bypass is placed at an intermediate station, as shown in figure 4-4, it is possible to run two vehicles on the shuttle and the capacity is doubled. If, however, the same idea is tried with two intermediate stations and four vehicles, the capacity does not double again but returns to the value for a simple shuttle of the same length. It is shown, therefore, that the advantage of including two or more intermediate bypass stations is not to increase capacity but to keep the capacity from reducing as the total line length increases.

In the next major section, section 4.2, the question of limitations on system capacity due to vehicles stopping at stations is considered. The criterion upon which the calculation is made is to keep the minimum distance between vehicles or trains greater than the required stopping distance if a failure should occur. For the case of a direct flow-through station, which may be either on-line or off-line, the results are summarized in a single dimensionless graph, figure 4-7. Here, the minimum time headway T can be found as a function of vehicle or train length L, station dwell time t_D, line speed V_L, normal and emergency deceleration, a and a_e, and the k-factor, where k is the ratio of the minimum distance between vehicles to the stopping distance of one vehicle. The case of end-of-the-line or back-up stations is then considered because this configuration is often used in line-haul systems to save space at the ends of the line. A dimensionless formula, equation (4.2.21), for the minimum time headway is given, and it is shown that, for the same line speed, the back-up station increases the minimum headway, but that, by reducing the line speed near the end stations, the headway possible at intermediate stations can be maintained.

Table 4-5 Classification of Transit Systems

	Shuttle	Loop	Line-Haul	Network
Stations:				
On-Line	A	A	A	A[a]
Off-Line	N/A	A	A	A
Lines:				
One-Way	A	A	N/A	A
Mixed	A	N/A	N/A	N/A
Two-Way	A	A	A	A
End Stations:				
Loop	N/A	N/A	A	N/A
Back-up	A	N/A	A	N/A
Service:				
Group	A	A	A	A[a]
Individual	N/A	A	A[b]	A

A—Applicable.
N/A—Not Applicable.
[a]In small networks only.
[b]Not for very high capacity.

The major section of the chapter, section 4.3, is devoted to loop systems. Here, basic performance equations are developed related not only to loops, but also to line-haul systems, which can be considered as collapsed loops, and to network systems, which comprise a multiplicity of connected loops. Six different types of loop systems, listed in table 4-5, are considered. Trip time matrices, demand matrices, and flow vectors are defined and it is shown how to find from them the average trip lengths and the required number of vehicles. The average trip length ratios, given in table 4-1, show that the capacity in a two-way system increases over that of a one-way system not only because there are two lines, but because of the decrease in average trip length. Thus, in comparing loops of say eleven stations, the capacity of a two-way system will be increased over that of a one-way system by a factor of $2(1.83) = 3.66$. With on-line stations, the required fleet size is the number of occupied vehicles required plus the extra vehicles needed in case of breakdowns. With off-line stations additional extra vehicles are needed to allow for redistribution of the vehicle fleet as a result of nonuniform demand. These are empty vehicles and the required number of them must be computed separately after the required number of occupied vehicles is found. Computation of the required number of occupied vehicles is summarized in table 4-2 for cases in which the average vehicle occupancy is known. For group systems, however, the number of occupied vehicles is found for a given schedule head-way from equation (4.3.5) and then the average vehicle occupancy is found from the equations tabulated in table 4-2. The required number of empty vehicles is determined from the demand and trip time matrices and is computed most easily by the diagrammatic method shown in figure 4-10, because the assignment of empty vehicles is not unique in loop systems.

In section 4.4, the theory of loop systems is applied to line-haul systems, considered as collapsed loops, and minor variations needed for the case of line-haul systems are given. Finally, the theory of network systems is considered in section 4.5. First, a series of geometric performance parameters, including the average trip length, is derived for a square network but in a form in which they are approximately applicable to any network. Figure 4-18 shows how the average trip length approaches a limit value as the network size increases. Then, the performance parameters—fleet size, average time headway, average line and station flow, and nonstop wait time—are derived in a form applicable to networks. Of these parameters, the nonstop wait time bears comment: It is the time one would wait on the average for a second party headed for the same station. If this time is short, then group service nonstop between stations is practical. If it is long, nonstop group service is not practical and should be replaced by either a group service that permits stops at a number of intermediate stations, or by individual nonstop service. Since the nonstop wait time increases with the size of the network, the practical service policy for large networks is either nonstop on-demand or multistop scheduled. The difference in trip time in these two cases is found by subtracting equation (4.3.10) from equation (4.3.9), that is, it is the number of stops multiplied by the excess time. In practical cases, from equation (4.3.2), the excess time is in the range of thirty to forty seconds. A computation of nonstop wait time is given for a particular case in figure 5-6.

Problems

1. A simple shuttle is to be built to carry a maximum of 1500 people per hour per direction between two points 500 meters apart. The maximum cruise speed of the vehicle is 48 km/hr. Each vehicle has two doors, one through which people egress and the other through which they ingress. Four people per second can move through each door. If the vehicle is filled at peak loading, what is the required vehicle capacity?

2. An elevator service is to be provided for a 120-ft, 10-story building. The maximum flow rate for which the elevator system is to be designed is 500 people in 10 minutes during the morning or evening period in which people are traveling only in one direction. If each elevator makes an

average of four intermediate stops, dwelling at each floor for 5 seconds, how many elevators are needed? The maximum lift rate is 200 ft/min, the acceleration is 0.5 g, and the capacity of each elevator is 10 persons.

3. Develop an expression for the capacity of an on-line station loop system with unidirectional stations in vehicles per hour if the vehicles are coupled into n-car trains and the length of each car is L_c. Plot the capacity as a function of n in the range $1 \leqslant n \leqslant 10$ for (a) standing-passenger vehicles in which $a_e = a$, and (b) seated-passenger vehicles in which $a_e = 2a$. In both cases assume $k = 2$, $V_L = 25$ m/s, $L_c = 15$ m, and $t_D = 15$ s.

4. A heavy-rail system is used as a line-haul transit system with back-up end stations ($L_{swx} = 95$ m) and eight-car trains. (a) Using the parameters of Problem 3 for standing-passenger vehicles, what is the capacity in people per hour if each car can hold 80 people and the average load factor is 60 percent. (b) By what percent is the capacity changed if the back-up end stations are replaced by loops, but the line speed around the loops must be reduced to 15 m/s? Did the speed reduction increase or decrease the capacity?

5. Assume that instead of coming directly into the station platform, the vehicles stop at a holding point where they wait for a platoon of n vehicles to load and leave together. The vehicles in the holding point then move forward together into the normal platform position. Determine the throughput of the station as a function of n and other pertinent kinematic parameters.

6. Consider the following loop systems. Distances between stations are given on the figure.

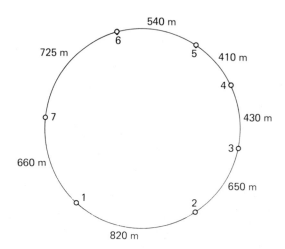

The demand matrix is as follows:

$$D_{ij} = \begin{bmatrix}
0 & 20 & 150 & 160 & 140 & 20 & 10 \\
40 & 0 & 130 & 170 & 160 & 30 & 20 \\
10 & 5 & 0 & 50 & 40 & 30 & 20 \\
15 & 10 & 40 & 0 & 30 & 20 & 10 \\
5 & 10 & 30 & 40 & 0 & 5 & 15 \\
15 & 5 & 120 & 140 & 160 & 0 & 10 \\
5 & 20 & 170 & 150 & 180 & 10 & 0
\end{bmatrix}$$

in which the units are people per hour.

Two different systems are to be considered, each in both one-way and two-way configurations:

System 1: On-line stations, standing-passenger vehicles operating in trains of two vehicles each to increase reliability. The line speed is 15 m/s, the vehicles can be assumed to be 10 m long, $k = 2$, and $a = a_e$.

System 2: Off-line stations, seated-passenger vehicles operating singly. The line speed is 10 m/s, the vehicles are 2.6 m long and accommodate 3 people. The average load factor is 1.5 people per vehicle and the dwell time is 5 seconds. Assume $k = 1$ and $a_e = 2a$.

Both types of vehicles can be loaded at a rate of two persons per second.

- a. For one-way, counterclockwise flow, compute from D_{ij} the flow into and out of each station and the total demand.
- b. Assuming the shortest length trip is always taken, separate the demand matrix into clockwise and counterclockwise components.
- c. For two-way flow, compute the flow from the street into and out of each station, considering the platforms from which vehicles are boarded for travel in opposite directions to be separate stations. This information is used to size the stations.
- d. Compute the total flow in each segment for one-way flow, and for two-way flow, on each track.

For System 1:

- e. Write a formula for minimum headway, T, based on station throughput considerations. (t_D is expressed as a function of vehicle capacity C_v.)
- f. For the one-way configuration, write a formula for C_v in terms of

minimum headway, T, assuming full vehicles on the busiest segment. Solve this equation, together with the equation from e for C_v and T. Round C_v up to the nearest multiple of five and call it the vehicle capacity, then round T up to the nearest multiple of 10 s and set the headway at this value. Compute t_D and round it up to the nearest multiple of 5 seconds. Compute the excess time T_{ex}.

g. Compute the circuit time and, as a matter of interest, the average speed. For the one-way configuration, compute the number of trains and the number of vehicles required.

h. For the one-way configuration, compute the average number of people per vehicle noting that it is the ratio of the average person-flow to the vehicle-flow.

i. For the two-way configuration, assume the same vehicle capacity as in the one-way system. Based on the flow of full vehicles in the busiest segment in each direction, compute the required headway in each direction. Compute the required number of two-vehicle trains and vehicles in each direction.

j. For the two-way configuration, compute the average number of people per vehicle in each direction.

For System 2:

k. Compute the excess time T_{ex}, and compute the average trip length for counterclockwise, one-way flow. Note that the corresponding matrix for clockwise flow is simply the transposed matrix.

l. Compute the average trip length for the two-way configuration in each direction.

m. Compute the number of occupied vehicles for the one-way and the two-way configuration.

n. Compute the excess-flow vector, EX_{v_j}, for the one-way and the two-way configuration.

o. Draw a diagram for the dispatching of empty vehicles for the one-way and the two-way configuration, and compute the required number of empty vehicles in both cases.

p. Based on the total flow of vehicles on the busiest link, compute the minimum operating line headway for the one-way or the two-way configuration, and compute the minimum nose-to-tail spacing.

q. If the failure deceleration rate is twice the emergency deceleration rate, and the control time constant is 0.6 s, compute the ratio of minimum nose-to-tail spacing to the minimum no-collision spacing.

r. Compute the maximum station throughput in vehicles per hour, and with $p_v = 1.5$ compare it with the maximum required flow into a station in vehicles per hour, making certain to account for the flow of empty vehicles. If the requirement exceeds the maximum permissible throughput, the station must have more than one loading berth.

s. If both types of vehicles cost $3000 per unit capacity (see figure 5-1), compute the fleet cost of each of the four configurations. Recompute the fleet cost of the two versions of System 2 for a line speed of 15 m/s.

References

1. John J. Fruin, *Pedestrian Planning and Design,* published in 1971 by the Metropolitan Association of Urban Designers and Environmental Planners, Inc., Box 722, Church Street Station, New York, N.Y. 10008.

2. K. Thangavelu, "Systems Analysis of Personal Rapid Systems," Ph.D. thesis, Department of Civil Engineering, Northwestern University, Evanston, Illinois June 1974.

3. Jack H. Irving et al., "Vehicle Management on Large PRT Networks," *Personal Rapid Transit III,* Audio Visual Library Services, University of Minnesota, Minneapolis, Minn., 1976.

5

Cost Effectiveness

This chapter is divided into three parts. First, equations applicable to parametric analysis of the cost of any transit system are given to the level of detail in which the cost of vehicles, guideways, stations, and central facilities are each represented by lumped variables. Cost analysis of each of these types of equipment can fruitfully be carried out in much more detail in subsystem analysis. Some of this kind of analysis is indicated in later chapters; however, for systems analysis, the above categories of equipment carry the analysis to the required depth. Second, equations for analysis of cost effectiveness are given and discussed; and, third, the equations of cost effectiveness are applied to the analysis of specific types of systems. This work is based on the author's paper in the book *Personal Rapid Transit III*[1].

5.1 Cost Equations

The cost equations are given in the following list of notations following definition of the terms.

C_{vc} = vehicle cost per unit capacity. If all passengers are seated, C_{vc} is the cost per seat. If standees are allowed, C_{vc} is the vehicle cost divided by the design capacity, not the crushload capacity. The vehicle cost is denoted per unit capacity because, as shown by figure 5-1, the vehicle cost per unit capacity is not correlated with vehicle capacity.

q_c = vehicle design capacity

C_g = guideway cost per unit length. If the system uses two-way integral guideways, C_g is the cost of the two-way integral guideway. For convenience, C_g also includes the cost of right of way.

C_s = station cost including right of way, but not including off-line ramps

C_{sf_o} = portion of cost of support facilities not proportional to the number of vehicles

C_{sf_v} = portion of cost of support facilities proportional to the number of vehicles, per vehicle

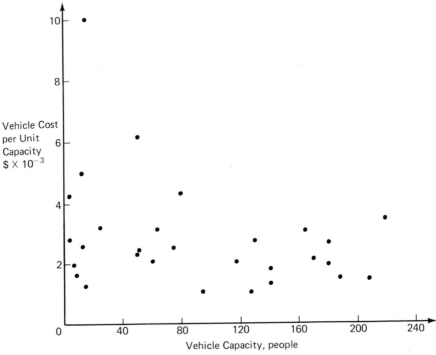

Figure 5-1. Guideway Transit Vehicle Cost per Unit Capacity (Data from 1975 Lea Transit Compendium)

l_r = length of an off-line ramp as determined by the theory of chapter 3

$\mathscr{L}$ = total guideway length. Given by equation (4.5.1) for network systems. If system uses two-way guideways, $\mathscr{L}$ is the total length of two-way guideways, not the one-way guideway length. Does not include off-line ramps.

n_s = total number of independent stations. Given by equation (4.5.4) for network systems.

N = the number of vehicles in the system. See equation (4.3.25).

Subscript o&m: This subscript is applied to the cost terms to denote the annual cost for operation and maintenance.

A_k = the amortization factor on the kth type of equipment, that is, the annual payment on the equipment for principal and interest divided by the initial cost. For convenience of readers not familiar with the economics literature, the formula for A_k is derived in Appendix A in terms of n_k, the life of the kth type of equipment, and r, the rate of interest on capital expenditure.

C_T = total initial cost of the system

$$C_T = (C_{vc}q_c + C_{sf_v})\,N + C_g\mathcal{L} + C_s n_s + C_{sf_0} \tag{5.1.1}$$

C_{v_a} = annual cost of vehicles per vehicle

$$C_{v_a} = (A_v C_{vc} + C_{vc_{o\&m}})q_c \tag{5.1.2}$$

C_{g_a} = annual cost of guideways per unit length

$$C_{g_a} = A_g C_g + C_{g_{o\&m}} \tag{5.1.3}$$

C_{s_a} = annual cost of an average station

$$C_{s_a} = A_s C_s + C_{s_{o\&m}} \tag{5.1.4}$$

C_{sf_a} = annual cost of support facilities

$$C_{sf_a} = A_{sf}(C_{sf_v}N + C_{sf_0}) + C_{sf_{o\&m}}N + C_{sf_{o\&m}} \tag{5.1.5}$$

C/yr = annual cost of system

$$C/\mathrm{yr} = C_{v_a}N + C_{g_a}\mathcal{L} + C_{s_a}n_s + C_{sf_a} \tag{5.1.6}$$

It is also useful to compute:

$(C/\mathrm{yr})_{\mathrm{cap}}$ = annual cost of amortization of capital equipment for entire system

$$(C/\mathrm{yr})_{\mathrm{cap}} = A_v C_{vc}q_c N + A_g C_g\mathcal{L} + A_s C_s n_s + A_{sf}(C_{sf_v}N + C_{sf_0}) \tag{5.1.7}$$

$(C/\mathrm{yr})_{o\&m}$ = annual system cost for operation and maintenance

$$(C/\mathrm{yr})_{o\&m} = C_{vc_{o\&m}}q_c N + C_{g_{o\&m}}\mathcal{L} + C_{s_{o\&m}}n_s + C_{sf_{v_{o\&m}}}N + C_{sf_{0_{o\&m}}} \tag{5.1.8}$$

5.2 Equations for Cost Effectiveness

Let t_d be the average number of trips per week day carried by the system.

Let t_{yr} be the average number of trips per year. Then in most cases

$$t_{yr} \approx 300 \, t_d \qquad (5.2.1)$$

The most basic cost effectiveness parameter is the *total cost per passenger trip* or the break-even fare. If this quantity is represented by C/tr,

$$C/tr = \frac{C/yr}{t_{yr}} \qquad (5.2.2)$$

The *cost per vehicle trip*, $(C/tr)_v$, is the cost per passenger trip multiplied by p_v. Then

$$(C/tr)_v = (C/tr)p_v \qquad (5.2.3)$$

The *cost per passenger kilometer, C/pkm*, is C/tr divided by the average trip length $<L_t>$ in kilometers. Thus

$$C/pkm = \frac{C/tr}{<L_t>} \qquad (5.2.4)$$

To determine the influence of freight hauling in addition to passenger hauling on the cost per passenger trip, let the number of freight trips per year, t_{yr_f}, be represented by

$$t_{yr_f} = et_{yr}/p_v \qquad (5.2.5)$$

Thus e represents the ratio of vehicle trips for freight movement to vehicle trips for passenger movement. The total cost per year will be increased because of the need to provide for freight vehicles; however, if some of the passenger vehicles are used for freight movement in off-peak hours, the ratio of the number of freight vehicles to the number of passenger vehicles need not be as high as e. Let this ratio be

$$e' = \frac{N_{freight}}{N_{pass}} < e \qquad (5.2.6)$$

Then, the cost per year as a function of the number of vehicles can be written in a form analogous to equation (5.1.6) in which N is multiplied by 1 + e' and n_s is increased if extra freight stations are added. As a first approximation, assume n_s is also multiplied by $1 + e'$. Then using equations (5.2.3), (5.2.2), (5.2.5), (5.2.6), (5.1.6) and (5.1.5),

$$C/tr = \frac{(C/tr)_v}{p_v} = \frac{C/yr}{P_v\left(\frac{t_{yr}}{p_v} + t_{yr_f}\right)} = \frac{C_1(1 + e') + C_2}{t_{yr}\,(1 + e)}$$

in which

(5.2.7)

$$C_1 = (C_{v_a} + A_{cf}C_{sf_v} + C_{sf_{vo\&m}})N_p + C_{s_a}n_s$$

$$C_s = C_{g_a}\mathscr{L} + A_{sf}C_{sf_o} + C_{sf_{oo\&m}}$$

where N_p is the number of vehicles needed for passenger service. With $e' \leqslant e$, it is clear that, because of the fixed facility costs, C_2, the addition of freight movement reduces the cost per passenger trip.

Consider an example. In a well-designed exclusive guideway system, $C_2 \approx C_1$. If, in the most extreme case, there are as many vehicle trips for freight movement as for passenger movement[2], $e = 1$. Finally, assume that half the freight trips are of such a nature that they can be handled by passenger vehicles in the off-peak hours. Then $e' = 0.5$. Substituting these three assumptions into equation (5.2.7) gives

$$C/tr = \frac{2C_1}{t_{yr}}\left(\frac{5}{8}\right)$$

Thus, in this extreme case, the cost per passenger trip is reduced to 62.5 percent of its value if there is no freight movement. Freight movement is not considered in the derivation of the following cost effectiveness parameters, but it can be considered on the basis of the above analysis as the need arises.

The next cost effectiveness parameter, of interest to the transit operator, is the *annual surplus*, S_a, where

$$S_a = t_{yr} \text{ (Average fare)} - (C/yr)_{o\&m} - (C/yr)_{cap} \qquad (5.2.8)$$

The two components of annual cost are broken out separately for emphasis because it is so common in contemporary transit studies to speak of a positive surplus when the annual revenue exceeds only the operation and maintenance costs. In capital intensive systems, $(C/yr)_{cap}$ exceeds $(C/yr)_{o\&m}$ often by a factor of more than two. Therefore, unless a system is under analysis in which the capital costs have been paid, it is not appropriate to refer only to an "operating surplus."

Another important cost effectiveness parameter is the *change in cost per trip if patronage is increased*. From equation (5.2.2), this is

$$\frac{\partial(C/\text{tr})}{\partial t_{\text{yr}}} = \frac{1}{t_{\text{yr}}}\left(\frac{\partial C/\text{yr}}{\partial t_{\text{yr}}} - \frac{C/\text{yr}}{t_{\text{yr}}}\right) \qquad (5.2.9)$$

If t_{yr} is increased without adding fixed facilities, but only vehicles, then, since the vehicle fleet increases in proportion to t_{yr}, C/yr is of the form

$$C/\text{yr} = a_1 t_{\text{yr}} + a_2$$

where a_1 and a_2 are independent of t_{yr}. Then

$$\frac{\partial C/\text{tr}}{\partial t_{\text{yr}}} = -\frac{a_2}{t_{\text{yr}}^2}$$

and the cost per trip decreases as patronage is added because a_2 is greater than 0. If, to attract additional patronage, additional fixed facilities are built, then the situation may be different. If patronage is attracted in proportion to the cost of the new facilities, a_2 is proportional to t_{yr}, and C/tr is independent of t_{yr}. If costs of the fixed facilities increase more rapidly than in proportion to t_{yr}, then equation (5.2.9) shows that C/tr increases as t_{yr} increases and these new facilities must be defended on a basis other than direct cost. In general, equation (5.2.9) shows that if a curve of C/yr versus t_{yr} is drawn, the cost per trip will decrease as t_{yr} increases only if the slope of the curve is less than the slope of a line from the origin of coordinates to the point in question.

The final cost effectiveness parameter is the *present value of future savings* if the system in question is built rather than if present trends are continued. Let $(CS/\text{yr})_n^{\circ}$ represent the cost savings in the nth year in the future in base year currency if the new system is built. Then

$$(CS/\text{yr})_n^{\circ} = (C/\text{yr})^{\circ}_{\text{trend system}} - (C/\text{yr})_{\text{new system}_{\text{cap}}} \qquad (5.2.10)$$
$$- (C/\text{yr})^{\circ}_{\text{new system}_{\text{o\&m}}}$$

in which the cost per year of the new system is separated into the cost for capital and the cost for operation and maintenance. The yearly cost of the trend system and the operating and maintenance costs of the new system increase year by year due to inflation; but, once bonds are secured, the capital cost per year for principal and interest is fixed. If the inflation rate is

i per year, the cost saving in the nth year in the future in nth year dollars is

$$(CS/yr)_n^n = [(C/yr)_{\text{trend system}}^\circ - (C/yr)_{\text{new system}_{\text{o\&m}}}^\circ](1 + i)^n$$
$$- (C/yr)_{\text{new system}_{\text{cap}}} \tag{5.2.11}$$

Then, if d is the discount rate, the present value of the savings in the nth year is

$$(CS/yr)_{pv,n} = \frac{(CS/yr)_n^n}{(1 + d)^n} \tag{5.2.12}$$

From Equation (5.2.11), it is clear that, due to inflation, the cost savings increases year by year if a substantial portion of the system cost is in capital rather than in inflating costs. The cumulative present value of future savings out to the Nth year is

$$PV_N = \sum_{n=1}^N \frac{(CS/yr)_n^n}{(1 + d)^n} \tag{5.2.13}$$

If the cost terms in equation (5.2.11) are independent of n, the summation of equation (5.2.13) can be written in closed form using the identity

$$x + x^2 + x^3 + \dots + x^N = x(x^N - 1)/(x - 1)$$

Then, equation (5.2.12) becomes

$$PV_N = [(C/yr)_{\text{trend system}}^\circ - (C/yr)_{\text{new system}_{\text{o\&m}}}^\circ] \times$$
$$\left(\frac{1 + i}{i - d}\right)\left[\left(\frac{1 + i}{1 + d}\right)^N - 1\right]$$
$$- (C/yr)_{\text{new system}_{\text{cap}}} \, 1/d \left[1 - \left(\frac{1}{1 + d}\right)^N\right] \tag{5.2.14}$$

Thus far, C/yr has included only the direct costs of the system. If the indirect costs due to factors such as air and noise pollution and land unavailable for other purposes are taken into account, as well as the direct cost to the traveler in terms of trip time, then PV_N becomes a true measure of the present value of the new system to society. This would seem to be a preferable measure of cost effectiveness of a new system to the more commonly used benefit/cost ratio because it quantifies the differences between new systems. Further usefulness of PV_N lies in the observation that, if the new system requires research and development to bring it into practical use, it is understandable that it would be justifiable to invest a small fraction of PV_N in research and development to realize the indicated cost savings.

5.3 Cost Effectiveness of Bus Systems

For bus systems that operate on surface streets, all of the annual costs are approximately proportional to the number of buses. Therefore let

$$C/\text{yr} = C_{b_a} N \qquad (5.3.1)$$

in which C_{b_a} is the total annualized cost of the bus system for capital equipment, driver wages, and central facilities. In 1975, in the United States, C_{b_a} was approximately \$50,000, of which approximately 80 percent was driver wages.

If the minimum bus headway is given as $T_{\min}$, the number of buses is given by the following equation, analogous to equations (4.3.5):

$$N = \frac{2\mathcal{L}}{V_{\text{av}} T_{\min}} \qquad (5.3.2)$$

Combining equations (5.3.1), (5.3.2), (5.2.2) and (5.2.1),

$$C/\text{tr} = \left(\frac{C_{b_a} \mathcal{L}}{150 V_{\text{av}} T_{\min}} \right) \frac{1}{t_d} \qquad (5.3.3)$$

If the bus system is a network of lines, define the daily trip density t_d by the equation

$$\tilde{t}_d = \frac{t_d}{A} \qquad (5.3.4)$$

in which A is the area covered by bus lines. Then, substituting equations (4.5.1) and (5.3.4) into equation (5.3.3),

$$C/\text{tr} = \left(\frac{C_{b_a}\beta}{75V_{av}T_{min}L} \right) \frac{1}{t_d} \tag{5.3.5}$$

Consider a typical example of a large bus network for which $\beta = 1$, $V_{av}T_{min} = 1$ mi $= 1.6$ km, and $L = 0.5$ mi (0.8 km). (This case corresponds, for example, to $V_{av} = 10$ mi/h and $T_{min} = 6$ minutes.) Substituting these values and $C_{b_a} = \$50,000$, into equation (5.3.5),

$$C/\text{tr} = (13.3\cancel{c}) \frac{10^4}{t_d} \tag{5.3.6}$$

Equations (5.3.5) and (5.3.6) apply for values of t_d up to the point of saturation, that is, up to the point where more trips can be handled only by adding more buses. If the bus system is saturated, N must be determined by equation (4.5.17) in which p_v is the saturation value of the average number of people per bus. Then, setting $f_p = 1$ and letting

$$T_{ex} + \frac{<L_t>}{V_L} = \frac{<L_t>}{V_{av}}$$

$$N = \frac{\sigma \tilde{t}_h <L_t> A}{p_v V_{av}} \tag{5.3.7}$$

Substitute equation (5.3.7) into equation (5.3.1), and then equations (5.3.1), (5.3.4) and (5.2.1) into equation (5.2.2) to give

$$C/\text{tr} = \frac{C_{b_a}\sigma <L_t>}{3000 p_v V_{av}} \tag{5.3.8}$$

and the headway corresponding to p_v is found by equating equations (5.3.2) and (5.3.7), with equation (4.5.1) substituted. Thus

$$T_{min} = \frac{40\beta p_v}{\sigma \tilde{t}_d L <L_t>} \tag{5.3.9}$$

in which it has been assumed that $\tilde{t}_d = 10\tilde{t}_h$. Assuming $C_{b_a} = \$50,000$, $\sigma = 1.05$, and $V_{av} = 16$ km/hr, equation (5.3.8) becomes

$$C/\text{tr} = \$1.75 \frac{<L_t>}{p_v} \qquad (5.3.10)$$

in which $<L_t>$ is in kilometers. Equating equation (5.3.10) and (5.3.6), it is seen that saturation of the bus system occurs when

$$\tilde{t}_d = 760 \frac{p_v}{<L_t>} \qquad (5.3.11)$$

Equation (5.3.6) and equation (5.3.10) for several values of T_{min}, $<L_t>$, and p_v are plotted in figure 5-2.

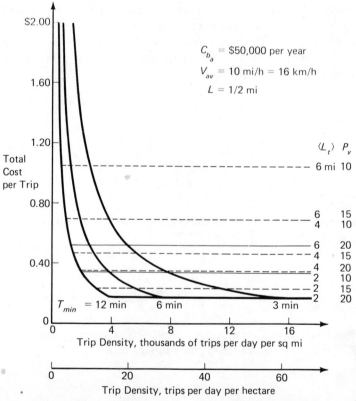

Figure 5-2. Total Cost per Trip of Bus Systems

Similar analyses can be carried through for the other cost effectiveness parameters, but for bus systems that does not seem worthwhile at this point. Understanding of the behavior of C/tr with trip density, trip length, minimum headway, and the saturation number of people per bus gives a good understanding of the cost effectiveness of bus systems.

The trip density can be interpreted by noting that

$$\bar{t}_d = m_t \, \tau_d \rho \tag{5.3.12}$$

in which ρ is the number of people per square mile, τ_d is the mobility, that is, the total number of trips per person per day, and m_t is the fraction of the number of daily trips taken by bus transit. If the bus network covers only a portion of the metropolitan area, $\bar{t}_d$ is composed of three types of trips:

1. Trips internal to the network
2. Trips from points outside the network to points inside
3. Trips from points inside to points outside

Analysis of this kind of trip distribution pattern is deferred to the next chapter.

5.4 Cost Effectiveness of Shuttles

In analysis of cost effectiveness of shuttles, the cost per vehicle trip is the most appropriate parameter. Combining equations (5.2.1) through (5.2.3),

$$(C/\text{tr})_v = \frac{C/\text{yr}}{300 t_d/p_v} \tag{5.4.1}$$

In the case of a simple shuttle, $N = 1$ and $n_s = 2$. Therefore equation (5.1.6) can be written

$$C/\text{yr} = C_{vs_{sf_a}} + C_{g_a}\mathscr{L} \tag{5.4.2}$$

in which

$$C_{vs_{sf_a}} = C_{v_a} + 2C_{s_a} + C_{sf_a} \tag{5.4.3}$$

It is convenient to express t_d/p_v in terms of capacity. The capacity of a shuttle is given by equation (4.1.4) in which $D_s = \mathscr{L}$ and the velocity and times are given in seconds. Let

$$T_{\text{ex}} = t_D + \frac{V_L}{a_m} + 1 \tag{5.4.4}$$

and

$$t_d/p_v = 10\alpha \left(\frac{1800 V_L}{\mathscr{L} + V_L T_{ex}} \right) \tag{5.4.5}$$

in which α is a factor between zero and one, and it is assumed that the daily number of vehicle trips is ten times the number of peak-hour vehicle trips. Substituting equations (5.4.2) and (5.4.5) into equation (5.4.1),

$$(C/tr)_v = C_0(1 + C_1\mathscr{L})(1 + C_2\mathscr{L}) \tag{5.4.6}$$

in which

$$C_0 = C_{vs_{sf_a}} T_{ex}/5.4(10)^6\alpha$$

$$C_1 = C_{g_a}/C_{vs_{sf_a}}$$

$$C_2 = 1/V_L T_{ex}$$

Thus, it is seen that the cost per vehicle trip for a shuttle is a quadratic function of the length of the shuttle. To give the reader a feeling for the cost per vehicle of a typical shuttle, consider the following example:

$$C_v = C_{v_c} q_c = \$80,000$$

$$C_s = \$100,000$$

$$C_g = \$1000/m$$

$$C_{sf} = \$50,000$$

Let the vehicles be amortized over an assumed life time of fifteen years and the fixed facilities over forty years, all at an interest rate of 6 percent. Then, from Appendix A, $A_v = 0.103$, and $A_g = A_s = A_{sf} = 0.066$. Let the annual operating and maintenance costs for the vehicle be 5 percent of the capital cost and for the stationary equipment be 2 percent of the capital cost. Then, from equations (5.1.2 through 5.1.5), and equation (5.4.3),

$$C_{v_a} = \$12,240 \qquad C_{g_a} = \$86/m$$

$$C_{s_a} = \$8600 \qquad C_{sf_a} = \$4300 \qquad C_{vs_{sf_a}} = \$33,740$$

Let $T_{ex} = 30$ s and $V_L = 10$ m/s. Then

$$C_0 = 0.187/\alpha \qquad C_1 = 0.00255 \qquad C_2 = 0.00333$$

Equation (5.4.6) is plotted in figure 5-3 for several values of T_{ex} and V_L, and for $\alpha = 1$. Thus, once the flow per day is determined as a fraction of capacity per day, the cost per trip may be found by dividing the values from figure 5-3 by α. The costs used are representative only, and computations made for specific cases should be based on manufacturer's data. The curves terminate at the low end at the minimum length for which the indicated line velocity is attainable at an acceleration of 1.25 m/s². (See the sentence below equation (2.4.6).)

5.5 Cost Effectiveness of Loop Systems

The number of occupied vehicles required in a loop system is given by table 4-2. In the present analysis, it is convenient to use the average velocity V_{av}, defined for loops by the equation

$$V_{av} = \frac{<L_t>}{\gamma T_{ex} + <L_t>/V_L} \tag{5.5.1}$$

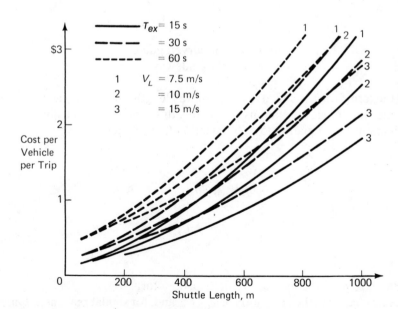

Figure 5-3. The Cost per Vehicle Trip of a Typical Shuttle (operating at capacity 10 hours per day 300 days per year)

in which the equations that give γ and $<L_t>$ are listed in table 4-2. Then, using the definitions given by equations (4.5.14) and (4.5.15), the total number of vehicles is

$$N = \frac{\sigma <L_t> t_d / 10}{f_p p_v V_{av}} \qquad (5.5.2)$$

in which $t_d = 10 \bar{D}_{peak}$ is the assumed daily travel. Equation (5.5.2) is applicable until the minimum headway, given by equation (4.3.6), is reached. If $\bar{t}_d$ is increased further, training or off-line stations must be used.

Using equations (5.1.6) and the definitions that lead to it, and (5.2.1), equation (5.2.2) becomes

$$C/\text{tr} = \frac{1}{300 t_d} \left[C_{c_a} q_c N + C_{g_a}(\mathscr{L} + 2l_r \mu n_s) + C_{s_a} n_s + C_{sf_{o_a}} \right]$$

$$(5.5.3)$$

in which

$$C_{c_a} = A_v C_{vc} + C_{vc_{o\&m}} + (A_{sf} C_{sf_v} + C_{sf_{vo\&m}})/q_c$$

$$C_{sf_{o_a}} = A_{sf} C_{cf_o} + C_{sf_{o\&m}}$$

$$\mu = \text{ratio of cost of curved guideway to} \\ \text{cost of straight guideway}$$

and the term $2l_r \mu n_s$ is added to the guideway length to explicitly account for off-line stations. If the stations are on line, this term is dropped and $f_p = 1$.

Substituting equation (5.5.2), equation (5.5.3) becomes

$$C/\text{tr} = \frac{C_{c_a} \sigma <L_t>}{3000 f_p V_{av}(p_v/q_c)} + \frac{C_{g_a} \mathscr{L} + C_{sf_{o_a}}}{300 t_d}$$

$$+ \frac{(2C_{g_a} l_r \mu + C_{s_a}) n_s}{300 t_d} \qquad (5.5.4)$$

in which p_v/q_c is the average vehicle load factor.

As indicated in the derivation of C_{vc}, C_{vc} and, for similar reasons, C_{c_a} are very weakly correlated with vehicle capacity. Hence, the first term in equation (5.5.4) depends on vehicle capacity directly only if vehicle size influences average speed and load factor. In on-line station systems, $f_p = 1$, but the intermediate stops lower V_{av} thus raising the vehicle cost component of the cost per trip. Larger vehicles must wait longer at stations to increase the load factor, thus reducing V_{av} while attempting to increase (p_v/q_c). If the stations are off-line, f_p may reduce to about two thirds but V_{av} increases substantially, for given V_L, due to elimination of intermediate stops (see figure 2-4). Also, as vehicle capacity decreases, the station dwell time required to obtain a significant daily average load factor decreases, thus increasing both V_{av} and p_v/q_c. If the service is on demand such that the vehicle leaves the station with only one party aboard, it is apparent that the first term in equation (5.5.4) is minimized. If the guideway is made bi-directional by permitting flow in opposite directions either side-by-side or above and below the guideway, the average trip length is substantially reduced, as indicated in table 4-1, thus reducing the vehicle cost term in equation (5.5.4).

The numerator of the third term in equation (5.5.4) increases due to addition of off-line stations because of the addition of off-line ramps. However, the station platform itself is generally shorter with off-line stations, thus reducing C_{s_a}. Moreover, the increased average trip speed, V_{av}, possible with off-line stations generally increases to t_d. Thus, the direction of the net change in C/tr due to addition of off-line stations requires detailed analysis of a range of specific examples.

For a given route length, $\mathscr{L}$, the second term in equation (5.5.4) depends mainly on C_{g_a} and t_d. The guideway cost per unit length, C_{g_a}, depends on three factors:

1. The weight per unit length of the vehicles
2. The cross sectional dimensions of the guideway
3. The maximum speed

In figure 5-4, the weights per unit length of operational and developmental transit vehicles are plotted as a function of design capacity. Lower weight per unit length of the vehicles permits reduction in guideway weight per unit length and hence in guideway cost. An even more effective way to minimize guideway cost, however, is to choose the guideway cross-sectional shape so as to minimize guideway weight per unit length. This subject is discussed in chapter 10.

The influence of maximum cruising speed on guideway cost is indicated by equation (3.6.21) which shows that, for a given guideway misalignment, the maximum lateral jerk is proportional to the cube of the speed. Thus, for specified maximum lateral jerk, the misalignment tolerances increase very rapidly with speed, thus requiring a more rigid, more accurately aligned, and hence more expensive guideway to accommodate higher speeds. In this regard, the comparison between on-line and off-line stations is signifi-

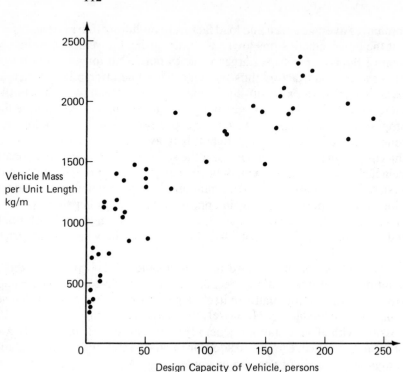

Figure 5-4. Transit Vehicle Mass per Unit Length
Source: 1975 Lea Transit Compendium

cant. With off-line stations, figure 2-4 shows that V_{av}/V_L is much closer to unity than with on-line stations. In typical cases, this ratio is in the neighborhood of 0.6 for on-line station systems and 0.95 for off-line station systems. Thus, for a given average speed, the maximum speed is considerably lower if off-line stations are used.

Finally, the patronage term t_d in the second and third terms of equation (5.5.4) is greatest and hence the guideway cost portion of C/tr least if the trip time is minimum, that is, if V_{av} is maximum. Thus, high V_{av} lowers all terms of equation (5.5.4). However, if V_{av} is increased by increasing V_L, C_{g_a} increases, as indicated above, and also C_{c_a} increases because higher V_L requires higher motor power, approximately in proportion to V_L^2. Also, l_r increases with V_L, as indicated by the theory of sections 3.4 and 3.5 Thus, there is a value of V_L that minimizes C/tr. Based upon detailed parametric analysis of the cost of guideways and vehicles, and of the dependence of patronage on V_{av}, the optimum value of V_L can be determined in specific cases. Determination of the optimum V_L for a range of practical cases is of fundamental importance in the cost effective design of guideway transit systems.

5.6 Cost Effectiveness of Line-Haul Systems

Since a line-haul system is a collapsed loop, the analysis of cost effectiveness follows the line of argument developed in section 5.5. The headway limitation is determined by the analysis of section 4.2 and may be different if the end stations are reversing as shown in figure 4-8 rather than if they permit unidirectional flow, as shown in figure 4-6. Equation (5.5.4) is used to compute the cost per trip, in which, for line-haul systems, $\mathcal{L}$ is the length of two-way lines and C_{g_a} is the annual cost per unit length of two-way lines.

In section 5.5, the terms of equation (5.5.4) were analyzed qualitatively to determine the variation of C/tr with various design options. Here, we will place some numerical estimates on the parameters in each of the three terms of equation (5.5.4). The costs assumed will be typical of several types of line-haul systems, and the purpose of the analysis is to obtain a feeling for the magnitudes and the ranges of variables needed to make the system economically feasible. Much actual cost data can be obtained from the Lea Transit Compendium[3] for specific systems of all types. However, to avoid reference to the equipment of specific manufacturers, the numbers assumed here must be considered representative only.

Consider the first term in equation (5.5.4), the vehicle cost per trip. From figure 5-1, a representative value of vehicle cost per unit capacity is about $2500 per unit capacity. Assume that the amortization factors are as computed in section 5.4, that the annual vehicle cost for operation and maintenance is 5 percent of the capital cost, and that the annual cost for support facilities is 30 percent of the annual vehicle cost. Then, from the definition below equation (5.5.3), $C_{c_a} = \$500$ per unit capacity per year. Consider an on-line station system. Then $f_p = 1$ and in typical modern cases $V_{av} = 60$ km/hr. Let $\sigma = 1.05$. Then

$$(C/tr)_{\text{vehicles}} = \$0.003 \; \frac{<L_t>}{p_v/q_c}$$

In line-haul systems $<L_t> = 8$ km is representative. The number of people per vehicle, p_v, comes from equation (5.5.2) and must be representative of rush period values. Assume $p_v/q_c = 0.2$. Then

$$(C/tr)_{\text{vehicles}} = \$0.12 \text{ (driverless vehicles)}$$

If each vehicle has a driver, add $30,000/q_c$ year to $C_{vc_{\text{o\&m}}}$. For typical train systems, assume the vehicle design capacity is 100 people per vehicle. Thus $C_{c_a} = \$800$ and

$$(C/tr)_{\text{vehicles}} = \$0.19 \text{ (driven vehicles)}$$

In this hypothetical case, there is a savings of 7¢ per trip by use of automatic control if the vehicles are large. With $q_c = 10$, the savings would have been $0.84 − 0.12 or 72¢ per trip. Thus there is a substantial advantage in going to automatic control only if small vehicles are contemplated. The actual savings is smaller than indicated if account is taken of the increased cost per vehicle due to automatic control equipment.

While the vehicle cost term in equation (5.5.4) appears to be independent of the patronage, t_d, equation (5.5.2) shows that p_v declines in proportion to t_d with vehicles operating at a fixed rush period headway. Thus, if t_d falls below the value used to compute N, in which computation p_v is assumed to be a reasonable fraction of q_c, $(C/tr)_{vehicle}$ rises because p_v falls.

In the above estimations, V_{av} was assumed to be 60 km/hr = 16.7 m/s. From equation (2.4.4) or figure 2-4, such a high average speed can be obtained only with wide station spacing and high line speed. For example, if in the rush period the dwell time averages 40 s, $a_m = 1.25$ m/s², and the station spacing is 2.4 km (1.5 mi), $V_{av} = 16.6$ m/s if $V_L = 30$ m/s. If increased access is desired by placing stops say one half mile or 0.8 km apart, then a V_L of 30 m/s can still be achieved but this results in an average speed of only 8.73 m/s (19.6 mi/h). Thus, the values of $(C/tr)_{vehicle}$ computed above must be multiplied by the ratio 16.6/8.73 = 1.9.

If the system under consideration is a street car with stops every quarter mile or 0.4 km, the maximum achievable speed at $a_m = 1.25$ m/s and $a_m/J = 1$ is (see equation (2.4.5)) $V_L = 21.7$ m/s = 48.9 mi/h. This is too high a maximum speed for street service. Assume instead $V_L = 35$ mi/h = 15.6 m/s. Then, from the same conditions, equation (2.4.4) gives $V_{av} = 5.06$ m/s (11.4 mi/h). If t_D is reduced to 10 seconds, $V_{av} = 8.14$ m/s (18.3 mi/h). Thus, in these cases, the vehicle cost per trip is increased by factors of 3.30 and 2.05, respectively.

If off-line stations are used in the same example with a trip length of five miles, $D_s = 8$ km in equation (2.4.4), and with $a_m = 1.25$ m/s², $t_D = 40$ s, and $V_L = 17$ m/s, $V_{av} = 15.2$ m/s. Thus, the average speed is only 10 percent below line speed. If $a_m = 2.5$ m/s², assuming seated passengers, and $t_D = 10$ s, $V_{av} = 16.4$ m/s or only 4 percent below line speed. As indicated in section 5.5, by obtaining an average speed only slightly below the line speed, the vehicle cost per trip can be kept low while not penalizing the guideway cost per trip by having to design for an excessively high maximum speed.

In estimating typical levels of the second and third terms of equation (5.5.4), it is necessary to develop a simple model for estimation of t_d. Thus, assume a line-haul system draws patronage from an area of length $\mathcal{L} + W$ and width W. Then, combining equations (5.3.4) and (5.3.12),

$$t_d = m_t \, \tau_d \, \rho A = m_t \, \tau_d \rho W(\mathcal{L} + W) \qquad (5.6.1)$$

In a typical case, assume $W = 2$ mi and $\mathcal{L} = 10$ mi. In typical U.S. urban areas, τ_d is roughly three trips per person per day. Assume a nominal case in which $\rho = 10,000$ people per sq mi and $m_t = 0.05$. Then $t_d = 36,000$ trips per day. This is typical of the trip attraction of rail rapid transit systems in the United States[4].

For elevated rail systems C_g is in the range of $10 million to $20 million per mile. For subways, the cost rises to the range of $40 million per mile, and for surface systems, it may be as low as $2 million per mile. Assume, as in section 5.4, $A_g = 0.066$ and $C_{g_{o\&m}}/C_g = 0.02$. Then, from equation (5.1.3), $C_{g_a} = 0.086\ C_g$. For convenience in this estimation, assume $C_{sf_{o_a}} = 0.2C_{g_a}\mathcal{L}$. Then the guideway cost per trip term in equation (5.5.4) is

$$(C/\text{tr})_{\text{guideway}} = \frac{C_{g_a}\mathcal{L} + C_{sf_{o_a}}}{300t_d}$$

$$= \left| \frac{0.103C_g\mathcal{L}}{300t_d} \right. \tag{5.6.2}$$

Substituting for t_d from equation (5.6.1) and then the numerical parameters listed under that equation,

$$(C/\text{tr})_{\text{guideway}} = 0.095(10)^{-6}C_g$$

Thus, if $C_g = \$2(10)^6$, $(C/\text{tr})_{\text{guideway}} = 19\cent$ per trip, and it is clear that even with modest guideway cost, the component of cost per trip due to the guideway is well above the component due to the vehicles. If a twenty-million-dollar-per-mile guideway is used, it can be justified only if the patronage is substantially higher. From equation (5.6.1), patronage can be increased by increasing the mode split m_t, by considering such a system only in very high population density corridors, or by increasing the area coverage. Assuming V_{av} is already as high as practical, m_t can be increased only by improving access to the system by drawing from a larger area. However, many studies of rapid rail including access modes indicate that, in most communities, a daily mode split of even 10 percent is highly optimistic[4]. With on-line stations, attempts to increase access and hence m_t by placing the stations close together result in lowered V_{av} and hence the sought-after increase in m_t is not impressive. V_{av} can be kept high and m_t at a maximum only with off-line stations, and nonstop, on-demand service. Even then, if the system only serves a narrow corridor and not an area, the expected increase in m_t is generally not impressive. From the analysis of $(C/\text{tr})_{\text{guideway}}$ it seems clear that the promise of guideway transit lies in keeping C_g under $2 million per mile and m_t as high as possible by providing minimum trip-time service.

Consider the station contribution to cost per trip. From equations (3.4.3) and (2.2.6), the length of an off-line ramp into off-line station is approximately

$$l_r = V_L \left[\left(\frac{32H}{J_n} \right)^{1/3} + \frac{V_L}{2a_m} + \frac{a_m}{2J} \right] \qquad (5.6.3)$$

For off-line station systems, assume for the present analysis that $a_m = J = J_n = 2.5$ m/s^2, $V_L = 15$ m/s, and $H = 2.5$ m. Then $l_r = 100$ m. For these systems, also assume that $\mu = 1.2$ and $C_g = \$2(10)^6$ per one-way mile or \$1250 per meter. Thus $C_{g_a} = 0.086\,(\$1250) = \$107.50$/m and $2\,C_{g_a}l_r\mu = \$25,800$ per year. For off-line station, small-vehicle systems, C_s has been estimated in the range of \$100,000. Thus, using the same amortization factor and ratio of capital to operating and maintenance costs as for guideways, $C_{s_a} = \$8600$ per year. Thus, for off-line station systems, we estimate the total station cost per year as

$$2\,C_{g_a}l_r\mu + C_{s_a} = \$34,400 \text{ per year}$$

But, for a two-way line-haul system, each "station" is two one-way stations with a cost of \$68,800 per year. With $\mathscr{L} = 16$ km (10 mi), we estimated $C_{g_a}\mathscr{L} + C_{sf_{0_a}} = 0.103\,C_g\mathscr{L}$, or with $C_g = \$4(10)^6$ per two-way mile $\times$ 10 miles, $C_{g_a}\mathscr{L} + C_{sf_{0_a}} = \$4.12(10)^6$ per year. If there is one station per mile, $n_s = 11$, and the total annual cost for stations if \$68,800\,(11) = \$757,000 or 18 percent of the guideway cost. If the stations are half a mile apart, their annual cost in this example is 35 percent of the guideway cost. Usually, the cost per two-way mile of guideway is not twice the cost of one-way guideway because of economies in placing two guideways on a single set of supports, but in the range of 30 percent less per unit length. If this is the case, the station cost is 26 percent and 50 percent of the guideway cost, respectively, in the above example.

If the stations are on-line, the platforms are generally larger and the structure larger. Costs of rail rapid transit stations are quoted in the range of \$500,000 to \$1 million and higher, which exceed the cost of off-line stations counting the off-line ramps. For this reason, and because of high guideway cost, the so-called "light rail" transit option is often considered. It is attractive if it does not require exclusive right of way, if the track can be conveniently laid at surface streets, and if enclosed stations are not needed. In these cases, the components of cost due to guideways and stations become manageable. Unfortunately, however, lower cost ways and stations usually mean interference with street traffic and hence reduced average speed, which increases the vehicle component of cost per trip.

If the line-haul system consists of forty-passenger buses operating in mixed traffic or on freeways, the major cost is the vehicle cost. Then, in the above example, the driver cost term in the cost per year is in the neighborhood of $30,000/40 = $750 and $(C/tr)_{\text{vehicles}}$ is approximately 21 ¢ per trip, if $V_{\text{av}} = 60$ km/hr, and rises in inverse proportion to V_{av}.

Again, it must be emphasized that the above calculations are representative only, and that conclusions for policy purposes should be based on analysis of specific situations. By following the above analysis, however, the reader can quickly estimate the cost per trip in specific cases. The other cost effectiveness variables derived in section 5.2 can be computed readily once the cost per trip and number of trips per year are known, and these need no further elaboration here.

5.7 Cost Effectiveness of Guideway Network Systems

In section 5.3, the cost per trip of network bus systems was discussed. Here, a similar analysis is carried forward for network systems in which automated vehicles run on exclusive guideways. For the analysis of network systems, equation (5.5.4) is still the basis, except that an additional term must be added to account for extra ramps at interchanges. Equation (4.5.6) gives a formula for the number of intersections in a network system.

Figure 5-5 shows two basic types of interchanges: the multilevel interchange and the Y-interchange. Both permit two perpendicular streams to go straight or turn through the interchange. The multilevel interchange has the advantages that traffic streams diverge before they merge, and both

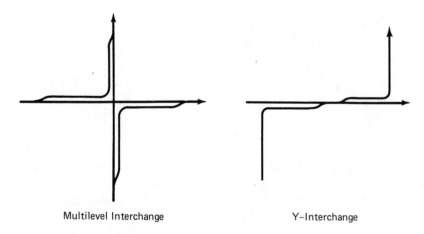

Multilevel Interchange   Y-Interchange

Figure 5-5. Network Interchanges

streams going straight through do not have to turn. It has the disadvantages, however, that the through guideways have to be at different levels, and the visual impact of guideways at one location may not be acceptable. The Y-interchange has the advantages of being all at one level and of minimum visual impact, but the disadvantages that the traffic streams must merge before they diverse, thus doubling the flow on the line through the interchange, and that the traffic on one of the lines must make unwanted turns through the interchange. In the cost analysis the difference is that the multilevel interchange uses four ramps and the Y-interchange two. Thus, define an interchange factor Z, where Z is equal to 1 for Y-interchanges and 2 for multilevel interchanges. Therefore, equation (5.5.4) becomes

$$C/\text{tr} = \frac{1}{300}\left\{ \frac{C_{c_a}\sigma <L_t>}{10f_p V_{av}(p_v/q_c)} \right.$$

$$\left. + \frac{1}{t_d}\left[C_{g_a}\mathcal{L} + (2C_{g_a}l_r\mu + C_{s_a})n_s + 2Zl_r\mu C_{g_a}n_I + C_{sf_{o_a}} \right] \right\} \tag{5.7.1}$$

The network values for $\mathcal{L}$, n_s, and n_I are given by equations (4.5.1, 4.5.4, and 4.5.6), respectively; and, from figure 4-18, let

$$<L_{av}> = \nu A^{1/2} \tag{5.7.2}$$

Using these equations and equation (5.3.4), equation (5.7.1) becomes

$$C/\text{tr} = \frac{1}{300}\left\{ \frac{C_{c_a}\sigma\nu A^{1/2}}{10f_p V_{av}(p_v/q_c)} \right.$$

$$\left. + \frac{(2\beta/L)[C_{g_a} + (2 + Z\beta)\mu C_{g_a}l_r/L + C_{s_a}/L] + C_{sf_{o_a}}/A}{t_d} \right\}$$

$$\tag{5.7.3}$$

To give a feeling for magnitudes, consider a specific example. A typical automated system suitable for network operation and for which cost data[5] is available is the Cabintaxi system under development since 1970 by DEMAG Fördertechnik and Messerschmitt-Bölkow-Blohm GmbH.

The parameters for this system are as follows:

q_c	=	3	σ	=	1.03
C_{ca}	=	$1450	μ	=	1.2
C_{ga}	=	$125/m	f_p	=	2/3
C_{sa}	=	$5590	V_{av}	=	10 m/s
C_{sfo_a}	=	$180,000	l_r	=	90 m
Z	=	1	p_v/q_c	=	0.5

In addition let the line spacing be $L = 800$ m. Then consider the two network sizes depicted in figures 4-16 and 4-17. Thus, for:

Figure 4-16

$$
\begin{aligned}
A^{1/2} &= 3l = 2400 \text{ m} \\
\beta &= 4/3 \\
\nu &= 1.21 \text{ for two-way flow (fig. 4-18)} \\
&= 1.44 \text{ for one-way flow}
\end{aligned}
$$

Figure 4-17

$$
\begin{aligned}
A^{1/2} &= 5L = 4000 \text{ m} \\
\beta &= 1.2 \\
\nu &= 0.99 \text{ for two-way flow (fig. 4-18)} \\
&= 1.21 \text{ for one-way flow}
\end{aligned}
$$

The costs given above are for two-way guideways and stations, with vehicles running above and below the guideway. With one-way guideways and stations, the cost of these facilities, in the Cabintaxi system, is reduced by about 25 percent.

The quantity 10 in the first term of equation (5.7.3) is approximate and has units of hours per day. Therefore, with V_{av} in meters per second, the first term must be divided by 3600 seconds per hour. The quantity $\bar{t}_d$ in equation (5.7.3) is not a true trip density because, in its definition given by equation (5.3.4), it is divided by the area bordered by the guideway. If, however, $\bar{t}_d$ is broken down into components, as indicated by equation (5.3.12), it is usual to think of ρ as the average number of people per unit area within the area served by the network area. Call this area A'. Then, for the network of figure 4-16, assume that $A' = (4L)^2$; and for figure 4-17, $A' = (6L)^2$, that is, $A'/A = (4/3)^2$ and $(6/5)^2$, respectively. Now, to be able to consider $\bar{t}_d$ in equation (5.7.3) as a true trip density, multiply $\bar{t}_d$ by A'/A.

With those modifications, equation (5.7.3) can be written in the form

$$C/\text{tr} = C_1 + C_2/\tilde{t}_d \qquad (5.7.4)$$

Values of C_1 and C_2 together with key geometric and performance parameters are given in table 5-1. In the table, it is assumed that the units of $\tilde{t}_d$ are trips per day per hectare (1 h = 10^4 m², 1 sq mi = 259 h).

The performance parameters for the data of table 5-1 are plotted in figure 5-6 as functions of trip density. The curves labelled "S" correspond to the network shown in figure 4-16 for a line spacing of 800 meters or one half mile, and the curves labelled "L" correspond to the network shown in figure 4-17 also for a line spacing of 800 meters. Data are plotted for each of these networks for both one-way and two-way lines.

In the upper graph of figure 5-6, the lines proportional to trip density give the fleet size. In each network more vehicles are required if the lines are one way because the trip length is longer in that case. In the two-way network, half of the vehicles are on each side of the guideway.

The average headway is derived from equation (4.5.18) except that for two-way lines, T_{av} is doubled because half of the vehicles are on each side

Table 5-1 Geometric, Performance, and Cost Parameters for a Typical Network System—$L = 800$ m, $V_{av} = 10$ m/s

$A^{1/2}$	$3L = 2.4$ km		$5L = 4$ km	
Guideway	Two-Way	One-Way	Two-Way	One-Way
v (fig. 4-18)	1.21	1.44	0.99	1.21
$<L_t>$, eq. (5.7.2)	2.90 km	3.46 km	3.96 km	4.84 km
$\mathscr{L}$ (eq. 4.5.1)	19.2 km		48 km	
n_s (eq. 4.5.4)	24		60	
$N/\tilde{t}_d$ (eq. 5.5.2)	8.50	10.15	26.10	31.91
$T_{av}\tilde{t}_d$ (eq. 4.5.18)	465 s (232 s)	195 s	379 s (189 s)	155 s
$f_{av}/\tilde{t}_d$ (eq. 4.5.19)	7.7 people/hr	18.5 p/hr	9.5 p/hr	23.2 p/hr
$fs_{av}/\tilde{t}_d$ (eq. 4.5.20)	2.13 p/hr	4.28 p/hr	1.92 p/hr	3.84 p/hr
$t_{nsw}\tilde{t}_d$ (eq. 4.5.22)	970 min	485 min	2766 min	1383 min
$C_1\$$	0.120	0.144	0.164	0.201
$C_2\$/\text{day-h}$	12.33	9.40	13.17	9.93

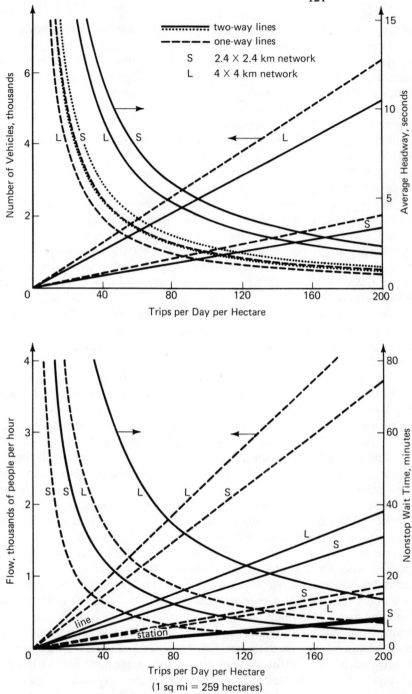

Figure 5-6. Average Performance Parameters in a Network System

of the guideway and the two groups of vehicles do not interact. If, however, the two-way network uses Y-interchanges, the average headway between merge and diverge points is not doubled. This headway is indicated by the dotted curves. It is seen in figure 5-6 that the average headway is a stronger function of provision of one-way or two-way guideways than of the size of the network. The capacity constraint on the system is due to the minimum headway, which is a fraction of average headway. The ratio T_{min}/T_{av} depends on the nonuniformity of demand, and the lines and stations should be located to make this ratio as near unity as practicable. Knowledge of T_{av} gives a feeling for the probable range of T_{min}, but T_{min} must be determined from a detailed operational simulation.

In the lower graph of figure 5-6, the lines proportional to trip density give the average line and station flow. The upper four lines marked "line," give the average line flow, and it is seen that even for the very high trip density of 200 trips per day per hectare (51,800 trips per day per square mile) the average flow is under 2000 persons per hour for two-way lines, but in the range of 4000 persons per hour for one-way lines. The maximum flows exceed these values by the ratio T_{av}/T_{min}, as discussed above. The average station flows can be compared with published data[6] from simulations on the maximum flows obtainable. With single-platform stations, flows of 600 to 1000 vehicles per hour are achievable according to the simulations.

The nonstop wait time, computed from equation (4.5.22) and presented as the family of hyperbolas in figure 5-6, is important from the viewpoint of the type of service provided. The reader is referred to the discussions following equation (4.5.22) for an interpretation of the meaning of T_{nswt}. Since the average trip time $<L_t>/V_{av}$ ranges, from table 5-1, between 4.83 min and 8.07 min, it is seen from figure 5-6 that the nonstop wait time is equal to or less than the average trip time only for densities above about 180 trips per day per hectare. The implication is that a service concept in which the first rider to board a vehicle must wait, say, at least T_{nswt} to see if another party can board going to the same stop will more than double the fleet size needed if the vehicle leaves when the first party boards. Such service will also substantially decrease patronage because the total trip time is more than doubled. Thus, group riding services require many intermediate stops, which also increase the total trip time and hence the cost of the vehicle fleet. Group services may in some cases be of interest in handling particularly high patronage between a pair or a small number of points if the headway requirements cannot be satisfied with single-party service; however, in these cases it should be determined if it would reduce the cost per trip by splitting the line into a pair of single party service lines.

Figure 5-7 shows the total cost per trip of the Cabintaxi system as a function of trip density. By comparing with figure 5-2 for given parameters, one can see under what circumstances the automated system has a lower cost per trip than a bus system, and it is seen that the comparison is favorable to the automated system for the higher range of trip densities, above about forty trips per day per hectare (10,400 trips/mi^2). It is cautioned that this comparison should not be taken too literally because of sensitivity to parameter changes and that specific conclusions should only be drawn from more detailed analysis of specific cases. In figure 5-7, it is seen that the two-way system is more expensive per trip for the large network below about 85 trips per day per hectare, and for the small network below about 130 trips. The two-way system is cheaper at high trip density because fewer vehicles are required and the vehicle cost term becomes more dominant as trip density increases. The larger network has higher cost per trip because the average trips are longer. Note that below 40 trips per day per hectare the estimated costs are very sensitive to errors in estimation of patronage.

At the bottom of figure 5-7, the modal split to the transit system is plotted as a function of trip density in accordance with equation (5.3.12). In this equation, the term ρ is to be interpreted not as the residential population density but as the number of people per hectare who live, or work, or shop, or seek recreation within the area of the transit network. If the network is placed in an area of major activity within the urban area, the latter density exceeds the residential population density by a large factor; however, if the network covers an entire city, the two average densities are roughly the same. Thus, it can be appreciated that, as the network grows, the cost per trip must increase if the modal split remains constant. However, a larger network puts more destinations within reach and can therefore be expected to increase the modal split, thus reducing the cost per trip. The plot of mode split versus trip density is made for the specific case of a mobility of three trips per person per day. This is representative of cities like Denver and Minneapolis, but, in cases in which a different value is more appropriate, the plot can be adjusted accordingly. The mode split in figure 5-7 includes trips totally within the network area as well as trips part within and part without. These mode splits will of course generally differ, and the differences must be taken into account in more detailed analysis.

A cost per trip in the range of thirty cents requires a trip density of eighty trips per day per hectare. With $\tau_d = 3$ and $m_t = 30$ percent, $C/tr = 30¢$ requires $\rho = 89$ people per hectare or 23,000 people per square mile. This is a low density for an active central business district, but $m_t = 30$ percent is well above that obtained by conventional distribution systems. Thus, to make the guideway system feasible, some auto-restrictive policies in the network area may be needed. If the network is used for freight movement, the cost per passenger trip may be reduced up to about 25 percent, as indicated in the discussion of equation (5.2.7).

The cost per passenger-kilometer, as defined by equation (5.2.4), is

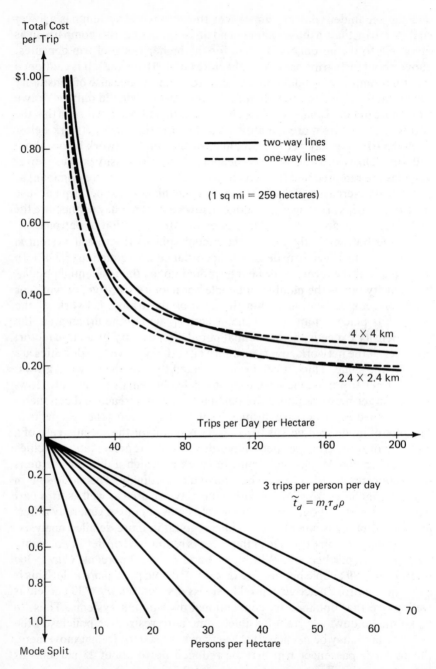

Figure 5-7. The Cost per Trip in a Network System

plotted in figure 5-8, based on the data of table 5-1. Note that there is a small economy of scale in this parameter, and that the one-way system is somewhat lower in cost per passenger-kilometer for all trip densities; whereas, if the comparison of costs is based on the trip, the one-way system is cheaper at low trip density but more expensive at high trip density. Again, at low trip density, the economic analysis is extremely sensitive to errors in estimation of patronage.

For network systems, it is worthwhile to consider the cost effectiveness parameter, PV_N, given by equation (5.2.13). Let the trend system in equation (5.2.10) be the auto system and assume the auto cost per vehicle-kilometer is in the range of 9$\textcent$ to 15$\textcent$ (15$\textcent$ to 25$\textcent$ per vehicle mile). Assume also that the average trip length is the same by both modes. Then

$$(C/\text{yr})_{\text{trend system}} = 300t_d \frac{<L_t>}{p_v} (C/\text{veh-km})_{\text{auto}} \qquad (5.7.5)$$

in which $t_d = \tau_d \rho A'$ is the total number of trips per day. Assume the new system is part auto and part automated network, and that the mode split to the automated system is m_t. Then

$$(C/\text{yr})_{\text{new system}} = 300t_d <L_t> \; [(C/\text{veh-km})_{\text{auto}} \; (1 - m_t)/p_v$$
$$+ \; (C/\text{pass- km})_{\text{net}} m_t] \qquad (5.7.6)$$

Substituting equations (5.7.5) and (5.7.6) into equation (5.2.10),

$$(CS/\text{yr})_n^\circ = 300 \; \bar{\imath}_d A' <L_t> \left[\frac{1}{p_v} \; (C/\text{veh-km})_{\text{auto}} - (C/\text{pass-km})_{\text{net}} \right] \qquad (5.7.7)$$

in which $\bar{\imath}_d = m_t \tau_d \rho$.

In this simple example, assume the system is all built at once and then that $(CS/\text{yr})_n^\circ$ is the same each year. The sum in equation (5.2.13) can then be written in the following closed form:

$$PV_N = \frac{(CS/\text{yr})_n^\circ}{d - i} \left[1 - \frac{1}{(1 + d - i)^N} \right] \qquad (5.7.8)$$

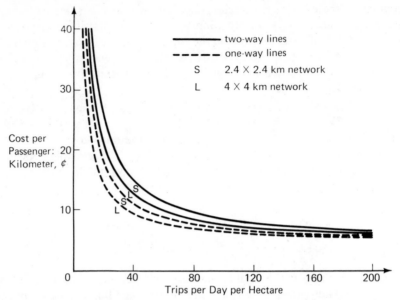

Figure 5-8. The Cost per Passenger Kilometer

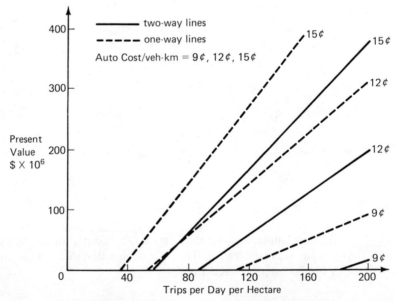

Figure 5-9. The Present Value of Future Savings If Network Is Built

For illustrative purposes, consider the specific example in which the discount rate d exceeds the inflation rate i by 2 percent, and $N = 20$ years. Then equation (5.7.8) becomes

$$PV_N = 16.4(CS/\text{yr})_n^\circ \qquad (5.7.9)$$

Economists do not agree on the most appropriate value for $d - i$, therefore a range of values must be used and the results compared. In figure 5-9, the present value of future savings over a period of 20 years is plotted for the 4 $\times$ 4 kilometer network of figure 4-17 for $p_v = 1.5$, for a range of auto costs, and for the range of trip densities for which PV_N is positive. It is interesting to note by comparing with figure 5-8 that the present value is negative in the range below 40 trips per day per hectare in which the cost curves rise steeply. It is also noted, from figure 5-8, that the present value would be less for the smaller network. A trip density of 40 trips per day per hectare corresponds at $m_t = 0.30$ to a density of 45 persons per hectare or 11,500 persons per square mile, or at $m_t = 0.50$ to a density of 27 persons per hectare or 6900 persons per square mile. Thus, for a wide range of existing urban densities, the automated system looks attractive from the standpoint of direct cost savings if mode splits in the indicated range are achievable. To achieve mode splits in this range, however, may require the imposition of policy restrictions on auto use such as high parking fees and narrowing of streets, by converting them partly or wholly into malls.

In a real situation, it would be desirable to build the network and put it into service stage by stage. Then, in the present value calculation, $(CS/\text{yr})_n^\circ$ changes from year to year and equation (5.2.12) must be used directly. Such a calculation is carried out in the author's paper in *Personal Rapid Transit III* for an exponential urban density model[1].

5.8 Summary

In this chapter, basic system cost equations are first derived applicable to any transit system. Then a family of cost effectiveness parameters are developed. The most fundamental of these is the total cost per trip, meaning the annualized capital cost plus annual operating and maintenance costs divided by the annual patronage. This parameter directly indicates the percentage of subsidy required for a given fare, and, if it is in a good range, the other parameters are usually satisfactory also. However, for a variety of purposes, other cost effectiveness parameters are derived. These are discussed as follows:

1. The cost per vehicle trip. This is of interest in comparing certain

systems, but is not a parameter of fundamental importance in the economics of transit systems.

2. The cost per passenger kilometer, which is of interest in comparing transit systems with the automobile, and is the most fundamental economic unit of transit performance.

3. The cost per passenger trip if freight is hauled on the transit system. If freight is hauled, more vehicles and more stations are needed, thus increasing the cost, but more revenue is generated, thus reducing the cost. Equation (5.2.7) includes both of these effects and shows, by the example given, that the potential for reduction of passenger cost per trip if freight is hauled is about 35 percent.

4. The annual surplus, which is of obvious interest to transit agencies, and to legislative bodies responsible for taxes to support the system if the surplus is negative, which is usually the case.

5. The added cost per trip required to attract one additional passenger per year. This marginal-cost parameter shows the point at which further expansion of the transit system cannot be justified on a direct economic basis. If all indirect costs are included with the direct costs, it is a true indication of the point at which to stop expansion.

6. The present value of future savings if the system is built. This parameter is developed by estimating the total transportation cost per year in each future year, say twenty years in the future, in the area in which a new transit system is to be deployed or extended, and is determined first without the new system and then with it. If the difference between these quantities is positive in a particular year, there is a cost savings in that year if the new system is built. If the savings in each future year is discounted to the present time and summed, the result is an indication of the size of research and development effort that can be mounted to bring the new system into being. If the cost includes all indirect as well as direct costs, and the accumulated present value is not strongly positive, the new system cannot be justified. This is a much stronger indication of the importance of the project to society than the more commonly used benefit/cost (b/c) ratio, which is too subjective in application. To use the b/c ratio, one must make a subjective judgment as to how far above unity it should be to justify the project, and it provides no quantitative information about costs.

In use of any of the cost effectiveness indicators, it is the responsibility of the analyst to compute a range of these indicators as a function of each of the variables to give the policy maker a sound basis for decision and a knowledge of the consequences of error.

In the third part of this chapter, the cost effectiveness equations are applied to each of the four basic types of transit systems listed in table 4-5. Network bus systems are discussed first. The cost per trip is given by equation (5.3.5) in terms of the scheduled headway and the trip density. But, as the trip density increases, a point will be reached at which the bus capacity is inadequate for the given headway. To increase patronage further, the headway must be reduced or lines must be placed closer together, in either case adding more buses in proportion to the added patronage. In this case, the cost per trip is independent of patronage and is given by equation (5.3.8) in terms of the saturation value of bus occupancy, that is, the maximum number of people the bus system can handle divided by the number of buses. Thus, the saturation value is well below the saturation occupancy of a given bus. For a typical case, the cost per trip of network bus systems is plotted in figure 5-2. The horizontal lines indicate the minimum cost per trip at saturation. The steeply rising curves, away from saturation, depict the situation of contemporary bus systems. As the population density has decreased, the trip density has decreased more than in proportion because lower density means longer service intervals at a given cost, and hence greater attractiveness of the automobile. Steeply rising cost per trip curves means rapidly increasing deficits, which lead to reduced service in terms of the number of buses or increased fares, either of which reduces patronage further.

Next, the cost effectiveness of shuttles is considered. Equation (5.4.6) shows that the cost per vehicle trip of a shuttle is a quadratically increasing function of the length of the shuttle. Thus, while relatively short shuttles have found practical applications, longer ones quickly become prohibitively expensive. Figure 5-3 shows a family of typical cases.

The cost per trip of loop systems is given by equation (5.5.4). Below it the variation of cost per trip with its parameters is discussed. A point worthy of emphasis is that, based on the data of figure 5-1, the capital cost of a vehicle per unit capacity is independent of vehicle capacity. Therefore the portion of the cost per trip due to vehicle capital cost is not a function of vehicle size but only of load factor, that is, relative occupancy. In most cases, the guideway cost term dominates. It is shown in chapter 10 that in urban applications the required guideway mass per unit length is proportional to the vehicle mass per unit length. Figure 5-4 shows that the mass per unit length of transit vehicles increases rapidly with vehicle capacity, indicating that minimum guideway size and hence cost is obtained with minimum vehicle size.

In section 5.6, equation (5.5.4) is applied to the analysis of the cost per trip components for line-haul systems. Typical numerical values of the various parameters are used to give the reader a feeling for the relative importance of vehicle, guideway, and station terms. It is shown that the unit cost of guideways must be very low compared to contemporary values if the guideway term is to reduce to the neighborhood of the other two terms. It is also shown that the introduction of automation is a significant factor in reduction of system cost only if the size of the vehicles is substantially reduced from current practice.

Finally, in section 5.7, the cost per trip equation is modified for use in analysis of the cost effectiveness of network systems. The result is equation (5.7.3). As a specific example, performance and cost effectiveness curves are developed for the case of a specific network system for which cost data is available. The basic performance parameters are shown in figure 5-6, and the cost effectiveness is shown by means of figures 5-7, 5-8 and 5-9. Note in particular that the nonstop wait time is, in almost all cases, too long to make it practical to have vehicles wait for a second party if the trip is to be nonstop. The cost per trip curves of figure 5-7 should be compared with the corresponding curves for bus systems, figure 5-2. It is seen that at high trip densities, the guideway system is cheaper. Note that, with the bottom chart relating trip density to mode split, figure 5-7 shows the range of parameters for which the guideway system is an economically justifiable alternative, and that in many cases the implication is that some form of auto-restriction policy is needed if the guideway system is to be economical. Figure 5-8 shows an economy of scale in going to large networks if the trip density does not decrease too much as the network size increases, and that the one-way line system gives a significantly lower cost per trip than the two-way line system. Finally, figure 5-9 shows how high the trip density must be if construction of the system is to be justified on a direct economic basis in comparison to an automobile system. Note from figures 5-7 and 5-8 that in the region of trip density in which the system is expensive, the cost per trip is very sensitive to errors in computing patronage; however, if the trip density is above about forty trips per hectare, the system is quite economical and insensitive to errors in computing patronage.

Problems

1. Municipal bonds at 4 percent interest are used to finance a public investment of $120,000,000 which has an estimated useful life of 40 years. What is the annual cost for capital and interest?
2. A city of 200,000 people with an average population density of 8000 people per square mile desires to install a network of scheduled bus lines using 60 passenger buses. The average line spacing for the network is 0.75 mi. It is determined that the average bus speed will be 11 mi/hr and that the average load factor can be no higher over the whole city than 25 percent. The average trip length can be taken as 40 percent of the square root of the area of the city. The cost parameters are those given in the text. It is proposed that a fare of 30¢ per trip be charged. Assume the mode split is 1.2 times the fraction of the area of the city that can be reached from an arbitrary point in the city without transferring, assuming that people will walk up to 0.25 mi from a bus line.

a. Write an equation for the modal split in terms of the area of the city (see section 6.8), and compute it for the given case.
b. Compute the total number of trips per day using parameters suggested in the text.
c. Compute the required number of buses if the transit authority choses to base the number on the average flow in the busiest hour.
d. Compute the headway in minutes needed to achieve the computed patronage.
e. Compute the cost per trip and the annual surplus per resident.
f. If the area of the city increases by 2 times and 5 times, what is the surplus per resident if the headway and density remain the same?
g. If the bus speed decreases by 30 percent due to increased street congestion, how does the annual surplus per resident change from that computed in *e*?

3. It is proposed to establish a line-haul commuter service between a major urban center and a satellite city 100 km away. Discuss the economics of this proposal in terms of the amount of travel needed to make it pay, the size satellite city implied, and the guideway cost. Use cost data discussed in the text.

References

1. J. Edward Anderson, "The Development of a Model For Analysis of the Cost Effectiveness of Alternative Transit Systems," *Personal Rapid Transit III,* Audio Visual Library Services, University of Minnesota, Minneapolis, Minn., 1976.
2. J. Edward Anderson, "An Overview of the Field of Personal Rapid Transit," *Personal Rapid Transit II,* Audio Visual Library Services, University of Minnesota, Minn., Minn., 1974, p. 4.
3. *Lea Transit Compendium,* N.D. Lea Transportation Research Corporation, Huntsville, Ala., 1975.
4. A.M. Hamer, *The Selling of Rail Rapid Transit,* Lexington Books, D. C. Heath and Company, Lexington, Mass., 1976.
5. *Nutzen-Kosten-Analyse für das Cabintaxi,* Text band, Wibera Wirtschaftsberatung Aktiengesellschaft für das Bundesminister für Forschung und Technologie, 15 July 1975.
6. *Personal Rapid Transit II,* op cit., pp. 439-478.

6

Patronage Analysis

In chapter 5, patronage was treated as a parameter in the cost effectiveness analysis. Such a procedure is useful for two reasons: (1) it separates the problem of analysis and discussion of cost effectiveness from the complex and controversial problem of determination of the patronage by treating patronage as a parameter; (2) it gives the systems analyst a good feeling for the range of patronage needed to recommend proceeding with detailed planning and design of a proposed system, for the variation of cost effectiveness with patronage, and for the accuracy with which patronage must be determined in specific cases; and (3) it enables the system analyst to explain the cost effectiveness behavior of the system to cognizant decision-making bodies with patronage viewed as a policy variable, which indeed it is in many cases.

In the state of transit development at the time of this writing, many engineers choose simply to ignore the problem of determining the patronage, and usually implicitly, to have faith that their system design will attract sufficient patronage to make it worthwhile. In the author's opinion, this attitude is at the root of most of the intense controversy over various transit options.

Patronage analysis is behavioral analysis, and is outside the range of knowledge and experience of most engineers. But the transit systems engineer simply must understand something of the technique of patronage estimation, and in planning the development of new systems he must understand the various behavioral factors that will influence people either to ride or not to ride his system.

The details of patronage analysis are very complex and are best left to specialists; however, the systems analyst must be able at least to make rough estimates to satisfy himself that the detailed calculations are reasonable. A good overview of the techniques of patronage analysis is given by Hutchinson[1]. References [1 through 8] will give the interested reader a good grasp of the problem of patronage analysis or demand estimation. In the design of new conventional systems for which operating experience can be used to calibrate the patronage models, the theory has been found to yield good results; however, in the planning and design of new transit systems thought to be able to increase patronage markedly, the extrapolation of existing models is risky and imprecise at best. Nonetheless, if progress is to be made toward solution of pressing transport problems, the problem must be treated in a variety of ways. Construction and operation of new systems in urban areas is of course the only acceptable final proof, but it is probable that much useful information can be obtained by carefully designed behavioral experiments and observations of human behavior in analogous situations, by analysis of all the steps the patron must take in making a trip on the new system, and by use of opinion surveys. An annotated bibliography of the literature is given in reference[9].

This chapter is intended as a first exposure to the problems of patronage analysis for new systems for which no operational experience is available. The material presented will assist the systems analyst to make rough preliminary estimates; however, again he should be cautioned to consult experts when making detailed estimates upon the basis of which decisions to invest funds are to be made.

6.1 Relationship between Yearly, Daily, and Peak-Hour Patronage

Three patronage parameters appear in chapter 5: the number of trips per year, per work day, and per peak hour. The first is the parameter of significance in determination of cost effectiveness and the third is needed for the estimation of capacity requirements. The second is a convenient intermediary value. In chapter 5 the following assumptions were made:

$$\text{Trips per year} = 300 \times \text{Trips per work day}$$

$$\text{Trips per work day} = 10 \times \text{Trips per peak hour.}$$

Since there are about 254 week days per year not counting holidays, the factor of 300 tacitly assumes that the traffic on an average one of the 111 weekend days or holidays is 46/111 or 41 percent of the traffic on a typical week day. The number 300 is close to that assumed by many consultants (some use 299 which looks more precise, but probably is not), but to determine it precisely would require far more extensive traffic surveys than usually can be afforded. In planning new systems in certain institutions, the factor of 300 may not be appropriate. For example, hospitals experience a more uniform traffic flow, and universities usually operate on fewer than 254 regular school days per year.

The ratio of daily to peak hour travel can be determined from graphs of traffic volume as a function of time of day. Such graphs are given by Meyer, Kain, and Wohl[10] for city-wide travel. The data presented shows that the factor of ten assumed in chapter 5 is high for auto drivers, but low for conventional transit. One may assume that the ratio for a new automated system may lie in between; however, that depends on the use of the system. If it is a line-haul system, primarily used to take people between home and work, the ratio may be closer to seven or eight. But if the system is a collector-distributor used more uniformly throughout the day, the ratio of daily to peak-hour travel may be higher than ten.

As indicated in chapter 5, the ratio of daily to peak-hour travel is used to estimate capacity requirements. Therefore, the value used is to some extent a matter of policy because it determines how much effort is to be expended to stagger the use of the system in rush periods.

6.2 Mobility

Equation (5.3.12) gives the trip density as a product of three terms: the modal split to transit, discussed in section 6.6; the daytime density of people in the service area of the transit system; and the factor τ_d called the mobility. The mobility is the number of trips per person per day, or some multiple of it. Zahavi, in reference[11], defines mobility as the number of trips per day per 100 residents. In table 6-1, his data is retabulated per resident. The table shows that τ_d varies from 1.65 in the high density area around New York City to 3.18 in Oklahoma City. The population weighted average value for three intermediate cities, Baltimore, Cincinnati, and Washington, is 1.99, and for the remaining smaller cities is 2.45. Thus, mobility is correlated with city size and density. Zahavi also shows that mobility increases with average trip speed in such a way that the most nearly constant parameter is the daily travel time budget. In other words, if the average speed of travel reduces, the average person takes fewer trips, that is, the mobility declines;

Table 6-1 Mobility in Various Cities
(Mobility = τ_d = trips per resident per day)

Tri-State	1.65	Springfield	2.17	Pulaski	3.09
Baltimore	1.72	Salt Lake City	2.48	South Bend	3.04
Cincinnati	2.17	Orlando	2.58	Columbia	2.79
Kansas City	2.00	St. Petersburg	2.17	Monroe	2.99
Indianapolis	2.14	Peoria	3.03	Fort Smith	2.26
S. E. Virginia	2.25	Baton Rouge	2.51	Rapid City	2.49
Oklahoma City	3.18	Knoxville	2.49	Washington	2.07

Source: reference [11].

or if the average speed of travel increases the mobility increases. The conclusion is that the estimate of patronage on a new automated system should not be based on the same center city mobility that exists prior to its installation but on a mobility adjusted according to the average speed provided by the new system compared with the average speed of travel prior to its construction. Thus, the assumption of a mobility of three trips per person per day, used in figure 5-7, is felt to be justified as a basis for preliminary estimates.

6.3 Required Precision of Patronage Estimates

Before spending a great deal of time estimating a difficult variable, it is important to estimate how accurately the variable must be known. Such an estimate can be obtained for the patronage variable by examining of cost per trip versus trip density, such as shown in figures 5-2, 5-7, and 5-8; or curves of present value versus trip density such as shown in figure 5-9. It is interesting to note from figures 5-7, 5-8, and 5-2 that, in the region of trip densities in which the system is cost effective in comparison with the bus or auto system, the cost per trip varies slowly with trip density; whereas in the low trip density region where the system is not comparatively cost effective, the cost per trip is very sensitive to changes in the estimate of trip density. For the automated network system assumed in figures 5-7, 5-8, 5-9, the transition occurs at about forty trips per day per hectare, and for the bus system of figure 5-2, the transition occurs at about twenty trips per day per hectare.

The meaning of the transition at forty trips in regard to the conditions in which it can occur is elucidated in figure 6-1, in which equation 5.3.12 is

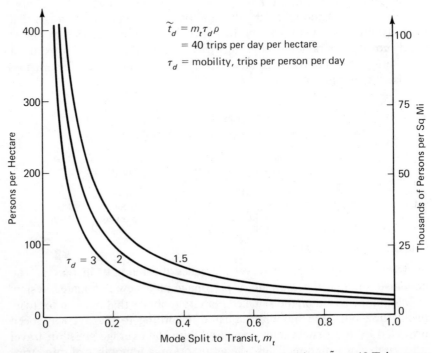

Figure 6-1. The Population Density Required to Achieve $\tilde{t}_d = 40$ Trips per Day per Hectare

plotted for $\bar{t}_d = 40$ trips per day per hectare, for three values of the mobility factor τ_d. Based on the discussion of section 6.2, it is reasonable to assume that the mobility lies within the range of the curves plotted. Then, the curves give the daytime population density in the transit service area required as a function of mode split to achieve a trip density of forty trips per day per hectare. It is seen that the required population density rises very rapidly after the mode split falls below about 20 percent.

The analyst can examine data on daytime population density independently to determine if, with reasonable mode splits, the system can be close to the range of cost effectiveness. If the judgment can be made that the mode split cannot be high enough for cost effectiveness, then the project can be abandoned without going through the expensive procedure of accurate mode split estimation. If the system is in the cost effective range, then fortunately the computation of patronage need not be precise for the economic analysis. It must of course be accurate enough to determine if capacity limitations will be approached.

In some cases, previous experience will indicate that with free competition from the automobile, the system cannot be cost effective. A policy decision can then be made in regard to the imposition of auto disincentives such a high parking fees to increase the transit mode split. However, as Zahavi points out, one must not assume that raising the mode split will automatically raise the transit trip density; because, if the transit system is too slow, auto disincentives may reduce mobility by a greater factor than the mode split to transit is raised. On the other hand, if the new automated mode has speed and service characteristics superior to the auto in the downtown situation, auto disincentives may not be necessary to attract an adequate mode split.

6.4 Trip Generation

The first step in patronage analysis is to estimate the total number of trips that could be served by the proposed transit system. In chapter 5, total trip density was defined as the product of the mobility and the density of people who live, work, shop, and seek recreation in the area served by the automated system. If the automated system is to serve a major activity center, this total person density can be many times the resident population density. The total travel is then the product of person density, mobility with the new system in place[a] and a suitably defined transit service area. The transit-service area includes at least the area within walking distance of stations, typically considered to be a quarter of a mile (0.4 km). This is

---

[a]Here the mobility is the ratio of the total number of trips within the transit service area to the daytime population of that area, and may bear no relationship to the values in table 6-1.

because data on bus travel indicates that only a very small fraction of bus trips either originate or teriminate more than this distance from bus stops. At an average walk speed of 2 mi/hr (3.2 km/h) a quarter of a mile is a fifteen-minute walk[12].

If the transit service area is taken to be a larger area, then it is a multimodal area and can be treated as such. If the patronage is based on the total daytime person density in the transit service area, then account is already taken of the fact that the people upon which the patronage estimate is to be based have somehow arrived within the transit service area. If they take the transit system under consideration, they are making a multimodal trip, at least for their trips into and out of the transit service area. This kind of trip is discussed in the following section. If the transit system is anticipated to use a feeder mode regularly and if it is region wide, then a secondary service area around each station should be defined consisting of the area beyond walking distance but within a distance from which trips can reasonably be expected to be drawn.

The outer boundary of the secondary service area is of course not sharply defined, but an indication can be obtained from data on specific operating systems. In the case of BART, data taken in 1975 showed that of all the people that ride the system, 26 percent arrive at the stations by foot, and 16 percent by bus. All but 2 percent of the remainder arrive by auto. On the other hand, of all of the people that leave BART stations, 68 percent walk to their destinations and 26 percent leave by bus. Thus, the effective service area of the destination station is substantially smaller than that of the origin station. In reference[13], Figure 1 (reproduced in this book as figure 6-2), access mode split curves are shown which are calibrated based on BART data. They show that very little bus patronage comes from beyond about 5 km (3 mi) of a station, and that the bus mode split is maximum at about 1.6 km (1 mi) from the stations. It can be argued that these data may not be representative because the schedules of bus service to BART stations are in need of improvement. Substantial improvements would, however, be expensive and, in the face of the need to improve BART patronage, have not been implemented. The curves of Figure 3, reference[13], show how the transit, auto driver and auto passenger mode split varies with the size of the access and egress transit service areas. If, for example, the mode split is computed for all trips in which both the origin and the destination are within 1 km (0.6 mi) of a transit station, only 9 percent of the trips can be expected to use transit with the assumptions made. Thus, Figure 3 shows how the transit mode split decreases as the size of the service areas increase.

The purpose of the preceding discussion was to indicate that the concept of a transit service area is useful in roughly estimating the potential transit patronage if account is taken of the fact that the mode split decreases if the service area around each station increases. Figure 4 of reference[13]

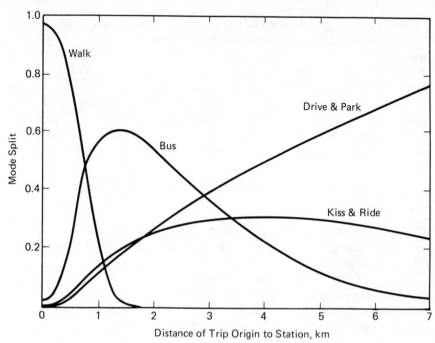

Figure 6-2. Access-Mode-Split Functions

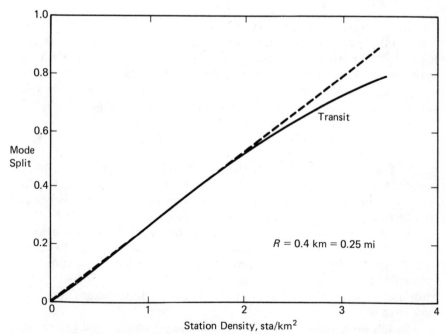

Figure 6-3. Transit Mode Split as a Function of Station Density

gives further insight into this phenomenon (reproduced here as figure 6-3). Here the transit mode split is plotted as a function of the inverse of the service area around each station, and it is shown that for service areas larger than that corresponding to the walking service area, the mode split is inversely proportional to the service area around each station. Thus, if A_s is considered to be the area around each station from which trips are drawn, and n_s is the total number of stations, the total transit service area is $A_{ts} = A_s n_s$. The mode split is approximately of the form $m_t = k/A_s$, in which k is independent of A_s. Then the total number of trips per day attracted to the transit system is

$$t_d = m_t \tau_d \rho A_s n_s = k \tau_d \rho n_s$$

Thus, the total patronage depends approximately on the number of stations and the mean population density at the stations, and not on the size chosen for the service area.

It is seen that the discussion of trip generation could not be divorced from a discussion of mode split, and that the problem of selecting the area from which transit trips are generated is secondary to the problem of determining the mode split for one particular service area.

6.5 Trip Distribution

The trip distribution is a matrix of origins and destinations of all trips, usually tabulated in terms of traffic assignment zones. In a macrosense, the trip distribution is needed in the analysis of a limited area automated transit system because the mode split may be different for trips with only one end in the transit service area, than for those with both ends so located. Thus, in general, the total number of trips on the transit system can be written

$$\text{Total trips} = m_{ii} t_{ii} + m_{io} t_{io}$$

in which m_{ii} is the mode split for the t_{ii} internal trips, and m_{io} is the mode split for the t_{io} trips which have one end outside the service area. Unless there is an auto disincentive within A_{ts}, it is likely that the inconvenience of transferring between modes will cause m_{io} to be considerably less than m_{ii}.

In a microsense, the trip distribution is the distribution to and from specific stations in the transit system. This distribution is needed to determine if capacity limitations are a problem at any of the station locations, or on any of the links. If this is the case, capacity may be increased by rerouting, or stations may have to be enlarged, or more stations and links may have to be added.

The full theory of trip distribution analysis is complex and extensive, and in any detailed analysis experts should be consulted. A good review of the methodology is provided by Hutchinson[1].

6.6 Mode Split Analysis—A Probability Argument

Anderson[13] has introduced the argument that the mode split to a transit system is proportional to the product of two probabilities: (1) the probability that the origin of the trip is within a reasonable distance of a station of the transit system; and (2) the probability that the destination is within a reasonable distance of a transit station. "Reasonable distance" does not necessarily mean walking distance, but it is the distance relative to the total length of the trip that will cause the traveler to feel it is worthwhile in comparison to an auto trip to go to a station by some means (auto, bus, walking), wait for and ride the major transit system, and then go to the destination by foot or by feeder bus. A reasonable distance will generally be small with respect to the length of the trip and less than the station spacing, otherwise the traveler will take a more direct route. Thus, if the average trip length is say, ten miles, it seems reasonable that the "reasonable distance" will not be more than one or two miles.

Each of the above probabilities is the total number of trip ends within reasonable distance of a station divided by the total number of trip ends in the urbanized area. If the trip end density is uniform, then each of the above probabilities is simply the station density, and it follows that the mode split is proportional to station density squared. With home-based trips, if the residential density is substantially uniform and the non-home ends of the trips are all concentrated at stations through judicious selection of station locations and concentrated development of work-shop-recreation locations, then the non-home trip end probability is unity and the modal split is proportional to the first power of station density. In the extreme of concentrated development of housing and other structures, both probabilities are unity and the mode split is maximum. For an automated system in a central business district in which the concentration of activity is relatively uniform, it would be expected that the mode split to the system will be proportional to the station density squared. For an entire urban area, a reasonable first approximation is that mode split is proportional to the first power of station density. Equation (4.5.5) shows that station density is proportional to L^{-2}, where L is the line spacing. With this assumption, equation (5.7.3) shows that for network systems, the cost per trip is a linearly increasing function of line spacing.

The above argument is useful to give a feeling for the gross behavior of mode split of network systems with line spacing, but it seems legitimate to apply it for gross estimates only for cases in which the behavioral attributes of the two modes compared are nearly the same. If significant differences exist in average speed, waiting time, availability, cost, physical or psychological comfort, or the like, the probability argument cannot be expected to be useful. These additional attributes form the subject of section 6.8.

6.7 Mode Split Analysis—The Logit Model

Experience has shown that the logit model for determination of choice between two or more alternatives is, at least in the transit mode choice situation, more satisfactory than other models[1]. The logit model is therefore gaining popularity in practical applications. It has the advantage that it is not ad hoc, but can be derived from fundamental considerations. It can be calibrated based on experience in such a way that it has been used successfully for predictions of mode split in some cases. The reader will appreciate the model, its strengths and limitations, and the discussion of section 6.8 on factors that influence patronage much better after having studied the following derivation of the logit model.

Let m be the mode split to the subject transit mode, that is, the fraction of the total number of trips taken by the subject mode. The mode split m is a function of various attributes $x_1, x_2, ..., x_q$, which are perceived by the individual traveler to a greater or lesser extent in all modes. For some modes, a specific attribute may be insignificant. For convenience and consistency, let each of the x_i be chosen in such a way that m is a monotone, continuous, decreasing function of x_i for all i. By definition, the function $m(x_1, x_2, ..., x_q)$ is bounded between zero and one, and by choice of the meaning of each attribute,

$$\frac{\partial m}{\partial x_i} < 0 \text{ for all } i$$

Then, the following postulates lead to the logit model:

1. The attributes can be treated as independent variables, that is, it is possible to vary only one of them while holding all others constant.

2. The mode split $m(x_1, x_2, ..., x_q)$ does not reach 0 or 1 for any finite value of any of the x_i, that is, m approaches 0 only as x_i approaches $+\infty$, and m approaches 1 only as x_i approaches $-\infty$, for all i.

Because of postulate 1, it is possible to consider the function $m(x)$, where x is any of the q attributes. Consider $m(x)$ in the neighborhood of a value of $x = x_1$ for which $m(x_1)$ is much less than 1. Then, because of postulate 2, an increase in x to $x_1 + dx$ causes dm to decrease but never to become negative. Therefore dm must be of the form

$$dm = -\alpha_1 f(m) dx \qquad \text{(a)}$$

in which α_1 is a positive constant; $f(m)$ is a monotone, increasing, continuous function for which $f(m) > 0$ for $m > 0$; and $f(0) = 0$. Then, $f(m)$ can be expanded into a series of the form[b]

$$f(m) = m^\nu (1 + c_1 m + c_2 m^2 + \ldots)$$

$$\approx m^\nu \qquad \text{(b)}$$

for very small values of m. If $\nu \neq 1$, equation (a) can be integrated into the following form for $0 < m_1 < m \ll 1$.

$$\alpha_1(x - x_1) = - \int_{m_1}^{m} m^{-\nu} dm = \frac{-1}{1 - \nu} (m^{1-\nu} - m_1^{1-\nu})$$

from which

$$m = [m_1^{1-\nu} - (1 - \nu)\alpha_1(x - x_1)]^{1/1-\nu}$$

There is always a finite value of $x = x_2(\nu)$ for which the term in brackets vanishes. Thus, if $\nu < 1$, $m(x_2)$ vanishes; and if $\nu > 1$, $m(x_2) = \infty$. Neither of these forms is admissible according to postulate 2. Therefore $\nu = 1$ and equation (a) becomes

$$dm = -\alpha_1 m \, dx \qquad m \ll 1 \qquad \text{(c)}$$

which satisfies postulate 2 for all dx for which $\alpha_1 \, dx < 1$.

It is useful to note that equation (c) makes sense from the behavioral viewpoint: If t_t is the number of transit trips, and t_T is the total number of trips,

$$m = t_t/t_T$$

---

[b]By permitting the constant ν to take any value, $f(m)$ can approach zero with any slope from zero to infinity. The coefficient of the first term in the power series expansion can be taken equal to unity because $f(m)$ is multiplied by an arbitrary constant in equation (a).

For $t_t \ll t_T$, t_T is affected very little by changes in t_t. Therefore

$$dm = \frac{dt_t}{t_T} - \frac{t_t \, dt_T}{t_T^2} \approx \frac{dt_t}{t_T}$$

Therefore, equation (c) becomes

$$\frac{dt_t}{t_t} = -\alpha_1 \, dx$$

This equation states that, if t_t is much less than t_T, a given change in attribute x causes a certain percentage change in t_t regardless of the size of t_t, that is, the portion of people who change their travel modes as a result of the change dx is proportional to the number of people who use the transit mode before the change dx. This is exactly what is to be expected if people make their decisions based on self interest and independent of one another.

For values of x for which $1 - m(x)$ is much less than 1, exactly the same line of reasoning that led to equation (c) can be applied, and the result is

$$d(1 - m) = +\alpha_2(1 - m)dx \qquad 1 - m \ll 1 \qquad \alpha_2 > 0$$

or

$$dm = -\alpha_2(1 - m)dx \qquad (d)$$

But, since in equation (d) $m \approx 1$, it may be approximated by

$$dm = -\alpha_2 m(1 - m)dx \qquad (e)$$

Similarly, since $1 - m \approx 1$ in equation (c), it may be approximated by

$$dm = -\alpha_1 m(1 - m)dx \qquad (f)$$

Equations (e) and (f) satisfy the postulates both near $m = 0$ and near $m = 1$, and lead to the same curve only if $\alpha_1 = \alpha_2 = \alpha$. Thus the differential equation of the modal choice curve is

$$\frac{dm}{m(1 - m)} = \frac{dm}{m} + \frac{dm}{1 - m} = -\alpha \, dx \qquad (g)$$

which integrates to

$$ln\left(\frac{1-m}{m}\right) = \alpha x + \gamma' \tag{h}$$

in which γ is a constant of integration. Solving for m, equation (h) becomes

$$m = \frac{1}{1 + e^{\alpha x + \gamma}} \tag{j}$$

If the modal choice is between two modes, x may be considered to be the difference in the attributes of the two modes, and one may in general write

$$\alpha x + \gamma = \alpha_1 x_1 + \gamma_1 - \alpha_2 x_2 - \gamma_2 = -U_1 + U_2$$

in which

$$U_i = -\alpha_i x_i - \gamma_i \tag{k}$$

Thus, if the two modes are equal in all respects, $m = 0.5$. Using equation (k), equation (j) can be written

$$m_i = \frac{e^{U_i}}{\displaystyle\sum_{k=1}^{2} e^{U_k}} \qquad i = 1, 2 \tag{6.7.1}$$

in which m_i is the mode split to the ith mode, and it is clear that $m_1 + m_2 = 1$. The form of equation (6.7.1) is readily extended to n modes. Thus

$$m_i = \frac{e^{U_i}}{\displaystyle\sum_{k=1}^{n} e^{U_k}} \tag{6.7.2}$$

The quantity U_i is called the utility of the ith mode, because m_i increases as U_i increases.

The analysis thus far has only considered one attribute. If there are q attributes, equation (h) can be extended to the form

$$\ln\left(\frac{1-m}{m}\right) = \sum_{j=1}^{q}(\alpha_j\,x_j + \gamma_j)$$

Hence the utility function for the ith mode can be written in the form

$$U_i = -\sum_{j=1}^{q}(\alpha_{ij}x_{ij} + \gamma_i) \qquad (6.7.3)$$

in which x_{ij} is the value of the jth attribute for the ith mode, α_{ij} is a weighting factor for the jth attribute when applied to the ith mode, and γ_i is a bias factor for the ith mode.

The above derived solution for $m(x)$ is not unique because, without violating the two postulates, equation (j) can be modified into the form

$$m(x) = \frac{F(x)}{1 + e^{\alpha x + \gamma}} + G(x)$$

in which, on substituting this equation into equation (g), as x approaches $\pm\infty$, $G(x)$ and $G'(x)$ vanish; as x approaches $+\infty$, $F(x)$ and $F'(x)$ remain finite; and as x approaches $-\infty$, $F(x)$ approaches 1 and $F'(x)$ approaches 0. Also, these functions are constrained by the fact that $0 < m(x) < 1$ for all x. Generalization of the logit model by introduction of the functions $F(x)$ and $G(x)$ permits the analyst to avoid the following two unrealistic properties of the logit model in cases in which it is applied to a situation in which there are more than two modes. The first is seen from equation (6.7.2) by dividing m_i by m_j. Thus

$$\frac{m_i}{m_j} = e^{U_i - U_j}$$

Since, U_i is a function of the attributes of the ith mode only, the ratio of the mode splits to two modes depends only on the properties of those modes and not on the properties of any other modes present. If a third mode is added, the model says that it attracts patronage from the other two modes in a strict proportion independent of the properties of the third mode. The first of these properties is called the "irrevelevant alternatives property," and the second the "new mode problem." The theory of avoidance of these problems is developed by McLynn[14], but as yet insufficient work has been done on calibration to determine the degree of improvement possible.

Thus far, nothing has been said about the nature of the attributes x_{ij}, which appears in the logit model. In most applications of the model, the only attributes taken are time and cost, and in others the attribute of auto ownership is included. Auto ownership is, however, not a continuous variable. It is better to account for it by doing separate mode splits in two groups of people: those with access to automobiles, and those without. The composite mode split is then

$$M = m_a f_a + m_{na} f_{na} \qquad (6.7.4)$$

in which f_a is the fraction of people with access to autos, $f_{na} = 1 - f_a$, and m_a, m_{na} are the corresponding mode splits. Experience with alternative transit modes gives one a great deal of unease in relying on a simple time-cost model, as it would seem that many other behavioral and attitudinal variables may play a significant role in determining the mode split. Recker and Golob (references[7] and [8]) give recognition to this difficulty and derive a logit model in which the attributes are descriptive ratings chosen to represent latent perception factors. These authors' analysis indicates closer predictions to observed behavior than those obtained using only the attributes of time and costs. While the increased mathematical difficulty of the model will reduce the access of transportation planners to it, it is a welcome step into a direction of greater reality.

The author developed a ten-dimensional logit model[13], based on only the time and cost attributes. The model includes both access and egress modes, and features a rapid means for rough calibration of the logit coefficients; however, insufficient data was available at the time to confirm its overall performance. Moreover, the magnitude of the errors that may result from the irrelevant alternatives problem are not known, and the neglect of behavioral attributes felt to be important may limit its usefulness to that of a mathematical structure for conveniently handling access, line-haul, and egress modes for a model of the type developed by Golob and Recker.

6.8 Factors That Influence Patronage

The personal decision as to whether or not a trip will be taken and, if so, by what mode depends on the characteristics of both the individual and of the transportation mode. When the individual has access to an automobile and the only alternative is a transit mode that is much slower, the decision is easy—the transit mode isn't given a second thought. In most U.S. cities the mode split to transit is in the range of from 3 to 5 percent; the vast majority of people give no thought to the possibility of using a bus or even to car pooling regularly, and changes in mode split are due to attracting or discouraging the marginal transit user—the person who doesn't have such easy access to an automobile, who changes residences or jobs to a location in which the use of transit is particularly convenient, or for whom auto travel is unusually unpleasant. As indicated in section 6.3, this low mode split range is the circumstance in which the cost per trip is particularly sensitive to policies or service features that encourage or discourage patronage. The cost effectiveness analysis of chapter 5 shows that automated guideway transit systems are worth considering only if the potential exists for increasing the mode split several fold. To accomplish such an increase requires careful consideration of all factors that influence patronage: the characteristics of the transit system, the characteristics of competing modes, and the attitudinal and behavioral characteristics of the potential patron. Increases in transit patronage can be produced by either of two ways: by making the transit system more attractive, or by making the alternatives less attractive. A third method is also tried: by marketing techniques to make the transit mode seem more attractive or acceptable compared with the alternatives without actually changing the physical characteristics of either. The third method was effective for a short while during the energy crisis of 1973, but soon the mode splits returned to their precrisis values. The promise of automated transit systems is that it may be possible to make them significantly more attractive than present transit systems, therefore the following discussion relates to methods of increasing patronage on transit by improving the characteristics of the transit system.

Availability of Information

If route and schedule information can be easily found so that potential patrons can feel at ease about getting to their destination on time, and equally important, if they are satisfied that they can get back again without being stranded, they may take transit much more often. If it is too difficult or too time consuming to find reliable information, transit will not be considered even though the alternative may be considerably more expensive. In many European cities, complete guides to the transit systems are easily available at newstands and elsewhere. They are easy to use even if the language is not understood, and often the complete schedule is posted at each bus or trolley stop. It is foolish to spend a great deal of money on transit improvements if an ample advertising budget is not to be provided.

Character of the Information

If the information received does not indicate that I can get where I need to go when I need to go, that I can return when necessary, and that the trip is sufficiently convenient and comfortable, I will choose an alternative which more closely fulfills my needs, or, as Zahavi reference [11]) points out, I may forego the trip. In other words, the transit network must be sufficiently comprehensive to meet a wide range of travel demands; the schedule of service must be frequent enough for a sufficiently large fraction of the day; and the service must be comparatively convenient and comfortable. A system that can take the patron directly to work but makes it impossible to make necessary side trips at lunch or on the way home will lose substantial patronage as a result. Some will counter that the appropriate recourse is to relocate all necessary services in concentrated clusters so that the side trips can be taken by walking. This solution has considerable merit in principle, yet the range of destinations that can be reached by walking is limited in most cities, and it is difficult in a free society to contemplate restructuring the city to a significant extent just to accommodate the needs of a transit system.

Some transit systems provide good rush-hour service, but, because of the high operating cost of keeping vehicles moving empty or almost empty in nonrush periods, the schedule frequency is reduced at those times from perhaps a vehicle every five minutes to one every half hour or one an hour. A person who works on a fixed schedule may accommodate to such an arrangement, but in circumstances in which the inconvenience or cost of driving to work is not too great, the flexibility of leaving work when desired is a strong deterrent to use of transit. Patronage analysis should take into account schedule variations, but all too often do not.

Perhaps the major inconvenience factor associated with conventional transit is the transfer. Consider the fraction of possible destinations in a city that can be reached without a transfer: To simplify the problem, consider a square city of area A and side $A^{1/2}$, and assume that a transfer is not needed if the origin or destination (trip end) is within a distance w of a transit line. Then, from a given point in the city, a trip can be made without transfer if the destination lies within either of two mutually perpendicular strips each of width $2w$ and length $A^{1/2}$, that is, the fraction of the area of the city that can be reached without transfer is $4w/A^{1/2}$. If the city streets are predominately curved, the length of each strip is longer than $A^{1/2}$, therefore the area that can be reached without transfer is larger. If the transit system is a network of lines with stops every two blocks or every quarter mile, if as indicated in section 6.4 the maximum walking distance is one quarter mile, and if walking distance is measured along city streets parallel and perpen-

Table 6-2 Fraction of Area Reachable without Transfer

$A^{1/2}$ (mi)	Percent of A Reachable without Transfer
5	15%
10	7.5
20	3.75
30	2.5

dicular to the transit lines, then the boundary of the strip within walking distance of bus stops is a sawtoothed line and the average value of w is $(3/4)(0.25 \text{ mi}) = 3/16 \text{ mi}$. Thus, the fraction of the area of the city that can be reached without transfer is

$$4w/A^{1/2} = 0.75/A^{1/2}$$

where $A^{1/2}$ is in miles. Some values are given in table 6-2.

For most major metropolitan areas, the value of $A^{1/2}$ is of the order of 15 to 30 miles. It is thus interesting to note that the fraction of the area reachable without transfers is in the same range the bus mode splits in most of those areas[15]. Navin[2] reports data synthesized from travel data in many cities which indicates that the transit travel behavior can be accounted for if it is assumed that people weigh the time required for a transfer in their choice of travel mode such that one minute of transfer time is equivalent to 6.6 to 10 minutes of riding time. Weighted thus, most mode split studies will indicate that only a small fraction of transit riders will regularly transfer. Consequently, the elimination of transfers in a network of guideways through the introduction of automatic switching capability removes a major deterrent to significant increases in mode split.

Station Accessibility

In the previous paragraph, it was assumed that the stations or stops of a network transit system were accessible by walking. With some transit systems, such as conventional line-haul systems, the stations must be widely spread to attain a sufficiently high average speed, and the cost per mile is too high to permit the system to be constructed in any but the highest density corridors. Thus, as discussed in section 6.4, to attract sufficient patronage the line-haul system must work in conjunction with a system of feeder buses or a background network of bus lines, ample parking facilities must be created at each station, and the process of transfer to and from the line-haul system must be as simple as possible. In the analysis of cost effectiveness, all of these types of facilities must be fully taken into account throughout the analysis and not as an afterthought.

Negotiation of the Station

Transit patronage is influenced by three basic station-related factors: the simplicity of paying the fare and finding the right vehicle, the feeling of personal security, and the waiting time. All of these factors require careful consideration from the viewpoints of the physiology and psychology of the patrons, and are dealt with in references [16]-[20]. In reference [18], the authors deal with the design of stations from the operations point of view, and call attention to a wide range of complexity in various automated systems which were under consideration in Denver. Their findings indicated that the scheduled, group-riding systems which use off-line stations and which were popular in conception at the time of the study provide considerable difficulty for the patron because the berth at which the vehicle must stop cannot generally be predicted before it must switch off the main line and into the station. Thus the patron cannot know in advance where to stand to wait for his vehicle. On the other hand, if the stations are on-line and the vehicles stop at every station, or if they are off-line and the service is on demand with each vehicle travelling directly to the destination, the patron may wait anywhere on the platform and board any vehicle. In these cases, the system operational design provides the patron maximum convenience in finding the right vehicle and removes the anxiety that he may not be headed towards the desired destination.

Fear of assault is often given as a reason for not riding a transit system. Thus, stations which have secluded corners and in which the potential patron may have to wait long periods in the off-peak periods provide an environment in which criminals may lurk awaiting their prey. On the other hand, stations with small, well-lighted areas easily monitored by television provide fewer opportunities for assault, particularly if the service is on demand so that in the off-peak hours particularly one boards a vehicle and leaves the station immediately. In this situation, loiterers are clearly identified.

In an automated transit system, wait time is of concern therefore for two reasons: the increased anxiety as a result of fear of assault, and the uncertainty in the total trip time. According to Navin[2], one minute of waiting time is perceived to be equivalent to 4.2 to 6.3 minutes of riding time.

Because the above factors are difficult to quantify in a patronage analysis, they are often ignored, but only at the peril of those responsible for the system design. It is necessary that all aspects of the design of transit stations and their operation be studied carefully by competent human factors specialists and social psychologists and that their recommendations be carried out. The analysis of cost effectiveness indicates that station costs are a relatively minor part of the overall cost of the system[13], therefore attention to human factors in station design and operation appear to offer the potential of significant dividends.

The Vehicle

The portion of the total trip spent in the vehicle can increase or decrease patronage depending on the physical and psychological comfort associated with it. Physical discomfort is due mainly to the spectrum of acceleration and jerk of the vehicle. In section 3.6 it was shown that the maximum lateral jerk due to a perturbation in the guideway is proportional to the cube of the speed. Therefore, for the sake of ride comfort the maximum speed should be held as low as possible; but to minimize travel time, the average speed must be as high as possible. These two contradictory requirements can best be resolved, as indicated in section 2.4, by minimizing the number of intermediate stops and by maximizing the normal rate of acceleration and deceleration.

The psychological comfort of the vehicle depends on the number and arrangement of seats and the degree to which a patron must be confronted with strangers. Fried and deFazio[19] shed some light on this question by observations on riders of the New York subway, and found that people do indeed arrange themselves in such a way as to minimize the possibility of eye contact with strangers. The whole question of personal space or psychic space in various cultures is discussed by Hall[20], and from the examples given in his book it is clear that the designers of transit vehicles need the assistance of the social psychologist before proceeding too far into expensive system development programs.

The two distinctly different psychological environments proposed in transit system design are the group-riding systems and the personal systems in which one cab is occupied only by people travelling together by choice. The moderately small group-riding systems, in which the cab holds six to twelve people, provides a transit environment similar to that of a dial-a-ride bus or an airport limousine, but without a driver. In semi-off-peak periods, the probability of being required to occupy such a cab with only one stranger is high and creates considerable anxiety in the minds of many people. The possibility of an uncomfortable encounter may be a strong deterrent to use of the system, and should be thoroughly investigated before proceeding too far into the development of such a system. On the other hand, the system in which each cab is used only by a group travelling together nonstop to the destination provides maximum personal security and freedom from anxiety, but is thought by some to foster loneliness in society. It is, however, the environment of the private automobile, but without the need or opportunity to drive. The possibility should not be overlooked that such an environment will provide a quantum jump in patronage and hence a significant increase in cost effectiveness. This is a particularly promising possibility for increased cost effectiveness since the small private party vehicle permits minimum wait time and minimum riding time because of the elimination of intermediate stops.

Egress

The final leg of the trip takes the patron from the destination station of the primary transit system to the final destination of the trip. Unless the patron is aware in advance of an acceptable way to make this trip, the total trip will not be taken by transit. Since a car will be available for this trip only rarely, the patron will have to rely on walking, a feeder bus, or a taxi. As indicated in section 6.4, in the BART system, 68 percent of the people who ride the system leave the stations by walking. Thus the effective transit service area for destination stations in the BART system cannot be much larger than the area accessible by walking.

6.9 Summary

This chapter is an introduction to the subject of patronage analysis and is intended to give the reader an intuitive feel for the subject. Detailed patronage analysis required for policy decisions about the deployment of particular transit systems is beyond the scope of this book. The first topic of discussion is the numerical values assumed in other chapters for the ratios of yearly to daily patronage and daily to peak-hour patronage, and it is emphasized that verification of figures used for the ratio of yearly to daily patronage requires much more detailed trip-making surveys than usually, if ever, undertaken. This is an irreducible error in most patronage analyses. Next, the concept of mobility is introduced and data is given on its values. It is emphasized that, in the design of new systems of high service level, the mobility is likely to be higher than existed before the new system is introduced.

The required precision of patronage estimates is the next topic of discussion. It is shown that, with guideway systems, the required precision is high in the range of trip density in which the system is uneconomical, and low when the system is economical. Next the problem of trip generation is discussed, and it is shown that the choice of boundary of the transit service area is unimportant in comparison to obtaining a good analysis of mode split for the area chosen, and therefore that the area within walking distance of stations is a good choice. The mode split is considered in two ways: First, by means of a basic probability argument; and, second, by deriving the logit mode split model from two postulates. The probability argument shows that if the trip distribution is close to uniformity, the mode split is proportional to the station density squared; and, in a real situation, that the mode split should be at least proportional to the first power of the station density, thus leading to the conclusion that the cost per trip in a network system increases at least linearly with the line spacing for line spacings greater than that which places all trip ends within walking distance of a station. Next, it is shown that the logit mode split model can be derived from two postulates: (1) That the mode split is a function of independent attributes, and (2) that the mode split, bounded between zero and one, does not vanish for any finite value of an attribute. It is also shown that the resulting formulation leads to the conclusion that, near zero and one, mode split decisions are made independently, consistent with the behavioral assumption that people act in their own interest. Finally, a series of factors that influence patronage are discussed, and, in particular, it is shown that there is a strong correlation between the percentage of the area of a city that can be reached by fixed route, fixed schedule bus and the actual bus mode splits achieved.

References

1. B.G. Hutchinson, *Principles of Urban Transport Systems Planning,* Scripta Book Company, McGraw-Hill Book Company, New York, 1974.

2. F.P.D. Navin, "Time Costs in Personal Rapid Transit," *Personal Rapid Transit II,* University of Minnesota, Minneapolis, Minn., 1974, p. 589-602.

3. "Behavioral Demand Modeling and Valuation of Travel Time," Special Report 149, Transportation Research Board, National Research Council, Washington, D.C., 1974.

4. "Travel Behavior," Report Number 446, Transportation Research Board, National Research Council, Washington, D.C., 1973.

5. "Transportation Demand and Analysis Techniques," Report Number 392, Transportation Research Board, National Research Council, Washington, D.C., 1972.

6. "Choice of Travel Mode and Considerations in Travel Forecasting," Report Number 369, Transportation Research Board, National Research Council, Washington, D.C., 1971.

7. T.F. Golob and W.W. Recker, "Attitude-Behavior Models for Public Systems Planning and Design," General Motors Research Publication GMR-1906, Warren, Michigan, June 19, 1975.

8. W.W. Recker and T.R. Golob, "An Attitudinal Mode Choice Model," *Transportation Research,* Vol. 10, No. 5, Oct. 1976, pp. 299-310.

9. Margaret E. Shepard, "Annotated Bibliography of the Application of Behavior and Attitude Research to Transportation System Planning and Design," General Motors Research Publication GMR-2089, Warren, Michigan February 1976.

10. J.R. Meyer, J.F. Kain, and M. Wohl, *The Urban Transportation Problem,* Harvard University Press, Cambridge, Mass., 1966, chapter 8.

11. Y. Zahavi, "Traveltime Budgets and Mobility in Urban Areas," Federal Highway Administration Report FHWA PL 8183, Washington, D.C., May 1974.

12. J.J. Fruin, *Pedestrian Planning and Design,* Metropolitan Association of Urban Designers and Environmental Planners, New York, 1971.

13. J.E. Anderson, "The Development of a Model for Analysis of the Cost-Effectiveness of Alternative Transit Systems," *Personal Rapid Transit III,* Department of Audio Visual Library Services, University of Minnesota, Minneapolis, Minn., 1976.

14. J.M. McLynn, "Disaggregate Modal Choice Models of Fully Competitive Type," Contract DOT-UT-20021, Office of Research and Development, Urban Mass Transportation Administration, Washington, D.C., December 1973.

15. *Urban Transportation Factbook,* American Institute of Planners and Motor Vehicle Manufacturer Association of the U.S., Detroit, Mich. 1974.

16. L.L. Hoag and S.K. Adams, "Human Factors in Urban Transportation Systems," *Human Factors,* 1975, 17(2), 119-131.

17. C. Tehan and M. Wachs, "The Role of Psychological Needs in Mass Transit," *High Speed Ground Transportation Journal,* Vol. 9, No. 2, 1975.

18. R.E. Johnson, H.T. Walter, and W.A. Wild, "Analysis and Simulation of Automated Vehicle Stations," *Personal Rapid Transit III,* Department of Audio Visual Extension, University of Minnesota, Minneapolis, Minn., 1976.

19. M.L. Fried and V.J. DeFazio, "Territoriality and Boundary Conflicts in the New York Subway," *Psychiatry,* Vol. 37, February 1974.

20. Edward T. Hall, *The Hidden Dimension,* Anchor Books, Garden City, New York 1969.

7

Requirements for Safe Operation

7.1 Introduction

A transit system is safe if no injuries result from its use. Injuries may result to passengers riding the vehicles, to persons moving into or out of vehicles or stations, or to passers-by. In this chapter, the possibilities of injury while riding or while moving in and out of the vehicles of a transit system are considered in order to develop design requirements for minimization of the probability of injury. Injuries due to equipment malfunctions that occur in the stations but away from the vehicles must, of course, be considered in the design of station equipment. Such design, while important, is outside the scope of this book. Injuries due to human intervention such as assault can be minimized by considering this factor in the architectural design of the stations[1], by providing ample lighting, by providing television monitoring at critical locations, by providing station attendants if the circumstances warrant it, and most importantly by designing the service concept of the system in such a way that waiting in stations is minimized especially in off-peak hours. The later consideration is an important reason for interest in on-demand service concepts. The probability of injury to passers-by is minimized by use of exclusive guideways either elevated or underground, or, if at grade, by use of fences to separate the system from the community.

It is unfortunately unrealistic to take the position that no injuries will ever result from the use of a properly designed transit system. Even with slow speed, large shock absorbing bumpers, thickly padded interiors, and elaborate fail-safe circuits in the control system, injuries may occur through some unusual and unforeseen circumstance, however low its probability. The price of overprotection may be unacceptable capital and operating costs, uncompetitive speeds, and unreliable service due to stoppages resulting from unnecessary actuation of safety devices. It is therefore incumbent upon the engineer to prepare and present objective data in understandable form on the probability of injury as a function of cost, patronage, and service dependability.

Discussion of the possibility that someone may be injured is socially acceptable when considering conventional transit where the death rate is in the neighborhood of one per one hundred million passenger miles, or when considering the auto system where the corresponding rate is approximately seven per one hundred million passenger miles. But when designing new

157

systems, many of the professionals involved feel very uneasy about suggesting that a failure mode or combination of failure modes may ever exist that could produce injury. This is one of the prices of attempting to innovate. One cannot design to be only as safe conventional transit. One must set a good deal more stringent criterion. Fortunately, by following the advice that stands out from the analysis of this chapter, the development of extremely safe transit modes appears economically feasible.

In section 7.2, we examine the kinematics of emergency situations in which a vehicle failure occurs that causes a vehicle to slow down or to speed up, or to fail to slow down when commanded. The analysis leads to conclusions as to the requirements of design and operation that will prevent collisions when only one failure occurs. The possibility always exists, however, that two simultaneous failures may occur in such a way that a collision between vehicles results. An example would be that the brakes on one vehicle lock and, simultaneously, the failure-monitoring system that is present to inform the trailing vehicle of the failure itself fails. As a result of this possibility, the process of collision needs to be studied to determine the design and operational conditions that minimize the probability of injury. The analysis of collisions begins in section 7.3 with the development of the characteristics of the constant force, constant displacement shock absorber, an ideal device for vehicle protection in collisions. Then, in section 7.4, simplified criteria for avoidance of injury are given. With this background, the problem of collision of the passenger with a constraint device in the vehicle is treated in section 7.5 to determine the maximum allowable collision velocity. In section 7.6 all of the elements of the collision problem are assembled to produce recommendations on the maximum tolerable collision velocity between vehicles as a function of intravehicle throw distance between passenger and padded surface, the thickness of the padded surface, and the stroke of the shock absorber. Finally, oblique collisions are treated in section 7.7.

Early work on the problem of safe operation of automated transit systems at close headways was performed by Bernstein and Schmitt[2] and by Stepner, Hajdu, and Rahimi[3]. The analysis of this chapter builds on the results of these authors, but is based mainly on simplifications and extensions of the work of Anderson[4]. The theory of safe operation of automated transit has also been developed by McGean[5,6], by Hinman and Pitts[7], and by Lobsinger[8]. The problem of collisions in small automated transit vehicles has been treated in detail by Garrard, Caudill, and Rushfeldt[9,10]. These references provide confidence that the simple approach given in section 7.5 is a good approximation and gives the essential ingredients of a safe design. The applicability of automotive crash testing to automated transit systems has been discussed by McGean and Lutkefedder[11], and by Miller and Shoemaker[12].

7.2 Requirements for Collision Avoidance

Three basic failure modes are treated in this section: (1) the brakes are applied unintentionally or a vehicle otherwise suddenly begins to decelerate; (2) a motor receives an unintentional command to accelerate; and (3) a vehicle entering a station fails to respond to a command to decelerate.

In the following analyses, deceleration is treated as a parameter. If this is the case directly, the implication is that the vehicle is supplied with knowledge of the deceleration and acceleration and that the braking system is controlled to brake at constant deceleration, commonly called "closed loop braking." If such feedback is not provided, open loop or constant force braking results. This means that the braking deceleration is not determined by the braking force alone, but also by the grade, wind, and condition of the guideway. Analyses that include all of these effects are given by McGean[5], Hinman[7], and Lobsinger[8]. To use the present analyses in the case of open loop braking, separate calculations of braking deceleration in terms of the above effects is required. Such calculations in detail are not essential to the understanding of basic system requirements for safe operation and are therefore not included. However, by consideration of a few examples, the reader should become convinced that the variation in braking deceleration is large if open loop braking is used, and therefore that such braking is suited only to low-capacity systems.

Sudden Deceleration

Consider two vehicles travelling in a cascade, the first of which fails in such a way to suddenly decelerate. A monitoring system either on board the vehicles or at wayside detects the failure and causes the trailing vehicles to begin to decelerate. The situation is depicted in figure 7-1. The failed vehicle, of length L_v and labeled "f," is moving at a line speed V_L when, at $t = 0$, it suddenly decelerates at a rate a_f and comes to a stop in a time $t_f = a_f/V_L$. At $t = 0$, the closest trailing vehicle, labelled "e" for emergency braking, is separated from the failed vehicle by a distance H_0 and travels at a slightly different velocity due to control tolerances. To make the computation conservative, a higher velocity, $V_L + \Delta V$, is assumed. A time t_c is required for braking action to begin. Then the deceleration of vehicle e begins to increase at a rate J_e up to a maximum value a_e. Finite jerk is taken into account in vehicle e and not in vehicle f because this is a conservative assumption, that is, it results in a larger value of minimum separation than would otherwise be the case.

The aim of the analysis is to determine the minimum time headway T_{min} that can be permitted if no collision is to occur as a result of a deceleration failure, and to determine the maximum collision velocity that could occur if

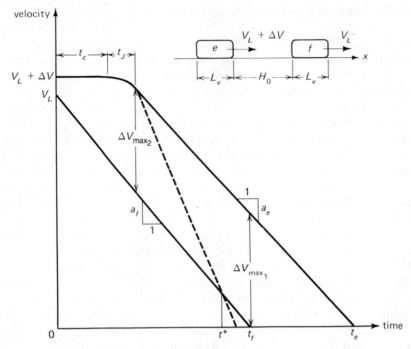

Figure 7-1. Velocity-Time Diagram for Determining No-Collision Headway in Sudden-Deceleration Failures

a closer headway is inadvertently attained. In terms of the minimum permissible nose-to-tail spacing, the minimum time headway (see equation (4.3.6)) is

$$T_{min} = \frac{H_{min} + L_v}{V_L} \qquad (7.2.1)$$

The results are functions of V_L, a_f, a_e, t_c, ΔV, J_e, and L_v. If $a_f > a_e$ the maximum collision velocity occurs if the vehicles are separated initially such that the collision occurs at the instant the failed vehicle stops (see figure 7-1). If $a_f < a_e$, the maximum collision velocity moves to the time $t = t_c + t_J$. If a_e increases sufficiently over a_f, the velocity-time lines of figure 7-1 cross before either vehicle has stopped. In either case, the nose-to-tail spacing between vehicles closes up at most by the amount represented by the portion of the area between the velocity-time lines of figure 7-1 for which $V_e \geqslant V_f$.

Consider the equation of motion of the failed vehicle. At $t = 0$ let its velocity be V_L and the position of its center of gravity be at a distance $x = H_0 + L_v$ ahead of the center of gravity of the trailing vehicle. The equation of motion of vehicle f and its integrals are

$$\ddot{x}_f = -a_f \tag{a}$$

$$\dot{x}_f = V_L - a_f t \tag{b}$$

$$x_f = H_0 + L_v + V_L t - \frac{a_f t^2}{2} \tag{c}$$

Setting $\dot{x}_f = 0$, equation (b) gives the time required for the failed vehicle to stop:

$$t_f = V_L/a_f \tag{d}$$

The motion of the trailing vehicle is more complex and must be divided into three time zones: $0 \le t \le t_c$, $t_c < t \le t_J$, and $t > t_c + t_J$. For the first region

$$\ddot{x}_e = 0 \tag{e}$$

$$\dot{x}_e = V_L + \Delta V \tag{f}$$

$$x_e = (V_L + \Delta V)t \tag{g}$$

For the second region, vehicle e begins to decelerate at a rate of change J_e, and the initial conditions are taken from the equations of motion of the first region at $t = t_c$. Thus

$$\dddot{x}_e = -J_e \tag{h}$$

$$\ddot{x}_e = -J_e(t - t_c) \tag{i}$$

$$\dot{x}_e = V_L + \Delta V - \frac{J_e(t - t_c)^2}{2} \tag{j}$$

$$x_e = (V_L + \Delta V)t - \frac{J_e(t - t_c)^3}{6} \tag{k}$$

By setting $\ddot{x}_e = -a_e$, equation (i) gives the boundary of region 2:

$$t_J = a_e/J_e \tag{l}$$

In the third region, $t \geqslant t_c + t_J$, vehicle e is uniformly decelerating at a rate a_e. Therefore the equation of motion and its integrals are

$$\ddot{x}_e = -a_e \tag{m}$$

$$\dot{x}_e = V_L + \Delta V - \frac{J_e t_J^2}{2} - a_e(t - t_c - t_J) \tag{n}$$

$$x_e = (V_L + \Delta V)t - \frac{J_e t_J^3}{6} - \frac{J_e t_J^2}{2}(t - t_c - t_J) - \frac{a_e}{2}(t - t_c - t_J)^2 \tag{o}$$

Setting $\dot{x}_e = 0$, equation (n) gives the time required for vehicle e to stop:

$$t_e = t_c + t_J + \frac{1}{a_e}(V_L + \Delta V) - \frac{a_e}{2J_e} \tag{p}$$

If $a_e < a_f$ the maximum possible collision velocity considering arbitrary initial separation is $\dot{x}_e$ at $t = t_f$. After substituting for t_f from equation (d) and t_J from equation (l), the result, from equation (n), is

$$\Delta V_{max} = V_L \left(\frac{a_f - a_e}{a_f} \right) + \Delta V + a_e t_c + \frac{a_e^2}{2J_e} \quad \text{for } a_e \leqslant a_f \tag{7.2.2}$$

If $a_e > a_f$, the maximum possible collision velocity is $\dot{x}_e - \dot{x}_f$ evaluated at $t = t_c + t_J$. (The reader can verify that the value of $\dot{x}_e - \dot{x}_f$ at $t = t_c$ is always less if $2a_f > a_e$.) Thus, using equation (l) in equation (b) and (j) evaluated at $t = t_c + t_J$,

$$\Delta V_{max} = \Delta V + a_f t_c + \frac{a_e}{2J_e}(2a_f - a_e) \quad \text{for } a_e > a_f \tag{7.2.3}$$

It can readily be seen that the two equations give the same result when $a_f = a_e$.

Consider the case in which the velocity-time lines do not cross before the vehicles stop, that is, $t_e > t_f$. Then if H_0 is sufficiently large so that the vehicles do not collide as a result of the maneuver, the space between them closes up an amount represented by the area between the two solid curves of figure 7-1. This close-up distance is therefore the minimum spacing that can be permitted between vehicles if a collision is not to occur, and is found by setting $H_0 = H_{min}$ and $x_f(t_f) - x_e(t_e) = L_v$. Substituting equation (p) into equation (o), and equation (d) into equation (c), and using equation (l), the minimum spacing is

$$H_{min} = \left(\frac{a_f - a_e}{2a_f a_e} \right) V_L^2 + \left(t_c + \frac{a_e}{2J_e} + \frac{\Delta V}{a_e} \right) V_L$$

$$+ \left(t_c + \frac{a_e}{2J_e} \right) \Delta V + \frac{\Delta V^2}{2a_e} - \frac{a_e^3}{24J_e^2} \qquad (7.2.4)$$

Substituting into equation (7.2.1),

$$T_{min} = \left(\frac{a_f - a_e}{2a_f a_e} \right) V_L + t_c + \frac{a_e}{2J_e} + \frac{\Delta V}{a_e} + \frac{L_v}{V_L}$$

$$+ \left(t_c + \frac{a_e}{2J_e} + \frac{\Delta V}{2a_e} \right) \frac{\Delta V}{V_L} - \frac{1}{24} \left(\frac{a_e}{J_e} \right)^2 \frac{a_e}{V_L} \qquad t_e \geq t_f \qquad (7.2.5)$$

If, in figure 7-1, the velocity-time lines cross ($t_e \leq t_f$), they do so at a time t^* which can be found by setting $x_e(t^*) = x_f(t^*)$. Using equations (n) and (b),

$$t^* = \frac{1}{(a_e - a_f)} \left(\Delta V + a_e t_c + \frac{a_e^2}{2J_e} \right) \qquad (q)$$

From equations (d) and (p), the condition for the case $t_e \leq t_f$ is

$$\frac{a_e - a_f}{a_e a_f} \geq \frac{1}{V_L} \left(t_c + \frac{a_e}{2J_e} + \frac{\Delta V}{a_e} \right) \qquad (7.2.6)$$

In this case, the two vehicles close up a maximum amount $x_f(0) - x_e(0) - [x_f(t^*) - x_e(t^*)]$ and then separate before stopping. The maximum close-up distance is the minimum nose-to-tail spacing H_{min} permissible at line speed if collisions are to be avoided in sudden deceleration failures. Using equations (c), (g), (o) and (q),

$$H_{min} = \frac{a_e^2}{2(a_e - a_f)} \left(\frac{\Delta V}{a_e} + t_c + \frac{a_e}{2J_e} \right)^2 - \frac{a_e}{2} \left(t_c + \frac{a_e}{2J_e} \right)^2 - \frac{a_e^3}{24J_e^2} \qquad t_e \leq t_f$$

$$(7.2.7)$$

For the case $t_e \lesssim t_f$, $H_{\min}$ is independent of V_L. Therefore it is not helpful to substitute equation (7.2.7) into equation (7.2.1) to get an algebraic equation analogous to equation (7.2.5). Instead, in the following numerical examples, we will deal with equation (7.2.7) directly.

It is necessary now to determine the importance of the various terms in equations (7.2.5) and (7.2.7) in typical numerical examples. Such analysis will permit the designer to concentrate attention on the most fruitful ways to minimize $T_{\min}$.

First consider the case $a_f \geq a_e$. From figure 7-1 it is clear that this case always implies that $t_e > t_f$. Physically, this case must hold for vehicles in which propulsion and braking is accomplished through wheels. This is because possible differences in the coefficient of friction between the wheels and the roadway make it necessary to assume in safety analysis that the failed vehicle can stop more quickly than the trailing vehicle. If the vehicles use rubber-tired wheels on a roadway, the coefficient of friction may be as high as about 0.8 on dry surfaces, but may not exceed 0.3 on wet surfaces[13, 14]. If standing passengers are permitted, a_e must be limited to about 2.5 m/s², but if all passengers are seated, $a_e = 5$ m/s² is practical but achievable only on dry surfaces.

In normal circumstances, passenger comfort dictates that J_e not exceed a_e in seconds units; that is, a_e should not build up to its steady value in less than one second. Equation (7.2.5) shows, however, that higher J_e reduces $T_{\min}$. Therefore, we will assume that in emergencies $J_e/a_e = 3$ s⁻¹ is permissible. For $V_L = 10$ m/s, a relatively low nominal value, the last term in equation (7.2.5) is only two milliseconds and can always be neglected. The second-to-last term in equation (7.2.5), the sum of three factors multiplied by $\Delta V/V_L$, is also always small if $\Delta V/V_L$ is small. Since the last term is also small, attention will be concentrated on the first five terms.

Table 7-1 shows some typical nominal values of the term in equation (7.2.5) for seated and standing passenger vehicles. The value of $t_c = 0.7$ s is typical of lags experienced in systems that apply traction through wheels, but does not include lags induced by discrete sampling of position, that is, it assumes a continuous flow of information on intervehicle spacing. Based on the work of Kornhauser[15], it is assumed that the velocity is controlled to within ± 0.5 m/s. It is seen that unless a_e is close to a_f, the first term in equation (7.2.5) dominates in determining $T_{\min}$. If the difference $a_f - a_e$ can be made small either by increasing a_e or by designing slip clutches into the wheels so that the maximum value of a_f is limited, the first term is reduced below t_c. Further significant reductions in $T_{\min}$ is seen to require reduction in both t_c and L_v. Finally the value of $\Delta V_{\max}$ computed from equation (7.2.2) is tabulated for the two cases, and it is seen that the design is not fault tolerant in the sense that if a vehicle inadvertently strays inside $H_{\min}$, the possible collision velocity is almost as large as the line velocity.

Table 7-1 Components of Minimum Headway for $t_e > t_f$

	Standing-Passenger Vehicle	Seated-Passenger Vehicle			Standing-Passenger Vehicle	Seated Passenger Vehicle
V_L(m/s)	15	15	$\left(\dfrac{a_f - a_e}{2a_f a_e} \right) V_L$ (s)		2.06	0.56
a_e(m/s^2)	2.5	5				
a_f(m/s^2)	8	8	$a_e/2J_e$ (s)		0.25	0.17
t_c(s)	0.7	0.7	$\Delta V/a_e$ (s)		0.20	0.10
J_e/a_e(s^{-1})	2	3	L_v/V_L (s)		0.67	0.47
ΔV (m/s)	0.5	0.5	T_{min} (s)		3.88	2.00
L_v (m)	10	7	ΔV_{max} (m/s)		13.2	10.5

Second, consider the circumstance in which a_f is reduced enough so that $t_f > t_e$. Then equations (7.2.7) and (7.2.2) apply. Also, equation (7.2.6) indicates how small a_f must be for this case to apply. Design to keep t_e below t_f requires greater sophistication in design than the opposite case. To insure that the failure deceleration is below the emergency deceleration in all weather conditions requires that braking not be done through wheels but by a linear system acting directly between the vehicle and the guideway, such as a linear electric motor or eddy current brake[16]. It also requires special care in the design of all surfaces between the vehicle and guideway so that in no circumstances can a failure cause the vehicle to stop quickly. For example, if wheels are used for suspension, they should be smooth and the roadway should be smooth. Moreover, the design should use seated passenger vehicles so that a_e can be kept as high as practical. Finally, by use of linear electric propulsion and braking combined with continuous position and velocity sensing, t_c can be reduced below 0.1 s.

With the design changes indicated in the above paragraph, consider the nominal values of the design parameters to be $a_e = 5$ m/s^2, $t_c = 0.1$ s, $J_e/a_e = 3$ s, $\Delta V = 0.5$ m/s, and $V_L = 15$ m/s. Then, from equation (7.2.6), the case $t_e < t_f$ holds if $a_f < 4.5$ m/s^2. As a result of attention to the design, as indicated above, let $a_f = 2.5$ m/s^2. Then, from equation (7.2.7),

$$H_{min} = 1/5(1.83)^2 - 0.20 = 0.47 \text{ m}$$

Or, for $a_f = 4$ m/s^2,

$$H_{min} = 3.15 \text{ m}$$

Thus H_{min} is very sensitive to a_f, and it is noted that it is independent of V_L. Using equation (7.2.1) T_{min} can be found. For very short-headway systems, L_v will be less than the values of table 7-1. Typical values range from 2.3 to 3 m[17]. Then, for $V_L = 15$ m/s and $a_f = 2.5$ m/s², T_{min} ranges between 0.18 and 0.23 s. If $a_f = 4$ m/s², T_{min} ranges between 0.36 and 0.41 s. Thus, by careful attention to the design so as to minimize a_f, very low headways are possible with no collisions in the event of a deceleration failure. From equation (7.2.3), ΔV_{max} ranges from 0.75 to 1.23 m/s. Thus, with improved design to permit short headways, the design becomes more fault tolerant in that the maximum collision velocities possible at even shorter headways are insignificant, as will be seen by the theory of section 7.6.

Sudden Acceleration

Consider a cascade of vehicles in which one vehicle suddenly fails in such a way that full motor power is applied. A separate monitoring system detects the failure, causes the motor power to be switched off, and applies the emergency brakes. The situation is depicted in figure 7-2. At $t = 0$, a vehicle, labelled "f", suddenly begins to accelerate at a rate a_f. For conservatism in estimating the minimum headway, assume that due to control system imperfections, vehicle f is travelling at $t = 0$ at a speed ΔV above the speed V_L of the vehicle immediately ahead. At $t = t_c$ the emergency brakes begin slowing the vehicle by applying a negative jerk J_e until the vehicle begins decelerating at a rate a_e. To minimize the close-up distance, vehicle f is permitted to decelerate at a_e until it crosses the velocity V_L. The velocity then must undershoot and return to V_L. The reduction in spacing between vehicle f and the lead vehicle ℓ is the cross hatched area in figure 7-2, and is labelled H_{min}. The minimum spacing between vehicles permissible if collisions are to be avoided is H_{min}. If the spacing is closer than H_{min} at $t = 0$, then a collision will occur at a maximum collision velocity of ΔV_{max}.

Because the velocity of vehicle ℓ does not change during the maneuver, ΔV_{max} and H_{min} do not depend on V_L. Therefore the problem of determining ΔV_{max} and H_{min} can be solved most easily in a reference frame that moves to the right at velocity V_L. In this reference frame take the initial position and velocity of vehicle f to be

$$x_f(0) = 0 \qquad \dot{x}_f(0) = \Delta V \qquad \text{(a)}$$

Then the equation of motion of vehicle f and its integrals are as follows: In the range $0 < t < t_c$,

$$\ddot{x}_f = a_f \qquad \text{(b)}$$

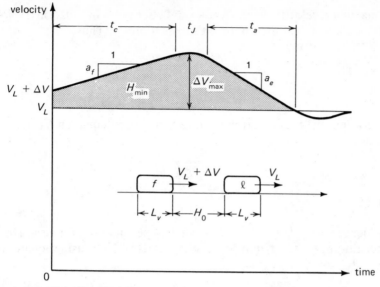

Figure 7.2 Velocity-Time Diagram for Determining No-Collision Headway in Sudden-Acceleration Failures

$$\dot{x}_f = \Delta V + a_f t \tag{c}$$

$$x_f = \Delta Vt + \frac{a_f t^2}{2} \tag{d}$$

In the range $t_c < t < t_c + t_J$

$$\dddot{x}_f = -J_e \tag{e}$$

$$\ddot{x}_f = a_f - J_e(t - t_c) \tag{f}$$

$$\dot{x}_f = \Delta V + a_f t_c + a_f (t - t_c) - \frac{J_e(t - t_c)^2}{2} \tag{g}$$

$$x_f = \Delta Vt_c + \frac{a_f t_c^2}{2} + (\Delta V + a_f t_c) (t - t_c)$$

$$+ \quad \frac{a_f(t - t_c)^2}{2} \quad - \quad \frac{J_e(t - t_c)^3}{6} \tag{h}$$

The maximum velocity occurs when $\ddot{x}_f = 0$. Set $\ddot{x}_f = 0$ in equation (f), solve for $t - t_c$, and substitute the result in equation (g). Thus,

$$\Delta V_{max} = \Delta V + a_f t_c + \frac{a_f^2}{2J_e} \qquad (7.2.8)$$

The jerk interval t_J is found by setting $\ddot{x}_f = -a_e$ in equation (f). Hence

$$t_J = \frac{a_f + a_e}{J_e} \qquad (i)$$

Consider the range $t_c + t_J < t < t_c + t_J + t_a$. The initial conditions are found by substituting $t - t_c = t_J$ into equations (g) and (h). Thus, using equation (i),

$$\dot{x}_f(t_c + t_J) = \Delta V + a_f t_c + \frac{a_f^2 - a_e^2}{2J_e} \qquad (j)$$

$$x_f(t_c + t_J) = \Delta V t_c + \frac{a_f t_c^2}{2} + (\Delta V + a_f t_c)\frac{(a_f + a_e)}{J_e}$$

$$+ \frac{1}{6}\left(\frac{a_f + a_e}{J_e}\right)^2 (2a_f - a_e) \qquad (k)$$

Hence, the equation of motion and its integrals are

$$\ddot{x}_f = -a_e \qquad (l)$$

$$\dot{x}_f = \Delta V + a_f t_c + \frac{a_f^2 - a_e^2}{2J_e} - a_e(t - t_c - t_J) \qquad (m)$$

$$x_f = \Delta V t_c + \frac{a_f t_c^2}{2} + (\Delta V + a_f t_c)\frac{(a_f + a_e)}{J_e}$$

$$+ \frac{1}{6}\left(\frac{a_f + a_e}{J_e}\right)^2 (2a_f - a_e) - \frac{a_e}{2}(t - t_c - t_J)^2$$

$$+ \left(\Delta V + a_f t_c + \frac{a_f^2 - a_e^2}{2J_e}\right)(t - t_c - t_J) \qquad (n)$$

The time interval t_a in figure 7-2 is found by setting $x_f = 0$ in equation (m). Therefore

$$t_a = \frac{1}{a_e}\left(\Delta V + a_f t_c + \frac{a_f^2 - a_e^2}{2J_e}\right)$$ (o)

Now, $H_{min} = x_f(t_c + t_J + t_a)$. Therefore, by substituting $t_a = t - t_c - t_J$ in equation (n) and using equation (o), we find after simplifying the algebra

$$H_{min} = \frac{\Delta V^2}{2a_e} + \left(\frac{a_f + a_e}{a_e}\right)\left[\Delta V\left(t_c + \frac{a_f + a_e}{2J_e}\right) + \frac{a_f t_c^2}{2}\right.$$

$$\left. + \left(\frac{a_f + a_e}{J_e}\right)\frac{a_f t_c}{2} + \frac{(3a_f - a_e)}{24}\left(\frac{a_f + a_e}{J_e}\right)^2\right]$$ (7.2.9)

To estimate the magnitude of H_{min}, note that H_{min} increases as a_f increases, but decreases as a_e increases. (This is most easily seen from figure 7-2.) Hence, to get an upper bound on H_{min}, overestimate a_f and underestimate a_e. It will be necessary again to treat seated- and standing-passenger vehicles separately. In both cases, note from the theory of section 2.3 that at line speed it is not economical to provide motor power ample for maximum acceleration at line speed. Therefore assume a_f is 50 percent of the service acceleration. As before, assume a_e is twice the service acceleration. Consequently, assume for standing-passenger vehicles

$$a_f = 0.5(g/8) = 0.63 \text{ m/s}^2$$

$$a_e = 4a_f$$

For seated-passenger vehicles, the rates are doubled. Thus

$$a_f = 1.25 \text{ m/s}^2$$

$$a_e = 4a_f$$

In both cases, let $J_e = 3a_e$ in units of seconds. Then equation (7.2.9) becomes

$$H_{min} = \frac{\Delta V^2}{8a_f} + \frac{5}{4}\left[\Delta V\left(t_c + \frac{5}{24}\right) + \frac{a_f}{2}\left(t_c^2 + \frac{5t_c}{12} - \frac{25}{1728}\right)\right]$$

As in the previous paragraph, let $\Delta V = 0.5$ m/s. Then for standing-passenger vehicles, we have for H_{min} and for ΔV_{max}, from equation (7.2.8),

$$H_{min} = (0.39t_c^2 + 0.78t_c + 0.17) \text{ m}$$

$$\Delta V_{max} = (0.63t_c + 0.53) \text{ m/s}$$

and, for seated-passenger vehicles

$$H_{min} = (0.78t_c^2 + 0.95t_c + 0.14) \text{ m}$$

$$\Delta V_{max} = (1.3t_c + 0.55) \text{ m/s}$$

For several values of t_c, H_{min} and ΔV_{max} are as given in table 7-2.

The corresponding minimum headways can now be found from equation (7.2.1). In all cases it is clear that the decelerating failure is more important than the accelerating failure in determining minimum headway.

Failure to Decelerate in a Station

Consider an off-line station with more than one series berth for loading and unloading passengers. It is desirable to cause the vehicles to stop close to one another to minimize the station platform length, and hence the station cost; however, too close a spacing may not be safe. The minimum permissible spacing, H_n, must be determined so that if a vehicle fails to decelerate to a stop when commanded, it will not, before emergency action is taken, collide with a stopped vehicle with a large enough velocity to cause injury to the passengers. The situation can be analyzed with the help of the velocity-time diagram of figure 7-3.

Table 7-2 Minimum Headway and Maximum Collision Velocity in Sudden-Acceleration Failures

t_c (s)	0.1	0.5	1
H_{min}, standees	0.25 m	0.66 m	1.34 m
H_{min}, no standees	0.24 m	0.81 m	1.87 m
ΔV_{max}, standees	0.59 m/s	0.85 m/s	1.16 m/s
ΔV_{max}, no standees	0.68 m/s	1.18 m/s	1.85 m/s

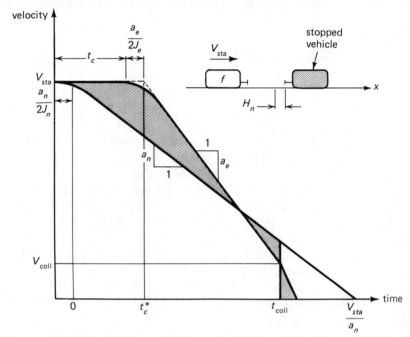

Figure 7-3. Velocity-Time Diagram for Determining Normal Stopped-Vehicle Separation in a Station

Assume the vehicles decelerate on an off-line ramp to a station velocity V_{sta} before entering the station-platform area. Within the platform area, the vehicle moves at V_{sta} until, at a certain point, it is commanded to decelerate at a normal rate a_n to stop a distance H_n behind a stopped vehicle. If the vehicle fails to decelerate when commanded, the failure is detected by a monitor and a separate system causes it to stop at a rate $a_e > a_n$, but emergency braking can be applied only after a certain control time delay t_c. The brakes on the stopped vehicle are locked so that if vehicle f hits it with a sufficiently small velocity, the vehicle will not move and is safe for passengers to load.

The maximum permissible collision velocity, V_{coll}, is determined by the conditions that the kinetic energy of the failed vehicle must be absorbed in the shock absorbing system if its maximum deflection is δ_s, and the intervehicle force transmitted by the shock absorbers is no greater than the braking force of the stopped vehicle, f_B. Thus

$$1/2m_f V_{coll}^2 = f_B \delta_s \tag{a}$$

Let the braking force be applied by the emergency brakes. Then

$$f_B = m_s a_e \tag{b}$$

in which m_s is the mass of the stopped vehicle. Combining equations (a) and (b),

$$\frac{V_{\text{coll}}^2}{2a_e} = \frac{m_s}{m_f}\delta_s \qquad \text{(c)}$$

Now consider the velocity-time diagram of figure 7-3. If vehicle f fails to stop when normally required and emergency action is initiated after a time delay t_c, vehicle f overshoots its normal position by the amount indicated by the crosshatched area above the normal acceleration line, then undershoots until it impacts the stopped vehicle at V_{coll}. Then, because of the force transmitted to vehicle f through the shock absorber, it decelerates to a stop at a higher rate, and the shock absorber deflection δ_s is represented by the crosshatched triangle to the right of the vertical line at the instant V_{coll} is reached. Computation of the distance H_n can be simplified by observing from equations (7.2.4) and (7.2.7) that the major effect of inclusion of finite jerk is to add $a_e/2J_e$ to t_c, since it was shown that the term $a_e^3/24J_e^2$ is very small. Assuming that the time interval t_c begins at the instant the vehicle normally begins to decelerate, jerk can be left out of the computation by replacing t_c by t_c^*, where

$$t_c^* = t_c + \frac{a_e}{2J_e} - \frac{a_n}{2J_n} \qquad \text{(d)}$$

With the above simplification, H_n can be found from figure 7-3 as follows: In normal circumstances the stopping distance from $t = 0$ is $V_{\text{sta}}^2/2a_n$, and vehicle f will stop a distance H_n from the next vehicle. In a failure, the vehicle may travel an additional distance H_n before colliding with a stopped vehicle at velocity V_{coll}. From figure 7-3, the total distance traveled from $t = 0$ is the area under the emergency velocity-time line between $t = 0$ and $t = t_{\text{coll}}$. This distance is

$$V_{\text{sta}}t_c^* + \frac{(V_{\text{sta}} - V_{\text{coll}})^2}{2a_e} + V_{\text{coll}}\frac{(V_{\text{sta}} - V_{\text{coll}})}{a_e}$$

Simplifying this expression, the normal spacing is

$$H_n = V_{\text{sta}}t_c^* + \frac{V_{\text{sta}}^2 - V_{\text{coll}}^2}{2a_e} - \frac{V_{\text{sta}}^2}{2a_n}$$

Substituting equations (c) and (d),

$$H_n = V_{\text{sta}}\left(t_c + \frac{a_e}{2J_e} - \frac{a_n}{2J_n}\right) - \frac{(a_e - a_n)}{2a_e a_n} V_{\text{sta}}^2 - \frac{m_s}{m_f}\delta_s \qquad (7.2.10)$$

In normal circumstances, $J_n = a_n$ in units of seconds. In an emergency we have assumed $J_e = 3a_e$. Thus, addition of the jerk terms reduces H_n. Assuming also that $a_e = 2a_n$, equation (7.2.10) becomes

$$H_n = V_{\text{sta}}\left(t_c - \frac{1}{3}\right) - \frac{V_{\text{sta}}^2}{4a_n} - \frac{m_s}{m_f}\delta_s \qquad (e)$$

To make $H_n < 0$, it is necessary that

$$t_c \leq \frac{1}{3} + \frac{V_{\text{sta}}}{4a_n} + \frac{m_s}{m_f}\frac{\delta_s}{V_{\text{sta}}} \qquad (f)$$

As a function of V_{sta}, the maximum value of H_n is determined by setting $dH_n/dV_{\text{sta}} = 0$. The value of V_{sta} at $H_{n_{\max}}$ is

$$V_{\text{sta}} = 2a_n\left(t_c - \frac{1}{3}\right) \qquad (g)$$

Substituting into equation (e),

$$H_{n_{\max}} = a_n\left(t_c - \frac{1}{3}\right)^2 - \frac{m_s}{m_f}\delta_s \qquad (h)$$

In the worst case, the stopped vehicle is lighter than the failed vehicle and is therefore more likely to move in a collision. Therefore, assuming nominally similar vehicles, let $m_s = 0.9\,m_f$. Assume also that $a_n = 2.5\ \text{m/s}^2$. Then, from equation (h)

$$H_{n_{\max}} = 2.5\left(t_c - \frac{1}{3}\right)^2 - 0.9\,\delta_s \qquad (i)$$

If $H_{n_{max}} = 0$, equation (i) gives

$$t_c = \frac{1}{3} + (0.36\,\delta_s)^{1/2} \tag{j}$$

Based on the work of the next section, let $\delta_s = 0.5$ m. Then, if $t_c < 0.76$ s, no spacing between vehicles is needed. If $t_c = 1$ s and $\delta_s = 0.5$ m, $H_{n_{max}} = 0.66$ m. The station speed corresponding to $H_{n_{max}} = 0$ is found by combining equations (g) and (j). Thus

$$V_{sta} = 3.0\,\delta_s^{1/2} \tag{k}$$

This is a very low velocity. With higher values of V_{sta}, $H_n < H_{n_{max}}$. For example, if $V_{sta} = 3$ m/s (6.8 mi/hr), $a_n = 2.5$ m/s^2, $\delta_s = 0.5$ m, equation (e) gives

$$H_n = 3t_c - 2.35 \text{ m}$$

Thus, if $t_c < 0.78$ s, no spacing is required. Note from equation (7.2.10) that if $a_e = a_n$ and $J_e = J_n$

$$H_n = V_{sta}t_c - \frac{m_s}{m_f}\,\delta_s \tag{l}$$

Thus, with $m_s/m_f = 0.9$ and $\delta_s = 0.5$ m, the time delay required to make H_n negative is

$$t_c < \frac{0.45}{V_{sta}}$$

The importance of rapid response time in minimizing station platform length is very apparent.

7.3 Constant Force, Constant Displacement Shock Absorbers

The possibility always exists that simultaneous failures of independent systems will cause collisions between vehicles in any transit system. Thus it is necessary to provide protection for the vehicles and passengers if collisions should occur. In the following sections, collisions are analyzed to determine design requirements for avoidance of injury to the passengers. The analysis is dependent on the design characteristics of the shock absorber used on the vehicles. If the reader is to appreciate the practicality of the characteristics used, it is necessary to understand the theory of the constant force, constant displacement hydraulic shock absorber. The following analysis of such a shock absorber is based on the work of Appel and Tomas[19].

The constant force characteristic of a shock absorber is optimum because it permits the relative kinetic energy of collision to be absorbed with a minimum stroke. Use of minimum stroke shock absorbers reduces their cost, reduces the vehicle length, and reduces the length of the station platform. The system cost therefore decreases with decreasing length of shock absorbers that provide a given level of protection. The constant displacement characteristic means that the maximum stroke of the shock absorber occurs for all collision velocities, thus causing smaller deceleration during collisions at smaller collision velocities. Thus, the passengers are not subjected to greater deceleration than necessary to reduce the relative velocity between vehicles to zero. If a collision should occur at a relative velocity greater than the design maximum, the relative kinetic energy of collision cannot all be absorbed by the shock absorber. As described in reference[10], the additional energy must be absorbed by the vehicle frame, and the cost of repair can be reduced by use of a replaceable crushable structure in front of each vehicle. It appears that such a combination protection system would be less expensive than providing hydraulic shock absorbers with a sufficiently long stroke to accommodate the largest conceivable collision velocity.

Fluid Flow Analysis

A schematic of a hydraulic shock absorber is shown in figure 7-4 in the necessary detail. The applied force on the piston is F_p, the maximum stroke is δ_{sa}, and the variable x is used to represent the stroke at any point. As a result of F_p, hydraulic fluid is forced through an orifice in the piston, and dissipates the work input $\int_0^x F_p dx$ in turbulence of the fluid to the left of the piston. The constant force, constant displacement characteristic may be achieved by using a variable area orifice. As indicated in figure 7-4, variability can be obtained by positioning a variable diameter rod along the axis of a hole in the piston, thus creating a variable area annular orifice. In the position shown in the figure, the relative velocity between the two cylinders is high, thus requiring a large fluid momentum exchange (large orifice area) to maintain a constant force. As x approaches δ_{sa}, it is desired that the relative velocity vanish, thus requiring the orifice area also to vanish.

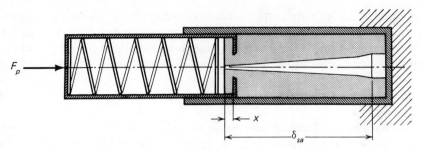

Figure 7-4. A Hydraulic Shock Absorber

Following a collision, the shock absorber will return to its initial position if a relatively weak spring is mounted in the moveable piston. Thus, no maintenance action is required following a collision that does not cause crushing of the structure.

Let the pressure difference across the orifice be Δp. Then if A'_p is the annular surface area of the end of a relatively thin-walled piston and the spring is relatively weak, $\Delta p A'_p = F_p$. If the velocity of the fluid passing through the orifices is V_{fl}, then, by applying Bernoulli's theorem across the orifice,

$$F_p = \Delta p A'_p = \frac{\rho}{2} \ (V_{fl}^2 - \dot{x}^2) A'_p \tag{a}$$

in which ρ is the density of the hydraulic fluid, and $\dot{x}$ is the velocity of the fluid on the right of the piston with respect to the piston. From the continuity equation

$$\dot{x} A_p = V_{fl} A_0(x) \tag{b}$$

in which A_p is the total area of the piston and $A_0(x)$ is the variable area of the orifice. Eliminating V_{fl} between equations (a) and (b),

$$F_p = \frac{\rho \dot{x}^2}{2} \left(\frac{A_p^2}{A_0^2} - 1 \right) A'_p \tag{7.3.1}$$

Momentum and Energy Conservation in a Collision

Consider figure 7-5. A collision occurs at $t = 0$ between two vehicles of masses m_1 and m_2 in the reference frame of vehicle 1. The collision velocity

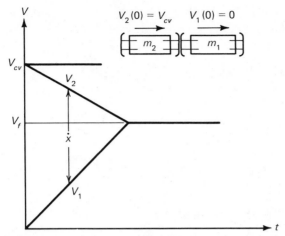

Figure 7-5. Velocity-Time Diagram of a Collision

is V_{cv} and, for $t > 0$, $V_2 - V_1$ is the velocity of vehicle 2 with respect to vehicle 1.

The costs of shock absorbers and their mounting structures can be reduced if several small shock absorbers are used rather than one large one. Therefore, assume two shock absorbers are placed side by side at the front and rear of each vehicle as shown in figure 7-5. Thus, if F is the total force between vehicles, $F = 2F_p$. The total stroke of the shock absorbers involved in a collision is $2\delta_{sa}$, and the relative velocity between vehicles is

$$2\dot{x} = V_2 - V_1 \tag{7.3.2}$$

During the collision, momentum is conserved. Therefore

$$m_1 V_1 + m_2 V_2 = m_2 V_{cv} \tag{7.3.3}$$

and the final velocity is

$$V_f = \frac{m_2}{m_1 + m_2} V_{cv} \tag{7.3.4}$$

The work done in compressing the plunger on one of the shock absorbers is $\int_{0|}^{x} F_p \, dx$. (At this point, F_p is retained as an arbitrary function in order that deviations from constant F_p as a result of approximations in the function $A_0(x)$ can be determined.) The work of compression is equal to the reduction in the kinetic energy of the system. Thus

$$W(\delta_{sa}) = 4\int_0^x F_p \, dx = \frac{m_2 V_{cv}^2}{2} - \frac{m_1 V_1^2}{2} - \frac{m_2 V_2^2}{2} \qquad (7.3.5)$$

The total work of compression is

$$W(\delta_{sa}) = 4\int_0^{\delta_{sa}} F_p \, dx = \frac{m_2 V_{cv}^2}{2} - \frac{(m_1 + m_2)}{2} V_f^2$$

Substituting V_f from equation (7.3.4),

$$4\int_0^{\delta_{sa}} F_p \, dx = \frac{1}{2}\left(\frac{m_1 m_2}{m_1 + m_2}\right) V_{cv}^2 \qquad (7.3.6)$$

or, if F_p is constant,

$$\delta_{sa} = \frac{1}{8}\left(\frac{m_1 m_2}{m_1 + m_2}\right) \frac{V_{cv}^2}{F_p} \qquad (7.3.7)$$

The Equation for the Variable Orifice Area

It is now necessary to express x^2 in equation (7.3.1) in terms of x and δ_{sa}. To do this, square equations (7.3.2) and (7.3.3) to give

$$4\dot{x}^2 = V_1^2 - 2V_1 V_2 + V_2^2$$

$$2m_1 m_2 V_1 V_2 = m_2^2 V_{cv}^2 - m_1^2 V_1^2 - m_2^2 V_2^2$$

Eliminating $2V_1 V_2$,

$$x^2 = \frac{1}{2m_1 m_2}\left[(m_1 + m_2)\left(\frac{m_1 V_1^2}{2} + \frac{m_2 V_2^2}{2}\right) - \frac{m_2^2 V_{cv}^2}{2}\right]$$

Substitute the kinetic energy during the collision from equation (7.3.5), and then the initial kinetic energy, $m_2 V_{cv}^2/2$, from equation (7.3.6). The result is

$$x^2 = 2\left(\frac{m_1 + m_2}{m_1 m_2}\right)\int_x^{\delta_{sa}} F_p(x)\,dx \qquad (7.3.8)$$

If x^2 is eliminated between equations (7.3.1) and (7.3.8), the result can be expressed in the form

$$\left[\frac{A_0^2(x)}{A_p^2 - A_0^2(x)}\right]F_p(x) = \beta\int_{x/\delta_{sa}}^{1} F_p(\xi)\,d\xi \qquad (7.3.9)$$

in which ξ is the dimensionless dummy variable x/δ_{sa}, and

$$\beta = \left(\frac{m_1 + m_2}{m_1 m_2}\right)\rho A_p' \delta_{sa}$$

In equation (a), δ_{sa} is given by equation (7.3.7) in terms of the maximum value of V_{cv}, $V_{cv\,\text{max}}$, and the corresponding maximum force, $F_{p\,\text{max}}$. It is meaningful to express $F_{p\,\text{max}}$ as

$$F_{p\,\text{max}} = \frac{F_{\text{max}}}{2} = \frac{m_2 a_{\text{max}}}{2} \qquad (7.3.10)$$

in which a_{max} is the deceleration vehicle 2 experiences during the collision at maximum V_{cv}. Substituting equation (7.3.10) into equation (7.3.7),

$$\delta_{sa} = \frac{1}{4}\left(\frac{m_1}{m_1 + m_2}\right)\frac{V_{cv\,\text{max}}^2}{a_{\text{max}}} \qquad (7.3.11)$$

Substituting equation (7.3.11) into equation (a)

$$\beta = \frac{\rho V_{cv\,\text{max}}^2}{4 m_2 a_{\text{max}}} A_p' \qquad (7.3.12)$$

Note, from equation (a), that β is a little smaller than the ratio of the mass of the fluid in one of the shock absorbers to the reduced mass of a vehicle, $m_1 m_2/(m_1 + m_2)$. Thus, in a practical design β is much less than 1.

If F_p is constant, it drops out of equation (7.3.9), and the result may be written in the form

$$\frac{A_0(x)}{A_p} = \left[\frac{\beta(1 - x/\delta_{sa})}{1 + \beta(1 - x/\delta_{sa})} \right]^{1/2} \tag{b}$$

Thus

$$A_0(0) = \left(\frac{\beta}{1 + \beta} \right)^{1/2} A_p \tag{c}$$

Dividing equation (b) by equation (c),

$$\frac{A_0(x)}{A_0(0)} = \left[\frac{(1 + \beta)(1 - x/\delta_{sa})}{1 + \beta(1 - x/\delta_{sa})} \right]^{1/2} \tag{d}$$

Let r_0 be the radius of the hole in the left-hand cylinder in figure 7-4, and $r_r(x)$ be the radius of the variable diameter orifice rod. Then

$$A_0(0) = \pi[r_0^2 - r_r^2(0)] \tag{7.3.13}$$

and

$$\frac{A_0(x)}{A_0(0)} = \frac{r_0^2 - r_r^2(x)}{r_0^2 - r_r^2(0)} \tag{e}$$

Substituting equation (d) into equation (e) and solving for $r_r(x)$, we have

$$\frac{r_r(x)}{r_0} = \left\{ 1 - \left[1 - \frac{r_r^2(0)}{r_0^2} \right] \left[\frac{(1 + \beta)(1 - x/\delta_{sa})}{1 + \beta(1 - x/\delta_{sa})} \right]^{1/2} \right\}^{1/2} \tag{7.3.14}$$

Equation (7.3.14) is plotted in figure 7-6 for the case $r_r(0) = 0$ and $\beta = 0.01$. Note that the slope $r_r'(x)$ approaches infinity at both $x = 0$ and $x = \delta_{sa}$. A change in β of 20 percent changes the profile by less than 0.1 percent. Therefore the constant force characteristic is insensitive to small parameter changes in equation (7.3.12). A constant taper rod is clearly suggested

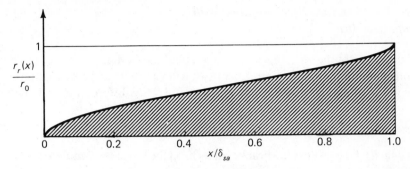

Figure 7-6. The Shape of a Variable Diameter Orifice Rod Varied in a Manner to Produce Constant Force in a Hydraulic Shock Absorber

from figure 7-6 as an inexpensive approximate shape. The force variations corresponding to the parameters of a constant-taper rod or other approximate shape can be found as described in the following paragraph. Once $A_0(0)$ is determined, A_p can be found from the cubic equation that results by substituting equation (7.3.12) into the square of equation (c). Substituting

$$A_p' = A_p - A_0(0) - A_r(0) \tag{7.3.15}$$

where

$$A_r(0) = \pi r_r^2(0)$$

the cubic equation can be written in the form

$$(p^2 - 1)[p - 1 - A_r(0)/A_0(0)] = \frac{1}{\gamma A_0(0)} \tag{7.3.16}$$

in which

$$p = A_p/A_0(0)$$

and

$$\gamma = \frac{\rho V_{cv_{max}}^2}{4 m_2 a_{max}} \tag{7.3.17}$$

The Equation for Force Variation with
Imperfect Orifice Variation

If the shape of the variable diameter rod that makes A_0 vary with x does not conform exactly to equation (7.3.14), F_p will vary with x. The variation can be found, if $A_0(x)$ is given, from equation (7.3.9) by differentiating it. Thus

$$[\ ]'F_p + [\ ]F_p' = -\beta F_p \tag{a}$$

in which [ ] represents the bracketed term on the left side of equation (7.3.9) and the primes denote differentiation with respect to $\xi = x/\delta_{sa}$.

Equation (a) can be rearranged in the form

$$\frac{dF_p}{F_p} = -\frac{d[\ ]}{[\ ]} - \frac{\beta d\xi}{[\ ]} \tag{b}$$

Integrating from 0 to x, the result can be written in the form

$$\frac{F_p(x/\delta_{sa})}{F_p(0)} = \frac{[\ ]_0}{[\ ]_{x/\delta_{sa}}} \exp\left[-\beta \int_0^{x/\delta_{sa}} \frac{d\xi}{[\ ]_\xi} \right] \tag{7.3.18}$$

in which

$$[\ ]_{x/\delta_{sa}} = \frac{A_0^2(x/\delta_{sa})}{A_p^2 - A_0^2(x/\delta_{sa})} \tag{7.3.19}$$

Thus, if it is found that cost can be saved by manufacturing a simpler shape than given by equation (7.3.14), equations (7.3.18) and (7.3.19) determine the consequent force variation.

Solution Procedure

The solution procedure now consists of the following steps:
1. Determine if the design is to be based on a collision with a fixed barrier or a moving vehicle. If the former, set $m_1/(m_1 + m_2) = 1$ in equation (7.3.11). If the later, assume m_2 is somewhat less than m_1, say $m_2 = 0.9\,m_1$. Then $m_1/(m_1 + m_2) = 1/1.9$.

2. Determine the design values of $V_{cv_{\max}}$ and $a_{\max}$ from system considerations and from the analysis of section 7.6.

3. Compute the stroke length from equation (7.3.11) and the maximum design force from equation (7.3.10).

4. Chose r_0 large enough so that the tolerances that must be held in manufacturing the variable diameter rod are reasonable, and chose $r_r(0)$ from design considerations. Then compute $A_0(0)$ from equation (7.3.13).

5. For a given hydraulic fluid density ρ, compute γ from equation (7.3.17), A_p from equation (7.3.16), and A_p' from equation (7.3.15).

6. For the above computed values of δ_{sa} and A_p, determine the buckling load for the shock absorber[20]. If it is several times $F_{p_{\max}}$, the design can proceed; otherwise A_p must be increased until buckling is not a problem. The thickness of the cylinder walls of the shock absorber must also be determined from buckling considerations.

7. Compute β from equation (7.3.12) in which A_p' is given by equation (7.3.15), and then the shape of the variable diameter rod from equation (7.3.14). If an approximate shape is desired, compute the consequent force variation from equations (7.3.18) and (7.3.19).

7.4 Criteria for Avoidance of Passenger Injury
In Collisions

Garrard, Caudill, and Rushfeldt[10] report the results of an extensive literature survey aimed at determining results of auto crash testing that may be applicable to small automated transit vehicles. The results indicate that precise injury criteria are subject to debate, and because of the many ways a person could impact a padded surface, no simple criterion can be expected to guarantee complete avoidance of injury. Nonetheless, criteria have emerged that can provide practical guidance in the safe design of automated transit vehicles.

The degree of injury depends on the magnitude, rate of change, and duration of acceleration. Experiments have suggested the following maximum values of deceleration and jerk for automotive restraint systems[10]:

Belt-strap restraints: 30 g's and 1500 g/s
Airbags: 60 g's and 3000 g/s
Airbelts: 50g's and 2000 g/s

The constraint on jerk indicates that the rate of rise and fall of the force-deflection curve of a padded dash cannot be too steep.

To take into account limitations on human tolerance to duration of deceleration, the Severity Index (SI) was developed by C.W. Gadd of the

General Motors Research Laboratory, and is used by the National Highway Traffic Safety Administration as a basis for a safety criterion. The definition of SI is

$$SI = \int_0^t a^n \, dt \qquad (7.4.1)$$

in which a is the deceleration in g's, n is an experimentally determined parameter with a recommended value, $n = 2.5$, and t is the duration of the acceleration pulse. The design guidelines developed in this chapter are based upon both the above mentioned deceleration and jerk limits and on the Severity Index. A value of SI = 1000 s is the "threshold of danger to life for internal head injury in frontal blows"[10]. It is further pointed out, however, that "experiments with human volunteers have indicated that severity indices of 1000 seconds are routinely sustained in collisions with no ill effects." Because of uncertainties mentioned above, the design recommendations given in the following section will be based on SI less than 500 s.

7.5 Collision with a Constraint Device in a Decelerating Vehicle

Force-Deflection Characteristics

Before considering the parameter choices required for passenger protection in a collision, it is necessary to study the problem of collision of an unconstrained body with a constraint device in a decelerating vehicle. The body (passenger) could be assumed to be constrained by a lap and shoulder harness, an explodable airbag, or a padded dashboard.

The force-deflection characteristics of the constraint device must be chosen so that the acceleration and jerk limits presented in section 7.4 are not exceeded. (The Severity Index, equation 7.4.1) will be seen to limit the duration of the collision and hence the collision velocity.) The acceleration and jerk limits can be met if the constraint device has a force-deflection characteristic such as shown in figure 7-7.

The ratio F_ℓ/δ_ℓ is limited by the maximum tolerable jerk, and F_ℓ by the maximum tolerable deceleration, that is, $F_\ell = ma_\ell$, in which m is the mass of the passenger and a_ℓ the deceleration limit. Ideally, the constraint device does not spring back all the way but absorbs some of the energy of collision

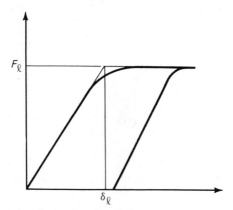

Figure 7-7. Idealized Force-Deflection Curve for a Constraint Device

in crushing. If the dash were to absorb all of the energy, the force would drop to zero at the instant of maximum deflection, and hence an infinite jerk pulse would occur. Some characteristics of energy absorbing materials applicable to padded dashboards are given in Table 1 of reference [12].

The Equivalent Problem

To determine the conditions under which the injury avoidance criteria can be met, it is necessary to study the problem of collision of a mass with a surface having the force-deflection characteristic of figure 7-7. The work of reference[9] has shown that a one-dimensional treatment of the problem gives results in good agreement with experiment. Conceptually, the problem of collision with a constraint device in a decelerating vehicle can be simplified by recalling Einstein's Principle of Equivalence[21]. According to the Principle of Equivalence, the present problem can be solved in a frame of reference attached to the decelerating vehicle by assuming that that frame is at rest but that a gravitational field is imposed that would draw objects to the constraint surface at an acceleration equal to the deceleration of the vehicle. The problem under consideration is therefore equivalent to the problem, shown in figure 7-8, of a mass m falling from a height δ_{th}, equal to the throw distance between the passenger and the constraint, in a gravitational field $g_e = a_v$, where a_v is the deceleration of the vehicle. The mass m strikes the constraint device with a velocity

$$V_{cp} = \sqrt{2a_v\delta_{th}} \qquad (7.5.1)$$

and sinks an amount δ_{pd} before stopping.

186

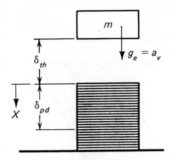

Figure 7-8. Collision of an Object with a Constraint

Solution Assuming Linear Force-Deflection Curve

Consider the motion in the linear portion of the force-deflection curve of figure 7-7. Then, if x is measured downward in figure 7-8 from the point of impact, the equation of motion is

$$m\ddot{x} = -\frac{F_\ell}{\delta_\ell} x + ma_v \tag{a}$$

Here ma_v is the equivalent weight of the mass m in the gravitational field a_v. The solution of equation (a) that satisfies the initial conditions $x(0) = 0$, $\dot{x}(0) = V_{cp}$, is

$$x = \frac{V_{cp}}{\omega_n} \sin \omega_n t + \frac{a_v}{\omega_n^2} (1 - \cos \omega_n t) \tag{b}$$

in which $\omega_n = \sqrt{F_\ell/\delta_\ell m}$. The jerk is obtained by differentiating equation (b) three times. Thus

$$\dddot{x} = -V_{cp}\omega_n^2\cos \omega_n t - a_v\omega_n\sin \omega_n t \tag{c}$$

The first term should normally be the largest since it is dependent on the collision. Thus, consider

$$|\dddot{x}(0)| \approx V_{cp}\omega_n^2 = \frac{V_{cp}F_\ell}{\delta_\ell m} \tag{d}$$

But $F_\ell/m = a_\ell$, the tolerable limit acceleration. Therefore

$$\delta_\ell = V_{cp} \frac{a_\ell}{J_\ell} \tag{e}$$

in which J_ℓ is the limit value of $|\ddot{x}(0)|$. The smallest value of J_ℓ/a_ℓ given in the data of section 7.4 is 40 s^{-1}. Therefore, the value of δ_ℓ that defines the break point in the force-deflection curve of figure 7-7 must come at a value $\delta_\ell = V_{cp}/40$ or greater if the jerk limit is not to be exceeded. But for a not unreasonably large value of $V_{cp} = 10$ m/s, $\delta_\ell = 25$ cm. This is large enough that the force-deflection curve is likely to be linear all the way, and the limits on acceleration and jerk should be determined by finding the maximum values of these quantities from equations (b) and (c). The acceleration is found by differentiating equation (b) twice. Thus

$$\ddot{x} = -V_{cp}\omega_n\sin \omega_n t + a_v\cos \omega_n t \tag{7.5.2}$$

The maximum value of $\ddot{x}$ is found by setting $\dddot{x} = 0$, solving for $\omega_n t$, and substituting in equation (7.5.2). The result is that the maximum occurs at

$$\tan \omega_n t = -\frac{V_{cp}\omega_n}{a_v} \tag{f}$$

and the magnitude of the maximum (using the identity $\cos \theta = 1/\sqrt{1 + \tan^2\theta}$) is,

$$|\ddot{x}|_{max} = V_{cp}\omega_n \sqrt{1 + \left(\frac{a_v}{V_{cp}\omega_n}\right)^2} \tag{7.5.3}$$

The maximum deflection also occurs at the value of $\omega_n t$ given by equation (f), and has a magnitude

$$|x|_{max} = \frac{a_v}{\omega_n^2} + \frac{V_{cp}}{\omega_n}\sqrt{1 + \left(\frac{a_v}{V_{cp}\omega_n}\right)^2} \tag{7.5.4}$$

In a similar way, the maximum jerk can be found by differentiating equation (c) and occurs at

$$\tan \omega_n t = \frac{a_v}{V_{cp}\omega_n} \tag{g}$$

On substituting this expression into equation (c), the maximum jerk is found to be

$$\left|\dddot{x}\right|_{max} = V_{cp}\omega_n^2 \sqrt{1 + \left(\frac{a_v}{V_{cp}\omega_n}\right)^2} \qquad (7.5.5)$$

It is seen that the maximum deflection and acceleration occur at the same time in the second quadrant (for $\pi/2 < \omega_n t < \pi$), but from equation (g), $\left|\dddot{x}\right|_{max}$ occurs early in the first quadrant. By dividing equation (7.5.5) by equation (7.5.3),

$$\omega_n = \frac{\left|\dddot{x}\right|_{max}}{\left|\ddot{x}\right|_{max}} \qquad (7.5.6)$$

If, from section 7.4, this ratio is set at 40, then, since $\omega_n = \sqrt{k/m}$ where k is the spring constant of the dashboard, k can be found for a given m. Since $\left|\dddot{x}\right|_{max}$ and $\left|\ddot{x}\right|_{max}$ increase as m decreases, the computation of k should be based on a small mass. For $m = 50$ kg, $k = \omega_n^2 m = (40)^2(50) = 8(10)^4$ N/m.

If the radical in equation (7.5.4) is eliminated by means of equation (7.5.3),

$$\left|x\right|_{max} = \frac{1}{\omega_n^2} \left(\left|\ddot{x}\right|_{max} + a_v\right) \qquad (7.5.7)$$

If the tolerable limits given in section 7.4 are assumed, the maximum deflection of the constraint device, which must be possible if the acceleration and jerk limits are reached, can be found. Assume the limits given for airbelts. Then, as before, equation (7.5.6) gives $\omega_n = 40$ rad/s. Then, with $\left|\ddot{x}\right|_{max} = 500$ m/s²,

$$\left|x\right|_{max} = \frac{(500 + a_v)}{1600} \approx 31 \text{ cm} \qquad (7.5.7a)$$

if a_v is much less than $\left|\ddot{x}\right|_{max}$, which is a desirable design condition.

Such a deflection may be possible with an airbag, but is probably too large for a fixed padded dash. Therefore, for a padded dash, $\left|x\right|_{max}$ must be lower. If the maximum dashboard deflection is given, it is necessary to know the impact velocity V_{cp} required to achieve it in terms of $|x|_{max}$. The desired relationship can be found by solving equation (7.5.4) for V_{cp}. Thus,

$$V_{cp} = \omega_n |x|_{max} \sqrt{1 - \frac{2a_v}{\omega_n^2 |x|_{max}}} \qquad (7.5.8)$$

This equation, together with equation (7.5.6) determines the maximum permissible V_{cp} based on the maximum permissible ratio of jerk to acceleration and the maximum available deflection of the constraint system.

If the constraint system is a tight seat and shoulder harness, δ_{th} in figure 7-8 is zero and, from equation (7.5.1), V_{cp} is zero. In this case, equation (7.5.8) gives the maximum permissible value of a_v:

$$(a_v)_{max} = 1/2 |x|_{max} \omega_n^2 \qquad (7.5.9)$$

In terms of the collision velocity between vehicles, and the shock absorber deflection, $(a_v)_{max}$ is given by equation (7.3.11).

Application of the Severity Index

Under the condition $a_v << V_{cp}\omega_n$, substitute equation (7.5.2) into equation (7.4.1). Then, with $n = 2.5$, SI can be written in the form

$$SI = \left(\frac{V_{cp}}{g}\right)^{2.5} \omega_n^{1.5} \int_0^\nu \sin^{2.5}\tau \, d\tau \qquad (7.5.10)$$

where $\tau = \omega_n t$, and $\nu = \pi$ if the constraint device behaves like a linear spring with no hysteresis, or $\nu = \pi/2$ if it is linear on the forward stroke but does not spring back and can exert no further force on the passenger after reaching maximum deflection. The latter behavior is produced by a force-deflection curve in which the force drops rapidly to zero once the relative velocity of the passenger with respect to the constraint vanishes. While such behavior cuts SI in half, it produces a very large forward pulse of jerk ($\overset{\cdots}{x}$), because the deceleration of the passenger reaches a maximum at the moment his velocity reaches zero. The effect is commonly felt in vehicles which brake to a halt at a constant braking rate (constant deceleration). At the instant the vehicle stops, the passengers suddenly lurch forward. In a collision with a constraint, the passenger is pressed against the constraint at the instant the motion of the passenger with respect to the vehicle stops, but forward motion is not needed for a sudden pulse of jerk to be felt. If it is true, however, that the duration of the pulse is the critical factor, then dropping the force suddenly to zero when $x = 0$ may be acceptable and has the advantage of not causing the passenger to be thrown backward. If, in a maximum collision, in which the acceleration and jerk limits are both reached during forward motion of the passenger with respect to the constraint, the limits are not to be exceeded on the return stroke, then the force-deflection curve (figure 7-7) cannot fall at a steeper slope than it rises, and the dashboard must retain a completely linear character. However, as compared to a constraint that returns no energy to the passenger, such a zero-hysteresis dashboard doubles the Severity Index and in addition throws the passenger backward. The SI and the throw-back phenomenon are reduced in a compromise solution in which the constraint is built somewhat thicker and also retains a significant amount of hysteresis. Equation (7.5.8), shows that, with a given V_{cp}, increasing the permissible deflection reduces ω_n, and therefore, from equations (7.5.3), (7.5.5), and (7.5.10), reduces the maximum acceleration, jerk, and SI, respectively.

Consider again equation (7.5.10). From equation (7.5.6) and the discussion below it substitute $\omega_n = 40 \, \text{rad/s}$. Also, let $g = 10 \, \text{m/s}^2$, and based on the above discussion, let $\nu = \pi/2$, but multiply the integral by 1.25 to allow for some hysteresis. Then, performing the integration numerically.

$$\text{SI} = 0.8 V_{cp}^{2.5}(1.25)\int_0^{\pi/2} \sin^{2.5}\tau \, d\tau$$

$$= 0.74 V_{cp}^{2.5} \qquad (7.5.11)$$

in which V_{cp} has units of meters per second. Solving for V_{cp}, equation (7.5.11) becomes

$$(V_{cp})_{\text{max}} = [1.35(\text{SI})_{\text{max}}]^{0.4} \qquad (7.5.12)$$

If, as suggested in section 7.4, $(\text{SI})_{\text{max}} = 500 \, \text{s}$, $(V_{cp})_{\text{max}} = 13.5 \, \text{m/s}$. This limit holds only if it is smaller than the value of $(V_{cp})_{\text{max}}$ given by equation (7.5.8).

The Airbag

If the constraint device is an airbag, the time available for it to deploy fully is the time required for m to fall a height δ_{th} from rest. Thus

$$\text{Deployment time} = \sqrt{\frac{2\delta_{th}}{a_v}} \qquad (7.5.13)$$

For example, if $a_v = 10\,g = 100\,\text{m/s}^2$ and $\delta_{th} = 10\,\text{cm}$, the deployment time is 45 milliseconds. If the undeployed airbag is stored a distance δ_s from the passenger, the average velocity of the bag during deployment is

$$\text{Average bag velocity} = (\delta_s - \delta_{th}) \sqrt{\frac{a_v}{2\delta_{th}}} \qquad (7.5.14)$$

If $\delta_s = 1$ meter and the above parameters are used, the average bag velocity is 20 m/s, which is well below sonic velocity of 300 m/s. Therefore, with reasonable dimensions, ample time is available for airbag deployment without causing harmful pressure waves.

7.6 Safe Velocities of Collision between Vehicles

In section 7.5, we have determined the limiting value of the tolerable collision velocity V_{cp} of a passenger with a constraint device if injuries are to be avoided. The limit is given by equation (7.5.8) in terms of the maximum permissible values of acceleration, jerk, and constraint deflection, or by equation (7.5.12) in terms of the Severity Index. The actual limit is of course the smaller of the values computed by these two formulas. To complete solution of the problem of requirements for a safe design, it is necessary to relate V_{cp} to the collision velocity between vehicles, V_{cv}. This relationship depends on the throw distance δ_{th} between the passenger and the padded surface at the moment of impact, the total stroke $2\delta_{sa}$ of the shock absorbers between vehicles, and the ratio m_2/m_1 of the masses of the two colliding vehicles.

The situation is shown in figure 7-9, in which it is assumed that the passengers are forward facing and seated. The two vehicles collide at $t = 0$. The passengers in the rear vehicle are thrown forward with respect to the vehicle, and the passengers in the forward vehicle are pressed into their seats. If the passengers face the rear, the situation of the passengers in the two vehicles is reversed in a collision between vehicles of the same mass. In a collision with a fixed barrier, the passengers are better protected if facing the rear, but preference for forward facing seats and the very low probability of a fixed barrier collision in a thoughtfully designed system lead us to assume forward-facing seats. If constant force shock absorbers are used, the velocity-time lines during collision are straight and the shaded area represents the total stroke of the shock absorbers, $2\delta_{sa}$, where δ_{sa} is given by equation (7.3.7). If, as recommended in section 7.3, constant force, constant deflection shock absorbers are used, δ_{sa} is a parameter, and the deceleration of the rear vehicle is

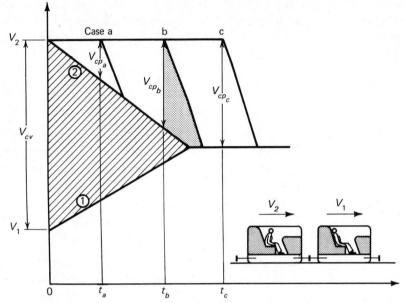

Figure 7-9. Velocity-Time Diagram of Vehicle and an Unconstrained Passenger during a Collision

$$a_v = a_2 = \frac{2F_p}{m_2} = \frac{V_{cv}^2}{2(2\delta_{sa})} \frac{1}{(1 + m_2/m_1)} \qquad (7.6.1)$$

in which, consistent with section 7.3, it is assumed that two side-by-side shock absorbers are placed on the front and rear of each vehicle.

In reference[9], it was shown that remarkably good accuracy in predicting the deceleration of the passenger during collision is obtained by assuming one-dimensional motion. At $t = 0$, the passenger, of mass m, is assumed to continue moving at velocity V_2 until collision with a constraint device occurs. If the throw distance δ_{th} is short, the passenger collides with the dash at a time such as t_a or t_b, while vehicle 2 is still decelerating. In this case, the collision velocity V_{cp} of the passenger with the dash is given by equation (7.5.1). If the throw distance δ_{th} is long, the passenger collides with the dash at a time such as t_c, after vehicle 2 and vehicle 1 reach the same velocity, and $a_v = 0$ during the collision. In this case, $V_{cp} = V_{cv} - V_f$, where V_f is given by equation (7.3.4). Thus

$$V_{cp} = V_{cv} \frac{1}{(1 + m_2/m_1)} \qquad (a)$$

Suppose first that the tolerance limit for avoidance of injury is dependent upon the acceleration and jerk limits of section 7.4. Then, the relationship between V_{cv} and the length parameters δ_{th}, δ_{sa}, and $\delta_{cd} = |x|_{max}$ is based upon equation (7.5.8). Once squared, this equation may be written in the form

$$V_{cp}^2 + 2a_v\delta_{cd} = \omega_n^2\delta_{cd}^2 \qquad \text{Case a}$$

$$V_{cp} = \omega_n\delta_{cd} \qquad \text{Case c}$$

$$\left. \begin{array}{c} \\ \\ \end{array} \right\} \quad \text{(b)}$$

in which δ_{cd}, a newly defined parameter, is the maximum deflection of the constraint device. For small throw distance, δ_{th}, V_{cp} is given by equation (7.5.1). Using this equation to eliminate V_{cp} from equation (b), Case a, and equation (7.6.1) to eliminate a_v, we obtain

$$V_{cv} = \omega_n\delta_{cd}(1 + m_2/m_1)^{1/2}[2\delta_{sa}/(\delta_{th} + \delta_{cd})]^{1/2} \qquad \text{(small } \delta_{th}, \text{ Case a)}$$
$$(7.6.2)$$

For large throw distance, δ_{th}, V_{cp} is given by equation (a) and the second form of equation (b) applies. Eliminating V_{cp} between these equations,

$$V_{cv} = \omega_n\delta_{cd}(1 + m_2/m_1) \qquad \text{(large } \delta_{th}, \text{ Case c)} \qquad (7.6.3)$$

The way equations (7.6.2) and (7.6.3) are to be interpreted is that V_{cv} is the maximum permissible collision velocity if δ_{cd} is the maximum available constraint deflection. On the other hand, for fixed δ_{cd} and δ_{sa} it is seen that larger V_{cv} than given by equation (7.6.3) can be tolerated if (see equation (7.6.2)) the throw distance δ_{th} is small enough so that

$$2\delta_{sa}/(\delta_{th} + \delta_{cd}) > 1 + m_2/m_1 \qquad (7.6.4)$$

This relationship can hold if δ_{sa}/δ_{cd} is larger than approximately one. To increase the tolerable collision velocity over that produced in case c, figure 7-9, it is necessary, for m_2 to be approximately equal to m_1, for the shock absorber length on one vehicle to be longer than the sum of the throw distance and the available constraint device deflection.

The above theory treats only Cases a and c in figure 7-9. In Case b, the vehicle is decelerating for only part of the period of collision. Thus the dotted area in figure 7-9, which represents δ_{cd}, is smaller than if the vehicle decelerated throughout the entire collision period. Thus, with a given δ_{cd}, V_{cv} could have been larger than if calculated by equation (7.6.2). Hence using equation (7.6.2) as an approximation for Case b is conservative.

In a collision between two vehicles of approximately the same mass, the situation is most severe if the rear vehicle (with forward-facing seats) is somewhat heavier than the forward vehicle. Thus, for collisions between two vehicles, let $m_2/m_1 = 0.9$. Then equations (7.6.2) and (7.6.3) become

$$V_{cv} = 1.95 \, \omega_n \delta_{cd} [\delta_{sa}/(\delta_{th} + \delta_{cd})]^{1/2} \qquad \text{(small } \delta_{th})$$

$$V_{cv} = 1.9 \, \omega_n \delta_{cd} \qquad \text{(large } \delta_{th})$$

$$(7.6.5)$$

In a collision with a fixed barrier, $m_2/m_1 = 0$, but there is no vehicle 1 to absorb half the energy. Thus, the total shock-absorber deflection is the deflection of the shock absorbers on vehicle 2. To take this into account replace $2\delta_{sa}$ by δ_{sa}. Then, for fixed barrier collisions,

$$V_{cv} = \omega_n \delta_{cd} [\delta_{sa}/(\delta_{th} + \delta_{cd})]^{1/2} \qquad \text{(small } \delta_{th})$$

$$V_{cv} = \omega_n \delta_{cd} \qquad \text{(large } \delta_{th})$$

$$(7.6.6)$$

Equations (7.6.5) and (7.6.6) determine the maximum permissible values of V_{cv} based on acceleration and jerk limits. Before discussing the results, it is necessary to determine the range of V_{cv} for which the Severity Index is below a specified maximum. The maximum value of V_{cp} in terms of SI is given by equation (7.5.12). For short throw distances, the relationship between V_{cp} and V_{cv} is found by substituting $2a_v$ from equation (7.6.1) into equation (7.5.1). Then

$$V_{cv} = V_{cp} \sqrt{2\left(1 + \frac{m_2}{m_1}\right) \frac{\delta_{sa}}{\delta_{th}}} \qquad \text{(small } \delta_{th}) \qquad (7.6.7)$$

(If $m_2/m_1 = 0$, replace $2\delta_{sa}$ by δ_{sa}.)

For long throw distances, the corresponding relationship is equation (a). Thus

$$V_{cv} = V_{cp}(1 + m_2/m_1) \qquad \text{(large } \delta_{th}) \qquad (7.6.8)$$

If V_{cp} from equation (7.5.12) is substituted into equations (7.6.7) and (7.6.8), the limit values of V_{cv} corresponding to the limit in SI can be found. Thus, for $m_2/m_1 = 0.9$,

$$V_{cv} = 2.20 \, (\delta_{sa}/\delta_{th})^{1/2}(\text{SI})_{max}^{0.4} \qquad \text{(small } \delta_{th})$$

$$= 2.14 \, (\text{SI})_{max}^{0.4} \qquad \text{(large } \delta_{th})$$

$$(7.6.9)$$

For $m_2/m_1 = 0$

$$V_{cv} = 1.59\ (\delta_{sa}/\delta_{th})^{1/2}(SI)_{max}{}^{0.4} \qquad \text{(small } \delta_{th})$$

$$= 1.13\ (SI)_{max}{}^{0.4} \qquad \text{(large } \delta_{th})$$

$$\left.\phantom{\begin{array}{c}a\\a\end{array}}\right\} (7.6.10)$$

Assuming, from section 7.4, a maximum value of $(SI)_{max} = 500$ s, equations (7.6.9) and (7.6.10) become

		m_2/m_1	δ_{th}
V_{cv}	$= 26.4\ (\delta_{sa}/\delta_{th})^{1/2}$m/s	0.9	small
	$= 25.7$ m/s	0.9	large
V_{cv}	$= 19.1(\delta_{sa}/\delta_{th})^{1/2}$m/s	0	small
	$= 13.6$m/s	0	large

Now we are in a position to summarize the results. As indicated following equation (7.5.6), set $\omega_n = 40$ rad/s, and recall from the remark above equation (7.5.10) that the SI computation, of necessity, neglects a_v compared with $V_{cp}\omega_n$. This condition is most likely to be met when δ_{th} is large. When δ_{th} is small, neglect of the a_v term is seen, by following the derivation of equation (7.5.10), to overestimate SI if $\nu = \pi/2$ and underestimate SI if $\nu = \pi$. Without more detailed analysis the best that can be said is to assume SI is in error if δ_{th} is small in an amount dependent on the parameter $a_v/V_{cp}\omega_n$. With these caveats, the results are as follows:

1. Collisions with similar vehicles ($m_2/m_1 = 0.9$).
   a. Large δ_{th}
      V_{cv} is the smaller of $76\delta_{cd}$ or 25.7 m/s. Thus acceleration and jerk limit V_{cv} if $\delta_{cd} < 34$ cm, a relation which in most practical cases must hold.
   b. Small δ_{th}
      V_{cd} is the smaller of

$$78\delta_{cd}[\delta_{sa}/(\delta_{th} + \delta_{cd})]^{1/2} \text{ or } 26.4(\delta_{sa}/\delta_{th})^{1/2}\text{m/s}$$

   If the second value is close to the first, the exact integration of equation (7.4.1) should be used.
2. Collisions with an immovable barrier ($m_2/m_1 = 0$).
   a. Large δ_{th}
      V_{cv} is the smaller of $40\delta_{cd}$ or 13.6 m/s.
      Thus the acceleration and jerk again limit V_{cv} if $\delta_{cd} < 34$ cm.

b. Small δ_{th}

V_{cv} is the smaller of

$$40\delta_{cd}[\delta_{sa}/(\delta_{th} + \delta_{cd})]^{1/2} \text{ or } 19.1 \, (\delta_{sa}/\delta_{th})^{1/2}\text{m/s}.$$

Consider the physical significance of these results. If the constraint device is a fixed padded dashboard, assume that a maximum practical $\delta_{cd} = 15$ cm. Then for $m_2/m_1 = 0.9$ and large throw distance, V_{cv} must be restricted to below 11.4 m/s. Thus, if the line speed is below this value and the worst collision is a vehicle moving at line speed colliding with a similar vehicle standing still, a fixed padded dashboard provides adequate protection. If fixed barrier collisions are possible, it must be possible to slow the vehicle to 6 m/s before collision.

If higher line speeds are to be used, adequate protection requires smaller δ_{th} than possible with a fixed padded dashboard. Assume the constraint device is a seat/shoulder harness. Then $\delta_{th} \approx 0$ and, if $m_2/m_1 = 0.9$,

$$(V_{cv})_{\max} = 78(\delta_{cd}\delta_{sa})^{1/2}\text{m/s} \tag{7.6.11}$$

In this case, δ_{cd} is the maximum stretch of the seat/shoulder harness. Assume $(\delta_{cd})_{\max} = 30$ cm. Then $(V_{cv})_{\max} = 42.7 \, \delta^{1/2}_{sa}\text{m/s}$. If $\delta_{sa} = 0.5$ m, values of V_{cv} up to 30 m/s or 67 mi/hr can be sustained without injury if the vehicle is not crushed. Check the SI criterion. In this case, $V_{cp} = 0$, therefore integration of equation (7.4.1) should be based on the second term of equation (7.5.2). Substituting into equation (7.4.1), the result may be written in the form

$$(V_{cv})_{\max} = [4\delta_{sa}g(1 + m_2/m_1)]^{1/2}(\omega_n\text{SI}/\textstyle\int\cos^{2.5} d\tau)^{0.2}$$

$$= 48.7[\delta_{sa}(1 + m_2/m_1)]^{1/2} \tag{7.6.12}$$

for values used above. Then if $m_2/m_1 = 0.9$ and $\delta_{sa} = 0.5$ m, $(V_{cv})_{\max} = 47.5$ m/s. Since this is greater than 30 m/s, computed above, $(V_{cv})_{\max}$ is still determined by the acceleration and jerk criterion.

If the constraint device is an airbag, δ_{th} is not zero but a few centimeters, and δ_{cd} may be larger. In this case $(V_{cv})_{\max}$ may be somewhat larger.

If the collision is with a fixed barrier and we wish $(V_{cv})_{\max} = 30$ m/s, then if $\delta_{cd} \approx 30$ cm and $\delta_{th} << \delta_{cd}$, we have

$$30 = 40(0.3 \, \delta_{sa})^{1/2}$$

so that we must have $\delta_{sa} \geq 1.88$ m. Since this is generally impractically long, it is impractical to provide protection in fixed barrier collisions at 30 m/s.

The advantage of the airbag in severe collisions, but the undesirability of deploying it in mild collisions suggests a solution in which the airbag is triggered, for example, by a pressure device attached to the hydraulic cylinder of the shock absorbers at a given pressure, and hence given deceleration level. For a given stroke, δ_{sa}, deceleration level, and mass ratio, equation (7.6.1) determines the value of V_{cv} at which the airbag is deployed. The corresponding pressure differential is then given by equation (7.3.1). Because an oblique collision may not involve the shock absorber, the airbag may be triggered by an inexpensive accelerometer designed to actuate at a given rate of deceleration, again determined by equation (7.6.1).

7.7 Oblique Collisions

Because of the possibility of wedging vehicles into the guideway, the worst type of collision in a guideway transit system is an oblique collision. Fortunately, however, the probability of such a collision is very low. It is the product of three probabilities: (1) the probability of a sudden deceleration failure, (2) the probability of a simultaneous failure in a braking or failure detection system, and (3) the probability that both failures happen to occur at a merge point in the guideway. Nonetheless, it is prudent to be aware of the consequences of such a collision and the measures necessary to minimize the probability of injury to the passenger.

Consider a collision at a merge point as shown in figure 7-10. A vehicle of width w and velocity V traveling on a straight piece of track, the centerline of which is the x-axis, collides with a vehicle with the same width and velocity merging with it on a spiral section. From equation (3.2.11), the equation of the spiral is

$$y = \frac{J_n}{6V^3} x^3 \qquad (a)$$

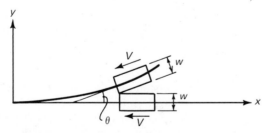

Figure 7-10. Geometry of an Oblique Collision

At the point of collision, $y \approx w$ because the angle of collision, θ, is small. For the same reason, θ is approximately

$$\theta \approx \frac{dy}{dx} = \frac{J_n}{2V^3} x^2 \qquad \text{(b)}$$

For $y = w$, solve equation (a) for x and substitute into equation (b). The result is

$$\theta = \frac{dy}{dx} \bigg|_{y=w} = \frac{3}{6^{1/3}} \frac{(J_n w^2)^{1/3}}{V} \qquad (7.7.1)$$

Assume each vehicle is equipped with crushable bumpers on the sides designed to compress an amount δ_y in an oblique collision at normal line speed V. When the side bumper on each vehicle has compressed an amount δ_y, the forward motion of both vehicles has stopped. Thus, the oblique collision is equivalent to a fore-aft fixed barrier collision in which the shock-absorber deflection δ_{sa}, using equation (7.7.1), is

$$\delta_{sa} = \frac{2\delta_y}{\theta} = 1.21 \frac{\delta_y V}{(J_n w^2)^{1/3}} \qquad (7.7.2)$$

For standing-passenger vehicles, $J_n = 1.25$ m/s² and $w = 2.4$ m. Thus $J_n w^2 = 7.2$. For seated-passenger vehicles $J_n = 2.5$ m/s² and $w \approx 1.7$ m. Again, $J_n w^2 = 7.2$. Thus equation (7.7.2) becomes

$$\delta_{sa} = 0.63\delta_y V \qquad (7.7.2a)$$

With this value of δ_{sa}, the maximum tolerable collision velocity V_{cv} can be found from the results of section 7.6 for the case of collision with an immovable barrier. For a given V, it is necessary to choose δ_y, δ_{th} and δ_{cd} so that $V_{cv} \leq V$.

7.8 Summary

Headway requirements for collision avoidance in on-line station systems depend on the kinematics of deceleration into stations, and was treated in section 4.2. In off-line station systems, the headway requirements for station flow can be determined by use of the same theory. Chapter 7, therefore, deals only with safe operation on line in off-line station systems.

It is divided into two parts. In the first part, section 7.2, the problem of the kinematic and design characteristics needed to avoid collisions in the presence of one major failure is treated. To determine these characteristics, two types of failure are treated: (1) the sudden deceleration, and (2) the sudden acceleration. Because it could be treated by the same approach, a third problem is treated: The failure of a vehicle to decelerate to a stop in a station when commanded. The result of analysis of the two types of on-line failures leads to the conclusion that the minimum headway for a given set of design characteristics is determined by the deceleration failure, not by the acceleration failure. The reason is that, in an economical design, the power available for acceleration at line speed will permit only about half the average acceleration to occur. Thus there is ample time to detect the failure and shut off the power before a collision occurs.

In a deceleration failure the minimum headway depends on the choice of design characteristics. The first choice is between constant force braking and constant, controlled deceleration braking. In the first case, variations in vehicle weight, wind, grade, and guideway coefficient of friction enter into the computation of minimum headway[5,8] and make the predicted minimum headway quite variable. If controlled deceleration braking is used by means of a feedback control mechanism, a more reliable and lower prediction of minimum headway is possible. If traction through the wheels is employed, the minimum headway is about four or five seconds if standing passengers are permitted, or about two or three seconds if all passengers must sit. If traction through wheels is replaced by linear electrical propulsion and braking, if care is taken in the design to eliminate causes of sudden stops (such as the locking of high friction wheels), and if advantage is taken of the electric braking to lower the overall time constant for application of the brakes to about one-tenth second or less, then the minimum headway reduces to less than one quarter second at 15 m/s.

If the emergency braking system fails to operate when one of the above types of failure occur, then it is not possible in general to avoid a collision. Thus, in the second part of chapter 7, the problem of determination of the design and kinematic conditions required to avoid injury to the occupants is considered. The basic design elements for minimization of injury are shock absorbers on the vehicle and passenger constraint mechanisms such as a padded dashboard, a seat/shoulder harness, or an airbag. The most efficient shock absorber is one that produces constant force throughout its displacement to minimize the length required and also produces full stroke for all collision velocities to cause the vehicle to decelerate at a rate no greater than needed. These characteristics can be attained by use of a variable orifice hydraulic shock absorber, the characteristics of which are developed in section 7.3. In section 7.4 criteria for avoidance of injury in terms of maximum deceleration, maximum jerk, and severity index are developed. With this background, the tolerable velocities of impact of the passenger with the constraint mechanism are developed in section 7.5, and it is shown that the force-deflection curve of these devices should be linear on the increase to avoid exceeding the jerk limit. In section 7.6, the tolerable range of collision velocities both between vehicles and with a fixed barrier are determined. The results are summarized at the end of section 7.6 in terms of three characteristic lengths: the throw distance between passenger and constraint mechanism, the deflection of the constraint mechanism, and the stroke of the shock absorber. The conclusions are that, if the constraint mechanism is a fixed padded dashboard, practical values of the above three lengths will permit collision without injury with a vehicle of ten percent greater mass if the collision velocity is below about 11 m/s. If an airbag or seat/shoulder harness is used, the safe collision velocity with a vehicle of ten percent greater mass increases to about 30 m/s. If the collision is with a fixed barrier, the limit collision velocities must be reduced to almost one half the above values. The final topic, treated in section 7.7, is the problem of oblique collisions. It is shown that such a collision is equal in severity to a fore-aft collision with a fixed barrier if the shock absorber stroke is equal to the lateral crushing capability of the vehicles divided by the collision angle. Since this angle is quite small (about 12 degrees), the equivalent shock absorber length is over one meter. At 10 m/s a fixed padded dashboard is an adequate constraint; however, at 15 m/s an airbag or seat/shoulder harness is needed.

References

1. Larry S. Bell, "Prevention of Crimes of Assault and Acts of Vandalism on Demand-Responsive Automated Transportation Systems," in *Personal Rapid Transit III*, Audio Visual Library Service, University of Minnesota, Minneapolis, Minn., 1976, p. 423.

2. H. Bernstein and A. Schmitt, "Emergency Strategies for Safe Close-Headway Operation of PRT Vehicles," in *Personal Rapid Transit*, Audio Visual Library Service, University of Minnesota, Minneapolis, Minn., 1972, p. 351.

3. D.E. Stepner, L.P. Hajdu, and A. Rahimi, "Safety Considerations for Personal Trapid Transit," in *Personal Rapid Transit*, op. cit., p. 451.

4. J.E. Anderson, "Theory of Design of PRT Systems for Safe Operation," *Personal Rapid Transit II*, Audio Visual Library Service, University of Minnesota, Minneapolis, Minn., 1974.

5. T.J. McGean, "Headway Limitations for Short Term People Mover Program," in *Personal Rapid Transit II*, op. cit., p. 349.

6. T.J. McGean, *Urban Transportation Technology*, Lexington Books, D.C. Heath and Company, Lexington, Mass., 1976.

7. E.J. Hinman and G.L. Pitts, "Practical Safety Considerations for Short-Headway Automated Transit Systems," in *Personal Rapid Transit II,* op. cit., p. 375.

8. David J. Lobsinger, "An Analysis of Minimum Safe Headway for No Collisions," in *Personal Rapid Transit II,* op. cit., p. 391.

9. W.L. Garrard, R.J. Caudill, and T.L. Rushfeldt, "Crashworthiness and Crash Survivability for Personal Rapid Transit Vehicles," in *Personal Rapid Transit II,* op. cit., p. 439.

10. W.L. Garrard, R. J. Caudill, and T.L. Rushfeldt, "Crashworthiness for High-Capacity Personal Rapid Transit Vehicles," Report No. MN-11-0037-74-1-UMTA (available from U.S. National Technical Information Service, Springfield, Va., PB 239-104/AS), October 1974.

11. T.J. McGean and N.W. Lutkefedder, "Application of Automotive Crash Survivability Research to Close-Headway PRT Systems," American Society of Mechanical Engineers Paper 73-ICT-52, September 1973.

12. P.M. Miller and N.E. Shoemaker, "Applicability of Automobile Crashworthiness Experiments to PRT Systems," in *Personal Rapid Transit II,* op. cit., p. 451.

13. D.F. Hays, and A.L. Brown, eds., *The Physics of Tire Traction—Theory and Experiment,* Plenum Press, New York, 1974.

14. *Skid Resistance,* National Cooperative Highway Research Program Report 14, National Research Council, Washington, D.C., 1972.

15. A.L. Kornhauser, P.M. Lion, P.J. McEvaddy, W.L. Garrard, "Optimal Sample-Data Control of PRT Vehicles," in *Personal Rapid Transit II,* op. cit., p. 362.

16. R.B. Fling and C.L. Olson, "An Integrated Concept for Propulsion, Braking, Control and Switching of Vehicles Operating at Close Headways," in *Personal Rapid Transit,* op. cit., p. 361.

17. *Lea Transit Compendium,* Vol. II, No. 4, N.D. Lea Transportation Research Corporation, Huntsville, Ala., 1975.

18. A.V. Munson, Jr., "Quasi-synchronous Control of High-Capacity PRT Networks," in *Personal Rapid Transit,* op. cit. p. 325.

19. H. Appel and J. Tomas, "The Energy Management Structure for the Volkswagen ESV," Society of Automotive Engineers Paper No. 730078, Warrendale, Pa.

20. S. Timoshenko, *Theory of Elastic Stability,* McGraw-Hill Book Company, New York, 1936.

21. A. Einstein, *The Meaning of Relativity,* Princeton University Press, Princeton, N.J., 1955, p. 57.

8

Life Cycle Cost and Reliability Allocation

8.1 Introduction

The life cycle cost of a system is the sum of the acquisition cost and the support cost. The acquisition cost is the purchase price plus the interest cost (see Appendix A); and the support cost is the cost of labor, equipment, spare parts, and the associated logistics required to operate the system and to keep it in operation during its useful life. Every chapter in this book deals directly or indirectly with the problem of minimization of the acquisition or support cost of transit systems, and it is found that the costs vary widely depending on the choice of a large number of parameters. In this chapter, the variation of the costs with subsystem reliability is considered.

In a given transit system, defined by the types of components used and the service provided, the acquisition cost will generally increase with the built-in reliability of the components and subsystems, as shown in figure 8-1. On the other hand, the support costs reduce as reliability increases

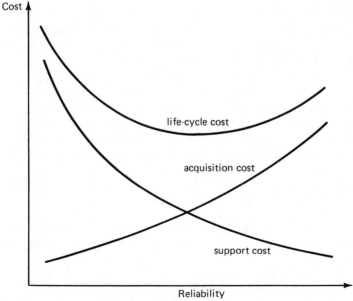

Figure 8-1. Life-Cycle Cost

203

because the frequency of maintenance declines. Thus the life cycle cost, as shown in figure 8-1, exhibits the character of a U-shaped curve with a single minimum point. Each subsystem, such as a motor, a controller, a braking system, or a wayside computer also possesses a similar life cycle cost curve. If each subsystem is designed so that its life cycle cost is minimum, the system life cycle cost is a minimum. If the system reliability is adequate at minimum life cycle cost, no further analysis is needed; however, the more usual situation is that in which system reliability must be increased. The problem then presents itself as to how to allocate subsystem reliabilities in such a way that the system life cycle cost is minimized at the required level of system reliability. This is a standard Lagrangian minimization problem, the solution of which is the main subject of this chapter. After completing this work, the author became aware that a similar approach had been developed by Everett[1]. The author's own original analysis of this problem has also been published.[2].

To solve the minimization problem in a meaningful way for transit systems, it is necessary to define a meaningful and accepted measure of system reliability, and to establish a means of classification of failures. System reliability is commonly measured in terms of "availability," and is treated in the next section. Classification of failures then follows.

8.2 Availability and Unavailability

Service availability in transit systems has been the subject of a great deal of analysis[3]; however, at the time of writing no completely accepted methodology has developed nor can it develop without considerably more operational experience with automated systems. Nonetheless, a logical formulation is possible which can be described in enough detail for the purpose of this chapter. The common definition of transit system availability is the ratio of the nominal trip time to the nominal trip plus the average time delay due to failures. To take into account variations in availability in various parts of the system at various times of day and on various days, the following definition of service availability A is more suitable:

$$A = \frac{PH_{yr}}{PH_{yr} + PHD_{yr}} \qquad (8.2.1)$$

in which PH_{yr} is the number of passenger-hours of travel per year on the transit system, and PHD_{yr} is the number of passenger-hours of delay due to failures per year.

Define "unavailability" as

$$\epsilon = \frac{PHD_{yr}}{PH_{yr}} \qquad (8.2.2)$$

In a perfect system, ϵ vanishes. If ϵ is much less than 1, as it must be if the system operates satisfactorily, equations (8.2.1) and (8.2.2) gives

$$A = \frac{1}{1 + \epsilon} \approx 1 - \epsilon \qquad (8.2.3)$$

Thus the sum of availability and unavailability is practically equal to one. Unavailability is the more useful measure of system performance because, as shown in section 8.5, it is the weighted sum of failure rates, and such a formulation is advantageous in the solution for the constrained minimum life cycle cost.

The quantity PH_{yr} can be expressed in the form

PH_{yr} = (Person-trips/yr)(Average trip time)
$\qquad$ = (Equivalent work days/yr)(Trips/work day) $<L_t>/V_{av}$

$$\approx 300t_d \frac{<L_t>}{V_{av}} \qquad (8.2.4)$$

in which t_d is the number of trips in an average work day, $<L_t>$ is the average trip length, and V_{av} is the average trip speed (see chapter 4). In the form given by equation (8.2.4), PH_{yr} is directly obtained from data normally available. A meaningful expression for PHD_{yr} depends upon the following definitions of subsystems and classes of failure.

8.3 Subsystems of an Automated Transit System

To make the analysis specific and therefore more meaningful, consider that an automated transit system will generally contain the types of equipment listed below:

Basic Components (without listed subsystems):
  1. Vehicles
  2. Guideways
  3. Stations

Vehicle Subsystems:
  1. Automatic vehicle door
  2. Propulsion system
  3. Control system including sensors and actuators
  4. Power conditioning and/or supply system
  5. Braking system

6. Switching system
7. Failure detection system

Wayside Subsystems:
1. Passenger processing equipment in stations (fare collection, destination selection, ticket vending, turnstiles)
2. Automatic station doors
3. Station entry monitors
4. Station-operated vehicle dispatchers
5. Merge point communication and control units
6. Diverge point communication and control units
7. Wayside switches
8. Wayside vehicle presence sensors
9. Wayside-to-vehicle, vehicle-to-wayside communication equipment
10. Central empty vehicle dispatcher
11. Central trip register and dispatcher
12. Central power supply

8.4 Classes of Failure

Each subsystem may, in general, fail in ways which produce different consequences in terms of the average number of passenger-hours of delay. These different modes of failure will be defined as different "classes of failure," and they need to be distinguished in this analysis in order to compute the number of passenger-hours of delay, and then the unavailability.

Some examples of classes of failure are the following:

Vehicle failure classes:
1. Vehicle is permitted to continue to nearest station, where passengers must egress. Vehicle is dispatched to maintenance. The number of passenger-hours of delay is the time lost by p_v passengers in transferring to second vehicle.
2. Vehicle is required to reduce speed but is permitted to continue to nearest station, where passengers must egress. Vehicle is dispatched to maintenance. The number of passenger-hours of delay is as computed in Class 1 plus time lost by people in a string of vehicles required to slow down while the failed vehicle advances to nearest station.
3. Vehicle stops or is required to stop and is pushed or towed by adjacent vehicle to nearest station. After people in the two affected vehicles egress, failed vehicle is pushed or towed to maintenance. The number of passenger-hours of delay is computed as in Class 2 but time delay is longer.

4. Vehicle stops and cannot be pushed or towed by adjacent vehicle. Must wait for rescue vehicle. The number of passenger-hours of delay is computed as in Class 3 but the total time delay is much longer and depends on the availability of alternative paths.

Merge point command and control unit failure classes:
1. Vehicles can proceed through merge point at reduced speed.
2. Vehicles must stop until unit is repaired.
3. Collision occurs.

Diverge point command and control unit failure classes:
1. Occasional vehicle is misdirected.
2. Entire stream of vehicles is misdirected.

8.5 Passenger-Hours of Delay per Year and Unavailability

Let

p = the number of different subsystems, as identified in section 8.3

q_i = the number of classes of failure of the ith type of subsystem

r_i = the number of i-type subsystem in the transit system

T_i = the number of hours the i-type subsystems are in service per year. If the subsystem is aboard a vehicle, T_i is the number of hours per year a vehicle is in service. Let this number be T_v. Typically T_v is about 10 hours/day times 300 days per year, or 3000 hours/year. If the subsystem is at wayside and the system operates 24 hours per day, $T_i = T_w = (24)(365) = 8760$ hours per year. If the system operates say six days a week and 18 hours per day, $T_w = 5616$ hours per year.

$MTBF_{ij}$ = mean time between failures of the ith class of the jth type of subsystem

The $MTBF$ of interest in transit systems is that which occurs due to random failures of maintained equipment. Unlike a spacecraft, a transit system can and should undergo periodic checks at a frequency greater by a factor of at least five than the failure rates to diagnose potential failures and to replace components that wear out. The time intervals between preventive diagnostics and maintenance are therefore short compared to the $MTBF$s. In this circumstance, the probability of failure in a given time increment is not strongly a function of time and can be assumed, in the service interval, to be random. Then the number of j-class failures per year of a piece of i-type equipment is simply $T_i/MTBF_{ij}$, and the total number of failures per year is

$$\sum_{i=1}^{p} \sum_{j=1}^{q_i} \frac{r_i T_i}{MTBF_{ij}}$$

Let τ_{ij} be the mean time delay of a person involved in a j-class failure of i-type equipment, and let n_{ij} be the mean number of people involved in such a failure. The $n_{ij}\tau_{ij}$ is the mean number of person-hours of delay due to a j-class failure of i-type equipment. Thus,

$$PHD_{yr} = \sum_{i=1}^{p} r_i T_i \sum_{j=1}^{q_i} \frac{n_{ij}\tau_{ij}}{MTBF_{ij}} \tag{8.5.1}$$

As indicated in the definition of T_i, there are generally two values for T_i, T_v for vehicle-borne equipment and T_w for wayside equipment. If there are N_v vehicles in the system, equation (8.5.1) can be written

$$PHD_{yr} = N_v T_v \sum_{i=1}^{p_{vs}} \sum_{j=1}^{q_i} \frac{n_{ij}\tau_{ij}}{MTBF_{ij}} + T_w \sum_{i=p_{vs}+1}^{p} r_i \sum_{j=1}^{q_i} \frac{n_{ij}\tau_{ij}}{MTBF_{ij}}$$

$$\tag{8.5.2}$$

in which p_{vs} is the number of types of vehicle-borne subsystems, and $p_{ws} = p - p_{vs}$ is the number of wayside subsystems. The unavailability is now obtained by substituting equations (8.2.4) and (8.5.2) into equation (8.2.2)

8.6 The Constrained Minimum Life Cycle Cost

The life cycle cost of a system is the sum of the installed costs of all subsystems plus the sum of the operating and maintenance (support) cost of all subsystems. Thus it is possible to express the life cycle cost (LCC) in the form

$$LCC = N_v \sum_{i=1}^{p_{vs}} LCC_i(x_{ij}) + \sum_{i=p_{vs}+1}^{p} r_i LCC_i(x_{ij}) \tag{8.6.1}$$

in which $x_{ij} \equiv MTBF_{ij}$ and the functional dependence of subsystem life cycle cost on reliability is explicitly indicated, that is, LCC_i is a function of the $MTBF$s for all classes of failure associated with i-type subsystems.

The problem posed is to minimize LCC subject to a constraint—the given value of ϵ, where ϵ is a function of all x_{ij}. To find the constrained minimum, a problem first solved by the French mathematician Lagrange (1736-1813), assume that ϵ is solved for one of the x_{ij}, say x_{mn}. Then, in principle, substitute x_{mn}, a function of all of the other x_{ij}, into LCC. In this case, the condition that LCC is minimum is

$$\frac{\partial LCC}{\partial x_{ij}} + \frac{\partial LCC}{\partial x_{mn}} \frac{\partial x_{mn}}{\partial x_{ij}} = 0 \qquad (8.6.2)$$

in which i and j take all values in the ranges $j = 1, ..., q_i$ and $i = 1, ..., p$ except for the single combination of values $i = m, j = n$. Since $\epsilon = \epsilon(x_{ij})$ is a given constant,

$$\frac{\partial \epsilon}{\partial x_{ij}} + \frac{\partial \epsilon}{\partial x_{mn}} \frac{\partial x_{mn}}{\partial x_{ij}} = 0 \qquad (8.6.3)$$

for all i, j except m, n.

Place the right-hand term in each of equations (8.6.2) and (8.6.3) on the right side of the equal sign and divide equation (8.6.2) by equation (8.6.3). The result can be expressed in the form

$$\frac{\dfrac{\partial LCC}{\partial x_{ij}}}{\dfrac{\partial \epsilon}{\partial x_{ij}}} = \frac{\dfrac{\partial LCC}{\partial x_{mn}}}{\dfrac{\partial \epsilon}{\partial x_{mn}}} = -\Lambda \qquad (8.6.4)$$

in which, because x_{mn} could be any of the x_{ij}, Λ has the same value for all ij. The constant Λ is called a Lagrangian multiplier.

From equation (8.6.1),

$$\frac{\partial LCC}{\partial x_{ij}} = r_i \frac{\partial LCC_i}{\partial x_{ij}} \qquad (a)$$

in which $r_i = N_v$ if the index corresponds to a vehicle subsystem. Similarly, from equation (8.2.2) and (8.5.1) ($x_{ij} \equiv MTBF_{ij}$),

$$\frac{\partial \epsilon}{\partial x_{ij}} = -\frac{r_i T_i n_{ij} \tau_{ij}}{PH_{yr} x_{ij}^2} \qquad (b)$$

Substituting equations (a) and (b) into equation (8.6.4), the Lagrangian multiplier becomes

$$\Lambda = \left(\frac{PH_{yr}/T_i}{n_{ij}\tau_{ij}} \right) MTBF^2_{ij} \frac{\partial LCC_i}{\partial MTBF_{ij}} \qquad (8.6.5)$$

in which the substitution $x_{ij} \equiv MTBF_{ij}$ has been made, and $T_i = T_v$ or T_w depending on the location of the equipment. The solution to the problem of the constrained minimum life cycle cost is determined by the condition that the quantity defined by the right side of equation (8.6.5) is the same for all failure classes of all subsystems.

Equation (8.6.5) contains three kinds of factors:

(1) PH_{yr}/T_i is the number of person-hours of travel on the system per hour of operation of i-type equipment, a factor determined from an understanding of the physical characteristics of the system and from an estimate of patronage.

(2) $n_{ij}\tau_{ij}$ is the number of person-hours of delay due to a j-class failure of i-type equipment. It is a matrix of values determined from classification of all failure modes, from estimation of the mean delay time due to each failure mode, and from estimation of the mean number of people involved in each failure mode. The latter factor, n_{ij}, is proportional to patronage, but since PH_{yr} is also proportional to patronage (see equation (8.2.4)), Λ is independent of patronage.

(3) The remaining factor in equation (8.6.5) depends on the reliability-cost relationship for each subsystem and is determined separately for each. The character of the function $\Lambda(MTBF)$ may be seen with the help of figure 8-1. When the slope of the life cycle cost curve is zero, $\Lambda = 0$. The solution lies to the right of this point since one would not consciously pay more for less reliability. The function $\Lambda(MTBF)$ is monotone increasing to the right of $\Lambda = 0$ if $\partial\Lambda/\partial MTBF > 0$ there. If $\Lambda(MTBF)$ is monotone increasing, it possesses a unique inverse $MTBF(\Lambda)$ and, as we will see, the problem of the constrained minimum life cycle cost has a straightforward and unique solution. To determine if $\Lambda(MTBF)$ is monotone increasing, consider the derivative of equation (8.6.5):

$$\frac{\partial\Lambda}{\partial MTBF_{ij}} = \left(\frac{PH_{yr}/T_i}{n_{ij}\tau_{ij}} \right) MTBF_{ij} \left(2 \frac{\partial LCC_i}{\partial MTBF_{ij}} + MTBF_{ij} \frac{\partial^2 LCC_i}{\partial MTBF^2_{ij}} \right)$$

Thus, $\partial\Lambda/\partial MTBF_{ij} > 0$ and possesses a unique inverse if both the slope and curvature of the function $LCC_i(MTBF_{ij})$ are positive, as is shown in figure

8-1. Since it likely that LCC_i approaches infinity as $MTBF_{ij}$ approaches infinity, it is unlikely that $\partial^2 LCC_i / \partial MTBF^2_{ij}$ is ever negative, but even if it is, the curve $\Lambda(MTBF_{ij})$ is still monotone increasing if

$$\frac{\partial LCC_i}{\partial MTBF_{ij}} > \frac{MTBF_{ij}}{2} \left| \frac{\partial^2 LCC_i}{\partial MTBF^2_{ij}} \right|$$

Without more information on the functions $LCC(MTBF)$ it is not possible to prove rigorously that the above inequality always holds, but it seems highly plausible and will be assumed in the following analysis. Thus it will be assumed that $\Lambda(MTBF)$ possesses a unique inverse $MTBF(\Lambda)$ as shown in figure 8-2, but to cover contingencies, it will be assumed that if $MTBF(\Lambda)$ is not unique the lowest value is to be used. Thus, as shown in figure 8-2, if Λ is plotted as a function of $MTBF_{ij}$ for each failure class of each subsystem, the optimum value of each $MTBF_{ij}$ for the minimization of system life cycle cost can be found if the solution value of Λ for the entire system is found.

The system value of Λ is found by satisfying the given constraint on system unavailability. Combining equations (8.2.2) and (8.5.1), we can now write

$$\epsilon(\Lambda) = \frac{1}{PH_{yr}} \sum_{i=1}^{p} r_i T_i \sum_{j=1}^{q_i} \frac{n_{ij} \tau_{ij}}{MTBF_{ij}(\Lambda)} \qquad (8.6.6)$$

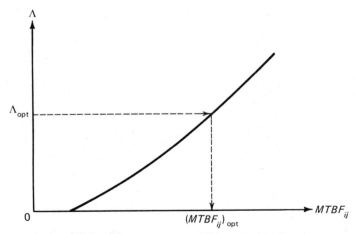

Figure 8-2. The Lagrangian Multiplier

in which the functional dependence of $MTBF_{ij}$ and hence of ϵ on Λ is indicated. Thus, the solution proceeds as follows: For each failure mode of each subsystem, $\Lambda(MTBF_{ij})$ is found and plotted. The inverse functions $MTBF_{ij}(\Lambda)$ are found from curves such as figure 8-2 and are used to compute the system curve $\epsilon(\Lambda)$ from equation (8.6.6). As indicated in figure 8-3, ϵ is maximum at $\Lambda = 0$ in the domain $\Lambda \geq 0$ and is monotone decreasing as Λ increases. The latter conclusion is a direct result of the facts (1) that all $MTBF_{ij}$ increases as Λ increases (see figure 8-2) and (2) that $\epsilon(\Lambda)$ is a sum of reciprocals of the $MTBF_{ij}$ (see equation (8.6.6)).

If $\epsilon_{\text{spec}} \geq \epsilon(0)$, where ϵ_{spec} is the specified level of system unavailability, $\Lambda = 0$ and the solution is obtained by setting all $MTBF_{ij}$ such that all $\partial LCC_i / \partial MTBF_{ij} = 0$. In the usual case, however, $\epsilon_{\text{spec}} < \epsilon(0)$. Then, as indicated in figure 8-3, the specified value of system unavailability yields a unique value $\Lambda = \Lambda_{\text{opt}}$. By entering the family of curves of Λ versus $MTBF_{ij}$ with Λ_{opt}, a unique set of values of $(MTBF_{ij})_{\text{opt}}$ are found. These values minimize system life cycle cost subject to the specified level of system unavailability.

If a given subsystem has only one class of failure there is a single set of curves like figure 8-1 for that subsystem. If in a certain subsystem there is more than one class of failure, it is implied in the above minimization process that it is possible to derive the curve $LCC_i(MTBF_{ij})$ for one particular value of j while holding the $MTBF_{ij}$ for all other j constant. It is not clear that this would always be possible, but if not, the implication would appear to be that the definition of subsystems must be further broken down.

Certainly the curves of LCC versus $MTBF$ are not easily obtained in the early phases of a design. Preliminary reliability allocations are, however,

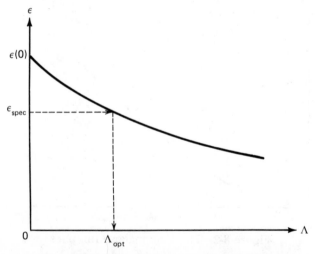

Figure 8-3. The System Constraint Function

necessary if a rational design is to ensue. Therefore, *LCC* versus *MTBF* curves must be estimated in successively more detail by a three-step process:

1. Parametric analysis of costs as functions of various system parameters
2. Refinement of costs by analogy with similar systems
3. Engineering cost analysis based on detailed designs

Out of such analysis, increasing refinement of the functions $\partial LCC_i/\partial MTBF_{ij}$ can be made, but at increasing engineering cost. As indicated in the next section, a preliminary allocation of subsystem *MTBF*s can be made without life cycle cost data; then, in section 8.8, it is shown how to obtain the next level of approximation based on preliminary values of $\partial LCC_i/\partial MTBF_{ij}$.

8.7 Approximate Solution to the Problem of Reliability Allocation

Equation (8.6.6) suggests the preliminary assumption

$$MTBF_{mn} = Cn_{mn}\tau_{mn} \qquad \text{(a)}$$

in which C is a constant and, to avoid confusion later, the dummy subscripts have been changed. This formula suggests that the *MTBF*s be allocated in proportion to the number of person-hours of delay due to a particular kind of failure. The constant C can be found by substituting equation (a) into equation (8.6.6). Thus

$$C = \frac{1}{\epsilon_{spec}PH_{yr}} \sum_{i=1}^{p} r_i T_i q_i \qquad \text{(b)}$$

Substituting equation (b) into equation (a)

$$MTBF_{mn} = \frac{n_{mn}\tau_{mn}}{\epsilon_{spec}} \frac{N_v T_v}{PH_{yr}} \sum \qquad \text{(c)}$$

in which

$$\sum = \sum_{i=1}^{p_{vs}} q_i + \frac{T_w}{T_v} \frac{1}{N_v} \sum_{i=p_{vs}+1}^{p} r_i q_i \qquad \text{(8.7.1)}$$

is the sum of the total number of failure classes defined for vehicle subsystems plus a weighting factor times the number of failure classes in all wayside subsystems.

In many cases n_{mn} can be expressed in the form

$$n_{mn} = \dot{n}_m \tau_{mn} \tag{8.7.2}$$

in which $\dot{n}_m$ is the mean flow of people involved in a failure of subsystem m. (Cases in which n_{mn} is not proportional to a flow are of lesser importance to system availability and, in any case, can be treated simply by substituting n_{mn} for $\dot{n}_m \tau_{mn}$.) Thus, equation (c) becomes

$$MTBF_{mn} = \frac{\dot{n}_m \tau_{mn}^2}{\epsilon_{spec}} \frac{N_v T_v}{PH_{yr}} \sum \tag{8.7.3}$$

The strong dependence of the required reliability on the time delay due to failure, τ_{mn}, is clearly evident from equation (8.7.3), thus indicating the importance of developing operational strategies in which failures can be cleared as quickly as possible. Since $\dot{n}_m$, N_v, and PH_{yr} are all proportional to patronage, the required $MTBF$ is proportional to patronage, a conclusion that is intuitively reasonable. Also, equation (8.7.3) shows that, for a given patronage, if N_v increases due to use of smaller vehicles, $MTBF_{mn}$ increases unless by design changes τ_{mn} is decreased enough so that the product $N_v \tau_{mn}^2$ does not change. Thus, if τ_{mn} varies as $N_v^{-1/2}$ the reliability requirements do not worsen in small-vehicle systems.

8.8. Approximate Solution to the Problems of Minimization of Life Cycle Cost and Reliability Allocation

Equation (8.7.3) allocates the reliability requirements in proportion to the number of person-hours of delay due to each type of failure, but makes no allowance for the possibility that the life cycle costs of some subsystems may change more rapidly with $MTBF$ than others. To account in as simple a way as possible for such variations, assume in equation (8.6.5) that, in the region of interest, the slopes of the curves of LCC_i versus $MTBF_{ij}$ are constant, that is, independent of $MTBF_{ij}$. Then equation (8.6.5) can be solved for $MTBF_{ij}$:

$$MTBF_{ij} = \left(\frac{n_{ij} \tau_{ij}}{LCC'_{ij}} \frac{T_i \Lambda}{PH_{yr}} \right)^{1/2} \tag{8.8.1}$$

in which

$$LCC'_{ij} \equiv \frac{\partial LCC_i}{\partial MTBF_{ij}}$$

If equation (8.8.1) is substituted into equation (8.6.6), the result can be solved for $\Lambda^{1/2}$. Thus

$$\Lambda_{\text{opt}}^{1/2} = \frac{1}{\epsilon_{\text{spec}}PH_{\text{yr}}^{1/2}} \sum_{i=1}^{p} r_i T_i^{1/2} \sum_{j=1}^{q_i} (n_{ij}\tau_{ij}LCC'_{ij})^{1/2} \qquad (8.8.2)$$

On substituting equation (8.8.2) into equation (8.8.1) and changing the dummy indices i,j to m,n in equation (8.8.1), the MTBFs are seen to be allocated according to the equation

$$MTBF_{mn} = \frac{n_{mn}\tau_{mn}}{\epsilon_{\text{spec}}} \frac{N_v T_v}{PH_{\text{yr}}} \sum_{mn} \qquad (8.8.3)$$

in which

$$\sum_{mn} = \left(\frac{T_m}{T_v}\right)^{1/2} \sum_{i=1}^{p_{vs}} \sum_{j=1}^{q_i} \left(\frac{n_{ij}\tau_{ij}}{n_{mn}\tau_{mn}} \frac{LCC'_{ij}}{LCC'_{mn}}\right)^{1/2}$$

$$+ \frac{(T_m T_w)^{1/2}}{T_v} \sum_{i=p_{vs}+1}^{p} \frac{r_i}{N_v} \sum_{j=1}^{q_i} \left(\frac{n_{ij}\tau_{ij}}{n_{mn}\tau_{mn}} \frac{LCC'_{ij}}{LCC'_{mn}}\right)^{1/2}$$

$$(8.8.4)$$

If subscript m corresponds to a vehicle subsystem, $T_m = T_v$ and the second double summation, dependent on the wayside subsystems, is weighted by the ratio $(T_w/T_v)^{1/2}$, which is greater than one if T_w is greater than T_v. If subscript m corresponds to a wayside subsystem, $T_m = T_w$ and $(T_w/T_v)^{1/2}$ factors out of equation (8.8.4). The second double sum is again weighted with respect to the first by the factor $(T_w/T_v)^{1/2}$. As indicated in section 8.5, in most cases $(T_w/T_v)^{1/2} \leqslant (8760/3000)^{1/2} = 1.7 > 1$. Thus the systems in operation longer weigh more heavily in determining the reliability requirements, as should be the case. It is also seen from equation

(8.8.4) that, since LCC'_{mn} is in the denominator, failure modes for which LCC increases more rapidly with $MTBF$ are allocated a smaller $MTBF$, the correct direction to minimize life cycle cost. Moreover, even without accounting for variations in LCC', equation (8.8.4) is more realistic than equation (8.7.1) in that failure modes for which $n_{ij}\tau_{ij}$ is larger weigh more heavily in determining the subsystem $MTBF$ requirements. Since the LCC' appear in equation (8.8.4) only under square-root signs, variations in the corresponding ratios have a diminished effect on the $MTBF$ requirements.

If all failure delay times are held constant except τ_{mn} and equation (8.7.2) can be used, $MTBF_{mn}$ is proportional to τ_{mn}, not to τ_{mn}^2 as is the case with equation (8.7.3); however, if all of the τ_{mn} are reduced in the same proportion, $MTBF_{mn}$ still reduces in proportion to τ_{mn}^2. If one of the τ_{ij} is large, all of the $MTBF_{mn}$ must suffer an increase in order to meet the specified system unavailability, ϵ_{spec}. This is clearly as it should be.

Note from equation (8.8.3) that, if equation (8.7.2) is substituted, $MTBF_{mn}$ is proportional to the ratio $\dot{n}_m/PH_{yr}$, that is, the ratio of flow rate in people per hour to person-hours of travel per year. This ratio is independent of patronage; however, N_v is proportional to patronage (see chapter 4). Therefore, the $MTBF$ requirements are proportional to patronage and to the number of vehicles in the system at a given patronage level. If the reliability requirements are not to increase in smaller vehicle systems (larger N_v), it is necessary that the operational control system be designed so that the squares of the delay times due to failures decrease in the same proportion as N_v increases, that is, that the product $N_v\tau_{mn}^2$ remain fixed. As the system size increases, PH_{yr} increases in proportion to N_v; therefore, the reliability requirements change as the system grows only insofar as the flow rates may be larger in a larger system.

Note in equation (8.8.3) that $MTBF_{mn}$ is inversely proportional to PH_{yr}. This may seem counterintuitive, but, from equation (8.2.2), at fixed ϵ an increase in PH_{yr} implies an increase in the number of person-hours of delay per year. An increase in the latter quantity clearly implies a decrease in $MTBF$ requirements.

8.9 Reliability Allocation in Sub-systems

A transit system is composed of vehicles, stations, wayside equipment, and central facilities. For the system as a whole, each of these systems is a subsystem. But a subsystem in this sense may be composed of "sub-subsystems." For example, if a vehicle is called a subsystem, its propulsion system, braking system, control system, and so forth, may be called "sub-subsystems." Each of these "sub-subsystems" can further be broken down into components or "sub-sub-subsystems." In application of the theory culiminating in equations (8.8.3, 8.8.4) the classification of subsystems is arbitrary. The user should, however, pick as "subsystems" the largest units for which specific failure consequences can be defined. Such a unit may be an entire vehicle because failures of its "subsystems" produce consequences such as defined in section 8.4 regardless of which "subsystem" failed. Similarly, several different types of station failures may cause identical consequences in terms of passenger delay. The requirement for selection of subsystems is that it be possible to derive a specific value of $n_{mn}\tau_{mn}$ for each of its classes of failure.

A "class of failure" may or may not be uniquely identified with a specific component or sub-subsystem failure. If it is, then the corresponding $MTBF_{mn}$ uniquely defines the required $MTBF$ of a specific component or subsystem. If not, any one of a number of failures can cause a failure of class "mn." In the latter case, one can write

$$MTBF^{-1}_{mn} = \sum_{k=1}^{K} MTBF^{-1}_{mnk} \qquad (8.9.1)$$

in which there are K "sub-subsystems" or components, the failure of any one of which will cause a failure of class "mn". Equation (8.9.1) states simply that the failure rate $MTBF^{-1}$ of a failure class or "system" is equal to the sum of failure rates of a series of independent units, the failure of any one of which produces a "system" failure.

But the theory of equations (8.8.3, 8.8.4) defines $MTBF_{mn}$. Then equation (8.9.1) may be considered as a constraint equation upon the basis of which the sub-subsystem $MTBF$s can be allocated to minimize the life cycle cost of the subsystem. Thus, replace ϵ in equation (8.6.4) by $MTBF^{-1}$. Then

$$\frac{\partial MTBF^{-1}}{\partial MTBF_k} = - \frac{1}{MTBF_k^2} \qquad (a)$$

Equation (8.6.4) now takes the form

$$\Lambda = MTBF_k^2 \ \frac{\partial LCC_k}{\partial MTBF_k} \qquad (b)$$

Following the derivation of equations (8.8.3, 8.8.4), solve equation (b) for $MTBF_k$. Thus

$$MTBF_k = \Lambda^{1/2}(LCC_k')^{-1/2} \qquad (c)$$

Substitute equation (c) into equation (8.9.1), solve for $\Lambda^{1/2}$ and drop the subscripts *mn* for brevity. Then

$$\Lambda^{1/2} = MTBF \sum_{k=1}^{K} (LCC'_k)^{1/2} \tag{d}$$

in analogy with equation (8.8.2). Now change the dummy subscript in equation (c) and substitute equation (d) into equation (c) to obtain the desired result:

$$MTBF_\ell = MTBF \sum_{k=1}^{K} \left(\frac{LCC'_k}{LCC'_\ell} \right)^{1/2} \tag{8.9.2}$$

Equation (8.9.2) shows that the *MTBF*s of each of a set of K sub-subsystems should be allocated in proportion to the known required mean time to failure of the subsystem, and weighted in inverse proportion to the square root of the corresponding slope of the sub-subsystem life cycle cost curve. If all of the LCC'_k are the same, then $MTBF_\ell = K(MTBF)$ as is to be expected, that is, if each of K components can fail in such a way as to produce a failure of the sub-subsystem of which they are a part, the failure rate of the sub-subsystem is greater than the failure rate of each of the components by the factor K.

Equation (8.9.2) together with equations (8.8.3, 8.8.4) lay the foundation for allocation of reliability requirements of all components and subsystems in a system of any degree of complexity.

8.10 Simultaneous Failures

The form of equation (8.5.1) assumes that failures act independently, that is, that if two failures were to occur simultaneously the total number of person-hours of delay would simply be the sum of the corresponding terms for independent failures. This is clearly not always the case because it is possible that the simultaneous occurrence of two independent failures could cause a collision. If precautions have not been taken in advance to minimize the consequences of collisions, the sum of the $n_{ij}\tau_{ij}$ for two simultaneously acting failure modes could greatly exceed the corresponding sum if the two failures occur at different times.

Strictly speaking, then, we should add to equation (8.5.1) terms corresponding to interactive failures. These terms will contain products of the $MTBF_{ij}$ in the denominators and, in the differentiation process leading to equation (8.6.5) and the subsequent equations for required $MTBF$s, will lead to fundamental complications—$\partial\epsilon/\partial x_{ij}$ becomes a function of all interactive failure modes, not just of x_{ij}. But, in a well-designed system, the probability of collisions involving greatly increased delay must be very small. Therefore, it is better to use the theory developed and to proceed iteratively to consider the consequences of simultaneous failures. The following procedure is recommended: First compute the required $MTBF$s from equation (8.8.3). Then, having the required $MTBF$s for individual failures, compute the $MTBF$s for simultaneous, interactive failures and estimate the corresponding $n_{ij}\tau_{ij}$ for them. If the corresponding contributions to equation (8.6.6) add significantly, to ϵ, then a new smaller ϵ_{spec} must be defined and the calculation repeated until the ϵ_{spec} plus the ϵ corresponding to collisions does not exceed the desired ϵ_{spec} counting all failures. A case of simultaneous failures is considered in section 9.5.

8.11 Summary

A method is developed for allocation of the reliability requirements of the subsystems and sub-systems of an automated transit system in such a way that life cycle cost is minimized. Besides a complete classification of the subsystems and their failure modes, the method requires knowledge of (1) the yearly number of hours of operation of the vehicle-borne and wayside equipment, (2) the mean number of person-hours of delay due to each failure (failure effects analysis), and (3) the slopes of the curves of subsystem and sub-subsystem life cycle cost versus $MTBF$.

The solution is given by equations (8.6.5) and (8.6.6); however, using it the numerical solution is graphical. An analytic approximation, adequate if the variation in the slopes of the life cycle cost curve are small, is given by equations (8.8.3, 8.8.4) and equation (8.9.2). The latter solutions have the additional advantage of providing a great deal of insight into the behavior of $MTBF$ requirements with various parameters, for example, the $MTBF$ requirements are:

1. Proportional to patronage
2. Independent of system size
3. Proportional to the square of the time delays due to failure
4. Proportional to the number of vehicles.
   Thus, if, with a given patronage, the vehicle size is reduced so that N_v increases, τ_{mn}^2 must be caused to decrease in the same proportion if the $MTBF$ requirements are not to worsen. Thus, more sophisticated control systems are required in small-vehicle systems than in large-vehicle systems.

References

1. Hugh Everett III, "Generalized Lagrange Multiplier Method for Solving Problems of Optimum Allocation of Resources," *Operations Research,* Vol. 11, No. 3, May-June 1963, pp. 399-417.

2. J.E. Anderson, "Life-Cycle Costs and Reliability Allocation in Automated Transit Systems," *High Speed Ground Transportation Journal,* Vol. 11, No. 1, Spring 1977, pp. 1-18.

3. *Proceedings of a Conference on Service Availability,* Transportation Systems Center, U. S. Department of Transportation, Cambridge, Mass., October 1976.

9

Redundancy, Failure Modes and Effects, and Reliability Allocation

9.1 Introduction

In the previous chapter, an equation for allocation of required subsystem reliability (equation (8.8.3, 8.8.4) was derived, thus providing a basis for allocating reliability requirements of the subsystems of a system in such a way that the system life cycle cost is minimized, subject to the constraint of a specified level of service unavailability. The theory requires classification of failure modes and determination of failure effects in terms of the delay times and the number of people involved in each failure. This task is outlined in the present chapter in enough detail to clarify the general method and to provide some numerical estimates of the reliability requirements.

In classification of failure modes for analysis of system reliability, failures are identified not according to which specific part fails, but according to the consequences in terms of person-hours of delay. Consequently, it is possible to aggregate many components and sub-subsystems into the set of subsystems specifically identified in equations (8.8.3, 8.8.4). For example, the entire vehicle can be considered as a subsystem possessing the failure classes defined in section 8.4. As discussed in section 8.9, if the failure of any one of K components or subsystems causes an m-class failure of the nth type of subsystem, then $MTBF_{mn}$ is given in terms of component failures by equation (8.9.1). This equation simply states that the failure rate of failures of the "mn" class is the sum of the failure rates of components that can cause it, that is, the probability of an "mn" failure is the sum of the probabilities of independent events that can cause it.

Equation (8.9.1) is the series law of failures. The corresponding parallel law is obtained by building redundancy into the system if the required value of $MTBF_{mn}$ cannot economically be achieved by single components or subsystems. The theory of redundancy is developed in the next section. Then, a set of subsystems of a transit system is defined and specific types of failure classes are considered in order to determine for each generally applicable formulas for the number of person-hours of delay. As a point of interest, the theoretical construct is then used to consider the problem of the most appropriate type of mechanism for escape from vehicles in case the need should arise. Finally, the various components of the theory are assembled to give a specific example of its application to the problem of reliability allocation.

9.2 Redundancy

A subsystem is redundant if two or more parallel units (components or subsystems) exist and if each is able to perform the function required of the subsystem without interference from the failed element, but possibly with minor degradation in service. Let $MTBF_u$ be the mean time between failures of either of the two parallel units. Then, the mean time between failures of either of the two units is $MTBF_u/2$.

Let τ be the time interval following a failure during which the failure of the second parallel unit is critical. If the subsystem is aboard a vehicle, τ is the mean time interval following the first failure required to get the vehicle off the line and into the maintenance shop; if the subsystem is at wayside, τ is the mean time required to fix it or replace it. If the entire system is to operate satisfactorily, it is necessary that

$$\frac{MTBF_u}{\tau} >> 1$$

If predictable failures due to wearing out of parts are eliminated by replacing all such parts at a fraction of their $MTBF$s, the remaining failures occur randomly and $MTBF_u/\tau$ can be interpreted as the number of subintervals τ during which the failure of a redundant element could with equal probability occur within the time interval $MTBF_u$. The failure of the second element of a redundant pair during τ then has a probability equal to twice the failure rate of a single unit divided by the number of time intervals $MTBF_{ss}/\tau$ in which, with equal probability, the second unit could fail. In other words, the $MTBF$ of both elements of the redundant pair is increased from $MTBF_u/2$ by the ratio $MTBF_u/\tau$. If $MTBF_{ss}$ is the mean time between failures of both elements of a redundant pair less than τ apart, that is, of the subsystem consisting of two parallel units,

$$MTBF_{ss} = \frac{MTBF_u^2}{2\tau} \qquad (9.2.1)$$

For example, if $MTBF_u$ is 100 hours so that on the average the failure of either of two units occurs once in 50 hours, and τ is 0.1 hour, there are 1000 time intervals each of length 0.1 hour during which the second failure could occur. Only if failure of the second element occurs in the specific interval immediately following failure of the first element, is a double failure of consequence. Thus $MTBF_{ss} = 50(1000) = 50,000$ hours.

The benefit of redundancy in systems that can be maintained at frequent intervals is enormously increased over that in systems, such as spacecraft, in which τ is essentially infinite. Thus the economics of redundancy in transit systems with failure monitoring is much different from that experienced in the aerospace field.

Trains

An example of redundancy in transit systems is the coupling of cars into trains so that failure of one car does not cause a line stoppage. In a two-car train, the mean time to failure of both cars within less than τ units of time is, from equation (9.2.1),

$$MTBF_{T_2} = \frac{MTBF_{car}^2}{2\tau} \qquad (9.2.2)$$

In a three-car train, the $MTBF$ for failure of any of the three cars is $MTBF_{car}/3$. The probability of failure of either of the remaining cars within the interval τ is $2\tau/MTBF_{car}$. Therefore the $MTBF$ for failure of two cars within less than τ is

$$\left(\frac{MTBF_{car}}{3} \right) \left(\frac{MTBF_{car}}{2\tau} \right)$$

The second car fails anywhere in the interval τ, therefore at a mean time 0.5τ following the first failure. The third car must carry the train the remaining time 0.5τ to the maintenance depot. The probability of its failure before arrival is $0.5\tau/MTBF_{car}$. Therefore, the $MTBF$ of all cars in the train before it can arrive at the maintenance depot is

$$MTBF_{T_3} = \frac{2MTBF_{car}^3}{3 \cdot 2\tau^2} \qquad (9.2.3)$$

By a similar analysis

$$MTBF_{T_4} = \frac{(2 \cdot 4)MTBF_{car}^4}{4!\tau^3} \qquad (9.2.4)$$

and it follows that

$$MTBF_{T_n} = \left(\frac{2 \cdot 2^2 \cdot 2^3 \ldots \cdot 2^{n-2}}{n!} \right) \tau \left(\frac{MTBF_{car}}{\tau} \right)^n \qquad (9.2.5)$$

in which we can write

$$2 \cdot 2^2 \cdot \ldots \cdot 2^{n-2} = 2^{(1+2+\ldots+\ n-2)} = 2^{(n-2)(n-1)/2}$$

It is of course recognized that the performance of an n-car train in which only one car is operative may be marginal; but the train can be kept moving, thus considerably reducing the passenger delay from the case in which the train stops. If $MTBF_{T_n}$ is given from system considerations (use of equations (8.8.3, 8.8.4)), the mean time to failure of each car must from equation (9.2.5) be

$$MTBF_{\text{car}} = \tau \left[\frac{n!\ MTBF_{T_n}}{2^{(n-2)(n-1)/2}\tau} \right]^{1/n} \tag{9.2.6}$$

Trains in Loop Systems

Consider a transit system in which N_t trains of n cars each move between on-line stations around a loop. A failure of any of the N_t trains causes shutdown of the system. Thus, from equation (9.2.5) the mean time between system shutdowns, $MTBF_{S_1}(N_t|n)$, is

$$MTBF_{S_1}(N_t|n) = \left[\frac{2^{(n-2)(n-1)/2}}{n!} \right] \frac{\tau}{N_t} \left(\frac{MTBF_{\text{car}}}{\tau} \right)^n \tag{9.2.7}$$

If the loop consists of two counterrotating one-way system, each of N_t trains of n cars, the system mean time between failures is found by substituting equation (9.2.7) for $MTBF_u$ in equation (9.2.1). Thus for a two-way loop,

$$MTBF_{S_2}(N_t|n) = \frac{MTBF^2_{S_1}(N_t|n)}{2\tau} \tag{9.2.8}$$

Suppose the system is designed so that $MTBF_{S_1} = 3000$ h or approximately one year. Suppose further that the mean time between inspections for failures is $\tau = 10$ hr. Then

$$MTBF_{S_2} = \frac{(3000)^2}{20} = 150 \text{ years} \tag{9.2.9}$$

if we assume 3000 hours of operation per year.

Now consider the problem of estimating the required *MTBF* of a single car in a train of cars. The equation for required *MTBF* is equation (8.8.3, 8.8.4). Let each of the N_t trains be the subsystems. Then, as a first approximation, assume that the N_t trains are the only subsystems in a one-way loop system, and that there is only one class of failure—a train stops. Then there is only one term in the summation of equation (8.8.4) and $\Sigma_{mn} = 1$. For the subject configuration, $N_v = N_t$, τ_{mn} is the mean time to restore service (*MTRS*) when a train fails, and n_{mn} is *MTRS* times the average total flow of people per hour into the system, t_h. Thus equation (8.8.3) becomes

$$MTBF_{T_{\text{req}}} = \frac{t_h(MTRS)^2 N_t T_v}{\epsilon_{\text{spec}} PH_{\text{yr}}} \qquad (9.2.10)$$

$MTBF_{T_{\text{req}}}$ is the required *MTBF* of a single train. To find the vehicle *MTBF* substitute $MTBF_{T_{\text{req}}}$ for $MTBF_{T_n}$ in equation (9.2.6), in which τ is the time interval between trips to the maintenance shop for inspection. Then the required MTBF of each car in a one-way loop is

$$MTBF_{\text{car}_{\text{req}}} = \tau \left[\frac{n! t_h (MTRS)^2 N_t T_v}{2^{(n-2)(n-1)/2} \tau \epsilon_{\text{spec}} PH_{\text{yr}}} \right]^{1/n} \qquad (9.2.11)$$

But from equation (8.2.4) PH_{yr} is the number of person-hours of travel per hour multiplied by the number of hours of travel per year. The latter quantity is simply T_v, therefore

$$PH_{\text{yr}} = (t_h T_{\text{trip}}) T_v \qquad (9.2.12)$$

in which t_h is the number of trips per peak hour, and T_{trip} is the average trip time. Thus, equation (9.2.11) becomes

$$MTBF_{\text{car}_{\text{req}}} = \tau \left[\frac{n! (MTRS)^2 N_t}{2^{(n-2)(n-1)/2} \tau \epsilon_{\text{spec}} T_{\text{trip}}} \right]^{1/n} \qquad (9.2.13)$$

In a typical case, assume $\tau =$ one day or 10 hours of operation of an average vehicle, $MTRS = 1$ hr, $T_{\text{trip}} = 6$ min (0.1 hr), and $\epsilon_{\text{spec}} = 0.01$. Then

$$MTBF_{\text{car}_{\text{req}}} = 10 \left[\frac{100 n! N_t}{2^{(n-2)(n-1)/2}} \right]^{1/n} \qquad (9.2.14)$$

For comparison, consider two cases: (1) There are five two-car trains ($N_t =$ 5, $n = 2$); and (2) the ten cars operate as individual units ($N_t = 10$, $n = 1$). Then

$$MTBF_{car_{req}} = 316 \text{ hr if } N_t = 5, \, n = 2$$

$$= 10,000 \text{ hr if } N_t = 10, \, n = 1$$

As a matter of interest, the meaning of ϵ_{spec} in terms of $MTBF_{S_1}$ (equation (9.2.7)) is found from the equation

$$MTBF_{S_1} = \frac{MTBF_{T_{req}}}{N_t} = \frac{(MTRS)^2}{\epsilon_{spec} T_{trip}} \qquad (9.2.15)$$

in which the second expression is from equation (9.2.10) with equation (9.2.12) substituted.

Using the numerical values below equation (9.2.13)

$$MTBF_{S_1} = 1000 \text{ hours}$$

or one failure every 100 days. If $\tau = 10$ hr, as before, equation (9.2.8) gives

$$MTBF_{S_2} = \frac{(1000)^2}{20} = 50 \, MTBF_{S_1}$$

The dramatic effect of redundancy on the vehicle $MTBF$ required to achieve a given level of service availability is very apparent.

Single Vehicles in Loop Systems

In the above calculations, it was assumed that n is the number of cars per train. Suppose the cars in a loop system operate singly but that each critical subsystem aboard a car is fully redundant. Then N_t is the number of individual cars, N_v, and $n = 2$. From equation (9.2.13), the required $MTBF$ is proportional to $N_v^{1/2}$. In small-vehicle systems, using all of the numerical values in the previous paragraph, $MTBF_{req}$ for each individual subsystem tends to be too high to be practical. The apparent difficulty can be solved, however, by examining equation (9.2.13) for $n = 2$:

$$MTBF_{\text{r.e.}} = (MTRS) \left(\frac{2\tau N_v}{\epsilon_{\text{spec}} T_{\text{trip}}} \right)^{1/2} \qquad (9.2.16)$$

in which $MTBF_{\text{r.e.}}$ is the $MTBF$ of the redundant element.

$MTBF_{\text{r.e.}}$ can be reduced if the system can be designed in such a way that both $MTRS$ and τ are reduced. The time τ the vehicle is on line with a failed redundant element can be reduced by introducing an independent failure-monitoring system, the failure of which will itself signal that the vehicle should be taken off the line. With a failure-monitoring system, τ becomes the time required to get the vehicle off the line and into the maintenance shop following indication of failure of one of the redundant systems or of the failure monitor. In this circumstance, $\tau = T_{\text{trip}}$, and equation (9.2.16) reduces to

$$MTBF_{\text{r.e.}} = (MTRS) \left(\frac{2N_v}{\epsilon_{\text{spec}}} \right)^{1/2} \qquad \text{(loop systems with} \qquad (9.2.17) \\ \text{failure monitoring)}$$

$MTRS$, on the other hand, is the mean time to restore service in the case of failure of both redundant elements. To reduce $MTRS$ to an acceptable value, it is necessary to introduce a means of rapid removal of a failed vehicle from the line. In a thoughtfully designed system, the vehicle will be pushable in almost all cases. Therefore, an automated pushing (or pulling) mode activated by the on-board failure-monitoring system should be added to the vehicle. (The availability of microprocessors permits the introduction of such devices on board each vehicle at modest cost.) With such a device, it is reasonable to reduce $MTRS$ to the order of one minute, that is, $MTRS = 1/60$ hr. For say $N_v = 300$ vehicles, $MTRS = 1/60$ hr, and $\epsilon_{\text{spec}} = 0.01$; equation (9.2.17) gives $MTBF_{\text{r.e.}} = 4$ hours. Since this is a very modest $MTBF$, much smaller unavailability is possible. For example, for $\epsilon_{\text{spec}} = 10^{-6}$, $MTBF_{\text{r.e.}} = 400$ hours required.

Single Vehicles in Network Systems

For network systems using single vehicles, it is necessary to recall that in equations (9.2.10) and (9.2.11), the appearance of t_h in the numerator was based on the assumption that the number of people involved in a failure is $(MTRS)t_h$. This is true in a loop in which $MTRS$ is long enough so that all vehicles are stopped. In a loop in which $MTRS$ is short, the number of people involved in a failure is more nearly $MTRSf_{\text{av}}$, whose f_{av} is the average line flow. Thus, if equation (9.2.17) is applied to cases in which

MTRS is small or to a network system in which only a portion of the flow is delayed, it should be replaced by

$$MTBF_{\text{r.e.}} = (MTRS)\left(\frac{2N_v f_{\text{av}}/t_h}{\epsilon_{\text{spec}}}\right)^{1/2} \tag{9.2.18}$$

In loop systems, $f_{\text{av}}/t_h = 0.5$ if the average trip goes half way around the loop, and the *MTBF* requirement is reduced $\sqrt{2}$.

In network systems, equation (4.5.19) gives

$$\frac{f_{\text{av}}}{t_h} = \frac{L<L_t>}{2\beta A}$$

and, from equation (4.5.17),

$$N_v = \frac{\tilde{t}_h A <L_t>}{p_v f_p V_{\text{av}}}$$

in which $\tilde{t}_h$ is the hourly trip density and A is the network area. With these substitutions, equation (9.2.18) becomes

$$MTBF_{\text{r.e.}} = (MTRS)<L_t>\left(\frac{\tilde{t}_h L}{p_v f_p V_{\text{av}} \beta \epsilon_{\text{spec}}}\right)^{1/2} \tag{9.2.19}$$

From figure 4-18 assume that for a large network

$$<L_t> \approx 0.8 A^{1/2} \tag{9.2.20}$$

Then, as a specific example, assume *MTRS* = 1/60 hr, $A = 256\,\text{km}^2$, $L = 0.8$ km, $p_v f_p = 1$, $\beta = 1$, $V_{\text{av}} = 50\,\text{km/hr}$, and $\epsilon_{\text{spec}} = 10^{-4}$. Then $<L_t> = 12.8\,\text{km}$, and

$$MTBF_{\text{r.e.}} = 27 \tilde{t}_h^{1/2} \tag{9.2.21}$$

if $\tilde{t}_h$ is the trip density in trips per hectare. From figure 5-7, assume $\tilde{t}_h = 60$ trips per hectare (15,000 trips per square mile) is an upper limit on patronage. Then $MTBF_{\text{r.e.}} = 209$ hours. Based on the work of C.L. Olson[1], this is a modest *MTBF*. If, however, a lower requirement is desirable, equation (9.2.19) shows that a lower value can be obtained by reducing *MTRS* below one minute. The work of Bernstein and Schmitt[2] indicates that a value

MTRS = 15 seconds may not be unreasonable, thus reducing $MTBF_{req}$ by a factor of four. $MTBF_{req}$ could be further reduced by reducing the ratio of τ to average trip length (see equation (9.2.16)). This can be done by dispersing small maintenance facilities throughout the network, but is probably not needed.

The above analysis shows that in large networks the simple expedients of

1. Redundancy in critical elements
2. Failure monitoring
3. Automated pushing

will reduce the *MTBF* requirements to readily obtainable levels, even if the time delays due to failure are of the order of 0.01 percent of travel time. This figure means that one hour of delay is experienced in 10,000 hours of travel. If the average regular user of the system takes 10 work trips per week of 15 minutes each for 50 weeks a year, the number of hours of travel per year is 125 hours. Assuming on that basis a total of 200 hours travel per year, $\epsilon = 10^{-4}$ means an accumulation of one hour of delay per person in 50 years.

The above analysis is of course preliminary since it neglects all wayside subsystems. Also, note from equation (8.9.2) that the *MTBF* requirements of the various individual vehicle-borne subsystems are higher than the above figures in proportion to the number of them.

9.3 Subsystems and Classes of Failure

In section 9.2, *MTBF* requirements were developed under the simplifying assumption that any wayside equipment is infinitely reliable. In a complete analysis, it is of course necessary to account for the finite reliability of wayside subsystems. As indicated in section 8.9 the subsystems should be defined as the largest units in the system for which meaningful values of person-hours of delay $(n\tau)$ due to each class of failure can be defined. Thus define the following types of equipment as the "subsystems":

1. Vehicles
2. Station entry monitoring equipment
3. Passenger processing equipment in stations
4. Merge point equipment
5. Diverge point equipment
6. Central communications and control equipment

For each of these subsystems, the classes of failure have to be defined separately. For the vehicle subsystem, the classes will be taken as those defined in section 8.4. For the remaining subsystems, the classes will be defined below.

The above analysis and that which follows is designed to apply to any type of transit system including systems with manually operated vehicles. In simpler systems certain terms are set to zero, as will be apparent.

9.4 Vehicle Failures

As indicated above, the classes of vehicle failure will be taken as those defined in section 8.4.

Class 1 Failures

In Class 1 failures, the number of persons involved in a failure is just the average number of persons per vehicle. Thus

$$n_{11} = p_v$$

The time delay, τ_{11}, is the time required to stop at a station, wait for a second vehicle, and resume the journey. Thus

$$n_{11}\tau_{11} = p_v \left(\frac{2V_L}{a} + t_{sd} \right) \tag{9.4.1}$$

in which t_{sd} is the station delay time.

Class 2 Failures

In Class 2 failures, the vehicle slows down, therefore all people in a string of vehicles that slows down are delayed. The number of person-hours of delay, $n_{12}\tau_{12}$, can be found by considering figure 9-1.

Assume that a vehicle slows down from line speed V_L to a speed V^* and cruises at V^* for a distance D^* at which time it leaves the main track. At this point, neglect the deceleration period. Then the time at which it leaves the main track is $t^* = D^*/V^*$. The time delay on line is

$$\Delta t_1 = t^* - t_a$$

$$= \frac{D^*}{V_L} \left(\frac{V_L}{V^*} - 1 \right) \tag{a}$$

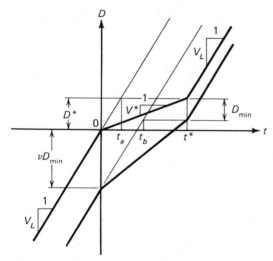

Figure 9-1. Distance-Time Diagram Used to Compute the Time Delay due to Slowdown of a Vehicle

in which $t_a = D^*/V_L$ is the time required to traverse D^* at V_L. In these calculations, neglect of jerk introduces an insignificant error, and the neglect of the acceleration periods can be accounted for by considering V^* to be the reduced velocity in the case of infinite deceleration. In significant cases, the error in neglecting the effect of finite deceleration is small. The passengers in vehicle 1 lose the additional time given by equation (9.4.1).

Assume a second vehicle is travelling a distance $\nu D_{\min}$ behind the first vehicle. $D_{\min}$ is the minimum nose-to-nose distance between vehicles and > 1. Then, at $t = 0$ (neglecting control lags) the second vehicle slows to a speed such that it achieves the minimum spacing, $D_{\min}$, at time t^*. (The velocity profile is of no consequence.) The time lost by the second vehicle is

$$\Delta t_2 = t^* - t_b$$

$$= \frac{D^*}{V_L}\left[\frac{V_L}{V^*} - 1 - (\nu - 1)\frac{D_{\min}}{D^*} \right] \tag{b}$$

in which $t_b = (D^* - D_{\min} + \nu D_{\min})/V_L$.

Assume a cascade of vehicles each spaced a distance $\nu D_{\min}$ apart. Then the time delay of the ith vehicle, Δt_i, is found by replacing $D_{\min}$ by $(i - 1)D_{\min}$ in equation (b). Thus

$$\Delta t_i = \frac{D^*}{V_L}\left[\frac{V_L}{V^*} - 1 - (i - 1)(\nu - 1)\frac{D_{min}}{D^*}\right] \tag{c}$$

The number of vehicles delayed n is found by assuming $\Delta t_{n+1} = 0$. Thus

$$n = \frac{1}{(\nu - 1)}\frac{D^*}{D_{min}}\left(\frac{V_L}{V^*} - 1\right) \tag{d}$$

If the average number of people per vehicle is p_v, the total number of person-hours of delay is

$$n_{12}\tau_{12} = p_v\left(\sum_{i=1}^{n}\Delta t_i + \frac{2V_L}{a} + t_{sd}\right) \tag{e}$$

Substituting equation (c), and performing the summation,

$$n_{12}\tau_{12} = \frac{P_v D^*}{V_L}\left[\left(\frac{V_L}{V^*} - 1\right)n - (\nu - 1)\frac{D_{min}}{D^*}\frac{n(n - 1)}{2}\right] + p_v\left(\frac{2V_L}{a} + t_{sd}\right)\Big] \tag{f}$$

Substituting equation (d)

$$n_{12}\tau_{12} = \frac{D^{*2}P_v}{2(\nu - 1)V_L D_{min}}\left(\frac{V_L}{V^*} - 1\right)\left[\frac{V_L}{V^*} - 1\right.$$

$$\left. + (\nu - 1)\frac{D_{min}}{D^*}\right] + p_v\left(\frac{2V_L}{a} + t_{sd}\right) \tag{g}$$

In most cases, the ratio D_{min}/D^* is much less than 1. Also note that the average flow f_{av} is

$$f_{av} = \frac{V_L p_v}{\nu D_{min}} \tag{9.4.2}$$

With these substitutions, equation (g) becomes

$$n_{12}\tau_{12} = \frac{\nu}{2(\nu - 1)} \left(\frac{D^*}{V_L} \right)^2 \left(\frac{V_L}{V^*} - 1 \right)^2 f_{av} + p_v \left(\frac{2V_L}{a} + t_{sd} \right)$$

(9.4.3)

Only the first term is in the form of a flow multiplied by a time delay squared (see equation (8.7.3)), but this is usually the dominant term.

It has been mentioned that the above analysis neglected the finite time required to change speed from V_L to V^*. Examination of the above analysis shows that if the position-time curve of vehicle 1 in figure 9-1 resumes speed V_L at t^*, the only change is that in equation (9.4.3) V_L/V^* is replaced by

$$\frac{V_L}{V^*} \rightarrow \frac{V_L}{V^*_{act}} \left[1 - \frac{(V_L - V^*_{act})^2}{aD^*} \right]$$

in which V^*_{act} is the actual reduced line speed. It is seen that the correction is small if D^* is large compared with twice the stopping distance from a speed $V_L - V^*_{act}$.

Class 3 Failures

In Class 3 failures, the failed vehicle, denoted vehicle 1, is assumed to stop on the guideway. Vehicle 2, behind it stops and then pushes it up to line speed. Vehicles 3, 4, and so on slow down, may stop, and then resume line speed. The position-time diagrams are idealized in figure 9-2. Assume that before failure, a cascade of vehicles travelling at velocity V_L is spaced at an average nose-to-nose distance of νD_{min} where, as before, D_{min} is the minimum nose-to-nose spacing. Vehicle 1 stops at $t = 0$. It waits until vehicle 2 can stop behind it and push it back to line speed. Vehicle 2 stops $\nu D_{min}/V_L$ units of time later. The stopping time is approximately V_L/a, where a is the deceleration rate. Therefore, counting the time required to stop and to resume speed, vehicle 2 is delayed $2V_L/a$ plus the delay time τ_p required for operation of the pushing mode. With these considerations,

$$\Delta t_1 = \frac{\nu D_{min}}{V_L} + \frac{2V_L}{a} + \tau_p + \tau_{11}$$

(a)

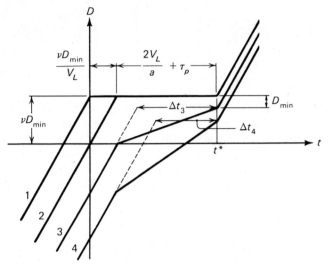

Figure 9-2. Position-Time Diagrams for Pushable Failure

in which τ_{11} (equation (9.4.1)) is added to account for the additional delay of passengers in vehicle 1 in transferring vehicles in the station nearest the failure. Similarly,

$$\Delta t_2 = \frac{2V_L}{a} + \tau_p + \tau_{11}$$

In analogy with the analysis of Class 2 failures,

$$\Delta t_3 = \frac{2V_L}{a} + \tau_p - (v - 1)\frac{D_{\min}}{V_L} \tag{c}$$

$$\Delta t_i = \frac{2V_L}{a} + \tau_p - (i - 2)(v - 1)\frac{D_{\min}}{V_L} \tag{d}$$

If n is the total number of vehicles delayed, the $(n + 1)$th vehicle is not delayed. Therefore,

$$\Delta t_{n+1} = 0 = \frac{2V_L}{a} + \tau_p - (n - 1)(v - 1)\frac{D_{\min}}{V_L}$$

and

$$n - 1 = \left(\frac{2V_L}{a} + \tau_p \right) \frac{V_L}{(v - 1)D_{min}}$$ (e)

If, as above, the average number of people per vehicle is p_v, and we take note of equation (9.4.1),

$$n_{13}\tau_{13} = p_v \left(\sum_{i=2}^{n} \left[\frac{2V_L}{a} + \tau_p - (i - 2)(v - 1)\frac{D_{min}}{V_L} \right] \right.$$

$$\left. + 8V_L/a + 2t_{sd} + 2\tau_p + vD_{min}/V_L \right)$$ (f)

If the sums of equation (f) are placed in closed form,

$$n_{13}\tau_{13} = p_v \left\{ (n - 1)\left[\frac{2V_L}{a} + \tau_p - \frac{(v - 1)D_{min}}{2V_L} (n - 2) \right] \right.$$

$$\left. + \frac{8V_L}{a} + 2t_{sd} + 2\tau_p + \frac{vD_{min}}{V_L} \right\}$$ (g)

Substituting equation (e) and simplifying the algebra

$$n_{13}\tau_{13} = p_v \left[\frac{V_L}{2(v - 1)D_{min}} \left(\frac{2V_L}{a} + \tau_p \right)^2 \right.$$

$$\left. + \frac{9V_L}{a} + 5/2\ \tau_p + 2t_{sd} + \frac{vD_{min}}{V_L} \right]$$

Finally, substitute equation (9.4.2). Then

$$n_{13}\tau_{13} = \frac{v}{2(v - 1)} \left(\frac{2V_L}{a} + \tau_p \right)^2 f_{av}$$

$$+ p_v \left(\frac{9V_L}{a} + 2.5\tau_p + 2t_{sd} \right) + \frac{p_v^2}{f_{av}}$$ (9.4.4)

If the vehicles are trained, p_v is the number of people per train. In almost all cases, the third term can be neglected, and often the second.

Equation (9.4.4) is valid unless the string of delayed vehicles is so long that some of them can be shunted around the delay by an alternate path or unless $(n - 1)vD_{min}$ exceeds the total length of track occupied by vehicles upstream of the point of failure. Thus, if D^* is the length of track occupied by vehicles upstream of the failure (analogous to the same symbol used in analysis of Class 2 failures), equation (e) applies if

$$D^* > (n - 1)vD_{min}$$

if this inequality is not satisfied, substitute

$$n - 1 = \frac{D^*}{vD_{min}} \tag{9.4.5}$$

and then equation (9.4.2) in equation (g) to obtain

$$n_{13}\tau_{13} = \frac{D^*}{V_L}\left[\frac{2V_L}{a} + \tau_p - \frac{(v-1)}{2v}\frac{D^*}{V_L}\left(1 - \frac{vD_{min}}{D^*}\right)\right]f_{av}$$

$$+ p_v\left(\frac{8V_L}{a} + 2t_{sd} + 2\tau_p\right) + \frac{p_v^2}{f_{av}} \tag{h}$$

When equation (h) applies, vD_{min} is much less than D^*. Therefore,

$$n_{13}\tau_{13} = \frac{D^*}{V_L}\left[\frac{2V_L}{a} + \tau_p - \frac{(v-1)}{2v}\frac{D^*}{V_L}\right]f_{av}$$

$$+ p_v\left(\frac{8V_L}{a} + 2t_{sd} + 2\tau_p\right) + \frac{p_v^2}{f_{av}} \tag{9.4.6}$$

This equation applies when

$$\frac{2V_L}{a} + \tau_p > \frac{(v-1)}{2v}\frac{D^*}{V_L}$$

an inequality which may be satisfied either if the flow is near saturation ($v = 1$), or if the delay time τ_p is unusually long. The first condition ($v = 1$) is not likely to happen in practical cases because merging becomes increasingly difficult as v approaches 1. On the other hand, a long pushing delay, if an automated pushing strategy is incorporated in the system, implies either a failure in the pushing mode or a Class 4 failure, that is, one in which the failed vehicle cannot be pushed.

Class 4 Failures

Based on the above discussion, $n_{14}\tau_{14}$ is given by equation (9.4.6), in which $\tau_p \rightarrow \tau_4$ becomes the time required to restore service—long compared to the other time intervals in equation (9.4.6). Thus

$$n_{14}\tau_{14} \approx \tau_4 \left(\frac{D^*}{V_L} f_{av} + 2p_v \right) + \frac{p_v^2}{f_{av}}$$

But $(D^*/V_L)f_{av}$ is the number of people in vehicles in the distance D^* between bypass tracks. This is generally large compared to p_v. Moreover,

$$\sqrt{\frac{\tau_4}{D^*/V_L}} \left(\frac{D^*}{V_L} f_{av} \right) >> p_v$$

since, if the vehicle cannot be pushed, $\tau_4 >> D^*/V_L$. Therefore $n_{14}\tau_{14}$ simplifies to

$$n_{14}\tau_{14} = \tau_4(D^*/V_L)f_{av} \tag{9.4.7}$$

in which D^* is either the mean distance from the failure to the nearest upstream alternative path or the length of the vehicle stream, whichever is shorter.

9.5 Station Entry Monitoring Equipment

Perhaps the most critical manuever in operation of a transit system is the one in which a vehicle or train approaches and stops behind another unloading and loading passengers. For on-line station train systems, this problem is discussed in section 4.2; and for off-line station systems with vehicles stopping behind one another, it is discussed in section 7.2. In this section, we consider the consequences of a combination of failures that causes a vehicle to fail to slow down on entry into a station. Such a failure implies a failure of all braking systems. With redundant systems, such a failure will be rare, but the station entry maneuver occurs with every vehicle-trip and is therefore of primary concern. One approach is to try to make the vehicle systems sufficiently reliable that the probability of station entry failure can be tolerated. Another approach, discussed here, is to add a station entry monitor to the equipment in each station. The monitor is designed to check the speed of each vehicle at one or more points while it is entering the station and to actuate an independent braking system if the speed is excessive.

The station entry monitors will of course add to the cost of the system, and themselves may fail, thus requiring the station to be bypassed until the repair is made. Thus the trade-off between increased reliability of vehicle-borne equipment to meet station entry requirements and the provision of station entry monitors need to be considered.

MTBF *between Collisions in Stations with No Monitor*

Let $MTBF_{vb}$ be the mean time between failures of the entire vehicle braking system. Assume that a vehicle-borne failure monitor detects the failure and, if the vehicle is not already committed to switch into a station, causes the switch to be locked in the position for station bypass, until the vehicle can be stopped safely. Thus failure of the braking system may cause a station collision only if it occurs after the vehicle is committed to enter the station.

The critical time t_{cr} during which the vehicle is committed to enter a station is the time interval from switch command to station stop. The switch command must occur far enough ahead of the station diverge point to permit the switch to be thrown, verification that it is thrown, and the vehicle stopped before the diverge point in case verification does not occur. At line speed V_L, the time to traverse the stopping distance $V_L^2/2a$ is $V_L/2a$. From equation (3.4.3), the time required to traverse the spiral section of the off-line track is $(32H/J)^{1/3}$. Finally, the time required to decelerate at the service rate to a stop is $V_L/a + a/J$. Thus,

$$t_{cr} = \text{time to switch and verify} + V_L/2a$$

$$+ (32H/J)^{1/3} + V_L/a + a/J \qquad (9.5.1)$$

For example, if $V_L = 15$ m/s, $a = 2.5$ m/s^2, $J = 2.5$ m/s^3, $H = 3$ m, and the switch/verify time is say 5 s, $t_{cr} = 18.4$ s.

If the average trip time is T_{trip}, then the fraction of braking failures in a specific vehicle that could result in in-station collisions is t_{cr}/T_{trip}. If there are N_v operational vehicles (or trains) in the system, the mean time between station collisions with no monitor in the whole system is

$$MTBF_{sc_{w/o \text{ monitor}}} \geq \frac{MTBF_{vb}(T_{\text{trip}}/t_{cr})}{N_v} \qquad (9.5.2)$$

The sign "$\geq$" indicates that a vehicle braking failure in the critical period sets up the conditions for a collision, but a collision does not occur in all circumstances, for example, when there are no parked vehicles in the station.

MTBF *between Collisions in Stations with Monitors*

Let the mean time between failures of the station monitor be $MTBF_{sm}$. If the monitor is inoperative, a failure detection system, operating with time delay t_{fd}, commands all approaching vehicles to bypass the station. Then only vehicles already committed to enter the station will do so. Thus it can be said that the station entry maneuver is unmonitored for vehicles within $t_{fd} + t_{cr}$ of the station, in which t_{cr} is given by equation (9.5.1). The number of vehicles in this critical period is simply $N_{cr} = (t_{fd} + t_{cr})/T_{sh}$, in which T_{sh} is the headway between vehicles entering the station. If the vehicles are equally spaced, the probability that one of the N_{cr} vehicles fails during the critical period is

$$P_{\text{veh. failure}} = \frac{(t_{fd} + t_{cr})}{MTBF_{vb}} \left(\frac{1 + 2 + \dots + N_{cr}}{N_{cr}} \right)$$

$$= \frac{(t_{fd} + t_{cr})(t_{fd} + t_{cr} + T_{sh})}{2MTBF_{vb}T_{sh}}$$

The reciprocal of this expression can be interpreted as the number of times the station monitor can fail for every time its failure is accompanied by a vehicle failure in the critical period. Thus, the mean time between potential collisions in a specific station is $MTBF_{sm}/P_{\text{veh. failure}}$. If there are n_s stations in the system, the mean time between potential collisions in the whole system is

$$MTBF_{sc_{w/\text{monitor}}} = \frac{2MTBF_{sm}MTBF_{vb}T_{sh}}{n_s(t_{fd} + t_{cr})(t_{fd} + t_{cr} + T_{sh})} \qquad (9.5.3)$$

Dividing by equation (9.5.2), the improvement in $MTBF_{sc}$ due to the station monitor is

$$\frac{MTBF_{sc\ w/monitor}}{MTBF_{sc\ w/o\ monitor}} = \frac{2N_v}{n_s} \frac{T_{sh}t_{cr}MTBF_{sm}}{(t_{fd} + t_{cr})(t_{fd} + t_{cr} + T_{sh})T_{tr}} \qquad (9.5.4)$$

in which

T_{sh} = station entry headway
t_{fd} = time constant of in-station failure detection system
t_{cr} = value given by equation (9.5.1)
T_{tr} = average trip time
N_v = number of vehicles
n_s = number of stations

Typical values might be $t_{cr} = 20\,\text{s}$, $t_{fd} = 10\,\text{s}$, $T_{sh} = 10\,\text{s}$, $T_{tr} = 10\,\text{min}$, $N_v/n_s = 10$. Then the right side of equation (9.5.4) becomes $20MTBF_{sm}$, in which $MTBF_{sm}$ is in hours. Thus, with redundancy in the station monitor, the $MTBF$ for station collisions can be improved by use of monitors by a very large factor, for example, for $MTBF_{sm} = 1000$ hours, by a factor of 20,000. Without the monitors, $MTBF_{vb}$ must be improved by the same factor to give the system performance possible with station monitoring.

Required MTBF of Station Monitors

In the previous paragraph, the mean time between in-station collisions in an entire system is related to the MTBF of the station monitors. The required $MTBF$ of the station monitor is determined by equations (8.8.3, 8.8.4) in which the n_τ and the LCC' corresponding to the monitor must be included. If the station monitor is inoperative, there are two choices: (1) all vehicles bypass the station until the monitor is restored to service; and (2) all vehicles passing the station slow down to a predetermined safe speed V^* until the monitor is restored to service. In the first case, persons destined for the failed station are rerouted to a different station and then must make their way to their final destination by alternative means; and persons initiating their trips at the failed station must either wait until the monitor is restored to service or go to another station. The number of people thus delayed is the sum of the flows originating and terminating their trips at the failed station, multiplied by the mean time to restore service. The time delay of each person is the additional time required to reach the destination via an alternate route. Thus

$$(n\tau)_{\text{station monitor}_1} = (f_{s_{\text{in}}} + f_{s_{\text{out}}})(MTRS_{sm})(\Delta \text{ trip time}) \qquad (9.5.5)$$

In the second case, the entire line flow f_{av} slows down for a period $MTRS_{sm}$, but there is no further delay of passengers passing the station in vehicles, or initiating or terminating their trips at the failed station. The corresponding $n\tau$ is given by equation (9.4.3) without the second term, and with $D^* = V^*t^*$ where, from figure 9-1, $t^* = MTRS$. The flow of passengers initiating trips at the failed station is delayed if the flow of vehicles into the station is inadequate to accommodate the initiating passengers. This flow includes both the occupied and empty vehicle flows into the failed station. The delay time is the same as the delay time of persons terminating at the failed station. With these factors in mind, the corresponding $n\tau$ for Case 2 is

$$(n\tau)_{\text{station monitor}_2} = \frac{\nu}{2(\nu - 1)}MTRS^2_{sm}\left(1 - \frac{V^*}{V_L}\right)^2(f_{\text{av}} + f_{s_{\text{in}}})$$
$$(9.5.6)$$

in which $f_{s_{\text{in}}}$ is the flow of passengers initiating trips at the failed station. Comparing with equation (9.5.5), the appropriate strategy can be determined. In terms of passenger discomfort and distress the (Δ trip time) associated with going to an alternative station should be weighted more heavily than the additional delay associated with slower movement through the station. Thus unless the line flow is much larger than the station flow and $MTRS$ is of the order of (Δ trip time), the best strategy is the second one.

9.6 Failures of Passenger-Processing Equipment in Stations

Patrons beginning their trips may be delayed at a station due to the following types of equipment malfunction:

1. Malfunction of automatic equipment such as destination selectors, fare collectors, and ticket dispensers
2. Malfunction of automatic equipment for assigning passengers to vehicles
3. Malfunction of automatic station doors leading from the station platform to the vehicle
4. Malfunction of automatic doors on the vehicle
5. Malfunction of starting equipment on vehicle

Patrons planning to end their trips at a certain station may be caused to bypass the station due to failure of station entry monitoring equipment, as described in section 9.5. They may also be caused to bypass the station due to malfunction of equipment described above which prevents the free flow of vehicles through stations. For example, failure of a vehicle to start moving after loading its passengers blocks the station. Once all station platforms behind the failed vehicle and all entering queue positions are filled, additional vehicles programmed to enter the station must be diverted to an alternate station. Thus, it is necessary in considering the required *MTBF* of station equipment to take into account as appropriate both the people initiating and terminating their trips at the malfunctioning station.

In group-riding transit systems, it is generally felt that automatic vehicle doors are necessary because no one individual can be expected to take responsibility for opening or closing the doors. In single-party, demand systems, on the other hand, manual doors may more likely be satisfactory. In either case, attainment of reasonable *MTBF*s requires that the doors be provided with a manual override both inside and outside to minimize both the number of people inconvenienced and the *MRTS*. If the vehicle doors are designed so they cannot lock and trap people inside, and that at worst a door malfunction is cause for dispatching the vehicle to a maintenance shop, they need not be considered further in this analysis.

To prevent people from accidentally or purposefully entering the path of vehicles moving through stations, and to improve the station climate, it has been thought that automatic station doors that slide open directly opposite the vehicle doors are a necessity. This is, of course, a degree of refinement not accorded many conventional transit systems. In new off-line station automated transit systems the vehicles move more slowly through the stations, and the wait time is minimum. Thus, the need for automatic station doors may in many cases be marginal. They can, however, be considered as one of the components in the following analysis. These doors should also be equipped with manual override devices which can be operated from either side.

For purposes of systems anlaysis, the failures that impede the flow of passengers as a result of malfunctions in stations can be divided into three classes:

1. Malfunctions that affect only the passengers initiating trips at the station in question
2. Malfunctions that affect incoming and outgoing passengers but do not divert passengers to other stations
3. Malfunctions that are serious enough to cause passengers to be diverted to other stations

Equipment on board a vehicle that affects its ability to start on command may be the same as that which could cause a malfunction while on line; but should still be included in the computation of required *MTBF* of the station equipment. The reason is that in the systems analysis, we compute the required *MTBF*s of the various classes of failures, not of specific components. The required *MTBF* of the components or subsystems is determined as indicated in section 8.9.

For Class 1 failures, the number of person-hours of delay can be found by considering figure 9-3, which shows the position-time lines of groups of passengers entering a station. Let p_g be the average number of people per group.

The first group entering the station following a malfunction is delayed τ_1 units of time. The second group, walking in at an average speed V_w, moves up to a minimum separation h_{min} behind the first group and waits until the malfunction is cleared. If T_h is the normal time headway between groups entering the station, the second group begins waiting $T_h - h_{min}/V_w$ units of time later than the first group. If T_{min} is the minimum time headway through stations, corresponding to the maximum flow rate of p_g/T_{min} people per unit time, the second group begins moving $T_{min} - h_{min}/V_w$ later than the first group. Thus the second group is delayed $\tau_1 - (T_h - T_{min})$. Similarly, the third group is delayed $\tau_1 - 2(T_h - T_{min})$. If q is the number of groups delayed, it may be seen from figure 9-3 that

$$q + 1 = \frac{\tau_1}{T_h - T_{min}} \qquad\qquad (a)$$

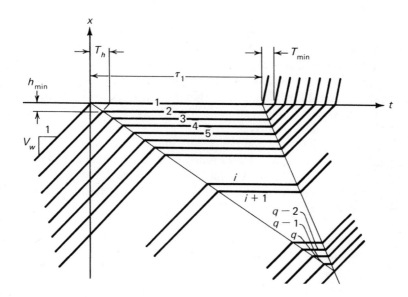

Figure 9-3. Position-Time Diagrams for Passengers Waiting for Service as a Result of a Delay of Duration τ_1

Then, the total number of person-hours of delay for Class 1 failures of station equipment is

$$(n\tau)_1 = p_g \sum_{i=1}^{q} [\tau_1 - (i-1)(T_h - T_{min})] \tag{b}$$

$$= p_g[q\tau_1 - (T_h - T_{min})(q-1)q/2]$$

$$= \frac{p_g\tau_1 q}{2}\left(\frac{q+3}{q+1}\right) \tag{c}$$

In cases of consequence, q is much greater than 1. Then, after substituting equation (a) into equation (c),

$$(n\tau)_1 = fs_{eq}\tau_1^2 \tag{9.6.1}$$

where

$$fs_{eq} = \frac{p_g}{2(T_h - T_{min})} \tag{9.6.2}$$

is an equivalent station flow. If the station is operating at maximum capacity when the failure occurs ($T_h = T_{min}$), $(n\tau)_1$ approaches infinity in theory, but in practice maximum flow will occur only for a short period so that the smallest average value of T_h is greater than T_{min}. If T_h varies with time, $(n\tau)_1$ can be found by direct summation of equation (b) for all values of q for which the summand is positive.

For Class 2 failures, the number of person-hours of delay is $(n\tau)_1$, given by equation (9.6.1), plus a corresponding term for the people terminating their trips at the failed station. The latter term is approximately of the form of equations (9.6.1) and (9.6.2) even if each vehicle carries more than one group. Thus

$$(n\tau)_2 = \frac{p_g}{2}\left(\frac{1}{T_{h_{in}} - T_{min}} + \frac{1}{T_{h_{out}} - T_{min}}\right)\tau_2^2 \tag{9.6.3}$$

in which T_{min} is the same value in both cases because of continuity of flow, and τ_2 is the mean time to restore service for Class 2 failures.

For Class 3 failures, substantially all of the vehicles terminating at the failed station are diverted to another station. The number of people thus involved is τ_3 times the flow into the station from the line, $fs_{in} = p_g/T_{h_{in}}$ in which $T_{h_{in}}$ is the equivalent minimum headway if there were only one group per vehicle. The delay time is the time added to the trip as a result of diversion to an alternate station. Thus

$$(n\tau)_3 = (n\tau_3)_1 + \frac{p_g\tau_3\Delta T_{trip}}{T_{h_{in}}} \tag{9.6.4}$$

in which $(n\tau_3)_1$ is as in equation (9.6.1) with τ_3 substituted for τ_1.

9.7 Merge Equipment Failures

Wayside merge equipment is needed to avoid collisions in car-follower systems by transferring the image of each car to the opposite branch of the merge, and in point-follower systems by sensing vehicle positions and commanding vehicles to slip slots. In either case, a failure of wayside equipment could in the worst case cause two vehicles to wedge together in the merge point. This is one of the worst types of system-caused failures in automated guideway transit (AGT) systems.

Failure monitoring is needed to minimize the consequences of merge equipment failures. If a failure occurs, the action can be either to stop the two streams of traffic entirely, or to slow them to a safe speed. In the latter case, the number of person-hours of delay is greatly diminished. Equations (9.4.3, 9.4.4, 9.4.6 and 9.4.7) apply directly to this case if account is taken of the involvement of two streams of traffic instead of one.

9.8 Diverge Equipment Failures

The purpose of wayside diverge point equipment is to read the destination of each car, determine the direction it should be switched, and cause the switch to be actuated. If the switch is in the track, the diverge point equipment includes the switch; if the switch is in the vehicle, it is included in vehicle-borne equipment.

Failures of diverge point equipment may be divided into two classes:

1. Some of the vehicles are misdirected and must either be rerouted or passengers must make their ways to their destinations by alternate routes.

2. The switch is locked in the middle thus requiring all vehicles to stop until it is restored to service.

In Class 1 failures, the number of person-hours of delay is

$$(n\tau)_1 = (\text{Misdirected flow})(\tau)(\Delta \text{trip time}) \tag{9.8.1}$$

in which τ is the mean time to restore service, and (Δtrip time) is the extra time needed to arrive at the destination by an alternate route.

In Class 2 failures, $(n\tau)_2$ is the same as a Class 4 vehicle failure and is given by equation (9.4.7).

9.9 Failures in Wayside Communications Equipment

In some types of automated transit systems all essential control equipment, except for wayside merge and diverge equipment, is aboard the vehicles. In this case the failure of wayside communications equipment, if there is any, may cause person-hours delay when some other failure has occurred or may decrease system capacity, thus causing delay in the peak periods. In other types of systems, the wayside communication link is essential to all control functions and its failure is of major consequence. To be meaningful, computation of $n\tau$ for these failures must be left to specific cases.

9.10 Failures in Central Control Equipment

Use of central control equipment in AGT systems may vary from complete control of the movement of every vehicle from a central facility, to supervisory functions in a central facility, to no central control.

Complete Central Control

If all control functions pass through a central control facility, a breakdown in this facility requires that all vehicles be stopped. Because of the excessive level of inconvenience this will cause, the system should be designed so that the vehicles can then move at slow speed under battery power into the nearest stations. Because of the possibility of a general power failure, such a back-up system is mandatory.

The corresponding value of $n\tau$ is composed of two groups of people: (1) those on the system at the time of failure; and (2) those seeking service. For the second group, the number of persons delayed is the total flow rate into the system t_h multiplied by the mean time to restore service, $MTRS$. Thus the number of person-hours of delay is

$$(n\tau)_2 = t_h(MTRS)^2$$

For the first group, the number of persons delayed is the number of persons riding the system at any one time. From equation (4.5.17), this number is t_h

times the average trip time, T_{trip}. The delay time depends on whether or not batteries are provided on each vehicle. If they are not provided, the delay time is $MTRS$. If batteries are provided, the delay time is the increase in trip time due to the decrease in speed from V_L to V^*. From equation (2.5.3) this time interval is approximately $(D_s/V_L)(V_L/V^* - 1)$ since the term V_L/a_m is generally small.

Summarizing, the total number of person-hours of delay due to a central control or power failure is

$$
\begin{aligned}
(n\tau)_{\text{central}} &= t_h(MTRS + T_{\text{trip}})MTRS & \text{no batteries} \\[6pt]
&= t_h[MTRS^2 + T_{\text{trip}}(D_s/V_L)(V_L/V^* - 1)] & \text{with batteries}
\end{aligned}
\quad (9.10.1)
$$

Central Supervisory Control

The consequences of failure can be reduced by decentralizing as much of the control as possible into the vehicles, stations, and switch points. It is still, however, desirable to exercise supervisory control at a central location for two reasons:

1. Prevention of overloads on specific lines and in specific stations by delaying the dispatching of vehicles to potentially overloaded stations
2. Optimum routing of empty vehicles

Central Register/Dispatcher

In the first function, rerouting along different paths to prevent line overloading can be accomplished by use of diverge point routing computers which communicate with downstream merge point computers. However, to avoid denying access to a station by vehicles programmed to that station because too many vehicles have been routed to it, central supervisory monitoring and control is necessary. The equipment is simple. All that is necessary is to communicate to a central register the estimated arrival times at the desired destinations of all trips ordered. If an arrival time comes into the station-i register too soon after the previous arrival time to station i, a communication is sent back to the origin station to order a specific time delay in dispatching of the vehicle so that the arrival rate does not exceed a specified value. Thus, before permitting a vehicle to leave a station, the station dispatcher asks permission of the central register. The central register then causes vehicles to be dispatched on a first-come, first-serve basis with time delays if needed. These delays will normally be too short to be recognized as delays.

The above-described central reigster function is simple enough to be inexpensively duplicated to reduce its required *MTBF*. If it doesn't work, the consequence is that a vehicle may arrive at its destination only to be aborted, that is, caused either to stop at an alternate station or to circle back for a second try. Causing vehicles thus to circle adds to the flow along lines already near their maximum flows, and thus may induce instability in a network AGT system. The problem is eased, however, by the existence of diverge point computers operating as described above. The number of person-hours of delay due to failure of the central register/dispatcher is best determined in a computer simulations of specific systems.

Empty Vehicle Dispatcher

The possibility of failure of a central computer/dispatcher which routes empty vehicles in an optimum way introduces a requirement for a suboptional but simpler empty vehicle dispatching scheme in which computer/ controllers at each station are able to rid the station of excess empty vehicles by dispatching them to the next station, and to call for empty vehicles from one or more stations up stream.

Failure of the optimal dispatcher may cause excess time delays because of a temporary local shortage of vehicles, particularly if it occurs during the rush period. Computer simulation of specific networks are again required to determine the number of person-hours of delay due to failures.

9.11 Escape Mechanisms

A means for escape from an AGT vehicle must be provided in two circumstances:
1. The vehicle is stuck on the guideway and cannot be removed in a reasonable time.
2. There is a fire on board.

The kind of escape mechanism that should be provided depends on the probability of each type of emergency and the cost and safety level of the mechanism. The control system enters the consideration of escape mechanisms insofar as it may reduce the probability of emergencies. As indicated in section 9.4, inclusion of a pushing mode in the longitudinal control system will greatly reduce the mean time between instances in which passengers must be removed from the vehicle. Addition of redundancy and monitoring equipment at merge and diverge points will greatly reduce the need for emergency escape at those points.

The most commonly mentioned escape mechanism is an emergency walkway along the entire length of the guideway. Such a walkway should be designed to be serviceable in inclement weather by the less agile members of society and permit people to walk safely a distance of up to half the station spacing. The advantages of emergency walkways lie in their simplicity and continual presence. Their disadvantages are cost and visual impact, both of which may significantly reduce the viability of the system. If escape mechanisms are not required very frequently, a small fleet of trucks equipped with hydraulic lifts may be satisfactory. A third mechanism, which also may simplify guideway maintenance, is a vehicle designed to run on the side of the guideway such as has been designed by DEMAG-MBB for their systems. See figure 9-4. One such vehicle in each loop of the system on standby at a station would be required.

In the case of fire, it may be equally satisfactory to cause the vehicle to proceed to the next station, usually no more than a minute away, as to let the patrons egress onto a walkway in highly unfavorable weather conditions. The extent to which the vehicles can be made fireproof and to which fire extinguishers can be provided will of course influence this tradeoff.

A long delay due to a vehicle stuck on the guideway is a Class 4 vehicle failure, and the number of person-hours of delay due to such a failure is given by equation (9.4.7). It can be anticipated that if the required *MTBF*s are computed to satisfy system requirements, the frequency of use of escape mechanisms will be very low. In this circumstance, the use of systems other than walkways appears warranted even though they involve a delay before egress is possible.

9.12 Reliability Allocation

The required reliabilities of the various subsystems and components can now be allocated by substituting appropriate $n\tau$ values such as estimated in sections 9.4-9.10 for all failure classes of all subsystems into equations (8.8.3, 8.8.4). The calculations require knowledge of the slopes of the life cycle cost curves LCC'_{ij}; however, to gain some insight and to illustrate application of the theory some simplifying assumptions about the LCC'_{ij} can be made. For some equipment it is not particularly expensive to increase reliability, that is, LCC'_{ij} is small and the corresponding equipment does not enter strongly into equation (8.8.4). In other cases, it may initially be sufficient to assume the LCC'_{ij} are all the same.

To develop a specific illustration, assume the only subsystems that need to be considered are the vehicles, the station monitors, the station passenger-processing equipment, and central control. For the first three subsystems, assume four, one, and three classes of failure, respectively, as

Figure 9-4. Service Vehicle in Operation on the Side of the Guideway of The Cabinlift System—at the Ziegenhain Hospital near Kassel, West Germany. Courtesy of DEMAG + MBB.

computed in sections 9.4, 9.5, and 9.6. For central control, assume one class of failure—a power failure. Let the subscripts in equations (8.8.3, 8.8.4) correspond to these subsystems and failure classes in the same order. Then in the application of equations (8.8.3, 8.8.4) it is more convenient to write them in the form

$$
\left.
\begin{aligned}
MTBF_{mn} &= \frac{(n_{mn}\tau_{mn})^{1/2}(T_m/T_v)^{1/2}}{\epsilon_{\text{spec}}t_h T_{\text{trip}}} \sum \\[2mm]
\sum &= N_v \sum_{j=1}^{4} (n_{1j}\tau_{1j})^{1/2} \\[2mm]
&+ \left(\frac{T_w}{T_v}\right)^{1/2}\left\{n_s\left[(n_{21}\tau_{21})^{1/2} + \sum_{j=1}^{3} (n_{3j}\tau_{3j})^{1/2}\right] + (n_{41}\tau_{41})^{1/2}\right\}
\end{aligned}
\right\} \qquad (9.12.1)
$$

in which it is assumed that all LCC' in equations (8.8.3, 8.8.4) are approximately equal, n_s is the number of stations, and PH_{yr}/T_v has been made specific by substituting equation (9.2.12). From section 8.5, it will be assumed in the following analysis that $(T_w/T_v)^{1/2} = 1.7$. To be specific, also assume that $\epsilon_{\text{spec}} = 10^{-4}$, that is, that each regular traveler on the average will experience one hour of accumulated delay every 10,000 hours. Assuming 200 hours of travel per year, this corresponds to one hour of delay every 50 years, or in other words, every fiftieth regular passenger will experience one hour of delay per year.

For the vehicle failure classes, the corresponding $n\tau$ are given respectively by equations (9.4.1, 9.4.3, 9.4.4, 9.4.7). In these equations, it is reasonable to assume for a first-order estimate that only the terms proportional to f_{av} are important. Then

$$
\sum_{j=1}^{4} (n_{1j}\tau_{1j})^{1/2} \approx f_{\text{av}}^{1/2}\left\{\left[\frac{\nu}{2(\nu-1)}\right]^{1/2}\left[\frac{D^*}{V_L}\left(\frac{V_L}{V^*}-1\right)\right.\right.
$$

$$
\left.\left. + \frac{2V_L}{a} + \tau_{p_3}\right] + \left(\tau_4\frac{D^*}{V_L}\right)^{1/2}\right\} \qquad (a)
$$

in which τ_{p_3} is the pushing delay time, and τ_4 is the time required to remove a nonpushable vehicle. From equation (9.5.6), for the monitor,

$$(n_{21}\tau_{21})^{1/2} = \left[\frac{\nu}{2(\nu - 1)} \right]^{1/2} MTRS_{sm}\left(1 - \frac{V^*}{V_L} \right) f_{av}^{1/2}(1 + fs_{in}/f_{av})^{1/2} \qquad \text{(b)}$$

From equations (9.6.1) through (9.6.4)

$$\sum_{j=1}^{3} (n_{3j}\tau_{3j})^{1/2} = (p_g/2)^{1/2}\left[\frac{\tau_1}{(T_{h_{in}} - T_{min})^{1/2}} \right.$$

$$+ \tau_2\left(\frac{1}{T_{h_{in}} - T_{min}} + \frac{1}{T_{h_{out}} - T_{min}} \right)^{1/2}$$

$$\left. + \tau_3\left(\frac{1}{T_{h_{in}} - T_{min}} + \frac{2\Delta T_{trip}}{\tau_3 T_{h_{in}}} \right)^{1/2} \right] \qquad \text{(c)}$$

From equation (9.10.1),

$$(n_{41}\tau_{41})^{1/2} = MTRS_{power}t_h^{1/2} \qquad \text{(d)}$$

in which it is assumed that batteries are used and, in the second form of equation (9.10.1), the second term is negligible.

As an illustration, let us compute the required *MTBF* for pushable vehicle failures in a loop system. Then $(n_{mn}\tau_{mn})^{1/2}$ is the sum of the second and third terms in equation (a) and $f_{av}/t_h = 1/2$. Assume the trip time is $T_{trip} = 0.1$ hour. For $(T_w/T_v)^{1/2} = 1.7$ and $\epsilon_{spec} = 10^{-4}$, equation (9.12.1), for $m = 1$, $n = 3$, becomes

$$MTBF_{13} = 5(10)^4\left(\frac{2V_L}{a} + \tau_{p3} \right) \frac{1}{f_{av}^{1/2}} \sum \qquad \text{(e)}$$

in which it is assumed that the average flow is at the rather high value of one half the maximum possible, that is, $\nu = 2$. To estimate the summation in equation (e), it can be assumed in equation (a) that τ_4 is by far the largest time parameter. Thus, only the right-hand term will be included. In equation (b) assume $V^*/V_L = 0.5$ and note that on the average $f_{av}/fs_{in} = n_s$, the number of stations. In equation (c) assume $p_g = 1.3$, $\tau_1 = \tau_2 \ll \tau_3$, and $T_{h_{in}} = 2T_{min}$. But $p_g/T_{h_{min}} = fs_{in}$. With these assumptions,

$$\frac{1}{f_{av}^{1/2}} \sum = N_v \left(\tau_4 \frac{D^*}{V_L} \right)^{1/2} + 1.7 \left\{ n_s \left[\frac{MTRS_{sm}}{2} \left(1 + \frac{1}{n_s} \right)^{1/2} \right. \right.$$

$$\left. \left. + \frac{\tau_3}{n_s^{1/2}} \left(\frac{1}{2} + \frac{\Delta T_{trip}}{\tau_3} \right)^{1/2} \right] + \sqrt{2} \, MTRS_{power} \right\} \tag{f}$$

In equations (e) and (f), assume D^*, the distance between stations, is 500 m, $V_L = 10$ m/s, $a = 2.5$ m/s. Then equation (e) with equation (f) substituted becomes

$$MTBF_{13} = 5(10)^4 \, \frac{(8 + \tau_{p_3})}{3600} \left\{ \left(\frac{50\tau_4}{3600} \right)^{1/2} N_v \right.$$

$$\left. + 1.7 \left[\frac{MTRS_{sm}}{2} \left(n_s^2 + n_s \right)^{1/2} + n_s^{1/2} \tau_3 \left(\frac{1}{2} + \frac{\Delta T_{trip}}{\tau_3} \right)^{1/2} + \sqrt{2} \, MTRS_{power} \right] \right\}$$

$$\tag{9.12.2}$$

Assume $N_v = 300$, $n_s = 7$. Then let the delay time for nonpushable failures be $\tau_4 = 1$ hour, the time to restore a station monitor to service be $MTRS_{sm} = 0.5$ hour, the $MTRS$ for a serious station failure be $\tau_3 = 0.5$ hour, and the $MTRS$ for a power failure chargeable to the system be $MTRS_{power} = 1$ hour. Further, assume $\Delta T_{trip}/\tau_3 = 1$. Finally, let the time to push be $\tau_{p_3} = 15$ seconds. Then, if the terms are listed in the same order as in equation (9.12.2),

$$MTBF_{13} = 319 \left\{ \begin{array}{ll} 35.4 & \text{vehicles} \\ \\ + \ 3.2 & \text{station monitors} \\ \\ + \ 2.8 & \text{passenger processing} \\ \\ + \ 2.4 & \text{control station} \end{array} \right.$$

$$= 14{,}000 \text{ hours}$$

This is too high an *MTBF* to be practical with single-chain components. With redundancy, equation (9.2.1) shows that the required *MTBF* of each redundant unit is

$$MTBF_{\text{unit}} = [2\tau(14,000)]^{1/2}$$

in which τ is the time required to get the vehicle off line after the failure has occurred. Let τ be the trip time of 0.1 hour, thus implying on-board failure monitoring. Then

$$MTBF_{\text{unit}} = 53 \text{ hours}$$

The above is an example calculation to illustrate the method. The numbers are guesses but are felt to be representative, and all elements in the system have not been taken into account.

9.13 Summary

In chapter 8, a theoretical method is developed to allocate the reliabilities of the subsystem of a general system in such a way that the life cycle cost is minimized while a given constraint on service availability is met. While it was not treated explicitly, the case in which some of the subsystem reliabilities are already known can be treated in a straightforward manner by replacing the unavailability factor ϵ by the net unavailability requirement of the subsystems with underdetermined reliabilities. By considering the subsystems as conglomerates of series-connected components, it was shown how the reliabilities of subsystems and components at all levels can be allocated in an optimum way.

The purpose of chapter 9 is to expand on and to illustrate the use of the theoretical method of chapter 8. It begins with the consideration of parallel connections between components, that is, redundancy. It is shown how to compute the reliability of systems of redundant members and that, with failure monitoring, redundancy greatly increases the service dependability of transit systems. Assuming only vehicle failures, the theory of redundancy is used to develop equations for the reliability of loop and network transit systems.

Next, the full application of the reliability allocation theory is initiated by developing formulas for the average number of person-hours of delay ($n\tau$) in a variety of classes of failure of vehicle and wayside subsystems. In specific systems, it may be possible to develop corresponding formulas for all significant failure classes; however, such a comprehensive treatment is not attempted. The purpose, rather, is to develop enough of the $n\tau$ formulas to illustrate application of the reliability allocation theory. In the final section of chapter 9, the reliability allocation theory is assembled and applied to a particular case.

Application of the reliability allocation theory is of fundamental importance both in the development and design of new transit systems and in the improvement of existing systems, and gives a great deal of quantitative insight into the most efficient and appropriate means of meeting system reliability goals at minimum cost. In particular, it shows the dramatic improvements in system reliability that can be made possible by introducing redundancy, failure monitoring, and rapid automated pushing of failed vehicles.

References

1. C.L. Olson, G.H. Fuller, and R.B. Fling, "Some Reliability, Dependability, and Safety Considerations for High-Capacity PRT Systems," *Personal Rapid Transit III,* Audio Visual Library Services, University of Minnesota, Minneapolis, Minn., 1976.

2. Harry Bernstein and Arthur Schmitt, "Emergency Strategies for Safe Close-Headway Operation of PRT Vehicles," *Personal Rapid Transit,* Audio Visual Library Services, University of Minnesota, Minneapolis, Minn., 1972.

10 Guideway Structures

10.1 Introduction

In transit systems that use exclusive guideways, the guideway is generally the largest cost item. Understanding of principles of guideway cost minimization is therefore crucial to the design of economical systems. Exclusive guideways may be either at grade, underground, or elevated; however, the analysis of this chapter is directed only to elevated systems. In spite of generally lower cost, at grade systems are not usually desirable in urban areas because of interference with cross traffic and increased difficulty to clear ice and snow. The cost per unit length of underground systems is roughly proportional to the cross-section area of the tunnel, and hence to the cross-section area of the vehicles. Because of the cost of relocating utilities, underground systems have been estimated generally to be three to five times as expensive per unit length as elevated systems; however, a study performed in Australia[1] indicates that for small-vehicle systems the cost of underground systems may compare favorably with the cost of elevated systems.

The material in this chapter is not intended to provide information needed for detailed design of elevated guideway systems. That would be a lengthier task than can be undertaken in a systems textbook. The objective is rather to provide insight into principles of cost minimization. Detailed methods of dynamic analysis, using computer simulations, have been developed under the auspices of the American Iron and Steel Institute (AISI)[2] and by several university groups[3,4,5,6]. The work of AISI, which includes a comprehensive treatment of ride comfort criteria, may be the most complete modern treatment of the design of steel guideways. The work of Snyder, Wormley, and Richardson[3] is directly useful, not only because they develop methodology for dynamic analysis of guideway-vehicle interactions, but because they give results that permit comparison of required guideway weight per unit length at different vehicle weights. The work of Paulson, Silver, and Belytschko[4] applies most directly to heavy-rail structures. Likins and his colleagues[5,6] include vehicle dynamics as well as guideway dynamics, as do Snyder et al., and also provide a method for minimizing the cost per unit length of a guideway, but for fixed cross-sectional configuration and fixed vehicle speed.

In the analysis of this chapter, it is assumed that the guideway cross section is rectangular for two reasons: (1) it is a basic cross section from

257

which certain specific conclusions can be drawn; and (2) it is sufficiently simply mathematically that the results can be understood in a general context. Various types of loading are considered to determine which loading conditions determine the beam design, and the parameter choices that minimize the beam weight per unit length and therefore its cost, are found.

10.2 Optimum Cross Section Based on Bending Stress

Relationship between Cross-Section Area and Moment of Inertia

Consider a beam of rectangular cross section with the dimensions shown in figure 10-1. If the maximum bending moment on the cross section is M and the maximum bending stress is σ, then it is well known from the theory of strength of materials that

$$\sigma = \frac{Mc}{I} \qquad (10.2.1)$$

in which $c = h/2$ and I is the moment of inertia of the cross section. For the cross section of figure 10-1,

$$I = 4t_1 \int_0^{(1/2)h} x^2 dx + 2w \int_{(1/2)h-t_2}^{(1/2)h} x^2 dx$$

$$= \frac{t_1 h^3}{6} + \frac{wt_2}{2} (h^2 - 2ht_2 + 4/3t_2^2)$$

Substituting into equation (10.2.1),

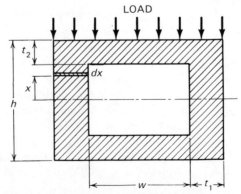

Figure 10-1. Cross Section of a Rectangular Beam

$$\frac{M}{\sigma} = \frac{I}{c} = \frac{t_1 h^2}{3} + \frac{wt_2}{h} \, (h^2 - 2ht_2 + 4/3t_2^2) \qquad (10.2.2)$$

It is convenient to introduce the dimensionless variables

$$\hbar = h/t_2$$

$$\alpha = wt_2/ht_1 \qquad (10.2.3)$$

$$\mathscr{I} = I/ct_1 t_2^2$$

Then, equation (10.2.2) can be written

$$\mathscr{I} = \hbar^2/3 + \alpha(\hbar^2 - 2\hbar + 4/3) \qquad (10.2.4)$$

The cross sectional area of the beam is, from figure 10-1,

$$A = 2(ht_1 + wt_2) \qquad (10.2.5)$$

or in dimensionless form

$$\mathscr{A} = A/t_1 t_2 = 2(1 + \alpha)\hbar \qquad (10.2.6)$$

By eliminating $\hbar$ between equations (10.2.4) and (10.2.6), it is possible to obtain an equation for $\mathscr{A}$ as a function of $\mathscr{I}$ with α as a parameter. Then, for a given $\mathscr{I}$, it is possible to determine for what value of α $\mathscr{A}$ will be a minimum. If $\mathscr{A}$ is a minimum, then for given wall thicknesses t_1 and t_2, A is a minimum, and the cost per unit length is a minimum.

First solve equation (10.2.4) for $\hbar$:

$$\hbar = \frac{3\alpha \pm \sqrt{(1 + 3\alpha)\left[3\mathscr{I} - \alpha\left(\dfrac{4 + 3\alpha}{1 + 3\alpha}\right)\right]}}{1 + 3\alpha}$$

Only the positive sign in the above equation has physical meaning. This may be seen by noting that for fixed α and fixed t_1 and t_2, h must increase as M increases. Substituting into equation (10.2.6) then leads to the result

$$\mathscr{A} = 2\left(\frac{1 + \alpha}{1 + 3\alpha}\right)\left\{3\alpha + \sqrt{(1 + 3\alpha)\left[3\mathscr{I} - \alpha\left(\frac{4 + 3\alpha}{1 + 3\alpha}\right)\right]}\right\} \qquad (10.2.7)$$

In figure 10-2, $\mathscr{A}/\mathscr{I}^{1/2}$ is plotted from equation (10.2.7) as a function of α with $\mathscr{I}$ as a parameter. Using $\mathscr{A}/\mathscr{I}^{1/2}$ as the ordinate reduces the range of the plotted variable by many orders of magnitude without reducing the generality of the results.

Optimum Width/Depth Ratio

Note from figure 10-2 that there is a value of α that minimizes $\mathscr{A}$ for fixed $\mathscr{I}$, that is, for fixed load and wall thicknesses there is a value of w/h which minimizes the cross sectional area and hence the cost of the beam per unit length. As the wall thickness becomes thin, $\mathscr{I}$ becomes very large. In the limit for very large $\mathscr{I}$, equation (10.2.7) simplifies to

$$\mathscr{A} = \frac{2(1 + \alpha)(3\mathscr{I})^{1/2}}{(1 + 3\alpha)^{1/2}} \tag{10.2.8}$$

Setting the derivative with respect to α equal to zero in equation (10.2.8) gives

$$\frac{\partial \mathscr{A}}{\partial \alpha} = 0 = \frac{2(3\mathscr{I})^{1/2}}{1 + 3\alpha}\left[(1 + 3\alpha)^{1/2} - \frac{3(1 + \alpha)}{2(1 + 3\alpha)^{1/2}}\right]$$

which is satisfied if $\alpha = 1/3$. Substituting $\alpha = 1/3$ into equation (10.2.8) shows that for thin-walled box beams the minimum cross-sectional area is found from

$$\mathscr{A}_{\min} = 4(2/3)^{1/2} \mathscr{I}^{1/2} = 3.27 \mathscr{I}^{1/2} \tag{10.2.9}$$

From figure 10-2, it is seen that as α increases, the ratio of $\mathscr{A}$ to $\mathscr{A}_{\min}$ increases as follows:

α:	1	2	3	4	5	6
$\mathscr{A}/\mathscr{A}_{\min}$:	1.06	1.20	1.34	1.47	1.59	1.70

The increased cost of the beam is in proportion to these numbers.

Figure 10-2 shows that for decreasing $\mathscr{I}$ (thicker-walled beams for a given load), the point of minimum $\mathscr{A}$ moves to values of α smaller than one third, and that for a value of $\mathscr{I}$ between 10 and $10^{1.5}$, α for minimum $\mathscr{A}$ vanishes. It is also noted that for thick-walled beams, the ratio $\mathscr{A}/\mathscr{A}_{\min}$ increases more rapidly as α increases than for thin-walled beams.

Required Wall Thickness

It is of interest to determine if there is an optimum way t_1 and t_2 can be chosen. To obtain a sufficiently high vibrational frequency (section 10.3), it is necessary to choose the ratio of h to the span sufficiently large, and in that way h is determined. Then, for a given α, the beam will support greater load if its wall thickness is greater. Thus the optimum wall thickness is the minimum value that will support the load.

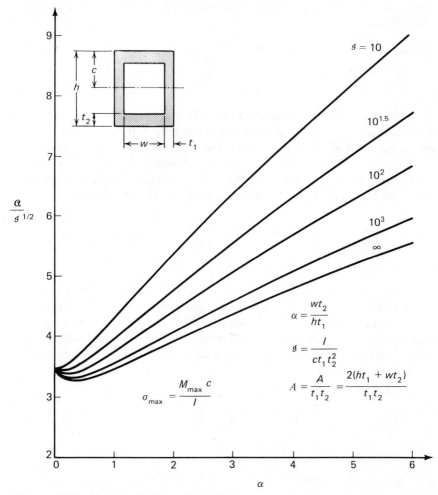

Figure 10-2. Required Cross-Sectional Area of a Box Beam at Given Maximum Static Load

If the minimum wall thickness is thin ($t << h$), equation (10.2.9) applies. Substituting the meaning of $\mathscr{A}$ and $\mathscr{I}$ given in figure 10-2,

$$A_{\min} = 3.27 \left(\frac{M_{\max}}{\sigma_{\max}} \right)^{1/2} t_1^{1/2} \qquad (10.2.10)$$

Thus $A_{\min}$ depends only on t_1 and not on t_2. This means that t_1 should be chosen as small as practical from the standpoints of fabrication, plate buckling (section 10.7) and plate vibration (section 10.8). On other hand, t_2 can be chosen to accommodate a desired ratio of w/h. Thus, from equations (10.2.3), for $\alpha = 1/3$,

$$\frac{t_2}{t_1} = \frac{h}{3w}$$

If, for ease of material procurement it is desired to make $t_1 = t_2$, then one must choose $h/w = 3$ to minimize cost per unit length. If, however, for some design reason it is desired to choose $h/w = 1$, say, then it is necessary to choose $t_2 = t_1/3$. But we have already chosen t_1 as thin as possible. Therefore t_2 must be at least as large as t_1, but clearly should be no larger. Thus, for thin walled box beams, one should make the choices

$$t_1 = t_2 = t$$

$$h = 3w$$

It is seen that if minimum guideway cost is desired, it is necessary to accommodate the vehicle design to the guideway and not vice versa.

The wall thickness required to meet static stress requirements can be found for $\alpha = 1/3$ by eliminating $\mathscr{A}$ between equations (10.2.9) and (10.2.6). Then, using the parameter definitions given in figure 10-2 and by equations (10.2.3), and setting $\alpha = 1/3$,

$$t = \frac{3M_{\max}}{2\sigma_{\max}h^2} \qquad (10.2.11)$$

An Example of Optimum Design of a Thin-Walled Beam

Consider a specific example. Assume a uniformly loaded simply supported beam with distance ℓ_s between supports. This load condition represents the case of a span loaded with vehicles with zero spacing between them, the worst static condition that must be considered. Then, from any text on strength of materials,

$$M_{max} = \frac{q\ell_s^2}{8} \qquad (10.2.12)$$

in which q is the load per unit length. If q_ℓ is the live load,

$$q = q_\ell + \rho g A \qquad (10.2.13)$$

in which ρg is the weight per unit length of the beam.
Substituting for A from equation (10.2.6) with $\alpha = 1/3$

$$q = q_\ell + 8/3\rho g h t$$

Substituting q into equation (10.2.12) and the result into equation (10.2.11) gives

$$t = \frac{3\ell_s^2}{16\sigma_m h^2} \, (q_\ell + 8/3\rho g h t)$$

Solving for t, we have

$$t = \frac{\dfrac{3q_\ell}{8\rho g h}}{\dfrac{2\sigma_m h}{\rho g \ell_s^2} - 1} \qquad (10.2.14)$$

Vanishing of the denominator gives the span length ℓ_s for which the beam can no longer support its own weight. Setting the denominator equal to zero and solving for ℓ_s gives

$$(\ell_s)_{max} = \left(\frac{2\sigma_m h}{\rho g} \right)^{1/2} \qquad (10.2.15)$$

We see that the maximum length for $q_\ell > 0$ depends on the material property $\sigma_m/\rho g$. For ordinary structural steel, the yield point is between 30 and 40,000 psi[7]. Therefore, assume a design stress $\sigma_m = 20,000$ psi $[140(10)^6 \text{ N/m}^2]$,[a] and $\rho = 484$ lb$_m$/ft^3[7760 kg/m^3]. Then $\sigma_m/\rho g = 1804$ m.

---

[a] 1 psi $= 6895$ N/m^2, 1 lb$_m$/ft$^3 = 16.02$ kg/m^3, 1 lb$_f$/ft $= 14.6$ N/m.

Thus, for a steel beam say 1 m deep, $(\ell_s)_{max} = 60$ m. For reinforced concrete beams, different values will be obtained depending on the arrangement of reinforcing bars and the degree of prestressing.

For a typical live loading $q_\ell = 300$ lb/ft (4470 N/m), the required thickness of a steel beam, computed from equation (10.2.14), is given in figure 10-3. The ratio of live load to dead load at maximum stress

$$\frac{q_\ell}{\rho g A} = \frac{2\sigma_m h}{\rho g \ell_s^2} - 1 \qquad (10.2.16)$$

is also shown as a matter of interest. Note that t is proportional to q_ℓ, but that $q_\ell/\rho g A$ is independent of q_ℓ.

Since $t/h < < 1$ in all cases in figure 10-3, the calculation based on equation (10.2.14) is valid. For concrete, t will be much larger and the

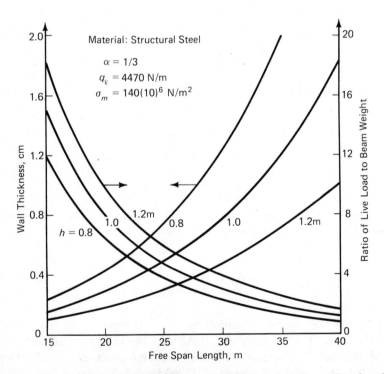

Figure 10-3. Required Wall Thickness of an Optimum Cross Section Steel Box Beam Uniformity Loaded

assumption $\mathscr{I} = \infty$ in use of figure 10-2 is not valid. In this case t can be found by iteration. For a given q_ℓ, σ_{max}, and h, assume a value of t and compute M_{max}/σ_{max}. Then compute $\mathscr{I}$ and from figure 10-2 select an appropriate α. Then $\mathscr{A}$ is determined. From equation (10.2.6) t can now be found. If the assumed and computed values do not agree, pick another value of t closer to the computed value and repeat the calculation until the two values converge.

Relationship between Live Load and
Weight per Unit Length

An important consideration in guideway design is to understand how the required beam weight per unit length and hence cost varies with q_ℓ. If α and h are held fixed, equation (10.2.6) shows that A is proportional to t. But, from equation (10.2.14) t is proportional to q_ℓ for $t \ll h$. Thus, for thin-walled beams, A, and hence the beam weight per unit length, increases in direct proportion to q_ℓ. Consequently the beam cost increases with q_ℓ. For thick-walled box beams strict proportionality does not hold and the function $A(q_\ell)$ must be found by iteration between equations (10.2.7) and (10.2.6), in which in $\mathscr{I}$ (equation (10.2.3)) M/σ is substituted for I/c, then M from equation (10.2.12) and q from equation (10.2.13).

Horizontal Wind Loading

Consider horizontal wind loading. From aerodynamic theory the horizontal wind pressure is $\frac{1}{2}\rho_a V_w^2$, in which ρ_a is the air density and V_w is the wind speed. Therefore the wind loading per unit length on the guideway alone with no vehicles is

$$q_{wind} = \frac{1}{2}\rho_a V_w^2 h \qquad (10.2.17)$$

The tolerable wind loading on a structure calculated for vertical loading is found with the help of figure 10-2 by noting that the appropriate value of α is the reciprocal of the value used in calculating the beam for vertical loading.

As an illustration, assume t is much less than h and $\alpha = 1/3$ for vertical load. Then, for horizontal wind loads $\alpha = 3$ and, from figure 10-2,

$$\mathscr{A} = 4.38\mathscr{I}^{1/2}.$$

Compare this equation with equation (10.2.9), in which $\mathscr{A}$ has the same value. $\mathscr{I}$ is proportional to M and hence to the load per unit length. Thus

$$q_{\text{wind}} = \left(\frac{3.27}{4.38}\right)^2 (q_\ell + \rho gA)$$

$$= 0.557q_\ell \left(1 + \frac{\rho gA}{q_\ell}\right)$$

Using the example of figure 10-3, $q_\ell = 4470$ N/m; and as an illustration assume $\ell_s = 30$ m. Then $q_\ell/\rho gA = 3.0$ and the tolerable wind load is

$$q_{\text{wind}} = 3320 \text{ N/m}$$

Substituting this value into equation (10.2.17), the wind speed corresponding to $q_{\text{wind}} = 3320$ N/m is

$$(V_w)_{\text{max}} = \left[\frac{2(3320)}{\rho_a h}\right]^{1/2}$$

But $\rho_a = 1.293$ kg/m³ at standard conditions, and, in the above example, $h = 1$ m. Thus

$$(V_w)_{\text{max}} = 72 \text{ m/s} = 161 \text{ mi/h}$$

With winds of even half this magnitude, it can be assumed that the system will be shut down and the vehicles stored in sheltered locations. Thus the added wind load on the vehicles need not be included. With, say $1/3(V_w)_{\text{max}}$, the system may, however, be operative. The wind load on the guideway alone will then be one ninth as much but the torsional load applied to the guideway through the vehicles must be taken into account. This problem is considered in section 10.6.

Double Guideway

Many guideway transit systems, both in development and in operation, use conventional wheeled vehicles which require wide guideways. Based on the above theory, an approach to optimum design of such a structure would be to use two parallel beams rigidly connected together. These could be I-beams, box beams, or some other shape. Let us compare these designs with a single box beam. The variables are the depth of the beams h, the thickness of the material t, and the span ℓ_s. The equations needed to compare designs are equations (10.2.2), (10.2.5), and (10.2.12). For simplicity, assume t is much less than h, and let $\alpha = 1/3$ for each beam. Then, from equations (10.2.2) and (10.2.5),

$$\frac{M}{\sigma} \approx \frac{2}{3}\,th^2 \tag{10.2.18}$$

$$A = \frac{8th}{3} \tag{10.2.19}$$

With the two-beam configuration, M is cut in half for each beam, and we wish to examine the effect of this reduction on the total cross-sectional area, that is, $2A$ for the two-beam configuration. Consider the following three cases.

Case 1: Fixed ℓ_s, t. Then h becomes $h/\sqrt{2}$ and A becomes $A/\sqrt{2}$. Hence the total cross-sectional area A_T becomes $\sqrt{2}A$, where A is the cross-sectional area of a single beam. Thus, with fixed ℓ_s and t, a two-beam configuration has 1.4 times the cross-sectional area of a one-beam configuration. Thus, if the material cost is proportional to the cross-sectional area, the two-beam configuration is 40 percent more expensive for the beams alone; however, the extra labor and material required to fasten the two beams together will increase the cost even more.

Case 2: Fixed ℓ_s, h. Now t becomes $\frac{1}{2}t$, and A becomes $\frac{1}{2}A$. Thus A_T remains the same. But if, for the single beam t is chosen as thin as possible for reasons of fabrication, it is unlikely that it is possible to reduce t by 50 percent. Thus, this form of the two-beam configuration is also more expensive than a single beam.

Case 3: Fixed t, A_T. In this case, equation (10.2.19) shows that h becomes $\frac{1}{2}h$, and equation (10.2.18) shows that M becomes $\frac{1}{4}M$. Thus two beams can carry only half the moment they must carry. But, from equation (10.2.12), if the maximum moment carried by the two-beam configuration is cut in half, ℓ_s must be reduced by $1/\sqrt{2} = 0.707$, that is, the span length must be reduced by 30 percent, thus requiring 30 percent more support posts.

In all three cases, it is seen that a guideway cost penalty is paid if conventional wheeled vehicles are to be used. Thus, long term interest in monobeam transit systems is justified. The difficult problem, however, has been to design the vehicle/guideway system in such a way that the vehicle can switch from one guideway to another with no moving parts in the track, that is, by means of in-vehicle switches. Several groups, reported in the Lea Transit Compendium[8], have succeeded in developing such switches.

10.3 Dynamic Loading—Single Vehicle Crossing a Span

In design of a guideway of minimum weight per unit length, it is necessary to understand the effect of motion of the vehicles on the maximum stresses in the guideway, and the vertical accelerations produced on the vehicle as a result of motion of the guideway. Also, knowledge of the amplitudes and frequencies of motion of the guideway is needed to make certain that the fatigue life of the guideway will be adequate. The objective of this section is to give some insight into these problems and the parameters that control them.

In this section, the simplest dynamic loading problem of interest is solved and discussed—that of a single vehicle crossing a flexible span. For mathematical simplicity, the dynamics of the vehicle are not taken into account. This permits concentration on guideway characteristics and will provide insight into choice of vehicle dynamic characteristics, but of course in a complete solution, vehicle dynamics must be considered. Such a treatment is given by Snyder, Wormley, and Richardson of MIT[3] for multiple vehicle crossings of a span. Therefore the important multiple vehicle case is treated in section 10.4 by discussion of their computer solutions.

Equation of Motion of a Flexible Span

Figure 10-4 depicts a vehicle of weight W and speed V about to cross a flexible simply supported span of length ℓ_s.

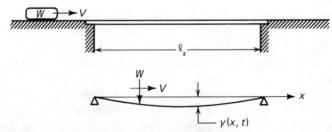

Figure 10-4. A Vehicle Cross a Flexible Span

In the present analysis, the vehicle will be treated as a point force W moving at speed V, and, for mathematical simplicity, the beam will be assumed to be undamped. Since the damping of a real beam is generally small, the undamped beam is a useful idealization. The deflection of the beam, $y(x, t)$, satisfies the partial differential equation[9]

$$EI \frac{\partial^2 y}{\partial x^4} + \rho A \frac{\partial^2 y}{\partial t^2} = f(x, t) \qquad (10.3.1)$$

in which E is the modules of elasticity, I and A have the meanings of the previous section, ρ is the mass per unit volume, and $f(x,t)$ is an arbitrary time-space-dependent force per unit length.

For a simply supported beam, the boundary conditions are

$$y(0, t) = y(\ell_s, t) = 0$$

$$\left. \frac{\partial^2 y}{\partial x^2} (0, t) = \frac{\partial^2 y}{\partial x^2} (\ell_s, t) = 0 \right\} \qquad (10.3.2)$$

and the initial conditions are taken as an undeflected beam at rest, that is

$$y(x, 0) = \frac{\partial y}{\partial t} (x, 0) = 0 \qquad (10.3.3)$$

Following reference[3], the solution of equation (10.3.1) can be expressed in the form

$$y(x, t) = \sum_{m=1}^{\infty} A_m(t) \sin \left(\frac{m\pi x}{\ell_s} \right) \qquad m = 1, 2, \ldots \qquad (10.3.4)$$

The form of the space function in equation (10.3.4) satisfies both the differential equation and the boundary conditions (10.3.2). Substitute equation (10.3.4) into equation (10.3.1), multiply by $\sin (n\pi x/\ell_s)$, and integrate from $x = 0$ to $x = \ell_s$. The result is that $A_m(t)$ satisfies the differential equation

$$\ddot{A}_m + \omega_m^2 A_m = \frac{2}{\rho A \ell_s} \int_0^{\ell_s} f(x, t) \sin m\pi x/\ell_s \, dx \qquad (10.3.5)$$

in which the dots denote time differentiation, and

$$\omega_m = \left(\frac{m\pi}{\ell_s}\right)^2 \sqrt{\frac{EI}{\rho A}} \qquad (10.3.6)$$

is 2π times the natural frequencies of vibration of the beam.

Solution with Vehicle as Point Load

The assumption that the vehicle behaves as a point force means that

$$\left. \begin{array}{lll} f(x,t)dx = W & \text{if} & x = Vt < \ell_s \\[2mm] = 0 & \text{if} & x \neq Vt \\[2mm] = 0 & \text{if} & t > \ell_s/V \end{array} \right\} \qquad (10.3.7)$$

Substituting equation (10.3.7) into equation (10.3.5) gives

$$\left. \begin{array}{ll} \ddot{A}_m + w_m^2 A_m = \dfrac{2W}{\rho A \ell_s} \sin \Omega_m t & t \leq \ell_s/V \\[4mm] = 0 & t > \ell_s/V \end{array} \right\} \qquad (10.3.8)$$

in which

$$\Omega_m = \frac{m\pi V}{\ell_s} \qquad (10.3.9)$$

The general solution of equation (10.3.8), for $t \leq \ell_s/V$, is

$$A_m(t) = C_1 \sin \Omega_m t + C_2 \cos \omega_m t + \frac{2W \sin \Omega_m t}{\rho A \ell_s (\omega_m^2 - \Omega_m^2)}$$

From equation (10.3.3), the initial conditions are $A_m(0) = \dot{A}_m(0) = 0$. Using these conditions to evaluate the constants C_1 and C_2,

$$A_m(t) = \frac{2W}{\rho A \ell_s \omega_m^2} \frac{1}{(1 - \beta_m^2)} \quad (\sin \beta_m \omega_m t - \beta_m \sin \omega_m t) \quad (10.3.10)$$

in which, from equations (10.3.9) and (10.3.6),

$$\beta_m = \frac{\Omega_m}{\omega_m} = \frac{\ell_s V}{m\pi} \sqrt{\frac{\rho A}{EI}} \tag{10.3.11}$$

is a dimensionless speed parameter.

Comparison with Static Solution

Equation (10.3.10) applies to the case $t \leq \ell_s/V$. The case $t > \ell_s/V$ will be solved later, but first it is useful to compare the above solution with the static solution for the same beam with a concentrated load at the center. From any text on strength of materials, the static midspan deflection ($y = \ell_s/2$) is

$$y(\ell_s/2) = \frac{1}{48} \frac{W \ell_s^3}{EI} \tag{10.3.12}$$

For the dynamically loaded beam, equation (10.3.4) gives for the midspan deflection

$$y(\ell_s/2, t) = A_1(t) - A_3(t) + A_5(t) - \ldots \tag{10.3.13}$$

ing equation (10.3.6), the dimensional coefficient in equation (10.3.10) is

$$\frac{2W}{\rho A \ell_s \omega_m^2} = \frac{2}{\pi^4} \frac{W \ell_s^3}{EI} \frac{1}{m^4}$$

Therefore, the ratio of dynamic to static deflection at midspan is, from equations (10.3.10), (10.3.12) and (10.3.13),

$$\frac{y(\ell_s/2,\, t)}{y(\ell_s/2)} = \frac{96}{\pi^4} \sum_{m=1,3,\ldots} \frac{(-1)^{(m-1)/2}}{m^4} \left(\frac{\sin \beta_m \omega_m t - \beta_m \sin \omega_m t}{1 - \beta_m^2} \right)$$

(10.3.14)

Note that $96/\pi^4 = 0.986 \approx 1$.

Because of the factor m^4, equation (10.3.14) is very nearly given by the first term:

$$\frac{y(\ell_s/2,t)}{y(\ell_s/2)} \approx 0.986 \left(\frac{\sin \beta_1 \omega_1 t - \beta_1 \sin \omega_1 t}{1 - \beta_1^2} \right) \qquad (10.3.14a)$$

The vehicle reaches midspan when $t = \ell_s/2V$. At this point, from equations (10.3.9) and (10.3.11), $\beta_m \omega_m t = m\pi/2$. Therefore equation (10.3.14a) becomes

$$\frac{y(\ell_s/2,\, \ell_s/2V)}{y(\ell_s/2)} \approx 0.986 \left(\frac{1 - \beta_1 \sin (\pi/2\beta_1)}{1 - \beta_1^2} \right) \qquad (10.3.15)$$

Equation (10.3.15) is plotted in figure 10-5. The maximum deflection is 1.520 times the static value and occurs when $\beta_1 = 0.373$. For higher values of β_1 (higher speed) the midspan deflection decreases with speed because the beam has insufficient time to respond to the presence of the vehicle. Below $\beta_1 = 0.373$ the maximum deflection may be larger or smaller than the static value depending on the phase relationship between the natural motion of the beam and the time of arrival of the vehicle at midspan. As the speed decreases to zero, equation (10.3.15) approaches $96/\pi^4$; however, the infinite series of equation (10.3.14) approaches $\pi^4/96$ when $t = \ell_s/2V$ because of the identity

$$\sum_{m=1,3,\ldots}^{\infty} \frac{1}{m^4} \equiv \frac{\pi^4}{96}$$

The maximum deflection of the beam generally occurs before or after the vehicle reaches midspan. These maxima can be found from equation (10.3.14a) but, from continuity, it can be assumed that they follow the envelope indicated by the dotted line in figure 10-5. The maximum midspan deflection while the vehicle is on the beam will probably be larger than 1.520 times the static value, but with the purpose of studying this problem in mind, enough has been learned without computing it exactly.

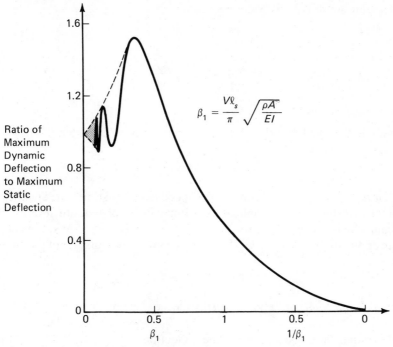

Figure 10-5. Maximum Midspan Deflection of Flexible Beam When Vehicle Is at Midspan

A Critical Speed

The value $\beta_1 = 0.373$ produces the maximum midpoint deflection when the vehicle is at midspan, therefore the corresponding speed can be called a critical speed. From equation (10.3.11) it is

$$V_{cr} = \frac{1.172}{\ell_s} \sqrt{\frac{EI}{\rho A}} \qquad (10.3.16)$$

For a thin-walled steel beam, equations (10.2.2, 10.2.5) show, for the optimum case $\alpha = 1/3$, that

$$\frac{I}{A} \approx \frac{th^3/3}{8th/3} = \frac{h^2}{8} \qquad (10.3.17)$$

Thus, equation (10.3.16) becomes

$$V_{cr} = 0.414 \, h/\ell_s \sqrt{\frac{E}{\rho}} \qquad (10.3.16a)$$

For steel, $E = 30(10)^6$ psi $= 21(10)^{10}$ N/m^2 and $\rho = 7760$ kg/m^3. Thus

$$V_{cr} = 2150 \, h/\ell_s \text{ m/s}$$

and for $h/\ell_s = 1/30$, $V_{cr} = 72$ m/s. This speed is several times the speeds of interest in urban transit applications, but will be of definite interest in designing high-speed intercity systems. For a speed of say 15 m/s, typical of urban applications, $\beta_1 = 0.373(15/72) = 0.078$ with the same set of parameters.

Motion of the Span after Vehicle Has Crossed

We have thus far considered only the deflection of the guideway while the vehile is at its center. It is possible that further motion of the vehicle will add energy to the guideway and hence increase the amplitude of its vibration. Thus, consider the case $t > \ell_s/V$. Then, the right side of equation (10.3.8) is zero and the solution is

$$A_m(t') = \frac{\dot{A}_m(0)}{\omega_m} \sin \omega_m t' + A_m(0) \cos \omega_m t' \qquad (10.3.18)$$

in which $t' = t - \ell_s/V$ and $A_m(0)$, $A_m(0)$ are found from equation (10.3.10) by substituting $t = \ell_s/V$. Taking into account from equations (10.3.9) and (10.3.11) that $\beta_m \omega_m \ell_s/V = m\pi$, and the expression above equation (10.3.14),

$$\left.\begin{aligned}
A_m(0) &= -\frac{2W\ell_s^3 \beta_m}{\pi^4 EI} \frac{\sin \omega_m \ell_s/V}{m^4(1 - \beta_m^2)} \\[2mm]
\frac{\dot{A}_m(0)}{\omega_m} &= \frac{2W\ell_s^3 \beta_m (\cos m\pi - \cos \omega_m \ell_s/V)}{\pi^4 EI} \frac{}{m^4(1 - \beta_m^2)}
\end{aligned}\right\} \qquad (10.3.19)$$

The maximum value of A_m after the vehicle has crossed the span is found by setting $\dot{A}_m(t') = 0$ from equation (10.3.18), solving for $\omega_m t'$, and substituting it into equation (10.3.18). Thus, $\dot{A}_m(t') = 0$ gives

$$\tan\omega_m t = \frac{\dot{A}_m(0)}{\omega_m A_m(0)} \qquad (10.3.20)$$

Using the trigonometric identity $\cos\theta = (1 + \tan^2\theta)^{-1/2}$, equation (10.3.18) can be written in the form

$$A_m(t') = \left[\frac{\dot{A}_m(0)}{\omega_m} \tan\omega_m t' + A_m(0) \right] (1 + \tan^2\omega_m t')^{-1/2}$$

Substituting equation (10.3.20),

$$(A_m)_{\max} = [A_m^2(0) + \dot{A}_m^2(0)/\omega_m^2]^{1/2} \qquad (10.3.21)$$

Substitute equations (10.3.19) into equation (10.3.21), taking into account that $\omega_m \ell_s/V = m\pi/\beta_m$. The result, as a ratio to equation (10.3.12), can be expressed in the form

$$\frac{(A_m)_{\max}}{y(\frac{1}{2}\ell_s)} = \frac{96\sqrt{2}}{\pi^4} \frac{\beta_m}{m^4(1 - \beta_m^2)} (1 - \cos m\pi \cos m\pi/\beta_m)^{1/2} \quad (10.3.22)$$

Substituting into equation (10.3.4) at $x = \ell_s/2$, the ratio of dynamic to static deflection is

$$\frac{y(\frac{1}{2}\ell_s)_{\text{dynamic}}}{y(\frac{1}{2}\ell_s)_{\text{static}}} = \frac{96\sqrt{2}}{\pi^4} \sum_{m=\text{odd}} \frac{(-1)^{(m-1)/2}}{m^4} \frac{\beta_m}{(1 - \beta_m^2)} \left(1 + \cos\frac{m\pi}{\beta_m}\right)^{1/2}$$

$$(10.3.23)$$

To illustrate the character of the motion, equation (10.3.23) is plotted in figure 10-6. It is seen that the peak amplitude ratio is 1.691 and occurs at $\beta_1 = 0.732$. This compares with a peak amplitude ratio of 1.520 at $\beta_1 = 0.373$ when the vehicle is at midspan. Thus the vehicle-at-midspan condition occurs at roughly half the speed, and equation (10.3.16) can still be considered the critical speed.

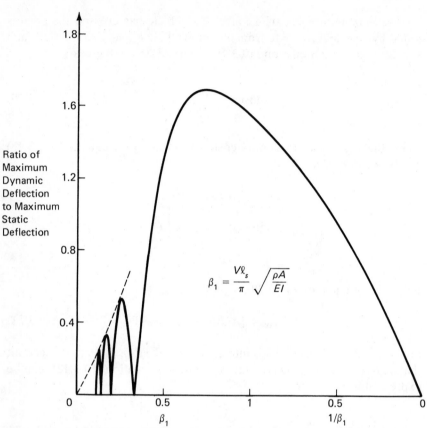

Figure 10-6. Maximum Midspan Amplitude of Vibratory Motion of Flexible Beam After Vehicle Has Crossed It

The Maximum Vertical Acceleration of the Vehicle

The limiting conditions in design of the beam are the maximum acceleration and the maximum dynamic bending stress. Thus formulas for these quantities are now developed.

The vertical acceleration as seen from the moving vehicle is the second total time derivative of $y(x,t)$. Thus

$$\frac{dy}{dt} = \frac{\partial y}{\partial t} + V \frac{\partial y}{\partial x}$$

$$\frac{d^2y}{dt^2} = \frac{\partial^2 y}{\partial t^2} + 2V \frac{\partial^2 y}{\partial t \partial x} + V^2 \frac{\partial^2 y}{\partial x^2}$$

Applying this operator to equation (10.3.4), then substituting $x = Vt$ and using equation (10.3.9) gives

$$\frac{d^2y}{dt^2} = \sum_{m=1}^{\infty} (\ddot{A}_m \sin \Omega_m t + 2\dot{A}_m \Omega_m \cos \Omega_m t - A_m \Omega_m^2 \sin \Omega_m t)$$

Substitute A_m and its derivatives from equations (10.3.10). Taking into account equations (10.3.9) and (10.3.11), and the identity above equation (10.3.14),

$$\frac{d^2y}{dt^2} = \frac{2W\ell_s V^2}{\pi^2 EI} \sum_{m=1}^{\infty} \frac{1}{m^2(1 - \beta_m^2)} \ [2(\cos^2 \Omega_m t - \sin^2 \Omega_m t)$$

$$+ \left(\beta_m + \frac{1}{\beta_m}\right)\sin \omega_m t \ \sin \Omega_m t - 2\cos \omega_m t \ \cos\Omega_m t]$$

Use of trigonometric identities reduces this expression to a sum of single cosine terms

$$\frac{d^2y}{dt^2} = \frac{2W\ell_s V^2}{\pi^2 EI} \sum_{m=1}^{\infty} \frac{1}{m^2} \left[\frac{2\cos 2\Omega_m t}{1 - \beta_m^2} \right.$$

$$\left. + \frac{1}{2\beta_m}\left(\frac{1 - \beta_m}{1 + \beta_m}\right)\cos(\omega_m - \Omega_m)t - \frac{1}{2\beta_m}\left(\frac{1 + \beta_m}{1 - \beta_m}\right)\cos(\omega_m + \Omega_m)t \right]$$

Note from equation (10.3.11) that β_m varies as $1/m$. Therefore the first term of the above equation is proportional to $1/m^2$, but the second and third terms are proportional to $1/m$. Hence, for $m > 1$ the first term can be neglected in rough estimations. Using equation (10.3.11), factoring out $2\beta_1$, and noting from equation (10.3.16a) that β_1 is small at urban speeds, d^2y/dt^2 can be written in the approximate form

$$\frac{d^2y}{dx^2} = \frac{W}{\rho A \ell_s} \, \beta_1 \Bigg\{ 4\beta_1 \cos 2\Omega_1 t + \left(\frac{1 - \beta_1}{1 + \beta_1} \right) \cos(1 - \beta_1)\omega_1 t$$

$$- \left(\frac{1 + \beta_1}{1 - \beta_1} \right) \cos(1 + \beta_1)\omega_1 t$$

$$+ \sum_{m=2}^{\infty} \frac{1}{m} [\cos(1 - \beta_m)\omega_m t - \cos(1 + \beta_m)\omega_m t] \Bigg\} \qquad (11.3.25)$$

Since β_1 is much less than 1, the second and third terms of the first vibration mode dominate the above expression. For small β_1, $1/(1 \pm \beta_1) \approx 1 \mp \beta_1$. Then, using trigonometric identities, the second and third terms become approximately

$$2(\sin \Omega_1 t \, \sin\omega_1 t - \beta_1 \cos\omega_1 t \cos \Omega_1 t)$$

But $\Omega_1 t = \pi/2$ when the vehicle is at midspan, and ω_1 is much greater than Ω_1. Therefore, for β_1 much less than 1, the maximum value of this expression is close to 2. Therefore

$$\frac{1}{g} \frac{d^2y}{dt^2} \Bigg|_{max} \approx \frac{2W\beta_1}{\rho g A \ell_s} = \frac{2(W/g)V}{\pi \sqrt{\rho AEI}} \qquad (10.3.26)$$

In which g is the acceleration of gravity.

Minimizing the Maximum Acceleration

Equation (10.3.26) is valid only if β_1 is much less than 1, but from the example following equation (10.3.16a) this is usually true in urban applications. From equation (10.3.11), the condition of small β_1 requires that the material property E/ρ be as large as possible, the cross-sectional property I/A be as large as possible, and for optimized values of E/ρ and I/A, that the span ℓ_s be limited for a given speed, or vice versa. For a given value of β_1, equation (10.3.26) shows that the maximum acceleration depends on $W/\rho g A \ell_s$, the ratio of vehicle weight to span weight. But ρ, A, and ℓ_s have already entered into computation of β_1. Therefore, the acceleration can be held below a specified limit only by limiting the weight of the vehicle. As shown by the rightmost form of equation (10.3.26), the maximum acceleration is insensitive to variations in span length ℓ_s as long as the condition β_1 is much less than 1 is maintained.

As indicated above, the cross-section parameter I/A should be maximized to minimize the effects of dynamic loading. Or, for given I/A, the dimension of the cross section should be chosen to minimize A, hence the weight per unit length, and hence cost per unit length. Clearly, the cross section that maximizes I for given A is one in which the bulk of the material is as far from the neutral axis of the beam as possible. For a box beam (see figure 10-1) of given wall thickness, I is maximized if the aspect ratio $\alpha = w/h$ vanishes. This is, of course, an unobtainable condition because lateral stiffness must be provided.

On the other hand, we found in section 10.2 that to maximize the load-carrying ability under static conditions, I/c had to be maximized for a given cross section area and this leads to $\alpha = 1/3$. For this condition, equation (10.2.2) and (10.2.5) show that, for the box beam with thin walls,

$$\frac{I}{A} = \frac{h^2}{12}\left(\frac{1 + 3\alpha}{1 + \alpha}\right) = \frac{h^2}{8}$$

We must concern ourselves with horizontal loads; therefore consider that I/A for the same beam in the horizontal direction is found by interchanging w and h, where $\alpha = w/h$. Thus

$$(I/A)_{\text{horiz}} = \frac{w^2}{12}\left(\frac{1 + 3\cdot 3}{1 + 3}\right) = \frac{h^2}{8(5.4)}$$

Thus, from equations (10.3.6) and (10.3.11),

$$\frac{(\beta_1)_{\text{vert}}}{(\beta_1)_{\text{horiz}}} = \frac{(\omega_1)_{\text{horiz}}}{(\omega_1)_{\text{vert}}} = (5.4)^{-1/2} = 0.430$$

Thus, the natural frequency of the beam in the horizontal plane is 43 percent of its value in the vertical plane. The load in the horizontal plane on a straight piece of guideway is due mainly to wind, which is a low frequency load. There is also a load due to unbalanced vehicles, much smaller and much more variable than the vertical load.

In curves, the load is due to the centrifugal force WV^2/gR, which for comfort should be less than about $W/4$. Then, from the middle expression in equation (10.3.26), in the horizontal directions $W\beta_1$ becomes

$$\frac{W}{4} \cdot \frac{\beta_1}{0.43} = \frac{W\beta_1}{4(0.43)} = 0.58W\beta_1$$

Thus, without changing ℓ_s, the maximum acceleration in the horizontal plane is only 58 percent of its value in the vertical plane in the case of a box beam for which $\alpha = 1/3$. In conclusion, it appears that a beam aspect ratio α of one-third is large enough to provide adequate stiffness in the horizontal plane.

Weight Penalty for Deviation from Optimum Cross Section

While it is of fundamental importance to find the optimum properties of the cross section for minimum cost per unit length, it is also important to know how much the cost increases if a nonoptimum cross section is used. As before, we assume that the cost per unit length increases with A^b. Thus, we wish to find how A varies with α for a given value of IA, that is, for given maximum acceleration (see the rightmost form of equation (10.3.26)).

First, substitute $w = \alpha h$ into equation (10.2.5) and solve for h. The result is

$$h = \frac{A}{2t} \frac{1}{(1 + \alpha)}$$

Substitute this value of h into the equation for I, which is immediately above equation (10.2.2). Thus

$$IA = A^3 \left[\frac{A}{48t^2} \frac{(1 + 3\alpha)}{(1 + \alpha)^3} - \frac{1}{4} \frac{\alpha}{(1 + \alpha)^2} + \frac{t^2}{3A} \frac{\alpha}{(1 + \alpha)} \right] \quad (10.3.27)$$

---

[b]Bare material cost will increase in direct proportion to A; however, fabrication costs and auxiliary equipment costs do not increase so rapidly.

The dimensionless parameter A/t^2 must be large in all practical cross sections; therefore, for constant IA, A varies with α for fixed t according to the equation

$$\frac{A}{A_{1/3}} = 1.5 \left[\frac{(1 + \alpha)^3}{6(1 + 3\alpha)} \right]^{1/4} \tag{10.3.28}$$

in which $A_{1/3}$ corresponds to $\alpha = 1/3$. Some values of this expression are as follows:

α:	0	1/3	1	2	3	4	6
$A/A_{1/3}$:	0.96	1	1.14	1.34	1.52	1.69	1.98

Comparing with the values following equation (10.2.9), one can see that the cost of the beam increases more rapidly to satisfy the dynamic loading criterion than the bending stress criterion.

Thus, from the viewpoint of vertical dynamic loading only, the cost per unit length is 4 percent less for the ideal and impractical cases $\alpha = 0$, as compared to the bending optimum case $\alpha = 1/3$. If $\alpha = 1/3$ is taken as optimum, it is seen that a square beam costs 14 percent more, the case $\alpha = 3$ costs 52 percent more, and so forth. See footnote on page 280.

The Relationship between Beam Weight and Vehicle Weight at Maximum Acceleration

It is also of importance to understand how the cost of a guideway of a given shape varies with vehicle weight. Thus, for $\alpha = 1/3$ and A/t^2 much greater than 1, equation (10.3.27) shows that

$$IA = \frac{1}{24} \left(\frac{3}{4} \right)^3 \frac{A^4}{t^2}$$

Substituting into equation (10.3.26),

$$\frac{1}{g} \frac{d^2y}{dt^2} \bigg|_{max} = \frac{4.8(W/g)Vt}{(\rho E)^{1/2} A^2} \tag{10.3.29}$$

Thus, for given maximum acceleration, speed, material, and wall thickness, *the weight of the beam is proportional to the square root of the weight of the vehicles.*

The Relationship between Vehicle Weight and
Speed at Maximum Acceleration

From equation (10.2.5), we have for $\alpha = 1/3$, $A = 8th/3$. Substituting this value into equation (10.3.29) gives

$$\frac{1}{g} \frac{d^2y}{dt^2}\bigg|_{max} = \frac{0.68(W/g)V}{(\rho E)^{1/2}th^2} \tag{10.3.30}$$

As an example, consider the steel beam assumed in computing figure 10-3. For steel, $E = 30(10)^6$ psi $= 21(10)^{10}$ N/m² and $\rho = 7760$ kg/m³; therefore $(E\rho)^{1/2} = 4.0(10)^7$ kg/m²s. Assume $h = 1$ m and take the realtionship between t and ℓ_s from figure 10-3. Then, equation (10.3.30) becomes (t in *cm*)

$$\frac{1}{g} \frac{d^2y}{dt^2}\bigg|_{max} = 1.7(10)^{-6} \frac{(W/g)V}{t} \tag{10.3.31}$$

Note that, because of the direct relationship between t and the span length, ℓ_s, the acceleration decreases as the span increases. From the viewpoint of the fabrication problem, however, there is a minimum practical value of t. Suppose this is one centimeter. Using this value, figure 10-3 shows that the span must be less than 34 m. Assume this is true. Then, consider the tolerable acceleration.

Reference[2], section 4.5, gives standards for vertical vibration recommended by the International Organization for Standardization (ISO). These standards are given as a function of frequency and exposure time. For a transit guideway system the frequency of significance is simply the reciprocal of the time required to traverse a single span, $f_1 = V/\ell_s$. The highest value of f_1 for urban applications may correspond to say $V = 20$m/s, $\ell_s = 20$ m; or $f_1 = 1$ Hz. For frequencies below about $f_1 = 1.4$ Hz, the ISO standard recommends a low-frequency limit vertical acceleration for ride comfort of 0.0707 gee. Substituting this value into equation (10.3.31) with $t = 1$ cm gives

$$V = \frac{41600}{M_v} \tag{10.3.32}$$

in which $M_v = W/g$ in kg if V is in m/s. Thus, for a 1000 kg vehicle, the velocity should not exceed 42 m/s; or for a 2000-kg vehicle, V should not exceed 21 m/s, and so forth. The significance of these results is that, with the assumed geometric parameters for a thin-walled steel box beam, stress, not ride comfort, determines the design at urban speeds if only one vehicle passes over each span at one time and the vibrations of the span are not amplified by multiple passages of vehicles. The latter restriction is relaxed in section 10.4.

The Maximum Dynamic Bending Stress

The bending stress in a beam is given by equation (10.2.1) in terms of the bending moment M. From any textbook on strength of materials, M is given in terms of the deflection curve by

$$M = EI \frac{\partial^2 y}{\partial x^2}$$

Thus

$$\sigma = cE \frac{\partial^2 y}{\partial x^2} \tag{10.3.33}$$

From equation (10.3.4)

$$\frac{\partial^2 y}{\partial x^2} = -\sum_{m=1}^{\infty} A_m(t) \left(\frac{m\pi}{\ell_s}\right)^2 \sin\left(\frac{m\pi x}{\ell_s}\right) \tag{10.3.34}$$

For $t < \ell_s/V$, $A_m(t)$ is given by equation (10.3.10). Thus $\sigma(x,t)$ is found by combining equation (10.3.33) and (10.3.34) and then by substituting equation (10.3.10). Using the relationship above equation (10.3.14), the result is

$$\sigma = \frac{8}{\pi^2} \frac{c}{I} \left(\frac{W\ell_s^2}{4}\right) \sum_{m=1}^{\infty} \frac{(\sin \beta_m \omega_m t - \beta_m \sin \omega_m t)}{m^2(1 - \beta_m^2)} \sin\left(\frac{m\pi x}{\ell_s}\right) \tag{10.3.35}$$

in which $W\ell_s^2/4$ is the maximum moment in a statically loaded and simply supported beam with a concentrated load at the center.

In the example used with equation (10.3.16a), it was shown that β_1 is much less than one in urban applications. Taking into account equation (10.3.11), equation (10.3.35) can therefore be approximated by

$$\frac{\sigma}{\sigma_s} = \frac{8}{\pi^2} \sum_{m=1}^{\infty} \frac{1}{m^2} \sin \Omega_m t \sin \left(\frac{m\pi x}{\ell_s} \right) \qquad (10.3.36)$$

This equation applies up to $t = \ell_s/V$. Therefore, from equation (10.3.9), $\Omega_m t$ reaches a maximum of $m\pi$. Consequently, $\sin \Omega_m t$ reaches its maximum of unity for all modes. The first mode ($m = 1$), for example, reaches its maximum when the vehicle is at midspan. Higher modes reach their maxima earlier. Without detailed calculations for a range of values of the parameters, it is not possible to calculate a precise maximum stress; however, it is seen that for the first mode $\sigma_{max}/\sigma_s = 8/\pi^2 = 0.81$, and for higher modes, the maximum stress falls off as $1/m^2$. Thus, it is unlikely that $(\sigma)_{max}$ will be much above the static stress, σ_s.

Consider the case $t > \ell_s/V$. From equation (10.3.22), the maximum value of A_m for this case, using equation (10.3.12), is

$$(A_m)_{max} \bigg|_{t > \ell_s/V} = \frac{W\ell_s^3}{EI} \frac{2}{\pi^4} \frac{2\beta_m}{m^4(1 - \beta_m^2)}$$

But, from equation (10.3.10), using the expression above equation (10.3.14), the maximum value of A_m when $t < \ell_s/V$ is

$$(A_m) \bigg|_{t < \ell_s/V} = \frac{W\ell_s^3}{EI} \frac{2}{\pi^4} \frac{1}{m^4(1 - \beta_m)}$$

Hence, after the vehicle passes over the span, the maximum stress does not exceed a factor $2\beta_m/(1 + \beta_m)$ times the maximum stress for $t < \ell_s/V$. For urban speeds, this factor is well under one, therefore the maximum stress is reached while the vehicle is on the span, and, as shown above, is close to the maximum static stress.

During the life of the guideway, it will undergo millions of cycles of stress. In a short-headway system, there may typically be 3000 vehicle passages in the peak hour over a given span, or about 30,000 passages per day. Assuming 300 full days of operation per year, there would be $9(10)^6$ passages per year. Thus, in a fifty-year life time, the guideway would have undergone in the neighborhood of 500 million cycles. It is clear therefore that the maximum stress must be kept well below the fatigue stress limit of the material. From reference[7], p. 5-11, the fatigue stress limit for an indefinite number of stress cycles is given for ordinary structural steel as 30,000 psi $(210 \cdot (10)^6 \text{ N/m}^2)$. Thus, the use of a design working stress limit of 20,000 psi, as has been done in all examples in this chapter, will insure long life of the structure without requiring more expensive special steels.

10.4 Dynamic Loading—Cascade of Vehicles Crossing a Span

Consider a cascade of vehicles crossing the span of figure 10-4 of equal weight W and spaced a distance ℓ_h apart. If each vehicle can be represented by a point load, the integral of equation (10.3.5) becomes

$$\int_0^{\ell_s} f(x,t) \sin m\pi x/\ell_s \, dx = W \sum_{i=1}^{N} \sin m\pi/\ell_s[Vt - (i-1)\ell_h]$$

$$(10.4.1)$$

in which N is the number of vehicles, but only those terms are included for which

$$0 \leq Vt - (i-1)\ell_h \leq \ell_s \qquad (10.4.2)$$

With the help of a trigonometric identity and equation (10.3.9), the right side of equation (10.4.1) may be written in the form

$$W(A \sin \Omega_m t + B \cos \Omega_m t)$$

in which

$$A = \sum_{i=p}^{q} \cos \frac{m\pi\ell_h i}{\ell_s}$$

$$B = \sum_{i=p}^{q} \sin \frac{m\pi\ell_h i}{\ell_s}$$

If $\ell_h > \ell_s$, there is only one vehicle at a time on the span, hence the sums in A and B have only one term. Moreover, between the passage of the first vehicle across $x = \ell_s$ and the arrival of the second vehicle at $x = 0$, the forcing function vanishes. If $\ell_h < \ell_s, p = q = 1$ for $0 \le Vt \le \ell_h; p = 1, q = 2$ for $\ell_h \le Vt \le 2\ell_h \le \ell_s$; and so forth. Thus the exact solution must be broken down into time steps corresponding to crossings of the vehicles across the boundaries of the span at $x = 0$ and ℓ_s.

No such solution will be attempted because it is easier to do on a computer, and Synder, Wormley, and Richardson of the department of mechanical engineering at MIT[3] have completed an even more realistic case—one in which each vehicle is represented by a pair of point forces at the front and rear wheels, and in which both structural damping and vehicle dynamics are included. We will discuss that solution, but before doing so, it is useful to study the characteristics of the mutliple vehicle solution in a general way: Motions of each mode m of vibration will be enhanced by successive passes of the vehicles if each vehicle arrives at $x = 0$ at the instant $y_m(x, t) = 0$ and $y_m(x, t) > 0$, that is, when the span is just ready to begin its downward motion. If the vehicle arrives at $x = 0$ when $y_m(x, t) = 0$ but $y_m(x, t) < 0$, the vehicle's weight will resist the motion of the span, and decrease the amplitude of motion.

The natural frequencies of vibration of the beam are given by equation (10.3.6), and the corresponding periods of motion are $2\pi/\omega_m$. Thus, if $\ell_h/V = 2\pi/\omega_m$ for mode m, that mode will be enhanced. If $f_1 = \omega_1/2\pi$, and equation (10.3.6) is substituted, the critical headways are

$$\frac{\ell_h}{V} = \frac{1}{m^2 f_1} \tag{10.4.3}$$

in which

$$f_1 = \frac{\pi}{2\,\ell_s^2}\sqrt{\frac{EI}{\rho A}} \tag{10.4.4}$$

is the fundamental natural frequency of vibration of the beam if its ends are simply supported.

The quantity ℓ_h/V is the time headway between vehicles. Thus, as the time headway decreases, large amplitude motion can first be expected when the time headway approaches $1/f_1$. Excitation of the second mode can be expected as V/ℓ_h approaches $4f_1$, and so forth. However, since vehicles must operate at a range of spacings down to the minimum permissible, the beam must be designed so that $V/\ell_h < f_1$.

To obtain a feeling for the magnitude of f_1, consider a numerical example based on the numbers used in computing V_{cr} from equation (10.3.16). Thus, using equation (10.3.17) and the value of E/ρ for steel, given after equation (10.3.16a) equation (10.4.4) becomes

$$f_1 = 2890 \ \frac{h}{\ell_s^2} \qquad (10.4.4a)$$

where the lengths are in meters. Notice that f_1 is independent of the thickness of the beam walls. If, for example, $h = 1$ m and $\ell_s = 20$ m, $f_1 = 7.23$ Hz, and $1/f_1 = 0.14$ s. On the other hand, if a longer span, say $\ell_s = 40$ m is desired, $1/f_1 = 0.55$ s.

In section 7.2 it was concluded, based on kinematical considerations, that a minimum headway of the order of 0.25 s is practical if the correct design choices are made. It is now seen that, with a steel beam one meter deep, this appears practical from the structural point of view for simply supported spans of 20 m, but not for spans longer than about 25 m. If the ends are constrained so that they cannot rotate under load, f_1 increases. For completely clamped ends, Timoshenko[9] shows that f_1 increases over the value given by equation (10.4.4) by the factor $(4.730/\pi)^2 = 2.267$. In this case, $1/f_1$ for $\ell_s = 40$ m decreases to 0.24 s. For short-headway transit systems, making the ends of the guideway at the supports rigid may be less expensive than reducing the post spacing or increasing the depth of the beam; however, considering the need for thermal expansion joints, this may be difficult.

An accurate assessment of the minimum practical headway, or of the design parameter choices required for a given headway, requires a detailed computer analysis such as performed by Snyder et al.[3]. Their results pertain to the performance of vehicles travelling on rough guideways as well as on flexible guideways. While the question of tolerable guideway roughness is of crucial importance in the cost of fabrication of the guideway, it is not considered further here. We consider rather the limitations reported by Snyder et al. due to flexible guideways. The results reported there are understood by means of the equation of criticality obtained by setting $m = 1$ in equation (10.4.3). Normalizing with respect to the span length ℓ_s, this equation can be written

$$\frac{\ell_h}{\ell_s} = \frac{V}{f_1 \ell_s} = V_c \qquad (10.4.5)$$

in which V_c is referred to by Snyder et al. as the "crossing-velocity frequency ratio." It is the ratio of the inverse of the crossing time, ℓ_s/V, that is the crossing frequency, to the fundamental frequency of vibration of the beam. When ℓ_h/ℓ_s, the dimensionless headway, reduces enough to equal V_c, the successive vehicle passages augment the natural vibration of the beam. The computer analysis of Snyder et al. indicates that, as more and more vehicles cross the span, the maximum amplitude of motion continues to build up, and reaches steady state only after the crossing of fifteen to twenty-five vehicles. Also, the maximum deflection of the span is increased after the twenty-fifth vehicle passes by a factor of 3.4/1.8 = 1.9 over the deflection after one passage. Thus, the maximum beam deflection and stress estimated above for the case of one vehicle crossing are approximately doubled.

Snyder et al. show a series of computer-drawn plots of the nondimensional maximum midspan deflection (y_{max}/y^*), where y^* is the static value given by equation (10.3.12), plotted as a function of V_c (equation (10.4.5)) for four values of ℓ_h/ℓ_s: 1.5, 1.0, 0.5, 0.25. Figure 10-7, taken from Snyder et al.[3] with permission, is a typical example. In this figure, $\ell_s = 30.48$ m and the structural damping ratio of the beam is 0.025. The deflections shown are the steadystate values achieved after fifteen to twenty-five vehicles have crossed the span. The plots can be envisioned as the resulting deflections if a cascade of vehicles at fixed headway ℓ_h continually increases its speed.

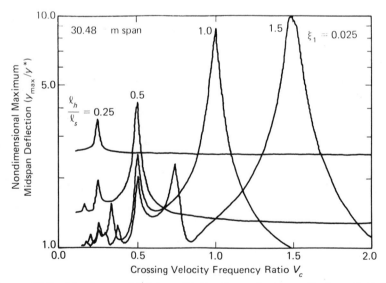

Figure 10-7. Maximum Midspan Deflections due to a Series of 1260-kg Vehicles Crossing a 30.48-m Span (from reference[3], Department of Mechanical Engineering, M.I.T.)

If $\ell_h/\ell_s = 0.25$, and V is very small, the deflection is the static value for vehicles equally spaced along the span. As V increases, y_{max} doesn't begin to increase noticeably until V_c gets within about 20 percent of the critical value of 0.25 (equation (10.4.5)). At $V_c = 0.25$ the deflection is about 1.4 times the static value. Then, after the speed has increased so that $V_c \approx 0.30$, the deflection is back to the static value and remains there through the remainder of the range of V_c shown.

If $\ell_h/\ell_s = 0.5$, y_{max} reaches a much higher maximum (6.9 times the static value) at the critical value of $V_c = 0.5$, but also peaks at $V_c = \frac{1}{4}$, and slightly at $V_c = 1/6$. The explanation for this behavior is seen by following the derivation of equation (10.4.3) and concentrating on the fundamental mode, $m = 1$. Thus, if the time headway between vehicles, ℓ_h/V, is equal to the period of motion $1/f_1$, each cycle of vibration of the beam is enhanced by the passage of each successive vehicle. But, the vibratory motion will also be enhanced, though to a lesser extent, if every other or every third, and so forth, vehicle arrives at the beginning of a period of motion of the beam. Thus, successively smaller resonances will occur when

$$\ell_h/V = 2/f_1, \; 3/f_1, \; \ldots$$

Or, in the notation of equation (10.4.5), successively smaller resonances occur when

$$V_c = \frac{\ell_h}{\ell_s}, \; \frac{\ell_h}{2\ell_s}, \; \frac{\ell_h}{3\ell_s}, \; \ldots \tag{10.4.6}$$

For $\ell_h/\ell_s = 0.5$, $V_c = 1/4$, 1/6, and so forth. For $\ell_h/\ell_s = 1.0$, resonances at $V_c = 1$, 1/2, 1/3, 1/4, 1/5, and 1/6 are visible; and for $\ell_h/\ell_s = 1.5$ resonances may be seen at $V_c = 1.5$, 0.75, 0.5, 0.375, 0.3, and 0.25. Equation (10.4.6) corresponds to equation 5.1 of reference [3] for $m = 1$.

Only the fundamental resonance, corresponding to $V_c = \ell_h/\ell_s$ produces an amplitude above the static value for $\ell_h/\ell_s = 0.25$. On this basis, therefore, the lower-speed resonances need not be avoided. It is important to note also, from figure 10-7, that the peak deflections increase in magnitude as the headway increases. Thus, with long headway systems it is particularly important to avoid operating a long stream of vehicles at $\ell_h = \ell_s V_c$.

Any elevated guideway transit system must be designed for the static loading condition of vehicles end to end on the guideway (equation (10.2.12). Thus, in the case where the minimum operating headway ℓ_h/ℓ_s is 0.25, the worst static condition produces a higher stress if ℓ_v is less than $\ell_h/1.4$, where ℓ_v is the vehicle length. If this condition holds, the resonant condition $V_c \ell_s = \ell_h$ need not be avoided for stress reasons. If the minimum operating headway $\ell_h/\ell_s = 0.5$, we must have $\ell_v < \ell_h/6.9$ if the static condition is to prevail, and so forth. If the system happens to operate with a long stream of vehicles at $\ell_h > (\ell_h)_{min}$, it may, with low probability, operate at one of the secondary resonant points of equation (10.4.6), but these resonances are not strong enough to be of concern. In any case, ride comfort will be increased if long streams of equally spaced vehicles are not permitted to form, that is, random spacing will improve ride comfort.

The MIT group[3] assumed a concrete guideway cross section of fixed shape and, in their computer runs, varied its size until both the stress criterion and the ride comfort criterion were satisfied. They found the required guideway cross sections by making computer runs of multiple vehicle crossings using three vehicle masses with the following characteristics:

Gross Vehicle Mass (kg)	1260	2700	4860
Passenger Capacity	4	6	12
Headway (s)	0.2	0.3	1.0
Flow (persons/s)	20	20	12

The results are shown in figure 10-8. Here we have plotted the required guideway mass per unit length as a function of vehicle mass for the two spans chosen in reference[3]: $\ell_s = 15.2$ m and 30.4 m, and for the cases of a single crossing and of multiple crossings sufficient to produce maximum amplitude of motion. Each of the twelve data points shown corresponds to a set of computer runs required to find the minimum guideway mass per unit length that satisfies both the stress and ride comfort criteria. For instance, the data point corresponding to figure 10-7 is the one for multiple crossings for which $M_v = 1260$ kg and $\ell_s = 30.4$ m. For this case, $f_1 = 1.49$ Hz and $\ell_h = (13.4 \text{ m/s}) (0.2 \text{ s}) = 2.68$ m. Hence,

$$V_c = \frac{V}{\ell_s f_1} = 0.296 \qquad \text{and} \qquad \frac{\ell_h}{\ell_s} = 0.088$$

In this case, ℓ_h is so small that ℓ_v cannot be much less than ℓ_h. Hence the dynamic load condition is likely to produce the greatest stress. From figure 10-7, it can be inferred, however, that for such a low value of ℓ_h/ℓ_s, the amplitude rise at $V_c = \ell_h/\ell_s$ will be quite small, and that the vehicles have passed over this minor critical point to reach $V_c = 0.296$.

Because of the different relationships to the resonant points in the various data points of figure 10-8 and in other configurations, one must not

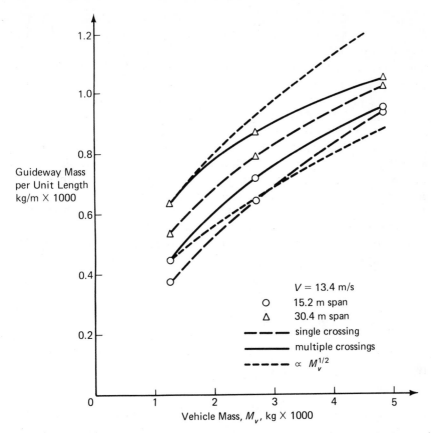

Figure 10-8. Guideway Mass per Unit Length Required to Meet Stress and Ride-Comfort Criteria

generalize the results of figure 10-8 too far; however, we can make the following observations:

1. The required guideway mass increases in going from single crossings to multiple crossings by about 20, 11, and 1.5 percent for vehicles masses of 1260, 2700, and 4860 kg, respectively. Thus, at least in this example, the analysis of multiple crossings is significant only in the smaller-vehicle cases, but the increase in guideway mass is small enough so that the single vehicle crossing, analyzed exactly, is of much interest in understanding the basic phenomena. (It must be remembered, however, that the MIT study also took into account vehicle dynamics.)

2. At a constant flow of persons per second, smaller vehicles will result

in a lower guideway mass per unit length and hence lower cost. Note that the data corresponding to the largest of the three vehicles corresponds to a flow only six tenths of the flow in the two other cases. Thus, if the flow with the largest-mass vehicle were increased to correspond to the other two cases, its guideway would be substantially larger.

From equation (10.3.29) it was concluded that the mass per unit length of the guideway is proportional to the square root of the vehicle mass if the ride comfort criterion governs over the stress criterion. To test this hypothesis in the case of the data of figure 10-8, dashed curves proportional to $M_v^{1/2}$ are drawn from the multiple crossing data points for the lightest vehicle. It is seen that the square-root assumption underestimates the guideway mass when $\ell_s = 15.2$ m, but overestimates it when $\ell_s = 30.4$ m. The differences are not surprising, however, because of: (1) the lower flow for the heaviest vehicle; (2) the fact that equation (10.3.29) is approximate; and (3) the fact that figure 10-8 applies for one specific velocity. The relationship

$$\text{GUIDEWAY MASS} \propto (\text{VEHICLE MASS})^{1/2}$$

is still a good rough approximation.

10.5 Limit Valve of Speed Based on Ride Comfort

Based on the analysis of section 10.4, it is useful to consider the following simplified analysis of ride comfort in vehicles in a cascade: Consider the case where ℓ_h/ℓ_s is much less than 1 and assume the guideway is uniformly loaded with a load per unit length $q = W/\ell_h$, where W is the vehicle weight. Based on figure 10-7, assume that for small ℓ_h/ℓ_s the resonant effects are small and, therefore, that the beam deflection is the static deflection with the load q. To increase ride comfort, assume that the beams are precambered to lie flat on their support posts when no vehicles are present. Thus, the deflection will be totally due to vehicle weight. To increase the beam natural frequency, clamp the ends of the beams on the support posts by overlaying steel sheets secured to the beams in such a way that thermal expansion can take place.

From any text on strength of materials, the maximum moment in such a beam is

$$M_{\max} = \frac{q\ell_s^2}{12} \qquad (10.5.1)$$

and the maximum deflection is

$$\Delta_{\max} = \frac{q\ell_s^4}{384EI} \tag{10.5.2}$$

With clamped beams, we can assume that the vertical displacement seen by a passenger is

$$y(t) = \frac{\Delta_{\max}}{2} \sin \omega t$$

where

$$\omega = 2\pi V / \ell_s$$

Hence, the maximum vertical acceleration is

$$a_m = \frac{\Delta_{\max}}{2} \ \omega^2 = 2\pi^2 \Delta_{\max} V^2 / \ell_s^2 \tag{10.5.3}$$

Assume the beam is designed to a certain maximum bending stress σ_m under the total load of vehicles end to end and beam weight. Then, from equations (10.2.1) and (10.5.1), the required moment of inertia is

$$I = \frac{h}{2\sigma_m} M_{\max} = \frac{h\ell_s^2}{24\sigma_m} \left(\frac{W}{\ell_v} + \rho g A \right)$$

in which $h = 2c$, ℓ_v is the vehicle length, and $\rho g A$ is the weight per unit length of the beam. Substituting this value of I into equation (10.5.2), and remembering that because of the assumed camber, $q = W/\ell_h$ in computing maximum deflection, equation (10.5.2) becomes

$$\Delta_{\max} = \frac{\sigma_m \ell_s^2 \ell_v}{16Eh\ell_h} \ \frac{1}{(1 + \rho g A \ell_v / W)}$$

Substituting this expression into equation (10.5.3) and solving for V, we obtain

$$V_{\lim} = \frac{2}{\pi}\left[\frac{2a_m Eh\ell_h}{\sigma_m \ell_v}\left(1 + \frac{\rho gA\ell_v}{W}\right)\right]^{1/2}$$ (10.5.4)

It is worthwhile to note from structural theory that if the beam had been simply supported, the factor of 12 in equation (10.5.1) would become 8, and the factor of 384 in equation (10.5.2) would become 384/5. Thus, E in equation (10.5.4) should be multiplied by $12/(8 \cdot 5) = 0.3$, and the maximum value of V for adequate ride comfort would reduce by $(0.3)^{1/2} = 0.548$.

We see that increasing the maximum stress σ_m lowers the limit velocity. This is because σ_m permits higher deflection. As expected, a heavier beam (greater ρgA) increases the limit velocity, heavier vehicles lower the limit velocity, and a shorter headway between vehicles lowers the limit velocity. The span ℓ_s does not enter directly, but through the parameter A, which must increase with ℓ_s at a given σ_m. The limit velocity can be increased most easily be increasing h.

As indicated in connection with equation (10.3.32) assume $a_m = 0.707$ m/s². Then for a one-meter-deep steel beam ($E = 21(10)^{10}$ N/m², $\sigma_m = 140(10)^6$ N/m²), equation (10.5.4) becomes

$$V_{\lim} = 29.3 \left(\frac{\ell_h}{\ell_v}\right)^{1/2}\left(1 + \frac{\rho gA\ell_v}{W}\right)^{1/2} \text{ m/s}$$ (10.5.5)

Thus, without computing the guideway/vehicle weight parameter, it is seen that for all headways the limit value of speed for adequate ride comfort is above the range of speeds of interest for urban applications. On the other hand, if the beams are simply supported, the factor 29.3 reduces to $29.3(0.548) = 16.1$ m/s $= 36$ mi/hr. In this case the parameter $\rho gA\ell_v/W$ is of interest for heavy vehicles at short headways. For steel, $\rho g = 77600$ N/m³. Assuming an optimum steel beam, equation (10.2.5) shows that $A = 8ht/3$. Assume $t = 1$ cm, $h = 1$ m. Then $\rho gA = 2069$ N/m. As an example, take the middle vehicle of figure 10-8. Then $W = 2700(10) = 27,000$ N. Thus $\rho gA/W = 0.077$ m⁻¹. Consider a minimum time headway of 0.25 second. Then, for $V = 20$ m/s, $\ell_h = 20(0.25) = 5$ m. Assume $\ell_v = 3$ m. Then for this case $\rho gA\ell_v/W = 0.23$ and $V_{\lim} = 23.0$ m/s (52 mi/hr) for simply supported beams. Since this limit speed is above the assumed speed, the beam is still determined by the bending stress criterion and not by ride comfort. With simple supports, however, the ride over the supports will contain higher frequency components than assumed and requires further study. To take into account the amplification produced near resonant conditions, a_m in equation (10.5.4) should be reduced in the same proportion that the amplitude is increased over the static value near resonance. If this adjustment is made to equation (10.5.4), it applies to the dynamic as well as to the static deflection conditions.

10.6 Torsion

Torsional Loads

A transit guideway can be loaded in torsion due either to wind forces or to centrifugal forces. Consider first the wind load. As an extreme condition, assume the maximum torque on the guideway to be determined by the condition that vehicles of height h_v are parked end to end on a span of length ℓ_s. Assume that at the support posts, the guideway is constrained from rotating. Then the torque is greatest at the support posts and is equal to one half the torque produced on an area $h_v\ell_s$. If h is the depth of the guideway, assume the point of application of the wind load is $(h + h_v)/2$ from the axis of twist of the beam. Then the torque due to wind is

$$T_w = \frac{\rho_a V_w^2}{8} \; h_v \ell_s (h + h_v) \qquad (10.6.1)$$

in which $\rho_a = 1.293$ kg/m² is the air density at standard conditions and V_w is the maximum wind speed perpendicular to the guideway.

A centrifugal torque is produced by vehicles travelling around a curved section of guideway at line speed V_L. If the vehicle weight is W and the maximum comfort level of lateral acceleration is a_ℓ/g, each vehicle produces a maximum torque

$$T_c = W \frac{a_\ell}{g} \frac{(h + h_v)}{2}$$

If the headway is ℓ_h, and ℓ_s is the unsupported span length around a curve, there can under normal conditions be ℓ_s/ℓ_h vehicles on one span. Then, as with equation (10.6.1), the maximum torque is less than

$$(T_c)_{\max} = \frac{W a_\ell}{4g} \; (h + h_v) \; \frac{\ell_s}{\ell_h} \qquad (10.6.2)$$

The actual torque is less than that given by equation (10.6.2) because the curvature of the guideway causes part of the torque to add to the bending moment at the support post, and only a component to be a true torque. Hence the present calculation is conservative.

The ratio of wind to centrifugal torque is

$$T_w/T_c = \frac{\rho_a V_w^2 h_v \ell_h}{2W(a_e/g)} \frac{(\ell_s)_{\text{straight}}}{(\ell_s)_{\text{curved}}} \qquad (10.6.3)$$

Assume the system operates normally up to say $V_w = 60$ mi/h (27 m/s), and consider two cases: (1) Standing passenger vehicles—assume $a_e/g = 0.125$ g, $W = 10,000$ lb$_f$ (45,400 N), $h_v = 2.4$ m, $\ell_h = 130$ m, and ℓ_s is the same for straight and curved track. Then, from equation (10.6.3),

$$\frac{T_w}{T_c} \approx 26$$

(2) Seated passenger vehicles—assume $a_e/g = 0.25$ g, $W = 2000$ lb$_f$ (9080 N), $h_v = 1.6$ m, $\ell_h = 10$ m, and ℓ_s is again the same in both cases. Then

$$\frac{T_w}{T_c} \approx 3.3$$

Thus, in both cases the wind torque is dominant and can be assumed to act with no centrifugal forces in computation of the maximum torsional stress, because it is not prudent to operate at normal line speed when the wind speed is maximum.

The Torsional Stress in a Box-Beam Guideway

Assume the guideway is a box beam with the dimensions shown in figure 10-1. Let $t_1 = t_2 = t << h$ and let the shear stress on the cross section due to the applied torque T be τ. According to Timoshenko and Goodier[10] , Saint-Venant showed that the cross sections of a noncircular beam warp in torsion. If they are restrained from warping, additional stress concentrations occur, and the following analysis must be modified. Thus, near constrained ends, more detailed knowledge of the means by which the supports resist torsion than available here must be available for a rigorous solution. Such a solution has been carried out by Ebner[11] but it will be assumed (1) that for relatively thick-walled beams (compared to aircraft wings) the correction is small, or (2) that it is possible to design end constraints that minimize stress concentration in torsion.

With these caveats, consider the beam of figure 10-1 and assume that the wall is thin compared with the depth h. In this case, Tomoshenko and Goodier indicate that, except at the corners (considered below), the shear stress τ can be assumed uniform. Then, the torque T can be expressed as

$$T = 2\tau t(hw/2 + wh/2) = 2\tau thw$$

Thus,

$$\tau = \frac{T}{2tA_c} \tag{10.6.4}$$

where $A_c \approx hw$ is the cross-sectional area of the beam.

The material cross-sectional area A is given by equation (10.2.5). The shear stress is minimum for a given guideway weight per unit length if A_c is maximized with A held constant. Thus, setting the variation of A equal to zero with t fixed results in $\delta w = -\delta h$. Then

$$\delta A_c = 0 = w\delta h + h\delta w = (w - h)\delta h$$

Thus, as should have been expected from symmetry, a box-beam guideway will resist a given load with the minimum weight per unit length if the beam is square. This is an important consideration, however, only if the torsional wind load is the dominant factor in determining the size of the guideway.

According to Timoshenko and Goodier, equation (10.6.4) is valid away from the corners of the box beam. At the corners, there is a shear-stress concentration dependent upon the ratio of the inside radius of curvature at the corners, a, to the wall thickness, t. On page 301, reference[10], a curve of the stress concentration as a function of a/t is given, calculated both on the basis of an approximate analytical theory and a numerical calculation by finite differences. For example, for $a/t = 1.0$, $\tau_{max}/\tau = 1.3$; and for $a/t = 0.5$, $\tau_{max}/\tau = 1.7$. To be safe, assume the stress concentration factor to be two, so that, from equation (10.6.4),

$$\tau_{max} = \frac{T}{tA_c} \tag{10.6.5}$$

Substituting equation (10.6.1) into equation (10.6.5), the maximum shear stress ($A_c = hw = \alpha h^2$) is

$$\tau_{max} = \frac{\rho_a V^2_w}{8\alpha} \frac{\ell_s}{t} \frac{h_v}{h}\left(1 + \frac{h_v}{h}\right) \qquad (10.6.6)$$

Assume $\rho_a = 1.293$ kg/m³, $V_w = 27$ m/s, $\alpha = 1/3$, $h = 1$ m, and $h_v = 2.4$ m. Then

$$\tau_{max} = 2884 \frac{\ell_s}{t} \frac{N}{m^2} = 0.410\ell_s/t \text{ psi}$$

Taking values of ℓ_s/t from figure 10-3, the following stresses are found:

$\ell_s(m)$:	20	30	40
τ_{max}(psi):	2830	1585	893
τ_{max}(N/m²):	19.9(10)⁶	11.2(10)⁶	6.3 (10)⁶

Thus, for a design based on bending stress, the shear stress is greatest where ℓ_s and t are the smallest. Since the design shear stress for structural steel[7] is about 12,000 psi (84(10)⁶N/m²), the design is in all cases determined by bending stresses, not shear stresses. If the minimum plate thickness is limited to say 1 cm for ease of fabrication, as assumed following equation (10.3.31), the maximum shear stress is even less for the smaller values of ℓ_s.

This conclusion leads to increased flexibility in design because the full box beam is not needed for resisting torsional loads. As an example, assume $w = 1/3$ m but that, for the portion of the box beam that resists torsion, h is reduced to the value h' such that τ_{max}, in equation (10.6.5), is equal to the design value. Then, substituting, $A_c = wh'$ and equation (10.6.1) for T, equation (10.6.5) can be expressed in the form

$$h' = \frac{\rho_a V^2_w}{8\tau_{max}} \frac{\ell_s}{t} \frac{h_v}{w} (h + h_v)$$

$$= 17.5(10)^{-6} \ \ell_s/t \text{ for } h_v = 1.6 \text{ m}$$

$$= 34.4(10)^{-6}\ell_s/t \text{ for } h_v = 2.4\text{m}$$

$$(10.6.7)$$

in which, in computing the lever arm for the wind torque, h is still taken as 1

m. Assume $t_{min} = 1$ cm, as suggested above. Then figure 10-3 shows that t is greater than t_{min} only above ℓ_s about 34 m. With this assumption, several values of h' are as follows:

ℓ_s(m)	t(cm)	h_v(m)	h'(cm)
20	1	1.6	3.50
30	1	1.6	5.25
40	1.84	1.6	3.80
20	1	2.4	6.88
30	1	2.4	10.32
40	1.84	2.4	7.48

Thus, a much shallower beam than a full box beam one meter deep will provide ample torsional strength. Note from equation (10.6.7) that h' is a quadratic function of the height of the vehicle, h_v, but that for full, unslotted box beams, extra vehicle height is not significant in torsion from the viewpoint of shear stress. (It may, however, be a factor in lateral vehicle stability.) If increased h_v adds to the weight of the vehicle; however, it will require a heavier beam. These conclusions indicate that the use of U-shaped beams to simplify switching, as is done in the design developed by The Aerospace Corporation[12] is a practical configuration.

Slotted Box-Beam Guideways

One of the most difficult design problems in narrow-beam transit systems is to develop a practical configuration that can permit vehicles to switch without moving a portion of the track. The requirement of movement of the track generally restricts the systems to long headways, hence large vehicles, hence to a large cross-section, high cost guideway. A method around this problem, employed in the design of the Rohr Monocab system in the United States, and the H-Bahn system in West Germany, is to slot the guideway so that a suspension bogie can ride inside the beam[13]. The subject of this subsection is the analysis of the torsional stresses in such a beam.

The theory of torsion of open channel sections is developed by Timoshenko and Goodier[10].

From this work, the maximum torsional stress in a thin-walled channel section and away from a corner is found to be the same as the maximum torsional stress in a bar of narrow cross section of thickness t and width b if the developed length of the channel cross section is b and its thickness is also t. Thus, reference[10] gives for the maximum shear stress of a channel section the formula

$$\tau = \frac{3T}{bt^2}$$

in which T is the applied torque. Just as with the development of equation (10.6.5), to account for stress concentrations in the corner, we will multiply the above value by two to obtain

$$\tau_{max} = \frac{6T}{bt^2}$$

For a thin-walled slotted box beam of depth h and width w, $b = 2(h + w)$ if we neglect the width of the slot. Then

$$\tau_{max} = \frac{3T}{(h + w)t^2} \tag{10.6.8}$$

In this case, the maximum stress is independent of the ratio w/h and depends only on the length of the perimeter.

Comparing with equation (10.6.5) with $A_c = wh$, we see that the slot increases the maximum stress by the factor

$$\frac{(\tau_{max})_{slot}}{(\tau_{max})_{no\ slot}} = \frac{3wh}{(h + w)t} \tag{10.6.9}$$

For beams with $h = 1$ m, $w = 1/3$ m, $t = 1$ cm, this ratio is 75. Thus, while the torsional stress in a full box beam was well below the design stress, it will dominate the design of a slotted box beam.

Substitute equation (10.6.1) into equation (10.6.8). Then

$$\tau_{max} = \frac{3\rho_a V_w^2}{8} \frac{h_v \ell_s}{t^2} \left(\frac{h + h_v}{h + w} \right) \tag{10.6.10}$$

As in the previous subsection, let $\rho_a = 1.293$ kg/m^3 and $V_w = 27$ m/s. Then

$3\rho_a V^2_w/8 = 353$ N/m² $= 0.05$ psi. Again assume a design shear stress of 12,000 psi or $84(10)^6$ N/m². To get a feeling for magnitudes, let $h = 1$ m, $w = 1/3$ m, and $\ell_s = 20$ m. Then from equation (10.6.10) the thickness needed to resist the torsional load is

$$t = 1.60 \text{ cm for } h_v = 1.6 \text{ m}$$

$$= 2.24 \text{ cm for } h_v = 2.4 \text{ m}$$

For a closed box beam, it was argued that the walls should be at least 1 cm thick to simplify fabrication. If this proves correct, the penalty in added weight per unit length and hence cost per unit length in using a slotted box beam is a factor of 1.6 for $h_v = 1.6$ m and 2.24 for $h_v = 2.4$ m. Recall from the previous subsection that these two values of h_v correspond to the use of seated- or standing-passenger vehicles, respectively. Thus, with slotted box beams, the penalty in guideway cost in using standing-passenger versus seated-passenger vehicles is a factor of $2.24/1.60 = 1.40$ or 40 percent.

An alternative design for a slotted beam configuration is to use a shallow box defined by equation (10.6.7) to resist torsion and thinner walls to contain the bogie. The fabrication cost of such a design would, however, increase.

10.7 Plate Buckling

If a box-beam guideway is built up of thin steel plates, it is necessary to ascertain that the side walls are thick enough so that they will not fail by buckling. The theory of buckling is given by Timoshenko[14]. To determine the critical buckling load of the side walls of a box beam, we must define the manner of support of the edges of the side walls and the manner of loading. These factors will differ with different vehicle support configurations, but before troubling to define them in detail it is useful to consider a simplified configuration which can be expected to produce buckling most easily. Then we can compare it with other configurations.

The simplest configuration of interest is a plate of length ℓ, width h, and thickness t simply supported along all its edges and subject to a uniform load per unit length N along the boundaries of length ℓ, in which we assume ℓ is much greater than h. Then, from reference[14], p. 329, the critical buckling load, converted to our notation, is

$$N_{cr} = \frac{\pi^2 D}{\ell^2}\left(\frac{\ell}{h} + \frac{h}{\ell}\right)^2 = \frac{\pi^2 D}{h^2}\left(1 + \frac{h^2}{\ell^2}\right)^2$$

in which

$$D = \frac{Et^3}{12(1 - \nu^2)}$$

is the place rigidity factor, where ν is Poisson's ratio and E is the modulus of elasticity. For structural steel $\nu = 0.3$ and $E = 21(10)^{10}$ N/m^2.

Thus, the critical buckling load for a steel plate for which h is much less than ℓ is

$$N_{cr} = 19(10)^4 \frac{t^3}{h^2} \text{N/m} \tag{10.7.1}$$

in which t is in centimeters and h is in meters. For the plate used in previous calculations for which $t = 1$ cm and $h = 1$ m,

$$N_{cr} = 19(10)^4 \text{ N/m} \quad (12,800 \text{ lb}_f/\text{ft})$$

Compare this result with figure 5-4, where a vehicle mass of 1000 kg/m exerts a force of 10,000 N/m. A pair of simply supported plates, idealizing a box beam, could support up to 380,000 N/m or a mass distribution of 38,000 kg/m—far higher than the mass per unit length of any of a wide range of transit vehicles. The actual edge conditions would stiffen the plate and decrease its load, and the load of the vehicles in most practical configurations is not applied directly to the top of the plates. Therefore, plate buckling plays no role in designing box-beam structures of the approximate dimensions considered above.

As a matter of interest, plate buckling would be important if N_{cr} were reduced by a factor of about 40(see figure 5-4). This would occur if t were reduced by $(40)^{1/3} = 3.42$ to about 3 mm. Such thin plates would be difficult to handle in a steel fabrication shop.

10.8 Plate Vibration

A final factor in design of thin-plate beams is the possibility that plate vibration will produce unwanted noise as vehicles pass. This problem can be analyzed by means of the theory of vibration of plates, developed by Timoshenko[9]. His equation (214) gives the frequencies of vibration of rectangular plates with simply supported edges. In the notation used here, these frequencies can be expressed in the form

$$f_{mn} = \frac{\pi}{2} t \sqrt{\frac{E}{12(1 - \nu^2)\rho}} \left(\frac{m^2}{h^2} + \frac{n^2}{\ell^2}\right) \qquad (10.8.1)$$

in which m and n are positive integers. For steel ($E = 21(10)^{10}$ N/m², $\rho = 7760$ kg/m³, $\nu = 0.3$), equation (10.8.1) becomes

$$f_m = 24.70t \left(\frac{m^2}{h^2} + \frac{n^2}{\ell^2}\right) \text{ Hz}$$

in which t is the thickness of the plate in centimeters and, as before, h and ℓ are the depth and length in meters, respectively.

Thus, for $t = 1$ cm, $h = 1$ m, and ℓ much greater than h, the lowest frequency ($m = n = 1$) is 24.7 Hz. The lowest audible frequency is about 20 Hz. Thus, corresponding to m, $n = 1$, 2, 3, ... , sound will be produced throughout the audible range if the beam is excited. Measures to prevent the production of unwanted noise depend on two factors: (1) design of the suspension system of the vehicles in such a way that the vibratory modes of the side walls are not excited; and (2) damping of the vibratory modes by application of an appropriate material to the walls of the plate.

If the vehicles use wheels, for example, the use of steel wheels on steel rails would appear to be the worst combination because imperfections in the rails attached to the guideway and in the wheels would act as forcing functions and would cause the plate walls of the guideway beam to vibrate audibly as the vehicles pass. Use of rubber-tired wheels would dampen the effect of imperfections, and the use of air or magnetic suspension would appear to remove high frequency forcing functions altogether.

The damping of structures by use of surface treatments is discussed by Plunkett[15,16]. For the present application, the work of reference[16] appears directly applicable. There it is shown that the application of a thin viscoelastic layer constrained by even thinner sheets of a stiff material such as steel or aluminum of optimum length provides a significant amount of damping to thin beams even though the surface treatment adds less than 3 percent to the weight of the beam. The optimum constraining layer length for damping of a thin beam is 3.28 $(t_1 t_2 E_2/G_1)^{1/2}$, where E_2 and t_2 are the elastic modulus and thickness of the constraining layer, respectively; and G_1 and t_1 are the shear modulus and thickness of the viscoelastic material, respectively. The amount of damping falls off rapidly if the length of the constraining layer deviates from optimum. Torvik and Strickland[17] have extended application of the method to plates with similar results.

10.9 Optimum Span Length

According to equation (10.2.14), the plate thickness of a box beam of constant depth and width must increase with the span length ℓ_s in a stress-limited design. Thus, the cost of the beam decreases as ℓ_s decreases, but smaller ℓ_s means more support posts; therefore, there is a value of ℓ_s that minimizes the cost of the guideway plus support posts. It is instructive to study this optimum design point.

To be specific, consider a thin-walled box beam design. The cost per unit length of the beam can be expressed as

$$C_g = C_{g0} + C_{kg}\rho 2(h + w)t(\ell_s) \qquad (10.9.1)$$

in which C_{g0} is the element of cost per unit length independent of ℓ_s, C_{kg} is the erected cost per kilogram of material, $2(h + w)t$ is the cross-sectional area of the beam, and $t(\ell_s)$ indicates the dependence of t on ℓ_s from equation (10.2.14). Assume, however, that t is not permitted to go below a value t_m taken in previous subsections as one centimeter.

Assume the posts are square cross-sectioned steel beams of side length h_p at the base, of wall thickness, t_p, and of height ℓ above the ground. Let the cost per post be

$$C_p = 4C_{pkg}\rho t_p \ell h_p \qquad (10.9.2)$$

in which it is assumed that the total cost of the post counting its base is proportional to the above-ground mass. But the dimensions of the base, h_p, depend on the applied moment, $M = F\ell$, where F is a force applied at the vehicle height. F can be due to either wind or to sudden braking of a stream of vehicles. Then, from equation (10.2.1) and equation (10.2.2) with $w = h \gg t$,

$$\frac{M}{\sigma_m} = \frac{F\ell}{\sigma_m} = \frac{I}{c} = \frac{4}{3}h_p^2 t_p$$

Thus

$$h_p = \left(\frac{3F\ell}{4\sigma_m t_p} \right)^{1/2} \qquad (10.9.3)$$

If F is due to wind,

$$F = \tfrac{1}{2}\rho_a V_w^2 (h + h_v)\ell_s$$

in which $(h + h_v)\ell_s$ is the cross-sectional area exposed to wind in one span length. If F is due to emergency deceleration of vehicles,

$$F = \frac{a_e W}{g} \frac{\ell_s}{\ell_h}$$

in which W is the weight of each vehicle, a_e is the emergency braking rate, and ℓ_h is the minimum headway of a stream of vehicles.

Based on the numerical values used in connection with equation (10.6.6), the maximum value of $\rho_a V_w^2 (h + h_v)/2 \approx 1600$ N/m. Assuming $a_e/g = 0.5$, $W = 12600$ N (see figure 10-8), and $(\ell_h)_{\min} = 5$ m, $a_e W/g\ell_h = 630$ N/m. Assuming that for heavier vehicles, ℓ_h increases in proportion to W, the wind load dominates. Substituting the wind load into equation (10.9.3), and then equation (10.9.3) into equation (10.9.2), the cost of each post is

$$C_p = 2C_{p_{\text{kg}}}\rho V_w \left[\frac{1.5\rho_a \ell^3 t_p (h + h_v)}{\sigma_m} \right]^{1/2} \ell_s^{1/2} \qquad (10.9.4)$$

Now the installed cost of the whole guideway per unit length can be expressed as

$$C_T = C_g + \frac{C_p}{\ell_s}$$

Substituting equations (10.9.1) and (10.9.4),

$$C_T = C_{g0} + A_1 t(\ell_s) + A_2/\ell_s^{1/2} \qquad (10.9.5)$$

in which

$$A_1 = 2\rho C_{kg} h(1 + \alpha) \qquad (10.9.6)$$

and

$$A_2 = 2C_{pkg}\rho V_w \left[\frac{1.5\rho_a \ell^3 t_p (h + h_v)}{\sigma_m} \right]^{1/2} \qquad (10.9.7)$$

The optimum span length is found by differentiating equation (10.9.5) with respect to ℓ_s and setting the result equal to zero. Thus,

$$\frac{dt}{d\ell_s} = \frac{A_2/A_1}{2\ell_s^{3/2}} \qquad (10.9.8)$$

gives the optimum value of ℓ_s.

As indicated above, it is necessary to take t at least as large as t_m which, from figure 10-3, corresponds to a specific value of ℓ_s, which we shall call ℓ_{s_m}. Then, from the form of equation (10.9.5), it is clear that the optimum value of ℓ_s must be at least as large as ℓ_{s_m}. Whether or not it is larger depends on whether or not the value of ℓ_s that satisfies equation (10.9.8) is larger or smaller than ℓ_s. If it is smaller, ℓ_s is the optimum value; if larger, the root of equation (10.9.8) is the optimum. Thus, assume $t(\ell_s)$ is the function given by equation (10.2.14) and express $t(\ell_s)$ in the form

$$t = \frac{ax^2}{1 - x^2} \qquad (10.9.9)$$

where

$$a = \frac{3q_\ell}{8\rho g h} = \frac{3W}{8\rho g h \ell_v} \qquad (10.9.10)$$

and

$$x = \ell_s/b \qquad (10.9.11)$$

where

$$b = \left(\frac{2\sigma_m h}{\rho g} \right)^{1/2} \qquad (10.9.12)$$

In the expression for a, we have assumed the live load per unit length is W/ℓ_v, where W is the vehicle weight and ℓ_v is its length. Now, from equation (10.9.9),

$$\frac{dt}{d\ell_s} = \frac{2ax}{b(1 - x^2)^2}$$

Substituting this expression into equation (10.9.8),

$$\frac{2ax}{b(1 - x^2)^2} = \frac{A_2/A_1}{2b^{3/2}x^{3/2}}$$

which may be written in the form

$$\mu = \frac{x^{5/2}}{(1 - x^2)^2} \qquad (10.9.13)$$

where

$$\mu = \frac{A_2}{4ab^{1/2}A_1} = \frac{2(C_{pkg}/C_{kg})V_w\ell_v(\rho g)^{5/4}[1.5\rho_a\ell^3 t_p(h + h_v)]^{1/2}}{3(1 + \alpha)W(2h)^{1/4}\sigma_m^{3/4}} \qquad (10.9.14)$$

Equation (10.9.13) is plotted in figure 10-9. Thus, after μ is found from equation (10.9.14), the optimum value of x is found as the corresponding value from figure 10-9. Then ℓ_s is found from equations (10.9.11) and (10.9.12). As indicated above, if this value of ℓ_s is less than ℓ_{sm}, ℓ_{sm} is the optimum value. Consider as an example a steel box beam for which $h = 1$ m, $\alpha = 1/3$. With $\rho = 7760$ kg/m³, $\sigma_m = 140(10)^6$ N/m², $V_w = 27$ m/s, and $\rho_a = 1.293$ kg/m³,

$$\mu = 15.9(C_{pkg}/C_{kg})\ell_v\ell^{3/2}t_p^{1/2}(h + h_v)^{1/2}/W$$

Assume $C_{\rho kg}/C_{kg} = 10$ to account for the cost of the entire post and its erection, and take W to be the smallest value given in figure 10-8, 12600 N. Then let $\ell_v = 2.6$ m, $h + h_v = 2.6$ m, and $\ell = 5$ m. Finally take $t_p = 0.02$ m to minimize possible damage in case of accidents, and we find $\mu = 0.084$. Then, from figure 10-9, $x = 0.335$. From equation (10.9.12), $b = 60.0$ m, Therefore, $\ell_s = 20.1$ m. But, if the wall thickness is limited to say 1 cm, figure 10-3 shows that the span is stress limited at $\ell_s = 32.8$ m. This is larger than the computed value of 20.1 m. Therefore, in this example, the guide-way cost is minimum if ℓ_s is taken as 32.8 m. If it were possible to use plates less than one centimeter thick without a corresponding increase in fabrication cost per unit mass of material, the total cost could be decreased.

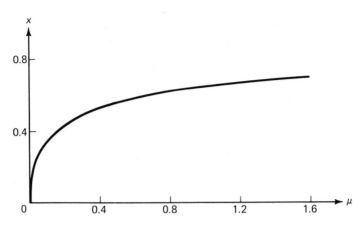

Figure 10-9. Span Length for Minimum Guideway Cost

10.10 Summary

The purpose of this chapter has been to examine the factors that have primary influence on the cost per unit length of elevated guideways, and to find optimum parameter choices where they exist that will minimize cost per unit length. Since the guideway is the single most expensive item in an exclusive-guideway transit system, the optimization of its parameters is of primary importance in minimizing the cost of the total system. While attention is devoted in this chapter exclusively to elevated guideways, it should be kept in mind that there may be circumstances in which at-grade guideways are satisfactory and would decrease system cost, and in which, in the case of small-vehicle systems, underground guideways may not be appreciably more expensive than elevated guideways [1].

The criteria for guideway design are primarily maximum stress and ride comfort; however, integration of the guideway into the system requires that consideration be given to the manner of switching and the manner of support of the vehicles by the guideway. To take advantage of the cost reduction possible with the use of small vehicles, it is necessary to consider switch mechanisms that do not require movement of a portion of the guideway; and, to provide adequate lateral stability and ride comfort, the dimensions of the guideway must not be too small. The results of this chapter indicate, however, that weight per unit length of the guideway increases too rapidly as parameters deviate from optimum to permit considerations of switching and lateral stability to dictate the basic guideway design. Rather, if weight and cost are to be minimized, optimum parameters must be chosen and then the switching and lateral stability requirements provided by clever design. Enough design and test experience has been accumulated to ascertain that these requirements are not incompatible. The visual appearance of the guideway is of course also an important factor in the design; however, this consideration is satisfied in a structurally optimum design because such a design has the smallest possible cross section.

It is not obvious a priori which stresses reach their design limits first in a given guideway design; therefore, all possibilities must be considered. The logical first step is to consider bending stresses produced by a static vertical load, assumed in the worst case to be due to vehicles at rest end-to-end on the guideway. Next, the dynamic loading due to motion of vehicles over the guideway is considered, first by studying the deflection, stress, and acceleration produced by a single vehicle of arbitrary speed and mass crossing a single, simply supported span, and second by studying the increased effects produced by cascades of vehicles crossing a span. The conclusion reached is that the static condition described above usually yields a higher stress than the dynamic stress produced with vehicles spaced farther apart, and therefore that, because the static yield point stress and fatigue limit stress are about the same in structural steel [7], the static condition of vehicles spaced end-to-end usually determines the design. Application of the ride comfort criterion then shows that at speeds higher than given by equation (10.5.4), the beam must be deeper than that required by the stress criterion.

Torsional stresses are next considered, and it is found that with a bending-optimum box beam, the torsional stresses due to wind and centrifugal forces are well below the design shear stress. Therefore only a small fraction of the depth of a bending-optimum box beam is needed to resist torsion, a conclusion that increases the flexibility of the choice of beam cross section. Slotted box beams are also studied in torsion, and it is found that for the same dimensions as a closed box beam, the shear stress is greater by a factor of about 75, thus requiring the walls of the beam to be substantially thicker. Finally, for thin-walled steel beams the possibility of plate buckling and plate vibration is examined. It is found that if the plate is thick enough so that its thinness will not cause fabrication problems (an intuitive judgement), buckling under the loads that can be produced by vehicles is not a problem, but that the plate can not practically be thick enough to avoid resonances in the audible range. Thus, it is necessary either to design the vehicle suspension system so that the plate vibratory modes will not be excited due to imperfections, or to apply an optimized vibration-damping layer to the surface of the beam. Such a treatment is described.

A number of numerical examples are worked out in this chapter to illustrate the method more specifically, and to give a feeling for the magnitudes of the various parameters. In all cases, the properties of ordinary structural steel are assumed. Perhaps the only other practical alternative is to use reinforced concrete; however, this is not done for three reasons: (1) the mathematics is much more straightforward for thin-walled beams (a good assumption for steel) than for thick-walled beams, which must be assumed with concrete; (2) there are more variables with concrete beams because of prestressing and placement of reinforcing bars; and (3) one example seems sufficient to illustrate the attainment of certain optimum conditions. Nonetheless, because of the low cost of reinforced concrete as compared to steel, its use should not be ignored and a similar solution should be carried through for concrete.

The results of chapter 10 will now be discussed in more detail: figure 10-2 gives the dimensionless material cross-sectional area $\mathscr{A}$ of a beam as a function of aspect ratio α for various values of a dimensionless loading factor $\mathscr{I}$. It is seen that for thin-walled beams the cross-sectional area of the beam for a given load is minimum if the aspect ratio if one-third. If the beam wall thickness is the same on all walls, this means that the width of the beam should be one-third the depth. As the wall thickness increases, the dimensionless loading factor $\mathscr{I}$ decreases and the optimum aspect ratio decreases. Thus, in all cases, a deep, narrow beam is indicated if the cost is to be minimized. By varying the parameter α in figure 10-2, one can see how the dimensionless area $\mathscr{A}$ increases away from the optimum condition. It can be expected that the cost per unit length of the beam increases with its cross-sectional area, that is, to the ordinate in figure 10-2; therefore this figure is basic to the determination of the relative cost of various beam designs. It is important to note that figure 10-2 is based on the fundamental bending stress formula, given by equation (10.2.1), and is independent of the manner or magnitude of loading.

Once the optimum aspect ratio of the beam is determined, its required thickness must be found as a function of load. If the wall is thin compared to the depth, the thickness is given by equation (10.2.14). For a given depth and span length, this equation shows that the required wall thickness is proportional to the live load per unit length. In the same circumstances, the cross-sectional area of the beam (and hence material cost per unit length) is proportional to the wall thickness. Therefore, if the beam is stress limited, which is the case for most urban application, *the material cost per unit length of the guideway is proportional to the weight per unit length of the vehicles*. Figure 5-4 shows the mass per unit length of forty-seven different transit vehicles of various capacity, and together with the above conclusion, illustrates a major reason for interest in small vehicles in automated transit systems.

The required wall thickness is plotted from equation (10.2.14) in figure 10-3 for a live load of 447 kg/m (300 lb/ft). Since the wall thickness is proportional to live load, it can readily be determined for other loadings. Some of the wall thicknesses plotted may, as mentioned above, be too thin from the viewpoint of ease of fabrication. If, for example, the thinnest permissible sheet is 1 cm, a beam one-meter deep is stressed to the design limit only if the spans are longer than 32.8 m. For shorter spans, the beam could tolerate a higher unit loading without exceeding the design limit; however, the cost then increases because more posts than necessary are used. If the guideway is built up of two parallel box beams in order to support ordinary wheeled vehicles, it is shown that for the same span length and beam-wall thickness, the total cross-sectional area and hence cost per unit length increases by about 40 percent.

Once static loading is understood, it is necessary to determine if the motion of the vehicles will set up resonant conditions that will make dynamic loading more severe than the worst static loading case of vehicles parked end-to-end on the guideway. As mentioned above, this case is treated by first examining the motions produced by a single vehicle crossing the span. As indicated from figures 10-5 and 10-6, the greatest deflection at any speed is only about 70 percent greater than the static value produced with one vehicle parked at the center of the span. Thus, unless the vehicles are almost as long as the free spans, the maximum static load will be greater than the single-vehicle dynamic load. For dynamic loading with single or multiple vehicles, the resonant conditions are determined by the natural frequencies of vibration of the unloaded beam. The natural frequencies are proportional to $(I/A)^{1/2}$, where I is the moment of inertia of the cross section and A is the cross-sectional area. Thus, for a given A, and hence a given cost per unit length, resonant conditions cause the least difficulty if I is a maximum. Maximum I, in turn, is produced if the beam is as deep and narrow as possible, but one must take into consideration the need for lateral stiffness. It is shown that for the bending-optimum aspect ratio of one-third, the natural frequency in the horizontal plane is 43 percent of its value in the vertical plane, a value judged sufficiently high.

From analysis of cascades of vehicles crossing a span, based on an analysis performed at the Massachusetts Institute of Technology, it is found that the ratio of dynamic deflection to static deflection with the same vehicle loading is greater if the vehicles are farther apart and diminishes markedly as the headway between vehicles decreases (see figure 10-7). It is also found that the maximum amplitude of beam motion is amplified with successive vehicle crossings by a factor of about 1.9 in 15 to 20 crossings at which time a steady-state condition is reached. Based on the MIT results, if the minimum operating headway is 0.25, 0.5 times the span length, the worst-case static stress will be greater than the maximum dynamic stress (at any speed) if the span length is greater than 5.6, 13.8 times the vehicle length. But, if the maximum vehicle speed is kept about 20 percent below the primary resonant condition (usually attainable), the maximum dynamic deflection is only a small amount greater than the static deflection for the case of vehicles spaced a fourth of a span apart, and it can be concluded that the maximum static stress determines the design.

Figure 10-8 shows that the guideway mass per unit length, determined under dynamic conditions, increases roughly as the square root of the vehicle mass for a given flow in seats per hour. But, if the static stress determines the design, the guideway mass increases as the first power of the vehicle mass, and this is the usual condition. If the static condition and not the dynamic condition determines the design, a simple formula (equation (10.5.4)) is found that determines the maximum speed for which the ride comfort condition is met. In most cases it is found that this speed exceeds the maximum speed of interest in urban applications, and hence that the design is determined from static stress considerations.

Torsional stress considerations indicate, as mentioned above, that a full box beam is not needed to resist the torsional loads, thus permitting some freedom in the design. If the beam is slotted, however, torsional loads are of prime importance. In this case, because of the added vertical height of standing-passenger vehicles and the accompanying increase in wind load, the use of standing-passenger vehicles adds about 40 percent to the mass per unit length of the beam required to resist the wind load.

Finally, a formula is found (equations (10.9.13, 10.9.14)) for the span length that minimizes the total cost of beams plus support posts.

References

1. *Personal Rapid Transit in Central Adelaide,* A Report for the Director General of Transport, South Australia, Loder & Bayly, Planning and Engineering Consultants (79 Power St., Hawthorn 3122), June 1976.

2. *Steel Structures for Mass Transit,* American Iron and Steel Institute, Washington, D.C., 1976.

3. J.E. Snyder, III, D.N. Wormley, H.H. Richardson, "Automated Guideway Transit Systems Vehicle-Elevated Guideway Dynamics: Multiple-Vehicle Single Span Systems," Report No. UMTA MA-11-0023-75-1, Department of Transportation, Washington, D.C., October 1975.

4. J.N. Paulson, M.L. Silver, and T.B. Belytschko, "Dynamic Three-Dimensional Finite Element Analysis of Steel Transportation Structures," Report No. DOT-TST-76-46, Department of Transportation, Washington, D.C., December 1975.

5. P.W. Likins, "Dynamic Interactions of PRT Vehicles and Elevated Guideways," Report No. DOT-TST-75-104, Department of Transportation, Washington, D.C., March 1975.

6. P.W. Likins, R.B. Nelson, D.L. Mingori, "Dynamic Interactions and Optimal Design of PRT Vehicles on Elevated Guideways," Report No.

DOT-TST-77-15, Department of Transportation, Washington, D.C., June 1976.

7. *Standard Handbook for Mechanical Engineers,* seventh edition, McGraw-Hill Book Company, New York, 1967.

8. *The Lea Transit Compendium,* N.D. Lea Transportation Research Corporation, Huntsville, Ala., 1976-1977.

9. S. Timoshenko, *Vibration Problems in Engineering,* second edition, D. VanNostrand Company, New York, 1937.

10. S. Timoshenko and J.M. Goodier, *Theory of Elasticity,* second edition, McGraw-Hill Book Company, New York, 1951.

11. Hans Ebner, "Torsional Stresses in Box Beams with Cross Sections Partially Restrained against Warping," National Advisory Committee for Aeronautics, Technical Memorandum No. 744, 1934, translated from *Zeitschrift für* Flugtechnik und Motorluftschiffahrt, Vol. 24, Nos. 23 and 24, December 14 and 28, 1933.

12. R.B. Fling and C.L. Olson, "An Integrated Concept for Propulsion, Braking, Control, and Switching of Vehicles Operating at Close Headways," *Personal Rapid Transit,* Department of Audio Visual Library Services, University of Minnesota, Minneapolis, Minn., 1972.

13. See the *Lea Transit Compendium,* op. cit., for details on these systems. With a bogie inside a box beam, an in-vehicle switch attached to the bogie can secure the bogie to one side of the guideway or the other without moving any elements of the guideway.

14. S. Timoshenko, *Theory of Elastic Stability,* McGraw-Hill Book Company, New York, 1936, chapter 7.

15. R. Plunkett, "Vibration Control by Applied Damping Treatments," *Shock and Vibration Handbook,* second edition, C.N. Harris and C.E. Crede, eds. McGraw-Hill Book Company, New York, 1976, chapter 37.

16. R. Plunkett and C.T. Lee, "Length Optimization for Constrained Viscoelastic Layer Damping," *The Journal of the Acoustical Society of America,* Vol. 48, No. 1, (Part 2), July 1970, pp. 150-161.

17. P.J. Torvik and D.Z. Strickland, "Damping Additions for Plates Using Constrained Viscoelastic Layers," *The Journal of the Acoustical Society of America,* Vol. 51, No. 3, March 1972, pp. 985-943.

11

Design for Maximum Cost Effectiveness

11.1 Introduction

In the previous chapters, specific topical areas of transit systems theory have been developed with a view to determining requirements, characteristics, and parameter choices that will increase cost effectiveness. The fundamental viewpoint taken of transit systems theory is not to take specific transit systems and transit concepts as they are known at the time of writing and explain how and why they work (although this is and must be an integral part of the process), but to consider the "transit system" as a multidimensional field of requirements, characteristics, and parameter choices all of which are subject to change, and to vary these factors until the cost effectiveness of the entire system is maximized. Such a process is very complex. It requires analysis by and interaction among many people of many disciplines over many years in a context in which many ideas are being tried in the laboratory, on test tracks, and in operation. Then it requires synthesis—the ultimate purpose of transit systems theory.

The previous chapters have laid groundwork felt by the author to be needed in synthesis of the design of a transit system of maximum cost effectiveness. Some areas which perhaps should have been covered are not covered in depth and, in some cases, not at all. Two examples are:

1. Computer simulations of operation of vehicles near and in stations, at interchanges, and in entire networks. Much of this kind of work has been done [1] and its existence has enabled the author to proceed with confidence in the development and explanation of the underlying algebraic theory in a form that can more easily be taught, and to offer the results of this chapter as realistic and practical possibilities.

2. Propulsion, braking and suspension. While many combinations of methods have been proposed and tested, and the choice of the best combination is important, the details are not felt to be needed in this book. The *requirements* for a propulsion and braking system are, however, of fundamental importance and are discussed in section 11.4. On the other hand, no similar reason has been found to consider suspension means and requirements on the same basis other than to note that the means proposed are wheels, air, and magnetic fields, and that some of them may be more suited to the optimum guideway configuration than others.

The synthesis of an optimum transit system is not a simple step-by-step process, it is a web of interconnected influences. But the exposition of it

315

must be necessity proceed step-by-step with a certain clumsiness associated with referencing back and forth in the argument. There is a certain danger in conveying the impression that the process is easier than it is, and in that all of the drama is washed away, hopefully to be told in other kinds of books. Moreover, it must be recognized that a single optimum system might not result, but different optima for different purposes. With these caveats, we proceed first by reviewing in this introduction the reasons for concentrating on automated guideway transit systems, and then, section by section, by developing a series of arguments leading to a system optimized to the extent possible in a book of this length.

Manually Driven versus Automated Transit

A great deal of information is available on the characteristics of transit systems in which the vehicles are driven by professional drivers. Rapidly rising deficits and poor service levels inherent to these systems indicate that continued attempts to expand transit service in this way will become increasingly unjustifiable. On the other hand, systems of manually driven vehicles using one of the riders as a driver (commuter vans) have proven economically viable, at least in the special circumstance in which both the origins and destinations of the trips taken by one vanload of people are closely clustered in comparison with the trip length. Attempts to expand this kind of service too far, however, run into the difficulty of increased circuity of the route and the increased unattractiveness this brings to the trip. Moreover, where commuter vans are used to carry people from suburban residential areas to inner city work places, they may because of their higher service level attract patrons away from the fixed route, fixed schedule bus system, thus further increasing its deficit. A conflict therefore develops which limits the extent to which commuter vans can be used.

The hope of overcoming some of these problems has turned interest to the potential of automated systems. In addition to offering the prospect of increased cost effectiveness, automated systems appear to permit increases in safety and reliability and to offer the prospect of twenty-four hour, on-demand service just as is obtained with elevators and escalators.

Exclusive versus Nonexclusive Guideways

Automated systems may, in theory, operate either on exclusive guideways or on nonexclusive guideways, that is, in mixed traffic. While there are some advocates of the latter approach, the problems of object detection and of recovery from a lateral steering failure in time to avoid a collision are sufficiently fundamental that such an approach has not been seriously considered except at very low speeds. Thus the logical choice for automated transit is to use exclusive guideways, either underground, elevated, or at-grade. At-grade guideways, while low in direct cost, suffer from the disadvantages that communities are divided by the lines, safety is a problem at crossings, and snow and ice are difficult to remove. Because of the low cost of at-grade systems, however, there are circumstances in which they are used. These exclusive guideway systems are usually referred to as automated guideway transit (AGT) systems. Their advantages are that they permit increased time reliability and safety, decreased trip time, and much decreased land use for transportation. Indeed, the latter factor may be the most fundamental reason for interest in AGT systems.

11.2 Guideways

The guideway is the most expensive component of an AGT system, therefore the optimization of its parameters is primary in cost minimization of the system. If the guideway is underground, minimization of the cross-sectional area of the vehicles and hence of the tunnels minimizes cost per unit length. If the guideway is elevated, the results of chapter 10 lead to the conclusion that the cost per unit length of the guideway will be minimized if the weight, size, and weight per unit length of the vehicles are minimized, and if the guideway is a deep, narrow monobeam. These conclusions run counter to much of contemporary practice, which is based on the use of duo-rail vehicles. Such systems, however, evolved from street vehicles in which the width between wheels is the only means of achieveing lateral stability. The use of deep, narrow monobeams clearly requires a completely different suspension system which must be designed from scratch. Several such designs are currently in test or in operation [2].

Much progress will be possible in the field of AGT systems once it is understood that the goal should be as described above. Practical use of the smallest vehicles for a given required capacity depends on development of design concepts in which minimum headway can be accomplished safely and reliably without excessive cost. These are the topics of chapters 7 through 9, and will be discussed below. Development of the best lateral suspension system using the vertical dimension of the guideway for lateral stability requires consideration of various mechanical design possibilities and the requirement of switching. Use of the smallest vehicles is possible only if the stations are off the main line. This conclusion is clear from the results of chapter 4, which show the capacities obtainable with on-line versus off-line stations. On-line station systems are inherently large-vehicle, high cost systems if adequate capacity is to be achieved. As a parallel, the freeway obtains its capacity from the fact that a flow of low capacity vehicles on the main line is uninterrupted by stops.

The practical use of off-line stations with small vehicles requires the development of a rapid and highly reliable switching mechanism. To decrease the *required* reliability of the switch and to increase the time available to throw it and verify that it has been thrown, the switch should be on board the vehicle rather than in the track. Many designs of such switches have been developed [3]. The problem of switching rapidly with a transit system using deep, narrow monobeams plagued designers for many years, and led most of them to abandon the idea of a rapid switch that does not require movement of a guideway element. In the past decade, however, this problem has been solved in several ways: (1) by use of a bogey inside the guideway from which the vehicle is hung [4], (2) by use of a U-shaped guideway with bottom-supported vehicles which obtain lateral stability from wheels riding on the inside vertical surface of the U-beam [5], and (3) by use of box beams but with a specially designed switch section in which the joining beams are cut so that the wheels which straddle the box beam can pass through but in which the bending stresses are carried by vertical plates outside the path of the wheels and joined to the inner beams by means of shear plates used as the tracks for the wheels [6]. The third configuration produces the most complex switch-section structure, but permits use of an optimum box-beam cross section away from the switches. The other configurations sacrifice somewhat the cost and weight of the beam away from the switch section but thereby achieve a structurally simpler switch section. At the time of writing, no truly comparative analysis of these configurations, considering all aspects of the interfaces with the vehicles, has been completed. Therefore it is not yet known which is the better choice.

11.3 Vehicle Fleet Costs

Figure 5-1 shows the reported initial cost per unit capacity of twenty-nine different guideway transit vehicles in development or in operation in various countries. By capacity is meant the design capacity of a vehicle in persons, that is, the number of seats plus the nominal number of spaces available for standees in uncrowded conditions. Some of the smallest vehicles included in figure 5-1 allow no adult standees at all. The conclusion of figure 5-1 is that the cost of a guideway transit vehicle per unit capacity is independent of capacity. This conclusion is rough because all of the costs in figure 5-1 have not been normalized to the same date and there has been no standardization of cost-reporting procedures. It does, however, make sense because the larger vehicles are manufactured by job-shop practices on an individual basis and require large machinery to move major parts; whereas, the smaller vehicles can be manufactured with higher production procedures and can be moved much more easily.

The cost of a vehicle fleet is the cost per unit capacity of a vehicle multiplied by the vehicle capacity multiplied by the required number of vehicles. The product of the latter two terms is the capacity in persons required of the entire fleet of vehicles. If the vehicle cost per unit capacity is constant, then *the fleet cost is proportional to the total capacity of the fleet and independent of the size of the vehicles.* But the total capacity required of a fleet of vehicles is simply the peak demand in people per unit of time multiplied by the average trip time and divided by the average load factor of a vehicle (see equation (4.3.26)). If the peak demand is considered given, the conclusion is that *the fleet cost is proportional to the average trip time divided by the average load factor.* Thus, the fleet cost is minimized by minimizing the average trip time (so vehicles can be used more often) and by maximizing the load factor (so each vehicle is used as intensively as possible).

From equations (4.3.2, 4.3.9 and 4.3.10), the average trip time can be written in the form

Average trip time = (average trip length) $/V_L$

+ (station dwell time + V_L/a_m + a_m/J)(number of stops)   (11.3.1)

in which V_L is the line speed, a_m is the service acceleration, and J is the comfort level of jerk. The factor a_m/J is, from chapter 2, about one second in all types of systems and is determined from comfort considerations. Because V_L appears in the denominator of one term and the numerator of another, there is a finite value of V_L that minimizes trip time; however, in most urban applications, this value is too high to be practical, and, in any case, the work of chapter 10 and section 3.6 shows that the guideway cost is strongly influenced by line speed. Thus there is a value of line speed that minimizes the total system cost, but it must be determined by considering both fleet cost and guideway cost. Once this value is determined, equation (11.3.1) shows that three operational factors determine the trip time: (1) the station dwell time, (2) the number of stops, and (3) the service acceleration. The station dwell time is minimized if the service is on demand with minimum delay of vehicles; the number of stops can be reduced to a minimum of one by using off-line stations and nonstop service; and the service acceleration can be maximized by using seated-passenger vehicles. These requirements are all compatible with and indeed made possible by the use of the smallest size of vehicle, and hence are compatible with the requirements of guideway-cost minimization. Moreover, as shown in chapter 3, the length of off-line ramps is minimized if the service acceleration is maximized, thus further reducing cost; and, from equation (4.5.22) and figure 5-6, on-demand, nonstop service is the only practical alternative in an off-line station, network system of anything but the smallest size.

Minimization of the fleet cost was shown also to require maximization of the average vehicle load factor. To maximize the load factor with on-demand, nonstop service in which people ride only with travelling companions, the vehicle must be as small as practical. The average number of people traveling in automobiles varies from about 1.2 during the rush period to about 2.1 in off-peak periods. Thus, the number of seats per vehicle should be more than two but probably not more than four. From the analysis of section 7.5, the author would judge that a three-seat vehicle with side-by-side seating is optimum. The fraction of a day's trips in which more than three people ride together is quite small (about three percent according to one survey), and in these exceptional cases, more than one vehicle per party can be used. The load factor also depends on the amount of deadheading in the system. As indicated in section 4.3, the amount of deadheading depends on the nonuniformity of demand in all systems. A more important factor, however, is the off-peak service and its relationship to total operating cost. If off-line station on-demand service is used, vehicles move only when there is demand for service. On the other hand, with on-line stations, the vehicles must move continuously on a schedule whether or not demand exists, for if they cease to run or decrease schedule frequency due to low demand, the service will appear more unreliable and patronage will drop further. Thus, lower load factors in a twenty-four hour period can be anticipated in large, scheduled vehicles than in small, demand activated ones, and hence the operating costs will be relatively higher in the larger vehicle system.

All of the system optimization requirements thus far discussed are seen to mesh without incompatibilities. Furthermore, the service level required of a system optimized by the considerations thus far discussed is the best that can be offered and will therefore maximize patronage. Before a conclusion can be reached, however, the operating and maintainance costs of the vehicle fleet per unit capacity per year must be examined. Based on data obtained from unpublished sources, it is evident that these support costs per unit capacity will fall slowly as the vehicle size increases. Whether or not the smallest vehicles gives the lowest cost per trip then depends on the relative load factor. Further research in this area is needed. The possibility of use of the smallest vehicles depends on the achievement of a sufficiently small headway safely and reliably. These requirements are discussed in the following sections.

11.4 Propulsion and Braking

The design requirements to permit safe operation at minimum headway are the subject of chapter 7. See section 7.8 for a detailed summary of these requirements. Among them is the requirement that direct, linear propulsion and braking be used instead of rotary propulsion and braking through wheels. It is shown in chapter 7 that, for seated-passenger vehicles, this change will reduce the minimum headway from about two to three seconds with rotary motors to about one quarter second with linear motors, that is, by a factor of at least eight. With 0.25-second headway and three seats per vehicle, the throughput is 43,200 seats per hour or, with a rush-hour load factor of 50 percent, 21,600 persons per hour. With automobile traffic on freeways, the maximum throughput per lane is about 2000 persons per hour. Therefore, 21,600 persons per hour is equivalent to over ten freeway lanes of traffic, a throughput far in excess of most requirements.

Three types of linear propulsion have been considered: (1) mechanical, (2) air, and (3) electric propulsion. Mechanical propulsion is used on moving sidewalks and ski lifts, applications for which speeds below about five meters per second are adequate. At speeds of interest for more general urban applications (say 10 to 25 m/s), friction losses and wear are too great for mechanical systems to be practical. Air propulsion, used on two developmental systems in the United States, is inherently noisy, and the means required to quiet the noise once generated make these systems uncompetitive for most applications. Electromagnetic propulsion, on the other hand, is quiet and applicable at any reasonable speed. Electromagnetic propulsion, besides satisfying requirements for safety at short headways, has the following advantages:

1. The guideway need not be heated to remove thin layers of ice or water because magnetic fields are unaffected by them.

2. If the vehicles use wheels, the tires can be smooth and the track smooth, thus minimizing noise as a cost to the community.

3. No moving parts, no wear, and minimum maintenance.

4. Grades up to 15 percent can be negotiated without difficulty; inded if there were no power limitation no grade would pose a problem.

Automated guideway systems have been developed using a variety of types of linear electric motors—linear induction motors (the most common), linear synchronous motors, and linear pulse dc motors. The later two types promise higher efficiency but are not as well developed as LIMs. More research and development is needed to determine which types of linear electric motors are the most cost effective, and to bring the designs into full commercial readiness. To minimize the weight of linear electric motors used on board vehicles, the heat transfer design of these motors must be improved as much as is practical. In-the-track motors can be lighter because they are pulsed and have some time to dissipate heat between passages of vehicles, but many more of them are needed. Hence, unless the throughput is very high, the cost trade-off will favor in-the-vehicle motors even though they increase the weight of the vehicles and create problems of power collection [7].

11.5 Standing versus Seated Passengers

Provisions for standees are made aboard trains, city buses, and streetcars; but not in taxis, limousines, and jitneys. Room for standees permits rush hour flows to be handled by "crush loading" each vehicle with standees and thereby increasing the capacity of a given fleet of vehicles. On the other hand, such service is not considered comfortable by most people and is avoided if alternatives are available. The alternative to increasing capacity by crush loading in special cases such as the termination of a sports event is to time these extra heavy demands in off-peak periods and to draw then from a pool of available vehicles, much as a fleet of taxis handle them now.

From the viewpoint of cost effectiveness, the considerations are as follows:

1. Figure 5-1 shows that, based on the design capacity of a fleet of vehicles, there is no economic advantage in automated systems in using larger vehicles that permit standees. Standing-passenger vehicles must be taller, wider, and generally longer than seated-passenger vehicles. As a result, as shown by figure 5-4, the larger vehicles, all of which permit standees, are much heavier per unit length than the smaller, seated-passenger vehicles. The consequence is, as shown by the work of chapter 10, that the guideway weight per unit length is greater in proportion to the increased vehicle weight per unit length. In addition, because of the larger profile of standing-passenger vehicles, the wind torques on the guideway are greater. Therefore, for systems in which torsion is critical (section 10.6), the guideway weight is further increased up to 40 percent if the vehicles are designed to accommodate standing passengers.

2. For standing-passenger vehicles, the safety considerations of chapter 7 cannot be applied—there is no way to protect standing passengers in a collision. Compared with seated-passenger vehicles in which passengers are protected as summarized in section 7.8, the required reliability of control and braking systems in standing-passenger vehicles must be increased in proportion to the increase in the probability of injury during a collision. In essence, with standing-passenger vehicles, the tacit assumption must be made that there will be no collisions. In the real world, regardless of the precautions taken, such an assumption is not realistic. If the same probability of injury as in a system with seated and protected passengers is insisted upon, the cost of the control and braking systems for standing-passenger vehicles must be greatly increased. These considerations, however, do not apply to seated-passenger vehicles in which there are long throw distances and no protection mechanisms—such vehicles must be treated in the above considerations as if they were standing-passenger vehicles.

3. It has already been mentioned in section 11.3 that the acceleration and deceleration ramps of off-line station systems must be longer if stand-

ing passengers are to be permitted because the tolerable acceleration and deceleration is only half as much. The formula for the length of one of these ramps is given by equation (2.2.6). Since a_m/J must be chosen equal to one second in both standing- and seated-passenger systems, and this factor is small compared with V_L/a_m, it is seen that the length of these ramps must be almost doubled if standing passengers are to be permitted.

No precise estimate of the ratio of cost of a standing-passenger vehicle system to a seated-passenger vehicle system on a completely comparable basis has been made; however, we can roughly estimate the ratio of guideway costs from figure 5-4. Compare a forty passenger vehicle with a three passenger vehicle. In these cases, the data of figure 5-4 is for standing-and seated-passenger vehicles, respectively. A forty passenger vehicle should be able to be built with a mass of say 1100 kg/m, and a three passenger vehicle with a mass of 300 kg/m. The ratio is 3.67, and from section 10.10, this should also approximately be the ratio of cost per unit length of the guideway. For the fleet cost, it is necessary to compare the increased cost of more reliable control and braking systems required of standing-passenger vehicles with the increased cost of providing for passenger protection in seated-passenger vehicles (see Chapter 7). Not enough data is available to make such a comparison; however, the cost of protection devices is included in the cost of the smallest vehicles of figure 5-1. In any case, the increased guideway cost with standing passenger vehicles is so great that the trade-off favors the specification of seated and protected passengers in an optimum AGT system. The comfort of the service provided with such a choice and the increased patronage it is likely to bring is a further dividend of the seated-passenger system.

11.6 Reliability

The process of synthesis of the characteristics of a transit system of maximum cost effectiveness has up to this section dealt with the acquisition cost of the system and not with its total life cycle cost. This is proper because it is easier to consider life cycle cost if we have specific configurations in mind. On the other hand, a configuration that is optimum from the viewpoint of acquisition cost may have to be discarded because of excessive support costs for operation and maintenance. Thus, consideration of the total life cycle cost must be an integral part of the synthesis process.

Consideration of life cycle cost includes all of the costs needed to keep the system operating at a specified level of reliability throughout its lifetime. The theory of life cycle cost minimization is developed in chapters 8 and 9. There, by a Lagrangian minimization process, it is shown how to find the optimum balance between acquisition and support costs for each subsystem in a transit system so that the life cycle cost of the entire system is minimized subject to a given level of service availability. The result is an equation (equations (8.8.3, 8.8.4)) for the mean time between failure of each subsystem that provides the proper balance and minimizes system life cycle cost. We called this the required reliability and spoke of allocation of reliabilities among the subsystems in such a way that the life cycle cost of the system is minimized.

Carrying the theory through rigorously to find the proper allocation of reliabilities requires knowledge of the rate of change of life cycle cost of each subsystem with respect to its mean time to failure. However, these quantities enter as the square root, which weakens their influence, and by making plausible simplifying assumptions about them it is possible to gain a great deal of insight into the means for achieving needed reliability. Indeed, without such a theory of reliability it would not be possible to proceed with confidence with a system of the general characteristics derived in the preceding sections.

To achieve sufficient reliability in small-vehicle systems, the theory shows that it is necessary to incorporate in the system the following features:

1. Redundancy in critical on-board components
2. Failure monitoring
3. Rapid automated pushing of failed vehicles

The theory of redundancy (section 9.2) shows, by equation (9.2.21), that with failure monitoring and automated pushing, the required reliability of each redundant element lies in an easily achievable range. The theory also shows (section 9.10) that reliability is improved if a minimum of functions are provided in the central facility and if as many of the control functions as possible are placed on board the vehicles. Because of the availability of low cost microprocessors, it can be expected that a high degree of sophistication in on-baord controllers, including the above three functions, will not raise the cost of each vehicle by a significant amount. Estimates by new-system developers of on-board control costs have been in the range of ten percent of the cost of the vehicle. Thus, while a great deal of effort is needed to fully commercialize small-vehicle AGT systems, the theory of reliability fully supports their feasibility without inordinate cost.

11.7 Dual Mode versus Captive Vehicles

The preceding paragraphs have concentrated on the basic characteristics of vehicles and guideways required to maximize cost effectiveness. Now we consider a basic configurational characteristic and its implications for the system as a whole. Dual mode [8] in its pure form is a system of vehicles and guideways designed so that the vehicles can be driven manually on the streets, but possess the needed control equipment to enable them to be operated automatically on the guideway. Thus, the need for a transfer to ride the automated system is completely eliminated, articles can be stored in the vehicles, and it would appear that such a system is ideal. The alternative is a system of automated vehicles captive to guideways, but such a system may require a transfer from a street vehicle to board it, and possibly another transfer at the terminal station. If it were not for seven fundamental difficulties with the pure dual mode concept, the captive vehicle configuration would hardly seem worth considering. But let us consider these difficulties and then examine the possibility of a compromise solution.

1. The first difficulty of pure dual mode is due to the requirement that the guideway would have to be wide enough to accommodate ordinary street vehicles—at least small ones. From the theory of chapter 10, this indicates immediately that the guideway would be a minimum of 40 to 50 percent more expensive than a monobeam guideway optimally designed for captive vehicles (section 10.2). The wider guideways would have greater visual impact and, in the region of the double guideway needed at the off-line ramp points, might be particularly objectionable. Thus, for reasons of both cost and visual impact, a less extensive network of guideways would be obtainable if the system were dual mode instead of captive vehicle. Some analysts argue that a less extensive network would be satisfactory if the system were dual mode, but this view caters to the auto owners and neglects the poorer members of society.

2. Dual mode vehicles would be propelled by rotary motors and braked through wheels. As indicated in section 11.4, the reduced friction obtained in wet weather would increase the minimum no-collision headway to about two seconds and therefore would limit the flow to 1800 vehicles per hour, only a little more than the capacity of a single freeway lane. To obtain a desirable capacity of say 6000 people per hour with no single-failure collisions (see section 11.11) the average number of people per vehicle would have to be at least 3.3, thus implying group riding and not the individual-owner vehicle implied by pure dual mode. The larger, group-riding vehicle would be heavier per unit of length and would therefore increase the weight and cost per unit length of the guideway in proportion. To obtain an average load of 3.3 people per vehicle would require, because of variations in demand, approximately a ten-passenger vehicle [9]. From figure 5-4, such a vehicle can be expected to weigh about 50 percent more per unit length than the smallest captive vehicle. Thus the guideway weight and cost would increase by the same factor, and, together with the increased cost for a wider guideway, would increase the guideway cost by a factor of about $(1.5)^2 = 2.25$ over the cost of an optimum captive-vehicle guideway. Moreover, in northern climates where ice could accumulate on the guideway, the guideway would have to heated. It would not do to apply salt to the surface for fear of shorting out the power rails. Thus the operating cost of a

dual mode system would exceed that of an optimized captive vehicle system.

3. Since dual mode vehicles would be driven on both ordinary streets and guideways, they would have to have provisions for both and would therefore inherently be more complex than either captive automated vehicles or ordinary automobiles, and would cost more than either. Pure dual mode vehicles would therefore be available only to the more affluent members of society. In early stages in which only small segments of the system were built, it could be used only for a small fraction of the trips one would make. Therefore the personal gain through reduced congestion and reduced trip time expected of the automated portion of the trip would as a whole be small, thus reducing further the incentive to purchase a dual mode vehicle. Use of the larger, group-riding vehicles, described in the previous paragraph, would reduce the attractiveness of a one-vehicle trip because of the circuity of the pick-up route needed to obtain a sufficiently high load factor to amortize the guideway.

4. At the entry points to the automated guideway, inspection stations must be placed to insure that the propulsion, braking, and control systems aboard each vehicle are functioning properly. A wheel-locking failure would be particularly severe with rotary drives because the automated pushing procedure would not work and an entire line would be blocked until the failed vehicle were removed. The inspection must be sufficiently comprehensive to check vehicles that have been off the line for a long period of time and to take into account that the control system may have been tampered with. Little is known about the time such an inspection precedure would take. But if it does take up to say a minute, the throughput of the station is severely restricted and the inconvenience of parking a street vehicle, walking through a captive vehicle station and boarding a ready and waiting vehicle may not be a greater deterrent to travel on the automated system. In a captive vehicle system, maintenance of the vehicles would be completely under the control of the system operator.

5. To accommodate all types of travelers, the dual mode stations would have to process both dual mode vehicles entering and leaving the system and captive vehicles at station platforms similar to those of a captive vehicle system. Thus a dual mode station is a captive vehicle station plus ramps going to and from the street, an inspection station, and an abort lane to remove disqualified vehicles. Such a station would take more land and would cost more than a captive vehicle station.

6. In downtown areas, congestion on the streets beyond control of the automated systems could cause the vehicles of a dual mode system programmed to exit at the congested location to back up onto the guideway. To prevent such a serious bottleneck, additional vehicles programmed to exit would have to be rerouted to another exit point and could, by their

presence, overload the guideway. Also, with the pure dual mode concept, each vehicle would have to be stored in the downtown area just as is the case with the present automobile system and little improvement in street congestion can be expected. For this reason, it has been suggested that a dual mode system operate in the downtown as a captive vehicle system, that is, with off-line stations only and no exit and entry ramps. But in such a case, a private dual mode vehicle would have to be shunted into an ordinary parking garage. Upon returning to the station at the end of the day, the dual mode vehicle owner would have to call his vehicle and wait perhaps five or ten minutes for its arrival. To avoid this problem, special multistory parking garages for dual mode vehicles could be built with exit and entry ramps right onto the guideway. Again this is an elitist approach and would add to the cost of the system. Furthermore, the volume of a dual mode parking garage would have to be several times larger than that for a captive vehicle system because of the requirement to retrieve a particular vehicle.

7. In a captive vehicle system, each vehicle could be used for up to six to ten trips during the rush period. Thus, when compared with a pure dual mode system, the captive vehicle system would require correspondingly fewer vehicles and would be much more conserving of scarce resources.

In the pure dual mode concept, it is seen that one problem is compounded upon another, and that the problems are fundamental and not likely to be solved by technological advances. Such a system is cost ineffective in comparison with an optimized captive vehicle system. To make dual mode work with adequate capacity, the vehicles must be larger than the optimum-sized captive vehicles—small buses essentially which operate in the mode of the commuter van. Thus the privacy aspect of dual mode is removed and with it its main advantage.

A compromise that would overcome difficulties 1 through 4 would be the use of pallets of optimum design to which small automobiles could be clamped. Very little engineering design has gone into this concept, however, and it does not solve difficulties 5 through 7.

11.8 Guideway Configurations

The process of optimization has up to this point settled on a system of small, seated-passenger vehicles designed to protect the passengers in case of collisions, and propelled by linear electric motors. The vehicles ride captive on monobeam guideways and use off-line stations as entry and exit points. Switching to the off-line stations and to other guideways is performed by switches on board each vehicle. To obtain adequate reliability, all critical on-board systems are redundant and failure monitored, and each vehicle is capable of engaging and pushing a disabled vehicle ahead of or possibly behind it. To obtain sufficiently low support costs, design simplicity must be maintained, but this is compatable with the use of linear drives. The theory of minimization of life cycle costs is essential here. The vehicles could ride either above the guideway, below it, or both; and would be suspended on wheels or magnetic fields, but probably not on air cushions because of the wide guideway they seem to require. Once such a basic configuration is established, many other optimizing decisions will be determined in an engineering development program.

The above design choices lead to a package of technology suited to an almost infinite variety of guideway configurations. Moreover, because of full switching capability, the system can begin as a single loop and be expanded loop by loop or line by line as needed. The capacity of an optimized system is adequate for almost all line-haul applications (section 11.4); and, because of the switching capability, radial lines can lead into collection and distribution networks in centers of major activity. As mentioned in section 11.1, sufficient computer simulation has been performed on a wide variety of line and network configurations to provide confidence that in most applications the above-mentioned configurations are fully practical. Because of the use of off-line stations, the productivity of a line-haul segment (which is provided by closely spaced stations) can be high.

The design of optimized network configurations, that is, the placement of lines and stations, is a science in itself. It is an iterative process fundamentally involving the use of behavioral mode split modeling and has not been treated in detail in this book. Nonetheless, the author does not slight its importance and has observed many cases in which faulty system design has resulted from inadequate attention to the difficult problem of patronage analysis.

11.9 Control

The control of AGT systems has received more attention in the literature than almost any other of its aspects [1]. The analytical aspects of obtaining adequate response under all conditions are well understood; however, the best means for obtaining reliable intervehicle positional and rate data on board each vehicle is probably yet to be developed. To satisfy safety requirements developed with train systems, these data must be present even if a vehicle lies dead on the guideway. Heretofore, however, insufficient attention has been paid to the coupling of such specifications with the probability of and consequences of failure. An optimized AGT system cannot be treated as if the vehicles were trains, tacitly assuming from a long tradition that the consequences of failure were the same. With redundant on-board elements, failure monitoring, modest speeds, lightweight vehicles, and passenger protection devices, an optimized AGT system bears no resemblance to a train system and the specification of its safety should be based on performance standards, not on design standards from another era. The problem of safety standards is an institutional one, but it also depends on development of adequate data based on the results of research and development.

11.10 Energy Conservation

Thus far the energy efficiency of an optimized AGT system has not been discussed. Clearly, with dimming prospects for continued availability of cheap energy, energy considerations enter very strongly into life cycle cost calculations and must be a primary concern in every phase of design. Let us consider the optimum design from the viewpoint of energy conservation.

1. Nonstop trips at uniform speed give a velocity profile that minimizes energy use. Trips with many stops require that the kinetic energy of the vehicle be restored after each stop. Equation (2.6.6) gives the energy consumed in a nonstop trip at constant speed once line speed is attained. If the trip has many stops, and D_s is taken as the total trip length, then the first term must be multiplied by the number of stops. By use of regenerative braking, some of the kinetic energy of the vehicles can be recovered as the vehicle is stopped.

2. Equation (2.6.6) shows that the energy per trip is minimized if the vehicle mass is minimized, a key requirement of the optimized system.

3. Equation (2.6.6) also shows that the energy per trip is minimized if the frontal area of the vehicles is minimized. If the vehicles were trained, however, the air drag term enters only once for each train and therefore is less than if the vehicles operate singly. But training of vehicles at stations increases the station dwell time and therefore the number of vehicles that have to be moved, in proportion to the increased average trip time. Also, from the discussion of equation (4.5.22), trained vehicles would require passengers to stop at intermediate stations, thus increasing the kinetic energy term of equation (2.6.6). If the vehicles travel nonstop between stations, Figure 2-4 shows that the line speed is lowered for a given average speed. Both the air drag and kinetic energy terms in equation (2.6.6) are proportional to the line speed squared. With all of these considerations, it is not at all clear that trained systems with the same average speed as an individual vehicle system would have a lower energy per trip. The trade-off calculations need to be made in specific circumstances. Certainly, in individual vehicle systems, greater attention should be paid to streamlining the vehicles to reduce the drag coefficient C_D in the air drag term of equation (2.6.6).

4. The use of off-line stations and on-demand service means that vehi-

cles need circulate only when demand exists. As discussed in section 11.3 in connection with the vehicle load factor, with systems using scheduled service, the vehicles must circulate to maintain schedules regardless of demand. Thus, in periods of low demand, substantially more energy is consumed by the system than if the vehicles moved only when trips need to be made.

5. The use of linear electric motors eliminates the problem of reduced traction if there is water, snow, or ice on the guideway. With rotary motors operating through wheels, the guideway must be kept dry to keep the level of traction acceptably high. In some applications, guideway-heating energy has been as high as propulsion energy. Linear electric motors, however, vary a great deal in efficiency. Two-sided linear induction motors use substantially less energy than one-sided motors because the magnetic flux paths are much more tightly coupled. The strength of the effective magnetic field is inversely proportional to the air gap, therefore suspension designs that permit the smallest air gap are to be preferred. Linear syncronous and linear pulsed dc motors promise higher efficiency than linear induction motors, but are not as highly developed. In all of these motors, end effects reduce efficiency and must be reduced by careful design. The optimum design of an AGT system clearly requires a strong research and development program on these motors.

11.11 Capacity Requirements

In section 11.7, it was mentioned that a capacity of 6000 people per hour per direction was desirable. As mentioned in section 11.4, the maximum capacity of a single freeway lane is about 2000 people per hour. This figure is obtained from surveys of traffic on freeways and is discussed in most traffic engineering textbooks. Three-lane freeways, common in many metropolitan areas as major line-haul transportation corridors, therefore have a capacity of about 6000 people per hour. Figure 5-6 shows that with a network system, the average flow reached 4000 people per hour only with the highest densities considered, which are far higher than obtained in most cities except within the central core. Equation (4.5.19) shows, however, that the flow is proportional to the average trip length. Therefore in very large spread cities, such as Los Angeles, flows on freeways higher than 6000 people per hour are routinely obtained. A guideway system is not expected to attract all of the line-haul traffic, indeed if half the rush hour traffic were attracted, it would in most cities be considered a resounding success. With these considerations in mind, it is clear that the specification of 6000 people per hour maximum flow for a suburb to downtown dual mode system will cover a wide range of applications, but that to achieve such a capacity with vehicles with rotary drives will require group-riding vehicles. On the other hand, if the guideway system is optimized, the calculation of section 11.4 indicates that it is not capacity limited.

Notes

1. *Personal Rapid Transit II,* Audio Visual Library Services, University of Minnesota, Minneapolis, Minn., 1974; and *Personal Rapid Transit III,* Audio Visual Library Services, University of Minnesota, Minneapolis, Minn., 1976.

2. *Lea Transit Compendium,* Vol. 2, No. 3, p. 25, and Vol. 2, No. 4, pp. 9, 17, and 37, N.D. Lea Transportation Research Corporation, Huntsville, Ala., 1975.

3. The systems referenced in Note 2 are the best examples.

4. Such a design is used by the H-Bahn and Monocab Systems referenced in Note 2.

5. Such a design is used in the High-Capacity PRT System developed by the Aerospace Corporation. See *Personal Rapid Transit,* op. cit., pp. 325-382; *Lea Transit Compendium,* op cit., Vol. 2, No. 4, pp. 9-12.

6. Such a design is used in the Cabintaxi System referenced in Note 2. See also "Cabintaxi: Urban Transport of the Future," *Elevator World,* April 1977. The detailed theory is developed by Dr.-Ing. Klaus Becker, in "Über den Einfluss von Fahrgeschwindigkeit und Streckennetz auf Verkehrsmenge und Kostenstruktur einer neuartigen Kabinenbahn," genehmigte Dissertation, Berlin, 1974.

7. Private discussions with developers of three new German AGT Systems indicates, however, that power collection problems for urban-speed systems are considered solved in Germany.

8. *Dual-Mode Transportation,* Special Report 170, Transportation Research Board, Washington, D.C., 1976.

9. This assumes a load factor of one-third, judged by the author to be reasonable on the average for group service with reasonable waiting time and counting deadheading. If, say an eight-passenger vehicle had been assumed, the argument that the dual mode guideway is substantially more expensive than a captive vehicle guideway is not changed.

Appendix A
Derivation of the
Amortization Factor

P = principal (original cost of equipment)
p = annual payment on principal and interest, assumed constant
A = p/P = amortization factor (see section 5.1)
r = annual interest rate
n = lifetime of equipment, or period over which loan is paid
I_i = interest payment at end of ith year
P_i = payment on principal at the end of ith year

$$p = I_i + P_i \qquad (A.1)$$

$$P = \sum_{i=1}^{n} P_i \qquad (A.2)$$

Interest paid at the end of the ith year is applied to the balance of principal owed during that year. Thus

$$I_i = r\left(P - \sum_{j=1}^{i-1} P_j\right) \qquad (A.3)$$

By using equation (A.2), we have from equation (A.3)

$$I_{n+1} = 0 \qquad (A.4)$$

If equation (A.3) is substituted into equation (A.1), the result may be written in the form

$$P_i = p - rP + r\sum_{j=1}^{i-1} P_j \qquad (A.5)$$

Thus,

$$P_1 = p - rP$$

$$P_2 = (p - rP)(1 + r)$$

$$P_3 = (p - rP)(1 + r)^2$$

By induction, assume

$$P_i = (p - rP)(1 + r)^{i-1} \qquad \text{for } i = 1, 2, ..., k \qquad \text{(A.6)}$$

Then, from equation (A.5),

$$P_{k+1} = (p - rP)\left[1 + r \sum_{j=1}^{k} (1 + r)^{j-1}\right]$$

$$= (p - rP)\left\{1 + r\left[\frac{(1 + r)^k - 1}{r}\right]\right\} = (p - rP)(1 + r)^k$$

Thus, P_{k+1} can be derived from equation (A.6) by substituting $k + 1$ for k. It is therefore proved that equation (A.6) holds for all k.

Now, substitute equation (A.6) into equation (A.1) and set $i = n + 1$. Using equation (A.4), the result is

$$p = (p - rP)(1 + r)^n$$

from which

$$\frac{p}{P} = A(r, n) = \frac{r(1 + r)^n}{(1 + r)^n - 1} \qquad \text{(A.7)}$$

Let I be the total interest paid.
Then

$$\frac{P + I}{P} = \frac{np}{P} = nA \qquad \text{(A.8)}$$

is the total payment for the equipment per unit of principal.
The present value of the total payment at year $i = 0$ is

$$PV = \sum_{i=1}^{n} \frac{p}{(1 + d)^i}$$

where d is the discount rate. Summing the series,

$$PV = \frac{p[(1 + d)^n - 1]}{d(1 + d)^n}$$

or, using equation (A.7),

$$\frac{PV}{P} = \frac{A(r, n)}{A(d, n)} \tag{A.9}$$

Index

337

About the Author

J. Edward Anderson is a professor of mechanical engineer at the University of Minnesota and president of the Advanced Transit Association. He received the bachelor's degree in 1949 in mechanical engineering from Iowa State University. His master's degree, also in Mechanical engineering, is from the University of Minnesota, and his PhD is from the Massachusetts Institute of Technology, with a thesis in magnetohydrodynamics . Dr. Anderson's professional career has been divided almost equally between industry and the university, and has included research and development in structures, instrument design, shock and vibration design, control, inertial navigation, operational computers, spacecraft design, explosion dynamics, magneto- and electro-hydrodynamics, heat transfer, and high-temperature gas dynamics. In the past nine years, he has studied, taught, and lectured on new transit systems and their societal impacts, and in the more general area of technology/society issues. He has authored the books *Magnetohydrodynamic Shock Waves*, MIT Press, International Edition by the University of Tokyo Press, Russian Edition by Atomizdat, Moscow; and *Magnetogasdynamics of Thermal Plasma*, Energia, Moscow. He was an editor of *Personal Rapid Transit* and General Editor of *Personal Rapid Transit II*, both distributed by Audio Visual Library Services, University of Minnesota.